THE COMPLETE
PATRICIA
CORNWELL
COMPANION

GLENN L. FEOLE, M.D.,
and DON LASSETER

BERKLEY BOOKS, NEW YORK

THE BERKLEY PUBLISHING GROUP
Published by the Penguin Group
Penguin Group (USA) Inc.
375 Hudson Street, New York, New York 10014, USA
Penguin Group (Canada), 10 Alcorn Avenue, Toronto, Ontario M4V 3B2, Canada
(a division of Pearson Penguin Canada Inc.)
Penguin Books Ltd., 80 Strand, London WC2R 0RL, England
Penguin Group Ireland, 25 St. Stephen's Green, Dublin 2, Ireland (a division of Penguin Books Ltd.)
Penguin Group (Australia), 250 Camberwell Road, Camberwell, Victoria 3124, Australia
(a division of Pearson Australia Group Pty. Ltd.)
Penguin Books India Pvt. Ltd., 11 Community Centre, Panchsheel Park, New Delhi—110 017, India
Penguin Group (NZ), Cnr. Airborne and Rosedale Roads, Albany, Auckland 1310, New Zealand
(a division of Pearson New Zealand Ltd.)
Penguin Books (South Africa) (Pty.) Ltd., 24 Sturdee Avenue, Rosebank, Johannesburg 2196,
South Africa

Penguin Books Ltd., Registered Offices: 80 Strand, London WC2R 0RL, England

This book is an original publication of The Berkley Publishing Group.

Copyright © 2005 by Cornwell Enterprises, Inc.
Cover art: Photograph of the author by Irene M. Shulgin, © Cornwell Enterprises, Inc.
Portions of "The Life of Patricia Cornwell" were written by Birger Nielson and have previously
appeared on his website, www.246.dk. They are used here with the permission of the author.
Cover design by Richard Hasselberger.
Text design by Tiffany Estreicher.

PRINTING HISTORY
Berkley trade paperback edition / January 2005

Library of Congress Cataloging-in-Publication Data

Feole, Glenn L.
     The complete Patricia Cornwell companion / Glenn L. Feole and Don Lasseter.—Berkley
  trade pbk. ed.
     p. cm.
  Includes index.
  ISBN 0-425-20131-7 (trade pbk.)
     1. Cornwell, Patricia Daniels—Handbooks, manuals, etc.   2. Novelists, American—20th
century—Biography—Handbooks, manuals, etc.   3. Detective and mystery stories,
American—Handbooks, manuals, etc.   4. Scarpetta, Kay (Fictitious character)—Handbooks,
manuals, etc.   5. Richmond (Va.)—In literature—Handbooks, manuals, etc.   6. Medical
fiction, American—Handbooks, manuals, etc.   I. Lasseter, Don.   II. Title.

PS3553.O692Z67 2005
813'.54—dc22

                                                                                              2004046205

PRINTED IN THE UNITED STATES OF AMERICA

10 9 8 7 6 5 4 3 2 1

Most Berkley Books are available at special quantity discounts for bulk purchases for sales promotions, premiums,
fund-raising, or educational use. Special books, or book excerpts, can also be created to fit specific needs.

For details, write: Special Markets, The Berkley Publishing Group, 375 Hudson Street, New York, New York
10014.

DEDICATION

To my wife, Tina, and my four children, Kelly, Ben, John, and Molly, who watched with patient incredulity as I sat and wrote for one year. We have shared years and years of stories and anecdotes and reading together, and I hope I have passed on my love of reading to you. All my love.

—GLENN L. FEOLE, M.D.

NOTE TO THE READERS

Source citations are provided throughout for referenced and quoted text sections. The cites for the quotes culled from Patricia Cornwell books have been taken from the paperback editions. The exceptions are *Trace* and *Blow Fly*—some of the pages referenced for these two titles have been taken from the hardcover editions.

As you read through certain sections of this book there may be timeline and incidental inconsistencies between the series books. In the end, for all the exacting specificity poured into the details, these Patricia Cornwell books we love are fiction and ultimately individual.

CONTENTS

PART THREE: A DOSE OF REALITY

PART FOUR: FINAL INVENTORY

FOREWORD

SEVERAL years ago, as I stood in my driveway, ready to leave my anachronistic solo pediatric practice in Westport, Connecticut, one of my patients ran up to me to say goodbye. She had heard that I was moving to Richmond and, clutching a large book in her hand, she told me, "Richmond. That's where my favorite author is. I've read all her books." She held up a book with a large color picture on the back. The photo featured an attractive, female helicopter pilot with short dirty-blond hair, a hint of a smile, and a leather bomber jacket. Given the photo's position, it had to be the author of the book: Patricia Cornwell. And, with that last name, she was probably a descendant of British royalty. What, I wondered, was a possible descendant of British royalty doing in Richmond, Virginia, flying helicopters and writing novels? Little did I know that I would find out for myself soon enough.

After wandering around in the Piedmont for two years, writing a book and pretending not to be a doctor, I called the medical examiner's office and asked if they just happened to need a doctor to be a medical examiner. My aim was to keep the medical wheels in my brain from rusting while my writing career careened wildly down, or up, the hill of success.

The person on the phone told me that they did in fact need such a doctor. So I drove downtown and met with Dr. Marcella Fierro, the chief medical examiner. The experience was like walking into the den of Nero Wolfe, or even into Sherlock Holmes's office on Baker Street. I sat there, like a sponge, and could feel my writer's instincts stir inside of me. It was the beginning, in many ways, of a new era in my life.

For a year, I quietly observed Marcella's incisive judgments, her pensive premonitions, her forceful charisma as she responded to my forensic observations from the many scenes of carnage that I visited. I soaked it all up. I even learned something despite myself. She patiently kept reminding me, like a mantra, that it's often a bad world out there.

In the course of that year, she also told me that she had a writer friend, a woman who just happened to be a helicopter pilot and perhaps of British royal descent, at least through marriage. And that's how I met Patricia Cornwell.

Patricia Cornwell sauntered down the hall of the M.E.'s office one day and the pieces fell into place in my mind—she was the writer on the back of the book my patient had shown me. But I had no idea what a celebrity I was meeting until I picked up a couple of books at one of Patricia's signings at a local bookstore in downtown Richmond. Instead of buying the books and leaving them at the Office of the Chief Medical Examiner (OCME) to be signed, which she happily does for the staff there, I drove over to the store instead.

I was on call that weekend as an M.E. and deluged with calls from the police. But I thought I'd just stop in at the store, get a quick signature from the author, and return to my calls. Imagine my shock when I got there. It was two hours before her scheduled appearance and already a thick line of people wound in and out of almost every aisle. The line then wound around the entire periphery of the store, out the back door, down the long sidewalk, and around the entire building to the other side where I had just entered. When Patricia Cornwell showed up, she had a smile and a pleasant word for each of her devoted fans. She made eye contact with each as she signed their books. I was impressed. This was a woman with a following. I dropped my books off at the counter to be signed later, when she was finished with the line of fans. That would take a while. I figured, given the size of the crowd, that my books might get signed by midnight.

I took away from that day a sense of how many readers Patricia Corn-well has touched. I became one of them myself, with an ever-growing addiction to her work that has resulted in this book. I hope you enjoy it.

Dr. Glenn L. Feole
2003

INTRODUCTION

As the author of a dozen nonfiction works depicting the horrors of real-life crime and the resolute efforts of law enforcement investigators, I was invited to examine fictional sleuthing in the novels of Patricia Cornwell from a distinctly nonfiction point of view. I launched into the project by reading her first Kay Scarpetta novel, *Postmortem*.

Like her legions of other fans, I was hooked.

What appeared to be a formidable task, reading twenty books by one author, turned out to be the most welcome research project of my career. Within just a few weeks, I journeyed delightfully through Cornwell's Scarpetta novels (eleven at the time, thirteen by the time this book was finished), three other crime novels, one biography, one nonfiction account of the case of Jack the Ripper, two cookbooks, and one novelette for children. Her protagonists and supporting casts became my familiar friends. I felt as if I had spent a great deal of time in Virginia, and intimately knew where these characters lived, worked, and died.

It soon became clear to me why bookstores are loaded with this author's novels, and why her admirers stand in lines for signed books and the chance to meet her. Cornwell occupies an unparalleled niche in the pantheon of accomplished writers. It is a privilege to contribute to a companion book for her inspired body of work.

One of the fundamental reasons for a companion book is to cast additional light on any esoteric terms and passages presented by an author. Patricia Cornwell's books, both novels and nonfiction, are perfect for this kind of detailed analysis. Her multilayered plots, enriched by technical idiom and numerous references to real people, locations, and historical events, add up to interesting complexity. Cornwell has clearly done her homework as reflected by her impressive knowledge of scientific and cultural subjects. The author pays tribute to her readers' intelligence by inserting varied material into her stories, including medical terms, ballistics, and legal quandries. She uses diverse scientific terminology. Cornwell places her characters in real cities, neighborhoods, restaurants, buildings, parks, and other sites. She imagines them not only with other fictional figures, but also with scores of bona fide people. The names of notorious real-life murderers are often mentioned.

This literary technique, intertwining real people with invented ones, and actual locations with imaginary ones, holds special appeal to me. It blurs the lines between fact and fiction, lending authenticity to both. Cornwell accomplishes this masterfully.

In reading the Scarpetta novels, it helped me considerably to take them in consecutive order. I strongly recommend that new readers do the same. This applies equally to the author's other novels.

I hope that I have managed not only to provide her faithful worldwide readers and fans with supplementary information, but have also given them a new understanding of the author's profound knowledge, research skills, and ability to tell richly layered stories loaded with authenticity.

Vladimir Nabokov wrote, "For me a work of fiction exists only insofar as it affords me what I shall bluntly call aesthetic bliss."

Patricia Cornwell knows how to present "aesthetic bliss."

Don Lasseter
2003

PART ONE

THE AUTHOR

THE LIFE OF
PATRICIA CORNWELL

PATRICIA Cornwell was born in Miami, Florida, on June 9, 1956, to Marilyn and Sam Daniels. Patricia's father was an appellate attorney; her mother was a secretary. In 1963, Patricia's parents divorced. Marilyn Daniels and the three children (Patricia and her two brothers) then moved to Montreat, North Carolina. Ruth and Billy Graham lived just two miles up the road from the family. It was Ruth Graham who gave young Patricia a leather-bound journal and told her to write. Patricia took the advice to heart.

Patricia grew up and went off to King College, Tennessee. She then transferred to Davidson College in Davidson, North Carolina, where she received her degree in literature. In 1979, she married Charles Cornwell, her former English professor. At the time of their marriage, Patricia was twenty-three and Charles was forty. (The marriage ended in divorce in 1989.)

The newly married Patricia started working as a reporter for the *Charlotte Observer*. Soon she became a police reporter, and her investigative work won awards. It was there that she saw a large slice of life that she was able to utilize later in her novels. Many of her experiences weren't pleasant. But she was a superb observer of life, and she was able to store her memories away to mine later as a fiction writer.

Her career as a writer of books began when Cornwell wrote *A Time for Remembering,* a biography of Ruth Bell Graham, the wife of evangelist Billy Graham. The work was published in 1983. This book is out of print now in its original version and is difficult to find, even in secondhand bookshops. (Less-than-perfect copies of this edition start at $75 as of the time of this writing.) A newer version of this book, *Ruth, A Portrait: The Story of Ruth Bell Graham*, was published by Doubleday in September 1997 and is generally more available.

In 1984, Patricia Cornwell took a job in the Virginia medical examiner's office. For six years she worked at the morgue, first as a technical writer, then as a computer analyst. She also volunteered to be a city cop. That's where she got her first taste of community policing.

Between 1984 and 1986, Cornwell wrote three novels based on her crime-desk experience, but the publishers to whom she submitted the manuscripts rejected them all. Disheartened, she wrote to Sara Ann Freed, then an editor at Mysterious Press, the one publishing house that had softened its rejection letter with encouragement. Freed told her to ditch the male detective who was then her central character. She suggested expanding Kay Scarpetta, originally a minor character in the work.

Cornwell took the editor's advice, reworked her material, and wrote a new manuscript. That manuscript sold to Susanne Kirk at Scribner, as did Cornwell's next five books. And so in 1990 Patricia Cornwell saw her first novel published to major international acclaim. *Postmortem* was the first novel to ever win the Edgar, Creasey, Anthony, and Macavity awards, as well as the French Prix du Roman d'Aventure, all in a single year. The book remains the only American crime novel to have ever won the coveted British Gold Dagger award.

Scribner acquired *Postmortem* in a two-book deal for a small four-figure advance after several other houses had turned it down. After *Postmortem* became a success, the price for Cornwell's work went up quickly. In March 1991 she signed a $385,000 deal for the paperback rights for *Body of Evidence.* This was the first big payday in what would soon become top-dollar book deals for the talented author.

Patricia Cornwell has divided her time between a number of homes over the past decade: Richmond, Virginia; Los Angeles, California; Greenwich, Connecticut; New York City; and Florida. The author has not forgotten her roots, though. She has kept her link to Davidson College active, and she sponsors scholarships for Davidson students with exceptional abilities in creative writing.

On March 1, 1996, six of Patricia Cornwell's books were included on the *USA Today* list of the twenty-five bestselling crime novels to date, including *The Body Farm, From Potter's Field, Postmortem, Cruel & Unusual, Body of Evidence,* and *All That Remains.*

Several of the Cornwell books seem to be loosely based on real crimes in the Virginia area, such as the Colonial Parkway murders and the Southside Strangler. Interested readers can find out more about these crimes in the section of this book called "That's a Real Killer."

In 1990, Patricia Cornwell earned a modest sum for her first Scarpetta novel, *Postmortem.* That soon changed. She recently signed a new contract worth $24 million for three future Scarpetta novels. The deal was brokered by Esther Newberg of ICM (International Creative Management).

In 1996 the Putnam Berkley Group (with Phyllis Grann as CEO) lured Patricia Cornwell to its list, and *Cause of Death* was published by Putnam in July 1996. The first non-Scarpetta novel, *Hornet's Nest,* was released in January 1997, followed in quick succession by *Unnatural Exposure* (1997), *Point of Origin* (1998), *Southern Cross* (1999), *Black Notice* (1999), *The Last Precinct* (2000), *Isle of Dogs* (2001), and *Blow Fly* (2003), as well as a nonfiction book on the real Jack the Ripper titled *Portrait of a Killer: Jack the Ripper—Case Closed* (2002).

For readers who are interested in finding out more about the author, Patricia Cornwell's official website can be found at www.patriciacornwell. com. One feature of the site is a list of Cornwell's favorite books by other writers—a fine way to get a window into Cornwell's mind. But reading the author's books remains the best way for someone to get to know Patricia Cornwell. As the author herself puts it, "It is important to me to live in the world I write about."

PATRICIA CORNWELL:
PROSE STYLIST

THE spectacular success of Patricia Cornwell's first published novel, *Postmortem,* is every writer's dream. It launched her career into the stratosphere of top American authors by garnering five major international awards:

John Creasey Award—British Crime Writers' Association

Edgar Award—Mystery Writers of America

Anthony Award—Bouchercon World Mystery Convention

Macavity Award—Mystery Readers International

French Prix du Roman d'Aventure

In other words, she hit the literary lottery jackpot.

Cornwell is widely quoted as saying, "It is important for me to live in the world I write about. If I want a character to do or know something, I want to do or know the same thing."

Thirteen of Cornwell's novels feature protagonist Dr. Kay Scarpetta, chief medical examiner of Virginia. Readers may find themselves confusing the two women. Sometimes, it's difficult to remember that this vast array of brilliant narrative is not from the fictional medical examiner herself, but from Cornwell. One might think, "Gee, this woman Scarpetta knows everything," and then come to the sober realization that this wisdom is really the author's. Cornwell is enigmatic about the issue. "Many of my readers think I am Scarpetta," she states in *Food to Die For* (p. 16). "But I am all of my characters."

In *Ruth, A Portrait,* Cornwell makes an interesting observation about the inspiration for Scarpetta. After she had completed the biography of Ruth Bell Graham, she needed new challenges. "I decided I had to find some other remarkable person who would put up with me for more than one crime. That's the genesis of Scarpetta, the heroine of my series. It is Ruth's fault," she said playfully. "She is responsible for people around the world knowing a lot more about blood spatter patterns, autopsies, and DNA" (p. 278, *Ruth, A Portrait*). In that case, the world owes a debt of gratitude to Mrs. Graham.

Certainly, Scarpetta's investigative expertise attests not only to Cornwell's knowledge of forensic medicine and police procedures, but also to her powerful storytelling techniques.

Every successful scene in a motion picture or a book must contain an element of tension. Cornwell demonstrates her grasp of this in her first novel by immediately creating a hint of antagonism between Scarpetta and Detective Pete Marino. The strain between them appears to stem from Marino's macho, misanthropic rejection of a woman meddling in what he perceives as a man's world of crime investigation.

Adversarial relationships provide a good source of tension, so Cornwell plays that theme early in *Postmortem* by creating conflict between Scarpetta and a female news reporter. In real life, distrust between news media writers and police agencies is not uncommon. The dilemma is unavoidable. Reporters work to satisfy a voracious appetite for instantaneous bulletins, preferably sensational ones. Law enforcement representatives must withhold any information that might compromise investigations. Cornwell understands this from experiences in her own work as a police reporter and in the Virginia medical examiner's office. She stirs disharmony into the mix of already simmering suspicions soon after the curtain rises on this drama of serial sex murders.

Crime novels must necessarily deal with the horror of people being killed. But some writers fail to examine the trauma to the victims' loved ones. Cornwell comes to grips with this in *Postmortem*. It can be seen when Scarpetta arrives at the crime scene, makes a preliminary examination of the evidence, and meets the husband of a sexually assaulted murder victim. The distraught survivor pleads with Scarpetta to shield his dead wife's nude and ravaged body from the view of investigative personnel inside the home.

Cornwell demonstrates compassionate knowledge of the unbearable horror endured by most family members when a loved one is slaughtered. Readers feel the husband's almost visceral pain. A murder victim's body loses all dignity when it becomes evidence to be photographed, examined, and cut during an autopsy. Respect for the corpse who was recently a breathing, vital person is sacrificed in the search for a killer. The resultant stress on family members is frequently so intense they must seek treatment for post-traumatic stress disorder. Cornwell does not shrink from this aspect of the story.

Sensitivity is important to Cornwell, as seen in her protagonist's empathy for the people on whom she performs autopsies. Scarpetta hates the dark humor she hears from detectives who observe postmortem examinations. When her niece makes a crass comment about the bodies, Scarpetta unleashes a scathing rejoinder. "'Imagine someone you love in a fucking morgue. Imagine people making fun of him, joking, making comments about the size of his penis or how much he stinks. . . . Maybe halfway into the goddamn job they threw a towel over his empty chest cavity and went to lunch. And maybe cops wandering in and out on other cases made comments about *crispy critters* or being *burned by a snitch* or *FBI flambé*. . . . Don't think I haven't heard it all. . . . Everything so . . . cold in the end. So don't you talk to me about autopsies'" (pp. 72–73, *Black Notice*).

Cornwell is also unafraid of plunging into the sensitive area of racial complexities. One example of this is seen with Scarpetta's housekeeper, Bertha. Cornwell uses dialogue to imply that the woman is African-American. Some readers may feel uncomfortable with the stereotypical portrait of this character, which seems influenced by the Oscar-winning Hattie McDaniel, who played Mammy in the film *Gone With the Wind*. It is not easy to bring up race while avoiding politically incorrect implications. The author weaves a narrow path here and deftly sidesteps any trouble.

Postmortem contains another racial encounter, and readers may squirm a little at this one. Scarpetta, investigating a case in which an African-American woman is murdered, telephones the victim's family to ask about an injury discernible on an X ray. A cultured female voice answers and identifies herself as the victim's sister. Scarpetta is confused because the woman doesn't "sound black." She asks, "'Mrs. O'Connor, are you black?'" and follows up with, "'Did your sister talk like you?'" Outraged, the woman hangs up on Scarpetta (p. 288, *Postmortem*).

Even though the author deliberately created this scene for specific purposes that will be revealed later in the book, the questions seem jarring, insensitive, and poorly phrased. The words also sound unlikely coming from an educated professional in an important high-profile position.

All authors wrestle with technical demands of the profession. Cornwell demonstrates extraordinary skill in perhaps the most important one-plot structure. Her intriguing plots are one of the reasons her books rocket onto the bestseller lists. She is an expert at building complex story lines with interlocking twists and turns.

Another difficult challenge for an author is the creation of powerful similes and metaphors. This element of writing can breathe life and color into otherwise monotonous passages. Similes not only must be cleverly original, but they must be appropriate to the setting. American authors John Steinbeck and Ken Kesey were masters at similes. Cornwell competes quite well with them in this discipline. A few examples:

- On approaching the electronically controlled gates of a forbidding mansion, someone pushes a button, and *". . . the gates open slowly like a raven's wings."*

- *". . . my nerves jump like water hitting hot grease."*

- *"Marino's sullenness is like a poisonous vapor."*

- *"My heart kicks like the sudden, unexpected kick of a brass drum."*

- *"Squirrels run errands up and down trees, tails curled like plumes of smoke."*

- Regarding a colleague's despondent expression, Scarpetta notes, *"[He] watches me with a tired look of sad nobility, as if he is Robert E. Lee remembering a painful battle."*

- Scarpetta removes a large X-ray film from its container: *"X rays sounded like saw blades bending as I pulled them out. . . ."* The reader can truly hear the strange pinging of a musical saw replicated by the bending celluloid sheets.

- Scarpetta is asked a difficult question and must be careful with her answer: *"I hold up the question like a ball I am about to serve, not sure of the angle or spin or how hard."*

She handles metaphors with equal dexterity:

- Cornwell implies evil in a powerful attorney's office by making all the furnishings, including the carpet, black.

- A character's facial features are strained: *". . . his eyes luminous in his wan El Greco face."*

- Scarpetta critiques another character's writing: *"Beryl wrote well, her prose sometimes breaking into song, but the story limped along on wooden feet."*

- View of New York City from an airplane: *"Below, the city was a dazzling circuit board with tiny lights moving along highways and tower lights winking red . . ."*

Phrases like these can truly make prose break into song and give the reader Technicolor word pictures.

Cornwell also knows the power of contrast, how to quickly change somber scenes into bright airy ones. In *Postmortem,* for example, she describes Scarpetta in her workplace where death and gore prevail. Then she quickly shifts gears to offer relief from the dark events and dreary laboratory by placing her protagonist in a bright, breezy mall. It's like a cool breeze on a humid day in Richmond.

Borrowing from literature and renowned philosophers, Cornwell finds a rich source for developing analogies.

- In *Point of Origin,* she turns to Herman Melville's *Moby Dick.* Scarpetta tries to convince her lover not to become obsessive in his quest to solve a crime. She pleads, *"'. . . don't turn into a Captain Ahab, okay?'"* (p. 190).

- In *Black Notice,* Scarpetta says, *"'Nietzsche was right . . . Be careful who you choose for an enemy because that's who you become most like'"* (p. 305). She refers to Friedrich Nietzsche (1844–1900), a German philosopher and poet who denounced religion and expressed belief in humanity's attaining perfection through forcible self-assertion.

- Also in *Black Notice,* Cornwell cites Greek mythology. Jay Talley observes that Lucy is trying to compete with Scarpetta's success, and says, *"'I think she has to be Icarus and fly too close to the sun because of you. I hope she doesn't push that myth too far and fall from the sky'"* (p. 363). In the ancient myth, youthful Icarus, attempting to escape from Crete, fashioned wings from wax and feathers, but he flew too high, too close to the sun. The heat melted his wax, and he suffered a fatal fall into the sea.

Yet another task at which Cornwell excels is the writing of dialogue. Conversations between her characters flow with ease and authenticity while delivering expository information. The author reveals an especially neat trick in *Postmortem,* in which she uses dialogue to create dissonance. While Marino is speaking, Scarpetta is thinking about something else. Both trains of thought, the one he vocalizes and the one she imagines, run alternately. The effect pulls the reader along on two separate highways simultaneously. The high-voltage scene ends with even more tension as Scarpetta excoriates a man who seems to be trying to help her.

Dialogue and expository narrative require a broad vocabulary, and Cornwell's supply of the right words is remarkable. She also spices her stories with plenty of profanity, for which she has taken some heat from at least one source. In *Ruth, A Portrait,* she speaks of the famous evangelist's wife and her reaction to the earthy material in Scarpetta's world. "Ruth has not so subtly suggested over the years that I use too many cuss words. I explain it's the characters who talk like that, not me" (p. 279). The raw language lends an aura of stark realism to the characters populating her novels.

Readers may wonder whether Cornwell bases any of her fictional work on real events. Most authors certainly incorporate life experiences into their work, but generally disguise it to avoid legal problems. Cornwell deliberately uses actual settings for most of her action.

In regards to using real-life crimes, *Postmortem* seems to bear a strong similarity to a 1987 Richmond, Virginia, case. Four young women, one of them a doctor, were raped and strangled. During the investigation, news reporters referred to the killer as the Southside Strangler. Authorities arrested Timothy Spencer. His 1988 trial, one of the first in the United States to introduce DNA evidence, resulted in his conviction and execution for three of the murders. DNA also cleared a man previously convicted of another murder Spencer may have committed. The Southside Strangler was executed on April 27, 1994.

If Cornwell did use this case as a model for *Postmortem,* she only smiles when asked about it and states that her crime novels are fictional.

Cornwell's meticulous research is evident in her novels and her nonfiction books. She has obviously visited many, if not all, of the locations she describes, and is intimately familiar with various minutiae of government organizations, professions, and people. For example, when her characters are in the chief medical examiner's workplace or Richmond's police headquarters, the narrative provides convincing detail, as textured and real as if it were playing out on a movie screen.

It is interesting to see that Cornwell makes Kay Scarpetta an epicurean cook who enjoys escaping to her kitchen, sipping wine, and preparing Italian cuisine. This foreshadows the author's subsequent books, *Scarpetta's Winter Table* and *Food to Die For.*

Authors who write a series of crime novels featuring the same protagonist are in constant search of refreshing approaches and new twists, seeking to keep the reader interested. Cornwell succeeds at this, and makes a notable change in the eleventh Scarpetta novel, *The Last Precinct.* In the preceding ten, she writes in the past tense. Readers of *The Last Precinct* will be carried along from the very first sentence with present-tense verbs: "*The cold dusk gives up its bruised color to complete darkness, and I am grateful that the draperies in my bedroom are heavy enough to absorb even the faintest hint of my silhouette as I move about packing my bags. Life could not be more abnormal than it is right now*" (p. 1).

Not only is this a marvelously gripping hook, but the verb tense lends an immediacy, as if the reader is actually watching it unfold. This technique is sometimes used by other authors to set a mood before reverting to the more traditional presentation of action in the past tense. If fans expect *The Last Precinct* to make that conversion, they are going to be surprised. The entire book is in the present tense. The switch certainly makes it different.

Another aspect of Cornwell's book structure is consistently striking. Readers will worry, as they approach the end of each story, with fewer and fewer pages to turn, that not enough space remains to clear up all the extant questions. The climaxes are always breathtaking and filled with jolting action. Somehow, though, the puzzles are solved, the red herrings disposed of, and the killer identified. But be warned. The Scarpetta books are a series, like an ongoing soap opera, and one book continues into the next. The protagonist and main characters appear in all of them, and even minor players and antagonists reappear. It is highly advisable to read the Scarpetta series in order.

Fans who are interested in Cornwell's personal life and how it ties into research for the novels should not overlook several insights she shares in *Food to Die For: Secrets from Kay Scarpetta's Kitchen.*

PATRICIA CORNWELL'S
WORKS:
A BIBLIOGRAPHY

ATRICIA Cornwell has averaged one Kay Scarpetta novel per year for the last fifteen years, starting with *Postmortem* in 1990 and ending, at the time of this writing, with *Trace,* published in 2004. She has also written three crime novels that do not feature Scarpetta: *Hornet's Nest* (1997), *Southern Cross* (1999), and *Isle of Dogs* (2001). In addition to this prodigious production, she has written one children's book, *Life's Little Fable,* and a Christmas tale involving Scarpetta, Marino, and Lucy, called *Scarpetta's Winter Table.*

Her first published work was nonfiction, a biography of Billy Graham's wife called *A Time for Remembering: The Story of Ruth Bell Graham,* published in 1983 and reissued as *Ruth, A Portrait: The Story of Ruth Bell Graham* in 1997.

Her most recent work of nonfiction was a close examination of one of history's most puzzling cases titled *Portrait of a Killer: Jack the Ripper—Case Closed,* published in 2002.

A CHRONOLOGICAL BIBLIOGRAPHY

A Time for Remembering: The Story of Ruth Bell Graham, 1983 (*Ruth, A Portrait: The Story of Ruth Bell Graham*, 1997)

Postmortem, 1990

Body of Evidence, 1991

All That Remains, 1992

Cruel & Unusual, 1993

The Body Farm, 1994

From Potter's Field, 1995

Cause of Death, 1996

Hornet's Nest, 1997

Unnatural Exposure, 1997

Point of Origin, 1998

Scarpetta's Winter Table, 1998

Southern Cross, 1999

Life's Little Fable, 1999

Black Notice, 1999

The Last Precinct, 2000

Isle of Dogs, 2001

Food to Die For: Secrets from Kay Scarpetta's Kitchen, 2001

Portrait of a Killer: Jack the Ripper—Case Closed, 2002

Blow Fly, 2003

Trace, 2004

THE KAY SCARPETTA SERIES

Postmortem

HARDCOVER EDITION:
New York: Charles Scribner's Sons, 1990
ISBN: 0-684-19141-5

PAPERBACK EDITIONS:
New York: Avon Books, 1991
ISBN: 0-380-71021-8

New York: Pocket Books, 1998
ISBN: 0-7434-7715-4

Postmortem begins in Richmond, Virginia, on June 6, 1983. Fittingly, considering the events that are about to unfold, it's raining—one of those torrential storms so common during southern summers. As the book begins, Kay Scarpetta is alone in her bed in the middle of the night, having nightmares. The reader soon discovers that she's earned her nightmares.

Scarpetta is forty years old, and she's been chief medical examiner of Virginia for roughly two years. In those years, she's seen what she thought was every kind of evil the human heart is capable of. Despite the horrors she's seen, her work is in many ways her life. She is divorced from Tony, her husband. She does have a romantic interest, Bill Boltz, who is the commonwealth's attorney for Richmond. But he isn't the only man in Scarpetta's life. Benton Wesley is an FBI profiler who also teaches at the National Academy in Quantico. Pete Marino is a detective-sergeant in Richmond and pushing fifty. All of these men are important to Scarpetta, professionally and personally, even though the relationships are far from smooth. Pete Marino, in particular, is a problem for Scarpetta. She doesn't understand him and he seems to actively dislike her. And, since he's the lead detective on many of her important cases, she needs to get along with him, something that simply isn't happening.

On the home front, Lucy, Scarpetta's niece, ten years old, is visiting her. But because of the havoc of Scarpetta's heavy caseload, Lucy and her aunt have had little time to spend together. While she waits for her aunt to find time for her, the talented youngster fiddles with high-school-level math and science for fun. In a charming scene that will nonetheless terrify anyone who has children around the house, Lucy tears into her aunt's home computer and reformats the hard drive. When Scarpetta realizes just how much data is on that machine, now lost forever, she nearly has a heart attack. Only after Lucy has her aunt thoroughly worked up does she admit that she backed up all the files before she acted.

All of these characters, introduced early in the book, will become central to the Scarpetta series, but for now Scarpetta's personal life has to be put on hold. She's got a killer to catch. A series of homicides has begun recently—less than two months before the book opens—and the strangled bodies of the victims have ended up in Scarpetta's morgue. Scarpetta is convinced that she's looking at the work of a serial killer. She's right, of course, but the murderer is leaving precious few clues behind. And her investigation is being sabotaged from within.

The computer at Scarpetta's lab has been broken into, and somebody is tampering with her evidence. It could be the killer covering his tracks—or it could be an enemy within the medical examiner's office. Or it could even be her much-despised boss, Alvin Amburgey. As far as Scarpetta is concerned, no one is above suspicion.

The victim, too, is bothering her. The young woman who died was a doctor, just like Scarpetta. She played the violin, she used her hands to heal, and a vicious killer tied her up. Something smells about this case—and it isn't merely the strange odor the killer left behind in the victim's bedroom.

Scarpetta can almost see her way into the killer's mind when the next victim presents evidence that tears through her theories. The killer has to be choosing his targets somehow. If only Scarpetta can find out how he selects his victims, she can find out who the killer is.

As the plot works to its surprising climax in a scene worthy of the best of the noir film directors, Cornwell brings her book to a masterful ending that knocked this reader's socks off.

Body of Evidence

HARDCOVER EDITION:
New York: Charles Scribner's Sons, 1991
ISBN: 0-684-19240-3

PAPERBACK EDITIONS:
New York: Avon Books, 1992
ISBN: 0-380-71701-8

New York: Pocket Books, 1999
ISBN: 0-671-03856-7

In October 1990, Scarpetta has the body of a brutally murdered novelist stashed in her refrigerator in the morgue. Reclusive author Beryl Madison had been tormented by threatening phone calls and the feeling that she was being stalked. She fled from Richmond to Key West to escape that feeling. She came back home, but her instincts were on the money, for she was murdered the night she returned to Richmond.

Life has gone on for the characters in Scarpetta's world. Marino has made lieutenant, complete with a brand-new LTD Crown Victoria to mark his increased stature on the force. Scarpetta and Marino go over the crime scene, step by step, but they find nothing. More important, they don't understand why a woman afraid for her life would let her killer into the security of her home.

As the case gets more complicated, so does Scarpetta's life. Help turns up in a very strange quarter—from lawyer Mark James, who dated Scarpetta back in school long ago and was once the love of her life. Scarpetta hasn't seen him for more than a decade.

Marino's concentration is split between clues to the murder and the agony of watching his new car get gradually trashed as the story develops. Starting with a missing cigarette lighter, and ending in a fiery inferno, the car's slow demise and its effect on Marino help build the tension, and yet are hysterically funny to anyone who has suffered through the torture of watching a new vehicle lose its shine.

The stakes get bigger when it becomes clear that Beryl's killer is fixated on Scarpetta. As her anxiety builds and her options shrink, Scarpetta has to find the killer before he finds her. Cornwell takes the reader through the dirty side of New York publishing, the secret pathways of money laundering, and the deranged mind of a psychopath.

All That Remains

HARDCOVER EDITION:
New York: Charles Scribner's Sons, 1992
ISBN: 0-684-19395-7

PAPERBACK EDITION:
New York: Avon Books, 1993
ISBN: 0-380-71833-2

On the last day of August 1992, Scarpetta has her hands full. Her plans for a peaceful Labor Day weekend have been trashed by an influx of bodies at the morgue. Most troubling among the corpses from car wrecks and shootings are a collection of bones—what remains of the victims of a particularly nasty murderer. A serial killer has been targeting couples for no apparent reason, burying their bodies in the Virginia woods. Now their bones are the only evidence. One of the most recent victims is the child of a political insider, a woman in charge of the president's war on drugs. Because this victim's mother has powerful connections, the pressure on Scarpetta to solve the case is unbearable.

This book showcases Cornwell's increasing mastery of the tools of her craft. The authentic small touches that are her trademark shine. There's the embarrassed trooper who tries to turn Scarpetta away from the roadside rest stop where the latest remains have been found because she doesn't look like a medical examiner. He tells Kay to "'Have a nice one'" (p. 6) as she goes to examine the scene, simply because he can't think of anything better to say after having made a fool of himself. The author's careful use of detail really comes to the fore in the stunning description of Scarpetta's examination of the bones for the tiniest clues that might identify the killer.

Cruel & Unusual

HARDCOVER EDITION:
New York: Charles Scribner's Sons, 1993
ISBN: 0-684-19530-5

PAPERBACK EDITION:
New York: Avon Books, 1994
ISBN: 0-380-71834-0

It's getting close to Christmas 1990, and Scarpetta is waiting for a corpse. Convicted killer Ronnie Joe Waddell is about to die in Virginia's electric chair, and Scarpetta and her staff are in the morgue, waiting to process the body.

As she waits for Waddell's body, Scarpetta is asked to consult on another case, this one a helpless thirteen-year-old boy. The boy's case bears striking similarities to the one that put Waddell on death row. But the convicted killer couldn't possibly have committed this recent crime. Scarpetta knows exactly where he was when the violence occurred, and he was in no position to have any part of it.

Another question haunts her—why did Waddell have a collection of cash register receipts with him, to be buried with him after he died? The receipts track purchases made shortly before Waddell's death. With Waddell securely behind bars when the charges were incurred, what could they possibly mean?

Scarpetta's personal life is again in a shambles. Mark James, the man she loved, was killed in a terrorist bombing in London, leaving a hole in her heart and an urge to avenge his death. As Marino puts it, "'You'd give them free autopsies if you could. And you'd want them alive and would cut real slow'" (p. 20). Scarpetta has the pressure of an unexpectedly grown-up Lucy visiting for the holidays, and now a whole new rash of crimes making her life miserable.

Waddell's death should have served to close the chapter on a string of murders. Instead, it's only the beginning of a new series of killings that seem to be related to Waddell—especially in the clues left behind. Waddell's fingerprints even turn up at a new crime scene, one that took place after his death.

With help from Scarpetta's friends and family, a clever killer will emerge from the shadows, and his name will become national news.

The Body Farm

HARDCOVER EDITION:
New York: Charles Scribner's Sons, 1994
ISBN: 0-684-19597-6

PAPERBACK EDITION:
New York: Berkley Books, 1995
ISBN: 0-425-14762-2

It's the fall of 1993, and Scarpetta's life is about to get complicated. Called in to assist in the investigation into the death of eleven-year-old Emily Steiner in the little North Carolina town of Black Mountain, Scarpetta has more questions than the available evidence can answer. On the surface, the crime bears the signature of the serial killer Temple Brooks Gault. But Scarpetta's not convinced that he's guilty this time.

At the top of Scarpetta's list of much-needed answers is a desperate desire to find out not just how Emily was killed, but when and where. The evidence provided by the little girl's corpse makes no sense. She's been missing for a week, yet the rate of decomposition isn't consistent with the estimated time of death. Not only that, but a strange mark on the corpse needs to be researched. Scarpetta's questions lead her to The Body Farm, a research facility in Tennessee that investigates questions about how long it takes a human body to decompose under various conditions.

Even as Scarpetta looks into the murder, another of the investigators on the case ends up dead in a most compromising way. A search of the crime scene turns up some improbable evidence. The author's complete understanding of forensic investigation and her deft handling of the dialogue among cops who have seen way too much of death and who fight it off with macabre humor are displayed at their finest in this scene.

Scarpetta has too many bodies, too many suspects, and she is convinced that the police department's most likely suspect is both innocent and completely defenseless.

Scarpetta's niece, Lucy, is following in her aunt's footsteps and working with the FBI as a computer maven. But a shocking crime has been committed upon the FBI's heavily guarded computer network, and Lucy is the main suspect. Scarpetta isn't sure what to believe. Her niece is telling her one thing, and the evidence is telling her another story. Lucy's guilt seems a foregone conclusion.

As Scarpetta works to solve the case against Lucy and to find the perpetrator of the murders in Black Mountain, a sinister presence makes itself known everywhere Scarpetta looks.

From Potter's Field

HARDCOVER EDITION:
New York: Charles Scribner's Sons, 1995
ISBN: 0-684-19598-4

PAPERBACK EDITION:
New York: Berkley Books, 1996
ISBN: 0-425-15409-2

It's Christmas Eve 1994, and Scarpetta's worst nightmares are about to come to life. Temple Gault has returned. His latest killing spree has started with a nameless woman's murder in New York's Central Park, but his ultimate target is Scarpetta. He has adopted her name to eat at one of Manhattan's fine restaurants. He's stolen her identity to pay for his meals. He's killed a cop because Scarpetta was getting too close to finding out the victim's name, and he stayed behind to watch her investigate the body. Scarpetta spots him, initiating a hair-raising chase through the tunnels of New York's subway system. Temple Gault seems to be everywhere.

Scarpetta suspects that Gault has tapped into some official information net as Lucy becomes involved in the case. A virus has infected the FBI computers, and it's feeding Gault everything he needs to know about their pursuit of him. As the plot builds to a showdown between Gault and Scarpetta, the psychological war between the good doctor and her brilliant nemesis rises to a fever pitch.

Cause of Death

HARDCOVER EDITION:
New York: G. P. Putnam's Sons, 1996
ISBN: 0-399-14146-4

PAPERBACK EDITION:
New York: Berkley Books, 1997
ISBN: 0-425-15861-6

It's New Year's Eve 1995, and it has been the bloodiest year in Virginia's history since the Civil War. As she prepares her annual summary of the past year's mayhem and murder, Scarpetta is called out to the Inactive Naval Ship Yard, a ships' graveyard of old naval vessels on the Elizabeth River, to examine the body of a scuba diver. When she arrives, she runs a gauntlet of bureaucratic obstruction, red tape, and inside joking among the men who make their living on the docks. It all reminds her of the troubles she had early in her career, when she was the lone woman in a field dominated by chauvinistic men. The author's descriptions of Scarpetta's state of mind as she deals with these difficulties will strike home with any reader who has ever felt like an outsider.

But Scarpetta perseveres. Cutting through the antics of anyone who tries to stop her, she enters the cold water and finds the body of an old acquaintance: Ted Eddings, an investigative reporter who investigated one story too many.

Scarpetta's first surprise is the whiff of cyanide she gets when she opens Ted's body—and suggests that she's looking at murder, not accidental death.

As Ted Eddings is laid out on the slab, one of the detectives working with her asks her if the loss of young lives ever gets to her. She replies, "'I can't let it get to me because they need me to do a good job for them'" (p. 34). It's a perfect Scarpetta moment, one that reveals Scarpetta's motivation that runs all through the series, and the reason that the books are so compelling.

But there's more to the mystery than the reporter's wrongful death. How did Scarpetta get the call reporting a wrongful death before the police did? That's just the tip of the iceberg in this strange case.

Kay's search for the killer leads her to an unlikely viper's nest of suspects with worldwide connections. And in the course of her investigation she discovers that her colleague and lover, Benton Wesley, has separated from his wife. It's a surprise for Scarpetta, one that he has neglected to share with her. But she must put aside her personal concerns and concentrate on the killer. It's clear there's a conspiracy at work—the only question is who will die next before Scarpetta can get to the bottom of it.

Unnatural Exposure

HARDCOVER EDITION:
New York: G. P. Putnam's Sons, 1997
ISBN: 0-399-14285-1

PAPERBACK EDITION:
New York: Berkley Books, 1998
ISBN: 0-425-16340-7

It's the fall of 1997, and Scarpetta is giving lectures in Ireland. She's gone there both to share her expertise with the local law enforcement agencies and also to examine a series of ten-year-old murders with eerie similarities to four cases that have cropped up in Virginia in the last year. She has no solid clues—no fingerprints, no dentition, no DNA to match the victims against. All she has is cut-up victims and the suspicion that the killer is adept with a meat saw. But the Irish cases are indeed similar enough that there must be a connection. All she has to do is find it.

She's also taken the Irish gig to keep her away from Benton Wesley, who is newly divorced. But as Marino says, " 'Comes a time when you got to call or fold . . .' " (p. 6). Scarpetta knows that's true, both for the case she's working and for her relationship with Benton. She returns to Virginia only to discover another dismembered body awaiting her in the Atlantic Waste Landfill. But this one's different.

Then the killer sends Scarpetta a message via the Internet: a picture of the dismembered body, including the hands and feet, of his latest victim—a photo so detailed that Scarpetta can see skin whorls and ridges in it. Finally, they might have a break in the case. They can identify the victim. But the source of the e-mail is troubling—going by the name of *deadoc,* the sender has clearly done everything possible to pattern a virtual self after Scarpetta.

Then Scarpetta contracts a virus that the victim was carrying and others may soon be sick if she can't solve the case.

As it is, the government's involved, the U.S. Army Medical Institute of Infectious Diseases and the CDC are looking at the virus, and the victim's house is being torched, along with everything inside, to stop the spread of infection. It's up to Scarpetta, since the killer is fixated on her, to set a trap to catch the killer. With the help of Lucy and Lucy's friend Janet, Scarpetta uses the Internet to close in on the perpetrator.

Point of Origin

HARDCOVER EDITION:
New York: G. P. Putnam's Sons, 1998
ISBN: 0-399-14394-7 (acid-free paper)
ISBN: 0-399-14412-9 (limited edition)

PAPERBACK EDITION:
New York: Berkley Books, 1999
ISBN: 0-425-16986-3

It's the summer of 1998, and Scarpetta's old enemies are surfacing everywhere. Carrie Grethen returns, mailing threatening letters to her. The killer who dismembered his victims is back and looking for new ways to get Scarpetta's attention. This time he's burying each of his crimes under an inferno. And it seems that Scarpetta's old enemies have something in common.

It's not the horror of these crimes so much as the choice of targets that worries Scarpetta. It seems a killer is closing in on the people she knows and loves, one by one. Everyone she knows is at risk: Benton Wesley, who wants to marry her. Lucy, who wants to emulate her. And all the people she has worked with for years.

A killer will put Scarpetta through a trial by fire in more ways than one—and nobody she loves is safe. In the end, her terrible sense of loss will drive her to find the culprits and bring them to justice.

Black Notice

HARDCOVER EDITION:
New York: G. P. Putnam's Sons, 1999
ISBN: 0-399-14508-7 (acid-free paper)
ISBN: 0-399-14522-2 (limited edition)

PAPERBACK EDITION:
New York: Berkley Books, 2000
ISBN: 0-425-17540-5

Scarpetta's old friend, Senator Frank Lord, has delivered one last message from Benton Wesley. It's a letter from Benton, one he wanted given to

Scarpetta (p. 2, *The Last Precinct*). The letter has brought back memories of Benton that Scarpetta has been suppressing, both of their times together and of all the crimes that kept them apart.

But, as always, crime gets in the way of Scarpetta's personal life. A decomposed body turns up in a shipping container en route from Belgium to Richmond. Scarpetta's postmortem turns up no answers, only questions—and an odd tattoo.

Not only is the autopsy a puzzle, it's clear that someone in Scarpetta's office is leaking information to the press. Her search for the identity of the killer and the identity of the snake in her office will lead her far afield. She'll see old friends and make new ones—on both sides of the Atlantic. She'll help Lucy through a terrible time as Lucy's partner in life and in HIDTA is wounded, and Lucy takes it badly. And, as the case heats up, Scarpetta heads to Interpol in France, and to a mission that could ruin her career . . . if she lives. Before matters come to a head, she'll find love and lose it, face the possibility that her career in Virginia may be over, and look a killer in the face on her own doorstep.

The Last Precinct

HARDCOVER EDITION:
New York: G. P. Putnam's Sons, 2000
ISBN: 0-399-14625-3

PAPERBACK EDITION:
New York: Berkley Books, 2001
ISBN: 0-425-18063-8

It's December 1999. Kay Scarpetta has been nearly murdered in her own home, and everybody around her is terrified. Scarpetta herself is merely strung out, jittery, in pain, and making the lives of those who love her miserable. She broke her elbow as she ran from the killer down an icy flight of stairs, so she's not in the best of shape physically, either. The police want her out of her house because it's now a crime scene, and the press is boiling with rumors about what is going on at her lab.

Scarpetta's stranded in the spotlight of her own success. As a series of events turns official suspicions on her, and an investigation headed by a formidable prosecutor is closing in on Scarpetta's life from every possible angle, she must find the truth—both about the crimes being committed by others and about the crimes being committed against her. And in the end she must decide what she herself holds dear.

The killer who assaulted Scarpetta in her home left a trail of other victims behind him—some in New York City. In Richmond, the commonwealth's attorney, Righter, may be after Scarpetta, and he's using Jaime Berger, the very woman whom Scarpetta helped investigate the murders in New York, as a weapon against her.

Blow Fly

HARDCOVER EDITION:
> New York: G. P. Putnam's Sons, 2003
> ISBN: 0-399-15089-7

PAPERBACK EDITION:
> New York: Berkley Books, 2004
> ISBN: 0-425-19669-0

It's the summer of 2003 and Scarpetta has fled Virginia, looking for peace, but she's soon drawn into a series of baffling murders in Florida. Still shaken from her experiences back in Richmond, she knows that she must figure out who she really is if she wants to heal. Her emotional balance governs not just her sense of self but also her effectiveness as an investigator. But she never seems to be able to make time for herself—the crime before her always takes precedence. In her quest for truth in a current case, she uncovers unexpected evidence, clues that bring her face to face with an international conspiracy and its connections to murders in Louisiana.

Trace

HARDCOVER EDITION:
> New York: G. P. Putnam's Sons, 2004
> ISBN: 0-399-15219-9

> New York: Berkley Books, 2005
> ISBN: 0-425-20420-0

Scarpetta left Richmond, Virginia, five years ago, turning her back on the city that was the scene of her greatest successes, and in the end her most stunning betrayal. She's been freelancing from her base in South Florida, when she is asked to return to Richmond to help with an odd case. She returns to the city that had once meant so much to her to find that nothing is as it seems. The person she thought invited her didn't. Her old lab is being demolished. The chief medical examiner is inept, and the case she was brought in to consult on is a shambles.

Lucy and Marino are busy with another case, an attempted rape by a stalker. So Scarpetta must get on with her investigation on her own.

The murder victim, a fourteen-year-old girl, can no longer speak for herself, and Scarpetta has only the smallest traces of evidence to work with. But she is determined to make the dead speak and to bring the killer to justice—no matter what it may cost her personally.

THE ANDY BRAZIL SERIES
Hornet's Nest

HARDCOVER EDITION:
New York: G. P. Putnam's Sons, 1997
ISBN: 0-399-14288-2

PAPERBACK EDITION:
New York: Berkley Books, 1998
ISBN: 0-425-16098-X

Markedly different in tone from the Scarpetta novels, and laugh-out-loud funny in places, this book looks at life in the Charlotte, North Carolina, police force. The story centers on the police chief, Judy Hammer, who is brilliant at her job and yet personally troubled; Hammer's deputy chief, Virginia West, who has built her whole life around the job; and reporter Andy Brazil, a sometimes-too-eager volunteer cop.

Southern Cross

HARDCOVER EDITION:
New York: G. P. Putnam's Sons, 1999
ISBN: 0-399-14465-X

PAPERBACK EDITION:
New York: Berkley Books, 1999
ISBN: 0-425-17254-6

Judy Hammer has been brought in to Richmond to clean up the city's police force. Still reeling from the recent death of her husband, she brings in her old friends Virginia West and Andy Brazil to help. And she needs their help, because she has to find the link between the desecration of a statue of Jefferson Davis, president of the Confederacy, and the murder of an elderly woman. There's a passel of problems in the town, and it seems that nothing, not even the Azalea Parade, can go on until they're solved.

Isle of Dogs

HARDCOVER EDITION:
New York: G. P. Putnam's Sons, 2001
ISBN: 0-399-14739-X

PAPERBACK EDITION:
New York: Berkley Books, 2002
ISBN: 0-425-18290-8

The governor of Virginia has declared war on speeders. And it's up to Judy Hammer, now the superintendent of the state police, to deal with the consequences. Nowhere is it pretty—but on the eccentric island of Tangier, thirteen miles off the Virginia coast in Chesapeake Bay, things have gone completely wacko. There's a thrill killer running around town, and she's as "unique" as her name. And then there are the crazy "mad dog hijackers" who are making the town's dogs run for their lives. The island has declared war against the mainland, and it's up to Judy and her friends to navigate the murky waters of politicians versus the people (and vice versa) and bring peace to the Commonwealth of Virginia.

NONFICTION

A Time for Remembering:
The Story of Ruth Bell Graham

HARDCOVER EDITION:
San Francisco: Harper & Row, 1983
ISBN: 0-06-061685-7

This is Cornwell's first book, a biography of evangelist Billy Graham's wife. The Grahams lived just a short distance down the road from Cornwell as she grew up. The book is a loving look at Ruth Graham, who had been a friend of the author's since she was a child, and who encouraged the young Patricia Cornwell to write. Ruth Bell Graham has often been hard to see in the shadow of her famous husband's career, but the author's portrait of her reveals what a vital force she has been in her husband's ministry. In addition, it shows what an amazing woman Mrs. Graham has been in shaping her own life and giving back love to the world in God's name.

Ruth, A Portrait:
The Story of Ruth Bell Graham

HARDCOVER EDITION:
New York: Doubleday, 1997
ISBN: 0-385-48879-3

PAPERBACK EDITION:
New York: Doubleday, 1998
ISBN: 0-385-48900-5

This is an updated and revised version of Cornwell's biography of Billy Graham's wife. Once again, the portrait of an indomitable and giving woman emerges from the gifted pen of Patricia Cornwell, who has known Ruth Graham since Patricia was seven years old.

Food to Die For:
Secrets from Kay Scarpetta's Kitchen

HARDCOVER EDITION:
New York: G. P. Putnam's Sons, 2001
ISBN: 0-399-14799-3

PAPERBACK EDITION:
New York: Berkley Books, 2003
ISBN: 0-425-19362-4

This book is something fans have long wanted—a fabulous look at how to make the scrumptious food that is described in Cornwell's novels. The cookbook also features quotes from the books, sidebars on the ingredients she uses, and advice on how to pick the finest tomatoes and the richest olive oils. In addition, it includes recipes from some of the restaurants featured in Cornwell's fiction, many of them created because fans of the books asked for them so often.

Portrait of a Killer:
Jack the Ripper—Case Closed

HARDCOVER EDITION:
New York: G. P. Putnam's Sons, 2002
ISBN: 0-399-14932-5

PAPERBACK EDITION:
New York: Berkley Books, 2003
ISBN: 0-425-19273-3

Patricia Cornwell used her own funds and her forensic expertise to take a close look at one of history's most horrific criminals. She used her literary acclaim and her unique access as a means to examine documents that haven't been examined in nearly a century. She ran modern investigative tests on all the original evidence presented in the case, and purchased and examined new evidence. Her conclusion—a shocking one that is well supported by the facts but is not popular with traditional Ripperologists—is that a famous artist of the day, Walter Sickert, was responsible for the killings. Sickert was a student of Whistler and Degas and a sometime actor. Like her gripping fiction, *Portrait of a Killer* takes the reader back to the streets of London in 1888, as well as deep into the methods of modern criminology, on the path of the notorious Jack the Ripper.

CHILDREN'S FICTION
Life's Little Fable

HARDCOVER EDITION:
New York: G. P. Putnam's Sons, 1999
ISBN: 0-399-23316-4

This children's picture book explores a fairy-tale world and teaches children that there are consequences for every action, no matter how perfect the world we live in. The book was written in response to the comments of a classroom full of second-graders that Cornwell visited in Los Angeles. A portion of the proceeds from the book are donated to literacy causes.

MISCELLANEOUS WORKS
Scarpetta's Winter Table

HARDCOVER EDITION:
Charleston, S.C.: Wyrick & Company, 1998
ISBN: 0-941711-42-0 (cloth)

This novella is a rare look at Scarpetta's softer side as she cooks her way through the days after Christmas with her family and friends. Recipes are introduced inside this novella from Scarpetta, Marino, and Lucy, as well as others, and a number of small domestic events occur while the characters cook their favorites. Including everything from Marino's run-in with a small boy who bombards his place with snowballs to the way to soothe a difficult family situation with superb food, the book is a charming Christmas gift to Patricia Cornwell's fans.

[Note: Due to space constraints, it would be impossible to include the publishers' information for every edition of every book.]

PART TWO

THE MAIN CHARACTERS

KAY SCARPETTA, MASTER SLEUTH

KAY Scarpetta, chief medical examiner for the Commonwealth of Virginia, is well educated, brilliant, professionally successful, wealthy, and divorced; she maintains an outward shell of calm dignity. Inside, though, she is a boiling cauldron of complexities.

Relationships are important to her, but not something at which she excels. She is extremely selective about the men she becomes involved with, and she revels in the feeling of being in love. Her track record in romance isn't exactly stellar. She often struggles with her emotions. She appears to have a cool, almost Victorian rejection of sexual arousal. This is in spite of the fact that she relishes her own sexual encounters. She can also surrender to passion in a sudden liaison. In the bedroom, she is an enigma. The men in her life are irresistibly attracted to her and sometimes frustrated by her as well.

Her relationships with her widowed mother and her one sister are a disaster, something that adds significant tension to her life. She has another family affiliation: Lucy, a niece to whom she is close.

Scarpetta is stubborn, driven, ambivalent about smoking, and a connoisseur of fine wines and a variety of liquors. She loves classical music. She has elegant tastes in furniture and home decor as well. In the kitchen, she can compete with a first-class chef, particularly when preparing Italian cuisine.

On the job, she can hold her own with chief executives and top government officials. Her strength and certainty are an integral part of her work life and serve to keep her centered. They are also a necessity, for her work life isn't easy. She is surrounded by death. She is also surrounded by men.

She is a woman.

And she works in a man's world.

This is a source of much difficulty for her. Her jaw tightens at the slightest hint of sexism. When she expresses this to a colleague, he reinforces her attitudes. "'You're a woman in a man's world. You'll always be considered an easy mark until the ole boys discover you have teeth. And you do have teeth. Make sure they know it'" (p. 245, *Postmortem*). Scarpetta learns to bare her fangs whenever she feels threatened by men.

Men envy her, become angry with her, lust for her, and cannot understand her. The relationships in her life seem doomed.

Her job, her values, and her principles are important to this woman. In *Cause of Death,* she makes her duties crystal clear: "'I'm Dr. Kay Scarpetta, the chief medical examiner,' I said as I displayed the brass shield that symbolized my jurisdiction over every sudden, unattended, unexplained or violent death in the Commonwealth of Virginia" (p. 9).

Even though she is scrupulously honest in professional dealings, Scarpetta tends to shade the truth about her age. In *Postmortem,* the first book about Scarpetta, she admits to being forty, while her niece, Lucy, is ten years old. In *The Last Precinct,* Lucy is twenty-eight, but Scarpetta has not yet reached fifty. The discrepancy may be intentional.

Born in Miami, Florida, about three years into the post–World War II baby boom, Scarpetta is of Italian Catholic heritage. "My ancestors are from Verona in northern Italy," she explains, "where a sizeable segment of the population shares blood with Savoyards, Austrians, Swiss. Many of us are blue-eyed and blond" (p. 386, *Cruel & Unusual*). She has inherited these characteristics, as well as her shapely figure. A size 8 dress fits her 5'5" frame perfectly.

Regarding her clothing and style, she says, "I do wear jeans. . . . I . . . dress like a proper chief or lawyer, usually in a tailored skirt suit or flannel trousers and a blazer. . . . I wear my blond hair short and neatly styled, am light on makeup and other than my signet ring and watch, jewelry is an afterthought. I don't have a single tattoo" (p. 307, *The Last Precinct*).

It may be a slight show of vanity that she seldom mentions her use of eyeglasses or that she is left-handed.

People who don't know Scarpetta very well may think she is too businesslike and that she reins her emotions too tightly. There are long-standing reasons for this ostensibly tough exterior, which appears even more impenetrable at Christmas. At age twelve, she lost her father on December 23. He had owned a small grocery store in Miami and provided a comfortable if not affluent living. A loyal family man, he was idolized by the elder of his two daughters. Scarpetta recalls, "His full name was Kay Marcellus Scarpetta III, and he insisted that his firstborn take this name, which has been in the family since Verona" (p. 254, *The Last Precinct*). Until he fell ill with leukemia, her life was happy. All of that changed into pained resignation as she watched him waste away. "I did not cry when my father died. He had been sick so many years I became an expert at cauterizing my emotions. When he finally died one evening at home, my mother's terrible grief drove me to a higher ground of detachment. . . ." (p. 161, *Body of Evidence*).

Death loomed ominously during her young, formative years. Even her favorite key lime tree in the backyard contracted citrus canker and died despite her devoted efforts to save it. It remained there, standing like a skeleton because Kay wouldn't let her mother cut it down.

Wrapping herself tightly against emotional trauma, young Kay focused even harder on academics, at which she already excelled as a straight-A student. But an event at St. Michael's Catholic School left more scars. A jealous classmate falsely accused her of cheating on a test, resulting in a cruel confrontation by the teacher, Sister Teresa. "There she was in her habit, towering over me like a giant frowning Antarctic bird wearing a crucifix" (p. 415, *The Last Precinct*). The nun made life miserable, lecturing Kay about the sins of cheating and coercing her to pray for guidance toward honesty. This experience planted a seed that would grow into a belief in meticulous truthfulness, except perhaps in divulging her age. No one is perfect.

By earning scholarships, Scarpetta advanced to Our Lady of Lourdes Academy, Cornell, Johns Hopkins, and Georgetown, taking degrees as a medical doctor and a lawyer. "I was one of four women in my class at Hopkins," she points out (p. 68, *Postmortem*). Breaking through the glass ceiling that holds some women behind in professional life is a point of pride with Scarpetta. "I was a small insect faced with a formidable male network web in which I might be ensnared but never a part" (p. 68, *Postmortem*). Nothing rankles her more than a perceived male attitude of superiority.

While pursuing her law degree at Georgetown, Scarpetta found a lover. She met Mark James, a tall, graceful, aristocratic hunk. "Even when we slept together our lovemaking did not permit many hours of rest . . . I was convinced we would be together forever" (p. 72, *All That Remains*). But when she graduated, she was "wearing someone else's engagement ring" (p. 75, *All That Remains*).

Scarpetta is coy about how many romantic liaisons she has experienced. "In truth, my lovers had been few" (p. 298, *The Body Farm*). She goes on to explain: "[T]hey had all been formidable men who were not without sensitivity and a certain acceptance that I was a woman who was not a woman. I was the body and sensibilities of a woman with the power and drive of a man, and to take away from me was to take away from themselves. So they gave the best they had, even my ex-husband, Tony [Benedetti], who was the least evolved of the lot, and sexuality was a shared erotic competition. Like two creatures of equal strength who had found each other in the jungle, we tumbled and took as much as we gave" (p. 298).

Does this revelation hint of a latent bisexuality? Her sister, Dorothy, seems to think so. In a drunken rage, Dorothy rails at Kay about her most recent lover. "'You were the *man* in that relationship, *Miss doctor-lawyer-chief*. I've told you before and I'll tell you again, you're nothing but a man with big tits.'" As Dorothy's anger spews even more, she yells, "'You're a closet diesel dyke'" (pp. 280–281, *Black Notice*).

On another occasion Scarpetta accidentally observes her gay niece with another woman and recalls it: "I could still hear them teasing in low playful voices and saw their erotic kisses on the mouth, deep and long, and hands tangled in hair. I remembered the strange sensation running through my blood as I silently hurried away, without them knowing what I had seen" (p. 13, *Point of Origin*).

In *The Last Precinct*, Anna, a confidante, asks about a woman with whom Scarpetta has conflicted feelings. "'Do you think she was sexually attracted to you?'" (p. 98).

Scarpetta gives it deep thought, wrestles with an answer, and finally responds. "'Possibly,' I equivocate." She claims, however, that she would have deflected any sexual advances by the woman. Wondering whether the questions are designed to see if she is homophobic, Scarpetta mulls it over in her mind. "I reach as deep as I can to see if I am uncomfortable with homosexuality." She decides, "'I'm okay with it. . . . It simply isn't my preference'" (p. 99).

After probing the subject even more, Anna gets right to the point. "'Have you ever felt attracted to a woman?'" (p. 100).

"'I have found some women very compelling,'" Scarpetta admits (p. 100), recalling crushes on female teachers. Finally, they allow the subject to peter out with no resolution. Scarpetta becomes the interrogator on a different line of inquiry.

Even if Scarpetta feels any attraction to her own gender, her romantic and sexual involvements are focused on men. But they are filled with pitfalls. Like her relationship with Mark, Scarpetta's marriage to Tony Benedetti fell apart, but not until it had consumed six years of her young life. Scarpetta recalls this while one of her subordinates offers coffee and fails to remember that she drinks it black. "My ex-husband never remembered either. Six years I lived with Tony and he couldn't remember that I drink my coffee black or like my steaks medium-rare, not as red as Christmas, just a little pink. My dress size, forget it. . . . I can't abide fluff, froth and frills. He always got me something in a six, usually lacy and gauzy and meant for bed. . . . [However, when] it came to his mother, Tony would somehow get it right" (p. 42, *Postmortem*).

Scarpetta's interactions with her own mother and her sister are fractious. Her ailing mother, who still lives in Miami, is acerbic and critical on the subject of Scarpetta's infrequent visits to see her. Her sister, Dorothy, Lucy's mother, is equally unpleasant. An author of children's books, Dorothy is a gadfly bouncing from man to man, an unsuccessful mother, and a thorn in Scarpetta's side. She recalls, "Dorothy . . . had been consummately narcissistic and irresponsible since the day she was born" (p. 161, *Body of Evidence*). "She was briefly married to a Brazilian twice her age who supposedly fathered Lucy. I say *supposedly,* because when it comes to Dorothy, only DNA would convince me of who she happened to be in bed with on the occasion my niece was conceived. My sister's fourth marriage was to a Farinelli, and after that Lucy stopped changing her name" (p. 29, *The Last Precinct*). During one of Dorothy's infrequent visits to Richmond, Scarpetta comments, "I was struck again by how much I disliked my sister. It made no sense to me that she was my sister, for I failed to find anything in common between us except our mother and memories of once living in the same house" (p. 248, *The Body Farm*).

The one relative Scarpetta loves is her niece, Lucy, whom Dorothy feels Scarpetta has tried to steal away and treat as her own daughter. Yet this relationship, too, is filled with bickering, misunderstandings, separations, and ongoing stress. As Lucy grows from a precocious, impertinent, ten-year-old redheaded computer genius to a brilliant adult techno-whiz, pilot, and millionaire, Scarpetta continues to adore her. With no misgivings at all, she accepts Lucy's homosexuality but constantly worries about her safety, especially when she joins the FBI.

In Scarpetta's own work, she is a perfectionist. She admits, "I tend to obsess over a task, any task" (p. 436, *The Last Precinct*). What guided her to choose a profession in which she would examine dead bodies in gruesome detail? Most coroners and chief medical examiners across the nation are men. Why would a woman select this field? Scarpetta offers some insight: "The career I . . . embarked on would forever return me to the scene . . . of my father's death. I would take death apart and put it back together a thousand times. . . . I would understand the nuts and bolts of it. But none of it brought my father back to life, and the child inside me never stopped grieving" (p. 162, *The Body of Evidence*).

In a sense, corpses speak to Scarpetta. Of course, corpses do not literally talk to Scarpetta, but she believes her job gives the departed individual one last opportunity to communicate through the discoveries a medical examiner can make. Their silent speech might provide many answers. Were they murdered? If so, how? Poison, blunt force trauma, shooting, strangling? Were they ill prior to their deaths? What environment surrounded them when they died? These and hundreds of other questions may be cleared up by human remains under the intense scrutiny of a competent investigator. For Scarpetta, it is more than a job.

An interesting difference between Scarpetta and her creator is revealed in *Postmortem*. Scarpetta states, "I no longer enjoy flying and opt for Amtrak whenever possible" (p. 41). Cornwell is known to fly her helicopter to book signings. Good books, though, require evolution of the characters, so Scarpetta not only shrugs off her fear of flying, but eventually imitates her creator by learning to pilot a helicopter.

A great deal of Scarpetta's working time is alongside police detective Pete Marino, who takes a dim view of her claim that bodies talk to her. A pair of murder victims had been found days after their car was located. Investigators had delayed reporting discovery of the car to Scarpetta. Chastising Marino, she said, "'If, God forbid, there is a next time, don't wait until the bodies turn up. . . . Let me know the minute the car is found.'"

Marino sarcastically snaps back, "'Yo. May as well start autopsying the cars since the bodies ain't telling us nothing'" (p. 28, *All That Remains*). Scarpetta thought his response an unsuccessful attempt to be funny.

They are an effective crime-solving team and rely on each other's skills. Even so, she is frequently negative about him, which is puzzling. No one has ever had a more loyal friend. He has saved her life several times, and nearly always responds immediately to her requests for his assistance. Yet she derides his appearance, criticizes him, expresses discomfort about his rough-edged social skills, makes fun of his speech, and is condescending about his politically incorrect viewpoints. She calls him "Marino," never "Pete," yet addresses her own employees by their first names. Without a doubt, they are opposites in many ways. Gradually, especially in the more recent novels, Scarpetta begins to show the poor fellow more appreciation for his unselfish, protective devotion to her safety and her reputation. It's clear that he also harbors underlying romantic and sexual feelings for her, but never openly expresses them.

Extreme dedication makes Scarpetta a superior medical examiner and crime solver. In her zeal for bringing killers to justice, she may exceed the activities of her real-life counterparts by doing considerably more than postmortem examinations of murder victims. She acknowledges the separation of authority: "I was well aware of the boundary separating my jurisdiction from that of the police" (p. 60, *Body of Evidence*). Still, she cannot resist joining crime-scene investigations, digging up evidence, traveling in search of clues, and performing independent sleuthing. Sometimes she finds herself issuing direct orders to police investigators. Rationalizing what might appear to be an infringement of the boundaries, she explains, "Though I had no right to tell [him] what to do, by Code I had jurisdiction over the bodies" (p. 85, *All That Remains*). Medical examiners do have the right to extend their work beyond forensic pathology, and Scarpetta stretches it to the limit. Maybe more M.E.s should do the same.

Her personal vices are more worrisome—particularly smoking. In the first chapter of *Postmortem,* she says, "Lighting a cigarette, I reached for the telephone and stabbed out my home number" (p. 20). *Postmortem* was first published in 1990, before a tidal wave of public intolerance about smoking reached its crest. A medical examiner who conducts autopsies, in which damage to lungs and other organs may readily be seen, would certainly understand how cigarettes ravage the human body. Many readers in the twenty-first century may blanch at Scarpetta's tobacco habit and hope that she will eventually give it up. And she does—several times.

It is easy to imagine the unpleasant odors of smoke and chemicals permeating Scarpetta's immaculate home and her office. Perhaps she will finally lose the habit for good.

The frequent mention of wine and liquor in Scarpetta's life brings to mind the question about possible alcohol abuse. Could her health be in danger? In *Black Notice,* she's in her home, preparing to conduct research. "I poured a double Scotch, walked into my study and turned on a light" (p. 48). Later in the same book, she returns to her hotel room feeling stress, "my hands shaking, my nerves jumping as if I had some awful disease. I got three Scotches from the minibar and poured all of them at once. I didn't bother to get ice. I didn't care if I felt like hell the next day because I knew I was going to anyway" (p. 345). Back in her Richmond home, she keeps an array of spirits in her home and there is enough drinking to occasionally deplete certain selections. In *All That Remains,* she comments, "We drank Scotch in my kitchen because I was out of bourbon" (p. 394). In *Body of Evidence* she is home alone and unable to sleep. "I downed another shot of brandy, then one more, and lay in bed staring up at the dark ceiling" (p. 264).

In addition to the hard stuff, she is a wine connoisseur. There is a revealing comment in *The Last Precinct:* "Sex is very much like wine, and if the truth be told, my encounters with lovers usually end up in the *village* section of the vineyard: low on the slope, fairly common and modestly priced" (p. 97).

Maybe Scarpetta has a need for alcohol as a way to relax and allow her sexual nature to surface. Sexuality is a powerful part of her psyche. In *All That Remains,* her former lover makes an unexpected appearance: "He took me in his arms, whispering my name, like a small cry of pain. . . . He kissed me as he pushed the door with his foot. It slammed shut with a bang. My eyelids flew open. Thunder cracked. Lightning lit up my bedroom again and then again as my heart pounded" (p. 297).

This symbolism is reminiscent of old movies, cutting away from the passionate lovers to scenes of crashing surf or a train thundering into a tunnel. More recent films, of course, don't use this sort of symbolism. They depict all the details blatantly. Cornwell never does that, but she does become more explicit.

"'Do you like sex?'" a friend, who is also a psychiatrist, asks in *The Last Precinct.*

"I laugh in surprise. No one has ever asked me such a thing. 'Oh yes, but it varies. I've had very good sex, good sex, okay sex, boring sex, bad sex. Sex is a strange creature. I'm not even sure what I think of sex. But I hope I've not had the *premier grand cru* of sex. . . . I don't believe I've had my best sex yet, my deepest, most erotic sexual harmony with another person. I haven't, not yet, not at all'" (pp. 97–98).

In *The Body Farm,* Scarpetta's description of a steamy encounter includes this passage: "As his fingers undid clothing and found me, they moved as if they knew a woman's body as well as a woman did, and I felt more than his passion. . . . I had told him in bed that I had never known a man to truly enjoy a woman's body, that I did not like to be devoured or overpowered, which was why sex for me was rare" (pp. 298–299).

To Scarpetta, men may not understand women's bodies, but there is certainly no mystery for her in men's bodies. One of the killers she pursues piques her curiosity: "I wondered if his genitalia were stunted, and if this might have something to do with why he undressed his victims only from the waist up. Perhaps to see normal adult female genitalia was to remind him of his own inadequacy as a male" (p. 360, *Black Notice*).

Certain male forms are admired by Scarpetta. About her deputy chief, a man who keeps his trim body in perfect shape, she muses, "I remembered our first company picnic at my house, when he had lounged in the sun with nothing but cut-offs on. I had been amazed and slightly embarrassed that I could scarcely take my eyes off him, not because I had any thoughts of bed, but rather his raw physical beauty had briefly held me hostage" (p. 141, *Point of Origin*).

Her job requires absolute knowledge of male physiognomy and sexual behavior in every aspect, including certain bizarre conduct. For example, autoerotic asphyxiation is brought up in *Body of Evidence, The Body Farm, All That Remains,* and *Black Notice.* Using her medical knowledge, Scarpetta must be able to recognize the signs of this peculiar cause of death. Autoerotic asphyxiation is the practice of deliberately reducing oxygen intake during masturbation, often with a scarf or rope tightened around the neck. The purpose is to heighten sexual pleasure during orgasm. This is reportedly achieved because low oxygen intake causes light-headedness that in turn lowers inhibitions. The risk is exacerbated because the carotid artery in the neck can be collapsed with very little pressure, resulting in almost instant unconsciousness. Death can follow within minutes. It is estimated that up to 1,000 people die annually in the United States from this dangerous practice.

Nothing is too strange to consider in a forensic pathologist's occupation.

In Scarpetta's case, the job should pay hazardous duty bonuses. More than once, she finds herself in face-to-face showdowns with killers, *High Noon* style. This diminutive woman uses a handgun as well as any sheriff on a dusty western street. It wouldn't be giving away any plot twists to note that she survives these violent encounters, albeit with the help of good old Pete Marino.

Kay Scarpetta is among the very best.

PETE MARINO,
DISGRUNTLED DETECTIVE

PETER Rocco Marino is tough. He's the consummate police detective, good at his job but always undermining his status with a vitriolic attitude about bureaucratic brass. The only high-level executive he tolerates is Scarpetta, whom he affectionately calls "Doc." From the outset, though, she seems to dislike Marino, sometimes almost loathing him. He deliberately needles her with offensive mannerisms and comments. The tension between them ebbs and flows. Will it turn stormy and violent like the Chesapeake Bay in a hurricane, or settle into a peaceful flow like the upper James River on a summer evening?

The two people share one similarity. Like Scarpetta, he is of Italian descent, but of the brown-eyed strain. Bright and perceptive, but moderately educated, he fractures the English language and peppers his conversation with profanity. His politically incorrect comments frequently include colorful homophobic expressions. Standing about six-two, he is a chain-smoker, an overweight meat-and-potatoes man, and one who appreciates a beer or bourbon but only while off duty. He drives a big blue Ford truck (p. 158, *From Potter's Field*), then later a Dodge Ram Quad Cab pickup. His wish list is short and simple. "'I've never been to Graceland,'" he says, and adds a desire to visit "'Alaska, Las Vegas and the Grand Ole

Opry'" (p. 122, *Unnatural Exposure*). The big, unkempt detective is fearless when facing down bad guys, but harbors phobias about AIDS and the effects of radiation.

In *Postmortem,* he is a sergeant with the Richmond, Virginia, police homicide unit. His duties while investigating murders usually put him in contact with Scarpetta, who is responsible for conducting autopsies of the victims.

Right off the bat, in the first book, Scarpetta expresses consternation about Marino. He telephones her with news of a murder. She is upset. "Ordinarily, the medical examiner on call is summoned to a death scene. But this wasn't ordinary. I had made it clear after [two previous killings] that no matter the hour, if there was another murder, I was to be called. Marino wasn't keen on the idea. Ever since I was appointed chief medical examiner . . . less than two years ago he'd been difficult. I wasn't sure if he didn't like women, or if he just didn't like me" (p. 2).

At the crime scene, Scarpetta describes Marino. "He was exactly the sort of detective I avoided when given a choice—a cock of the walk and absolutely unreachable. He was pushing fifty, with a face life had chewed on, and long wisps of graying hair parted low on one side and combed over his balding pate. At least six feet tall, he was bay-windowed from decades of bourbon or beer. His unfashionably wide red-and-blue-striped tie was oily around the neck from summers of sweat. Marino was the stuff of tough-guy flicks—a crude, crass gumshoe who probably had a foul-mouthed parrot for a pet and a coffee table littered with *Hustler* magazines" (p. 10).

It grates even more deeply on Scarpetta that Marino desecrates English grammar rules and openly expresses his opinions no matter how politically incorrect. He is his own man, though, and refuses to make any changes in his demeanor.

Many male readers of the Scarpetta series will immediately like Marino and say, "Right on, dude! Nothing wrong with beer and skin magazines. Hey, this guy has to deal with scum-of-the-earth maggots every working day of his life, so it's no wonder he gets a little bitter. So what if he does a combover and his necktie shows some wear and tear? He's not a fashion magazine model, he's a cop!"

Most female readers will probably agree with Scarpetta. On the other hand, some may be attracted to Marino.

It is not until a flashback in the third book, *All That Remains,* that the first meeting between Marino and Scarpetta is recalled. He had ambled into the laboratory where she was performing an autopsy on a murder victim. Very few words were exchanged between them. Then, "He strolled off without so much as a 'goodbye' or 'nice to meet you,' by which point our professional rapport had been established. I perceived he resented me for no other cause than my gender, and in turn I dismissed him as a dolt with a brain pickled by testosterone. In truth, he had secretly intimidated the hell out of me" (p. 127). So some light is cast on her reasons for disgruntlement with Marino.

At the beginning of the Scarpetta series, Marino is in an unhappy marriage and is the father of an estranged adult son, Rocky, who becomes a shyster lawyer. No wonder the aging detective is sometimes abrasive. In *Cruel & Unusual,* Scarpetta reveals a little more about Marino's early life. "He had survived a loveless, impoverished childhood in the wrong part of New Jersey, and nursed an abiding distrust of anyone whose lot had been better." She also notes, "Regardless of his loyalty to law and order and his record of excellent police work, it was not in his genetic code to get along with the brass. It seemed his life's journey had placed him on a hard road. . . . Marino was always angry about something" (p. 20).

Marino's wife finally leaves him. In *Cause of Death,* Scarpetta asks, "'Are you still upset about Doris?'"

He replies, "'I don't know if I ever told you about one of the last big fights she and I had before she left. . . . It was about those damn dishes she got at a yard sale. I mean, she'd been thinking about getting some new dishes for a long time, right? And I come home from work one night and here's this big set of blaze orange dishes spread out on the dining-room table.'" When Marino discovered the brand name of the dishes, one of his phobias kicked in. "'There was something in the glaze of this particular line that I come to find out will set a Geiger counter off.'"

Scarpetta tries to reassure him that no danger existed, but he snorts, "'I packed up all the dishes and dumped them without telling her where. . . . A month later she left'" (pp. 220–221).

One of the things Scarpetta frequently criticizes is Marino's bulging belly, which hangs over his belt. She keeps her own figure trim and admires men who do the same. But her disdain is motivated partly by her concern for his health. As a doctor, she realizes that his diet, high blood pressure, and excessive weight make him a high-risk candidate for a heart attack. When he begins to devour a grease-soaked steak biscuit from Hardee's,

Scarpetta asks, "'Do you have any idea how much sodium and fat you're ingesting right now?'" Marino replies, "'Yeah. About one third of what I'm going to ingest. I got three biscuits here, and I plan to eat every damn one of them'" (p. 78, *The Body Farm*).

Another point of contention between them is music. Scarpetta loves classical pieces; Marino worships Elvis and Patsy Cline. When an antagonist writes an online message suggesting that Presley died while on the toilet, Marino is outraged. He reads more of the unwelcome missive. "Elvis's many years of bad eating and pills . . . finally caught up with him, and he died of cardiac arrest in his luxurious bathroom in Graceland."

Incensed, Marino says, "'I wish people would leave Elvis alone'" (pp. 140–141, *Black Notice*).

Marino does have one other weakness. He is afraid to fly. This fear is mentioned several times in the series, especially when both Lucy and Scarpetta become helicopter pilots. He wants nothing to do with being in an aircraft unsupported by wings. In *Point of Origin,* he is coerced into a helicopter ride with Lucy at the controls and Scarpetta beside him. She notices that his seat belt is disconnected and asks, "'What happens if we hit severe turbulence when you're not belted in?'"

He snaps back, "'In case you ain't figured it out after all those bodies you've cut up, if this bird goes down, Doc, a seat belt ain't gonna save you. Not airbags either, if we had them'" (p. 20).

Marino's problems intensify after his wife deserts him. They eventually divorce. Lonely and depressed, Marino is involved in a few temporary relationships but nothing serious. It hurts him even more when his son is involved in defending a criminal Marino hates.

Several times in the series, Marino turns up at exactly the right moment to pull Scarpetta out of harm's way. Nearly every time she telephones him and asks him to come as soon as possible, he drops everything to join her. More than once, he saves her life. Could she show more gratitude?

Scarpetta feels surprise and a certain pity for him when she makes a business visit to his lonely house at Christmas and finds that he has covered it in "gaudy, outrageous" decorations. Inside is a lighted tree and wrapped presents, "almost all of them fake." He says, "'Least I can come home and something makes me happy. . . . Pizza's on the way. I got bourbon if you want some.'" When she asks for hot decaffeinated tea, he replies, "'You gotta be kidding'" (pp. 170–171, *Black Notice*).

On the job, he is promoted to lieutenant, then captain, but is un-comfortable in both roles. He prefers hands-on detective work.

Sometimes fatalistic, Marino comments on his mortality in *Cause of Death*: "'I'm afraid of dying. Every morning I get up and think about it, if you want to know. Every day I think I'm going to stroke out or be told I got cancer. I dread going to bed because I'm afraid I'll die in my sleep'" (p. 221). He also philosophizes about faith and life's end in *Point of Origin*, saying, "'You know how many guys I've known to drop dead of heart at-tacks or get killed on the job? How many of them do you think had faith? Probably every goddamn one of them. Nobody thinks they're gonna die, Doc. You and me don't think it, no matter how much we know. My health sucks, okay? You think I don't know I'm taking a bite of a poison cookie everyday? Can I help it? Naw. I'm just an old slob who has to have his steak biscuits and whiskey and beer. . . . So soon enough, I'm gonna stoop over in the saddle and be outta here, you know?'" He added that she would probably attend his funeral and "'tell the next detective to come along how it wasn't all that bad to work with me'" (p. 187, *Point of Origin*).

Who else would Marino share such personal thoughts with other than someone he considered his best friend? Scarpetta once said she wasn't sure if he didn't like women, or if he just didn't like her. This soliloquy by the aging detective should certainly have made his affection for her quite clear. Perhaps it did, as seen in her reply.

"'Marino . . .'" she says (never calling him Pete), "'. . . you know that's not how I feel at all. I can't even think of something happening to you, you big idiot.'"

Brightening, he asks, "'You really mean that?'"

"'You know damn well I do.'"

"'Know what, Doc? . . . I like you a lot, even if you are a pain in the fucking ass'" (p. 187).

Scarpetta reveals a bit more of a softening attitude in *All That Remains*. "It was hard for me to look at Marino now and imagine I had ever found him threatening. He looked old and defeated, shirt straining across his big belly, wisps of graying hair unruly . . . deep [facial] creases caused by the erosion of chronic tension and displeasure. . . . I gently touched his shoul-der" (p. 127).

Through the entire series, it slowly becomes evident that the rela-tionship between them is not as volatile as it once seemed. Scarpetta ex-presses contempt for Marino's appearance and habits, but probably feels a deep affection for the inner man, and certainly gratitude for his protection of her. He may very well be secretly in love with her but knows it can never be openly expressed. It's conceivable that he suppresses sexual fantasies about her as well. And she knows this.

In *The Last Precinct,* she comes to grips with these possibilities. "Marino yawns like a bear and pulls himself to his feet. He is made slightly unsteady by bourbon and smells like stale cigarettes, and regards me with a softness in his eyes that I might call sad love if I were willing to accept his true feelings for me" (p. 255).

This hard-bitten, iconoclastic man at last breaks down and acknowledges his real affection for Scarpetta in *The Last Precinct.* She is threatening to resign from her job and move from Richmond. Stunned by his reaction, Scarpetta describes it: "He shrugs and gets choked up. I can't believe it. Marino is about to cry" (p. 256).

The detective says, "'If you quit . . . Then what? I'm supposed to go down to the fucking morgue and you ain't there anymore? Hell, I wouldn't go down to that stink-hole half as much as I do if it wasn't for you being there, Doc. You're the only damn thing that gives any life to that joint, no kidding'" (p. 256).

Touched, Scarpetta is nice to him. "I hug him. I barely come up to his chest, and his belly separates the beat of our hearts. . . . I am overwhelmed by an immeasurable compassion and need for him. I pat his broad chest and let him know, 'We've been together for a long time, Marino. You're not rid of me yet'" (p. 256).

LUCY FARINELLI,
HIGH-TECH INVESTIGATOR

OBSERVING Scarpetta's close relationship with her niece, Lucy, is another pleasure of the series. It is initially very maternal and evolves into a deep friendship and a feeling of professional respect.

Caring about Lucy keeps Scarpetta grounded and striving to improve herself. Scarpetta seems to be the most open emotionally when she speaks of Lucy: "I placed my hand on her shoulder. 'I may not be the constant presence in your life that I wish I could be, but you are very important to me'" (p. 297, *Cruel & Unusual*). Scarpetta feels their roles expanding: "our relationship had become less mother-daughter as we evolved into colleagues and friends" (p. 112, *Unnatural Exposure*). Similarly, one evening they are talking in the dark and Scarpetta thinks, "For the first time in our lives, I talked to her as a trusted friend" (p. 337, *Unnatural Exposure*).

"Lucy's open adoration touched my heart as profoundly as it frightened me. She had caused me to experience a depth of feeling I had not known before" (p. 79, *Cruel & Unusual*). A poignant scene occurs when Scarpetta checks on Lucy, who is asleep. "It touched me that she was wearing a sweat suit that she had gotten out of one of my drawers. I had never had another human being wish to sleep in anything of mine" (p. 117, *Cruel & Unusual*).

"I understood her secret shame born of abandonment and isolation, and wore her same suit of sorrow beneath my polished armor. When I tended to her wounds, I was tending to my own. This was something I could not tell her" (p. 39, *The Body Farm*).

Scarpetta also worries about her influence on Lucy's lifestyle. When Lucy is interning at Quantico in *The Body Farm,* Scarpetta says, "Clearly, I had influenced her life, and very little frightened me quite as much as that did" (p. 4).

Lucy quits the FBI and ATF and creates a private investigative agency called The Last Precinct: "It's where you go when there's no place left" (p. 101, *Blow Fly*). Scarpetta senses she's troubled.

In *Blow Fly,* Lucy still can't reconcile her involvement in Benton Wesley's staged murder. Scarpetta doesn't suspect the truth and assumes Lucy is going through a terrible phase because she can't cope with Wesley's death (p. 100), Lucy blames herself for Scarpetta's unhappiness.

"'Please go south,' Lucy begged her, getting up from the bed and facing her with wet eyes and a red nose. 'For now. Please. Go back to where you came from and start all over.'

"'I'm too old to start over.'

"'Shit!' Lucy laughed. 'You're only forty-six, and men and women stare at you everywhere you go. And you don't even notice. You're one hell of a package'" (p. 136).

THE ANDY BRAZIL SERIES:
A CHANGE OF PACE

FTER the seventh Kay Scarpetta book, *Cause of Death,* Patricia Cornwell suddenly exited the fast lane of Scarpetta's adventures and moved to a twisting side road full of potholes and blind curves. She left Scarpetta, Pete Marino, and Lucy in temporary limbo. *Hornet's Nest* came out in January 1997 with a completely new set of protagonists: forty-two-year-old Deputy Chief Virginia West; her boss, unhappily married Chief Judy Hammer; and handsome wunderkind journalist and volunteer cop, Andy Brazil.

As the story progresses, flashes of Cornwell's usual brilliance emerge. Coining a memorable metaphor to describe a facial expression of anger, she writes, "He felt that bitter juice seep through his veins, the bile rising as his face reddened dangerously, his rage a solar flare on the surface of his reason" (p. 258, *Hornet's Nest*). Needing a powerful simile to express discomfort felt by a character in the presence of a dangerous woman, Cornwell penned, "He didn't want trouble, and [she] troubled him like an ice pick too close to his eye" (p. 251).

She returns to the sophisticated use of literary allusions as well. Late in *Hornet's Nest,* Cornwell describes Mayor Search and his impression of the budding journalist Andy Brazil. "This wasn't the typical smartass reporter

Search dealt with morning, noon, and night. The kid was Billy Budd, Billy Graham, wide-eyed innocence, polite, respectful, and committed. . . . [P]eople like this . . . died for causes, would do anything for Jesus, served a higher calling, were no respecter of persons, believed in burning bushes, and were not led into sin by Potiphar's wife" (p. 256).

The Bible and Herman Melville (1819–1891) are Cornwell's source for this philosophical passage. *Billy Budd* was Melville's final novel, incomplete at his death and not published until 1924. It tells the story of a handsome young sailor who is the center of struggles between good and evil, conscience versus law. Scholars have also seen it as a biblical allegory. Budd, the epitome of sweet innocence, accidentally kills his antagonist and suffers death himself. A 1962 film version of *Billy Budd* is regarded as a minor classic. Cornwell's readers may see Budd-like characteristics in Andy Brazil.

Evangelist Billy Graham's name appears frequently in Cornwell's work, possibly stemming from her first book, a biography of Graham's wife, and Cornwell's friendship with the Grahams.

"Potiphar's wife" is a reference to the Bible. In Genesis, Joseph, great-grandson of Abraham, is sold into bondage. Potiphar, an Egyptian "captain of the guard" for Pharaoh, buys the youth and gradually delegates authority to him. Potiphar's immoral, dissolute wife brings false charges against Joseph, who is cast into prison. Eventually he redeems himself by interpreting dreams of influential people. Art lovers will recognize the theme, which Rembrandt van Rijn depicted in a 1655 painting titled *Joseph Accused by Potiphar's Wife.*

In the Scarpetta series, stories unfold from the chief medical examiner's point of view. All events and people are seen through her eyes. In the Brazil novels, Cornwell institutes another sharp change by using frequent point-of-view shifts. Apparently wishing to reduce the jarring effect, she employs paragraph transitions with the use of word repetition. For example, at the beginning of *Hornet's Nest,* the reader observes action through Virginia West's eyes and thoughts as a corpse is examined at a crime scene. "Whenever the medical examiner touched the body, more blood spilled from holes in the head. West knew that whoever was doing this had no plan to *stop*" (p. 49). In the next paragraph's first sentence, Cornwell shifts point of view to Andy Brazil. "Brazil wasn't going to *stop,* no matter how much West got in his way . . ." (p. 49). By repeating the word *stop,* the author eases the sudden transition.

This technique is used frequently in all three books. Halfway through

Isle of Dogs, Andy Brazil says, "'Hate is hate. And I think it might be a good *plan* for me to address that in Trooper Truth [his website essays] soon'" (p. 176). Then Cornwell shifts to the point of view of a gang member named Cat: "Cat was unfolding his own *plan . . .*" (p. 176).

Quick point-of-view changes are risky in the hands of less adept authors, but Cornwell manages it handily. It may be a little over-the-top, though, when she shifts point of view to cats, dogs, and even crabs. It seems that the author is having a lot of fun with this freewheeling style. With that in mind, readers should relax and allow themselves to be carried along on this ride along an unfamiliar detour.

Cornwell does not forsake all of her previously applied devices. Just as she did in earlier novels, she infuses *Hornet's Nest* with unsettling conflict and tension, which keeps the reader turning pages. She dishes up stress in large doses as the protagonists grate on one another while sublimating sexual urges.

Two of the new characters, Judy Hammer and Andy Brazil, appear in all three books. The third one, Virginia West, plays a major role in *Hornet's Nest* and *Southern Cross.*

JUDY HAMMER

Judy Hammer is a strikingly attractive woman in her "early fifties" (p. 4, *Hornet's Nest*) when first introduced. She advances to fifty-five in the third book. Hammer is a mother of two grown sons and grandmother of their offspring. She is seen from Andy Brazil's point of view when he first meets her. "Brazil took in the short graying hair softly framing the pretty, sharp face, and the short stature and trim figure . . . [He] recognized her from television and photographs. . . . Brazil was awed, openly staring. He could get a terrible crush on this woman" (p. 47). This romantic reaction by the youthful Brazil may surprise some readers.

Tasteful and meticulous selection of clothing enhances her beauty. "Hammer was striking in a black silk suit with subtle pinstripes, and a black silk blouse with a high collar and black onyx beads" (p. 135, *Hornet's Nest*).

Assistant Chief Virginia West also sees Hammer's beauty. "Hammer didn't wear pants often, but today she was in them. Her suit was a deep royal blue, and she wore a red and white striped shirt and soft black leather shoes. West had to admit, her boss was stunning. Hammer could cover or show her legs without gender being an issue" (pp. 55–56, *Hornet's Nest*). Some readers may feel this passage suggests that West is sexually attracted to Hammer, but later events will dispel that notion.

Hammer and other characters in Cornwell's novels choose to wear Breitling watches, although Hammer prefers a "large scratch-proof Rado watch . . ." (p. 93, *Hornet's Nest*). Rado is a Swiss-made timepiece. The company claims to have launched the world's first scratch-proof watch in 1962.

Professionally successful as police chief in Charlotte, North Carolina, Hammer is troubled by her obese husband's depression and withdrawal into watching television, and concerned with his unhealthful eating habits. It is a major distraction for her. From Little Rock, Arkansas, Hammer still speaks with the same soft drawl of her youth when she met and married the intelligent, successful man whom she would surpass as he withered.

A total dedication to her work keeps Hammer from forming close relationships. In a self-analysis that reveals a lot about her, she states, "'I never had a friend. . . . Not in grammar school, when I was better than everyone in kickball. Not in high school, when I was good in math and the president of the student body. Not in college. Not in the police academy, now that I think about it'" (p. 192, *Hornet's Nest*).

After graduation, she advanced rapidly through the ranks, and was chosen by the mayor of Atlanta, Georgia, to become chief of police. She held the same position in Chicago before moving to Charlotte.

Even though jealous peers are resentful of her and rednecks dislike her role in "a man's profession," most people in the community respect her. When she is required to speak at a city council meeting packed with concerned citizens, she makes a strong impression. "All eyes were on the first police chief in Charlotte's history to make people feel important, no matter where they lived or who they were. Judy Hammer was the only mother some folks had ever known, in a way" (p. 206, *Hornet's Nest*).

Circumstances both tragic and enlightening will cause Hammer heartbreak, renewal of purpose, and changes in her life.

ANDY BRAZIL

Andy Brazil enters *Hornet's Nest* as an intelligent, exceptionally handsome, idealistic young journalist with a photographic memory. He is also a po-

THE ANDY BRAZIL SERIES: A CHANGE OF PACE   57

lice volunteer. Some readers may see him as a Clark Kent type, straight out of comic books. He lives with his withdrawn, alcoholic mother and still feels the pain of losing his police detective father twelve years earlier. He describes it: "'When I was ten . . . They said it was his fault. . . . Was in plain clothes, followed a stolen car out of his district, wasn't supposed to make a traffic stop. . . . The backup never got there'" (p. 134, *Hornet's Nest*). Drew Brazil, at age thirty-six, had been shot in the chest at close range and died instantly. The tragedy had destroyed Mrs. Brazil's life as well and cast a long-standing shadow over Andy's existence.

Faced with terrible loss and a ruined mother, young Brazil forges ahead and enters Davidson College. A school security guard, Mr. Briddle-wood, likes him. "He remembered Brazil as a kid, always in a hurry some-where with his Western Auto tennis racket and plastic bag of bald, dead tennis balls that he'd fished out of the trash or begged off the tennis coach. Brazil used to share his chewing gum and candy with Briddlewood, and this touched the security guard right down to his boots. The boy didn't have much and lived with a bad situation" (p. 78, *Hornet's Nest*).

Briddlewood and other generous people surreptitiously contribute to Brazil's educational expenses, hoping to provide opportunities for him.

Like Judy Hammer, Brazil makes no personal friends. He works long hours as a rookie journalist for the *Charlotte Observer,* and spends most of his spare time in his police volunteer duties. Unable to give up the only remaining symbol of his dead father, Brazil still drives an aging BMW owned by the late detective.

A librarian is impressed with the youngster. "She was well past sixty and believed that Brazil was the most beautiful human being she had ever met. He was nice and gentle and always thanked her" (p. 63, *Hornet's Nest*). Considering these traits, along with his athletic skills in running and tennis and his perfect physique, female readers may find it hard to be-lieve that Brazil has no girlfriends. Younger fans may not appreciate his selection of the woman with whom he eventually has a love affair, but older ones might heartily approve.

The *Charlotte Observer* (where Cornwell once worked) employs him to help prepare television listings. As an inexperienced reporter, Brazil makes remarkable headway, soon graduating to the crime beat. His editor takes a peek at one of the rookie's pieces in progress. "Packer scrolled through Brazil's latest and most masterful article. 'This is great stuff!' Packer was ecstatic about every word. 'One hell of a job!'" (p. 67, *Hornet's Nest*).

He lands an assignment to ride with Deputy Chief Virginia West in order to write firsthand articles about police activities. This draws him into the "Black Widow" killer's spreading web.

VIRGINIA WEST

Virginia West, deputy chief to Judy Hammer, is perhaps the most realistic character of the trio. She is sexy and beautiful and has a lover who doesn't entirely satisfy her. She likes greasy food from Bojangles (a restaurant chain featuring "Famous Chicken 'n Biscuits"), smokes, uses profane language, loves her cross-eyed Abyssinian cat, drinks beer, is a baseball fan, and lives alone. In her spare time, she works on home improvement projects, using carpenter tools like a handyman. Despite these characteristics, some of which are typically male habits, she is very much a woman.

Cornwell makes this clear. "West was forty-two, a woman who still turned heads and had never been married to anything beyond what she thought she was here on earth to do. She had deep red hair, a little unattended and longer than she liked it, her eyes dark and quick, and a serious body that she did not deserve, for she did nothing to maintain curves and straightness in the right places" (p. 3, *Hornet's Nest*).

In high school, West had excelled at tennis. The school "had no women's team back in those days" (p. 65, *Hornet's Nest*), so she joined the men's team. She had a powerful serve and "a slice backhand that could go through hot bread and leave it standing. All the boys had crushes on her and tried to hit her with the ball whenever they could" (p. 65). She never lost a match.

After joining the Charlotte police force, West became the first woman selected as rookie of the year. As she advanced, her dedication to the profession nearly cost her her life. As the first female homicide detective in Charlotte, she exchanged gunfire with a suspect. She killed him, but not before he winged her in the left shoulder. To West, this was just part of the job.

One aspect of her employment bothered her more than others. She hated attending autopsies. During one, she watched while repressing horrifying thoughts. "The morgue assistant was a big man who was always sweating. He plugged an autopsy saw into the overhead cord reel, and started on the skull. This West could do without. The sound was worse than the dentist's drill, the bony smell, not to mention the idea, awful.

West would not be murdered or turn up dead suspiciously in any form or fashion. She would not have this done to her naked body with people . . . looking on while clerks passed around her pictures and made comments" (pp. 58–59, *Hornet's Nest*).

West's nakedness would be explored in later erotic passages, but her partner's name will not be revealed here.

MYSTERY, SEX, AND HUMOR

Hornet's Nest, Southern Cross, and *Isle of Dogs* are constructed on three levels. First, they deal with relationships, usually thorny, between these protagonists, (though West is not in *Isle of Dogs*) and supporting players. Second, they come to grips with social conditions in both Charlotte, North Carolina, and Richmond, Virginia. This includes the plight of racial minorities, women competing in a male-dominated world, and a series of gruesome murders. Third, they openly explore sexual situations, both gay and straight. In *Hornet's Nest* alone, there are more than thirty passages of various lengths referring to sex of nearly every kind: rape, bondage/ domination, oral sex, prostitution, masturbation, incest, and even child molestation. Of course, criminal sexuality is treated as the disgusting behavior it is in real life. Both heterosexual and homosexual behavior is a common theme in all three books.

On the other extreme, Cornwell calls a skyscraper jutting above the Charlotte skyline a "sixty-story erection" (p. 90, *Hornet's Nest*). It could be argued there was no phallic intent in this case. An *Isle of Dogs* reference, though, leaves no room for doubt. The character involved is Thorlo Macovich, a black state police officer. "Macovich wished something magic would happen in his life to help him out of debt and ease his relentless, exhausting sexual cravings. Women and most men didn't have any idea what it was like to have a stallion between your legs that was always kicking, bucking, and snorting to get out of the stall, even when the *horsie,* as Macovich called it, was asleep. His lustful nature had trotted into his life at a very early age, and his father used to chuckle with pride and call his boy Thorlo Thoroughbred, not realizing that little Thorlo was developing a big problem that would eventually dominate his body and his life. . . . He had to have women who were sexually insatiable and skilled enough to stay in the saddle no matter how hard the ride" (pp. 144–145).

Male readers might not know whether to laugh or cry. The latter is more likely in a *Southern Cross* sequence. There is a dispute between two police officers, a man and a woman. Her frustration turns into a physical attack. She grabs his crotch and squeezes violently. Screaming, he tries to escape while the amused crowd offers comments. "'Go girlfriend . . . Yank it hard!'" "'Get him . . . in the nuts!'" "'Hey! Punch her! Man, fucking poke her eyes out!'" "'Pull that banana off the tree, girlfriend!'" "'Shift him into neutral, baby!'" "'Untie his balloon!'" (p. 292).

In *Isle of Dogs* a gang leader is startled by one of his underlings. "'You come in here one more time without asking and I'll blow your tiny dick off!'" (p. 181). A gentler allusion appears later in the same book. The governor, named Crimm, having achieved his position of power, thinks of his penis in terms of a diamond. "Having been born terribly short and homely with deteriorating eyes no longer mattered. Even the size of his diamond made little difference. It wasn't like the old days at the Commonwealth Club, where all the up-and-coming males would sit around the swimming pool naked . . . 'Not even half a carat,' Crimm remembered one of them whispering. 'It's the quality, not the size,' he replied. 'And how hard it is'" (p. 190).

References to breasts are a little less caustic. "She gave him a smirk as she bent over the cash drawer in a way that exposed her bulletlike headlights" (p. 239, *Isle of Dogs*).

Sex is dealt with on many levels in these stories. *Hornet's Nest* first takes a humorous approach as Virginia West busies herself with a home improvement project while her lover observes. "She slipped a nail from between her lips and looked at him, at his jeans. She rammed the hammer into her belt, and it was the only tool that was going to be intimate with her on this day" (p. 71). The same couple is the subject of another playful sexual reference. Cornwell must have been watching a football game when the inspiration for this passage struck her. A tryst between West and her male friend is interrupted. She is not interested in resuming it, while her lover is. "He and West had several downs yet to go, and he tackled her from behind, grabbing, fondling, and working his tongue into her ear. The play was incomplete as she broke free, leaving him yards behind and taking the ball with her. 'I'm tired,' she snapped. . . . He'd had enough of her poor sportsmanship and penalty flags" (p. 336).

The sexual content next turns a little more grim. A man lurking outside Virginia West's home thinks of raping her. "Bubba could only suppose that she was being screwed by her sissy boyfriend, and Bubba smiled as he imagined her getting screwed again by Bubba, as he sneaked closer to the front of the brick house" (p. 198, *Hornet's Nest*). An allusion to another kind of rape is also made through the same character. "Bubba could see it now. The pretty boy getting what he deserved, from the rear, from a manly man like Bubba, whose favorite movie was *Deliverance*" (p. 110). The 1972 cinematic classic, based on a book of the same title by James Dickey (who also plays a minor role in the movie), starred Jon Voight and Burt Reynolds. Four men take a wild canoe trip on the rapids of a Georgia river. At one point, Voight and Ned Beatty stop on the wooded shore and are accosted by a pair of filthy hillbillies. The assailants force Beatty's character to strip so one of the hillbillies can sexually assault him from the rear. Readers who have seen the movie will get a clear idea of what Bubba is contemplating.

Eroticism appears several more times in *Hornet's Nest*. Virginia West is a sexually experienced woman who entertains thoughts about the innocent Andy Brazil. "West wondered if Brazil had ever visited a topless lounge and sat stiffly in a chair, his hands in a white-knuckle grip on armrests, as a naked woman rubbed against his inner legs, and got in his face" (p. 84).

Some critics have described *Hornet's Nest* and the two subsequent books featuring Judy Hammer and Andy Brazil as "dark humor." There is little doubt of Cornwell's intention to sprinkle her prose with satire and prompt a chuckle here and there, but a grim element is present, too.

Most of the whimsy is based on misinterpretation of words by characters who read or hear them. It is reminiscent of the prison warden in Paul Newman's movie *Cool Hand Luke,* when he declares, "What we've got here is a failure to communicate."

Examples of this failure to communicate abound in all three books. *Southern Cross* has a black police officer pulling over a character named Bubba Fluck who has been hunting raccoons. When Bubba is ordered to step out of the car, he says, "'Officer . . . I've been up all night lost in the woods coon hunting.'

"The racial slur was astonishing.

"'Not a good time to say something like that, Mr. Fluck,' [says the officer] in an icy voice. . . . 'You hang 'em from trees or shoot 'em?'

"'We get 'em in trees if we can,' Bubba said. 'It's not legal to shoot 'em right now.'"

The officer "jerked open the door and looked down at Bubba. He wanted to beat him up. It occurred to him that he might be able to get away with it since this was Rodney King in reverse" (p. 248).

Another miscommunication takes place in *Isle of Dogs*. Goofy Governor Crimm, in his seventies, interprets his frumpy wife's secrecy about collecting trivets as possible infidelity. When she innocently recites that "variety is the spice of life," Crimm thinks his suspicions are confirmed. "The governor picked up on his wife's secret code and was shocked she would be so blatant, and he imagined her having sex with this Andy fellow, who probably would have nothing on but a duty belt" (p. 125).

Slapstick humor can also be found in these novels. In *Hornet's Nest*, Bubba (not the same man mentioned above) plans revenge on Virginia West by sneaking to her home late at night and using Super Glue to seal her entry door shut. "This idea had come from yet another of his anarchist manuals and might well have worked like a charm had circumstances not conspired against him as he unfolded his Buck knife and cut off the tip from the tube of glue. A car was coming, and Bubba wisely supposed it might be the cop returning home. It was too late to run, and he dove into the hedge. . . . [Later,] Bubba emerged from the hedge, his fingers glued together and left hand completely fastened to the right inner thigh of his fatigues. He rapidly hobbled away, looking remarkably like a hunchback. He could not unlock his truck or drive . . . this required his removing his pants, which he was in the process of doing when Officer Wood happened by on routine patrol, checking the park for perverts. Bubba was arrested for indecent exposure" (p. 199).

Other episodes, humorous in varying degrees, revolve around flatulence; the desperate need to urinate; poor eyesight; a rude, clumsy nurse; sexual situations; jealousy; language translation errors; an uncontrollable sphincter muscle; a dog typing words on the owner's computer; and mangled clichés. Like the definition of beauty or truth, any individual's sense of humor is completely personal and subjective. These episodes are sometimes uproarious.

RELATIONSHIPS

[Note: Be aware that this section contains spoilers. Essential plot elements are revealed as the relationships between the characters are examined.]

PATRICIA Cornwell's earlier novels show a more carefree Scarpetta. There is even mention of her dating. In *Body of Evidence,* she is having a drink with a retired judge who is making the moves on her (p. 8).

In the later Scarpetta novels, she is more experienced and subsequently a little more jaded about relationships. Speaking of Benton Wesley, with whom she is involved but whom she has not married, she thinks, "I had passed the midline of my life and would not legally share my earnings with anyone, including my lover and my family. Maybe I sounded selfish, and maybe I was" (p. 12, *Point of Origin*). For emotional support and for insight into her relationships, Scarpetta readily admits to seeing a psychiatrist occasionally (p. 75, *All That Remains*).

Her pattern of dealing with emotional problems is a familiar one: denial. After Wesley's death, Scarpetta realizes that her answer to this crisis is to run away from it and not face it. She tells Lucy, " 'For once I'm not going to slam the door on something and run. I've done it most of my life, beginning when my father died. Then Tony left and Mark got killed, and I got better and better at vacating each relationship as if it were an old house. Walking off as if I had never lived there. And guess what? It doesn't work. . . . If you've learned nothing else from me, Lucy, at least learn that. Don't wait until half your life has passed'" (p. 305, *Point of Origin*).

At Wesley's funeral, she also feels doubts about her decision not to marry him. "I wondered if my independence had been born of a seminal insecurity. I wondered if I had been wrong" (p. 396, *Point of Origin*).

"'You're awfully straight and narrow, aren't you, Kay?'" Teun McGovern said in *Point of Origin*. "'Unlike the rest of us, you never seem to use poor judgment or do anything wrong. You probably never overeat or get drunk.'"

Scarpetta responds, "'I hope that's not how I'm perceived. . . . I'm just more reserved because I have to be'" (p. 244).

COLLEAGUES AND LOVERS

Pete Marino

One of the joys of the Scarpetta series is getting to observe and savor the evolving relationship between Scarpetta and Pete Marino. They are opposites in terms of social status, taste, and even personality, with all the tension and humor that this involves. Over the years, they come to appreciate each other's strengths and weaknesses and develop a very caring relationship, although Marino is often in anguish over his unrequited love for Scarpetta.

But the start of their friendship was rocky. Scarpetta had a wary working relationship with Marino. In reflecting on the chauvinism that she faced in medical school, Scarpetta says, "I'd thought those days were behind me, but Marino brought all of it back" (p. 71, *Postmortem*).

In the second book in the series, *Body of Evidence,* Marino is much more attached to Scarpetta and is concerned about her. She seems to hide her feelings for him by being overly defensive. "I couldn't get rid of Marino. He insisted on walking me to my car. 'You got to keep your eyes open. . . . Maybe you should feel lucky I hover over you like a guardian angel'" (pp. 59–60). Scarpetta responds with, "I ignored him . . . I shot him one of my looks" (p. 60). Later on, when Scarpetta tells him of the demands that Mark James and Sparacino are making on her, she observes, "I think it was the first time I had ever seen Marino scared" (p. 140). He is worried for her. When the killer puts the murder victim's necklace on the doorknob of Scarpetta's back door, Marino asks Scarpetta, "'You want me to sleep on your couch tonight?'" (p. 264).

Both Scarpetta and Marino are lonely in *Body of Evidence.* "His wife was gone. His kids were grown. It was a gray, raw Saturday. Marino didn't want to go home to an empty house. I wasn't exactly feeling contented and cheery inside my empty house, either" (p. 122). She invites him over and makes spaghetti.

Scarpetta, knowing that Marino's wife is out of town dealing with her own dying mother in *All That Remains,* says, "'Sunday night—how about coming over for dinner? Six, six-thirty?' . . . 'Yeah, I could probably manage that,' he said, looking away, but not before I caught the pain in his eyes. . . . he had been unwilling to talk about his personal life" (p. 89).

Scarpetta and Marino get progressively closer in the third novel. When she forgets that she invited him to dinner, Marino doesn't want to upset her by pointing it out and says, "'Don't matter. Had a couple of things to follow up on, anyway.'" Scarpetta thinks, "I always knew when Marino was lying. He wouldn't look me in the eye and his face got red" (p. 101, *All That Remains*). Later, when Scarpetta says, "'Thank you for everything,'" he replies "'Huh?'" "I knew he'd heard me, but he wanted me to say it again." And she does say it again. "'I appreciate your concern, Marino. I really do'" (p. 103). Later, she comments, "For a fleeting moment I saw him as if I did not know him, my heart touched in a sad, sweet way. Marino had aged" (p. 126).

Concerned about Marino's high blood pressure, lack of exercise, stressful job, and being overweight, Scarpetta offers, "'Listen . . . Why don't we work on this together? We'll both cut back on coffee and get into exercise routines'" (p. 180, *Cruel & Unusual*). Later, "Marino reached for the salt but I got it first" (p. 244).

In *The Body Farm,* a different side of their relationship emerges. Marino and Scarpetta are at extreme odds. Her professional allegiance has shifted from Richmond to her new responsibilities as forensic consultant for the FBI at Quantico, and Marino is worried about their working relationship. He is also worried about a weakening of their friendship and is frankly jealous when Scarpetta shows an interest in Benton Wesley.

Wesley says, "'Marino has feelings for you that he can't handle, Kay. I think he always has'" (p. 75). Later, Scarpetta points out that "[Marino] took me to the Policeman's Ball" (p. 75). Later, during an argument with Marino, Scarpetta is so emotionally upset that she says, "'You're so damn possessive and jealous you're making me crazy,'" at which Marino, not one to mince words, lashes out at her, "'at least I'm not screwing anybody who's married'" (p. 217). Afterward, Scarpetta admits to herself that "I could never be romantically interested in him" (p. 218).

Marino, however, does branch off on his own, the first time since his divorce from his wife of thirty years. He starts a romantic relationship with Mrs. Steiner, the mother of the deceased girl in *The Body Farm;* sleeps over at her house several times; and has dreams of becoming the new chief of police in Black Mountain. The culmination of their romance is not the stuff that dreams are made of, however, and Scarpetta comes to his rescue.

In *From Potter's Field,* Marino has been dating a woman named Molly since Thanksgiving (p. 19). He is preoccupied with her and is no longer concerned about the affair that Scarpetta is having with Benton Wesley (p. 38). However, when Scarpetta receives a threat from the killer in the mail, he insists on sleeping at her house. "He put his head in his hands, and when he looked up at me his face was exhausted. 'You know how I'll feel if something happens to you? . . . It will kill me. It will, I swear'" (p. 172). Scarpetta says, "I was devoted to Marino but could not bear the thought of him in the house. . . . I had always known Marino had an interest in me that I could not gratify" (pp. 172, 175).

In *Cause of Death,* Marino and Scarpetta seem closer again. "By now Marino and I were more than partners or even friends. We were dependent on each other in a way neither could explain" (p. 128). Marino also shows more of his human side to Scarpetta when he tells her that he is having a panic attack and feelings of depression and impotence (pp. 220–221). He's also developing a deep fear of death.

Point of Origin is filled with Scarpetta's sorrow-filled affection for Marino, as she observes him aging and the poor condition he keeps himself in. "His shape was big and tired in the dark, and I suddenly was overwhelmed by sad affection for him. Marino was alone and probably felt like hell. . . . I supposed I was the only constant in his life" (pp. 185–186). She even shows up at his house and does his dishes when he is on the phone. There is also a lot of friendly humor directed at Marino in this novel. Their relationship has reached a deeper, more mature level as they both become older and more experienced. She doesn't really want him to sleep over at her house to "protect" her but asks him to do so out of kindness. Marino's response: "'That's what I'm thinking,' he said with feigned cool professionalism" (p. 186).

When Marino expresses his fears of dying and his poor physical shape, she says, "'I can't even think of something happening to you, you big idiot'" (p. 187). When Marino philosophically admits that he feels he has lived life to the fullest and is ready to die, she thinks, ". . . the image of his garish house at Christmas brought tears to my eyes" (p. 211).

In *Black Notice*, Scarpetta, moved by the letter Benton wrote her before he died, expresses her feelings more directly as she says, "'Marino, I really need you to come over. . . . It's very important to me. It's personal and very important.'

"It was so hard to say that to him. I didn't think I'd ever told him I needed him in a personal way. I couldn't remember the last time I'd said words like this to anyone but Benton" (p. 46).

When Marino suggests in *Black Notice* that Benton might still be alive, Scarpetta actually slaps him. "I'd never come even close to violence with anyone in my life, not anyone like this, not someone I knew and cared about." Marino says, "'I'm sorry'" (pp. 304–305).

However, Marino's jealousy turns tempestuous when he finds out that Scarpetta has slept with Jay Talley, a spoiled, rich womanizer in Marino's opinion. Scarpetta screams at him in anger (pp. 369–370, *Black Notice*). Marino actually tries to hit Talley. He sobs when Scarpetta tells him that he is really angry at Carrie Grethen and Newton Joyce. In his mind, there is also no one good enough for Scarpetta.

Scarpetta has a growing empathy for Marino's ways in *The Last Precinct*. She understands him at a deeper level. When his earthy language offends attorney Jaime Berger and she admonishes him, Scarpetta notes, "He wants to impress, belittle and bed Jaime Berger, and all of it is about his aching wounds of loneliness and insecurity, and his frustrations with me. As I watch him struggle to hide his embarrassment behind a wall of nonchalance, I am touched by sorrow" (p. 148). When Scarpetta tells Marino that she is quitting her job as chief medical examiner, he gets choked up and almost cries. They embrace and Scarpetta feels "an immeasurable compassion and need for him" (p. 256).

"Marino may look like a redneck, talk like a redneck, act like a redneck, but he is as smart as hell, sensitive and very perceptive" (p. 1). She admits that he still has feelings for her, as usual: "I have . . . always been aware that his respect for me is potently laced with insecurity and sexual attraction" (p. 5).

Throughout *Blow Fly*, Marino's deep feelings for Scarpetta continue. He is in love with her and is hurt that she does not feel the same about him (p. 105). "She has never been in love with him" (p. l75). Altruistically speaking, "he dreams of rescuing Benton and returning him to Scarpetta" (p. 112).

Because Scarpetta misses Benton so much, Marino has a "sick pain somewhere around his heart [that] topples him into deeper despair. He hurts deeply for her" (p. 146).

Marino is very sensitive to snobbery and class distinctions. In *Unnatural Exposure*, we learn that he lives in the Southside, an "other side of the tracks" neighborhood, while Scarpetta lives in the upper-class area of the West End in Windsor Farms. He finally verbalizes his feelings with regard to Scarpetta: "'You ever said anything nice about my truck? You ever gone fishing with me? You ever eat at my house? No, I gotta go to yours because you live in the right part of town'" (p. 124).

Rocky Marino (Rocco Caggiano)

Pete Marino has a troubled relationship with his son, Rocky. Marino has always refused to say anything to Scarpetta about his son until *The Last Precinct*. It turns out that he is a disreputable criminal defense attorney who is going to defend the man who tried to kill Scarpetta, Jean-Baptiste Chandonne (pp. 216–218). Rocky has a history of being a sore loser. Rocky changes his last name to spite his father and then Marino refuses to talk about him. In *Blow Fly*, Rocky even has plans to murder his father, a plan thwarted by Lucy.

Bill Boltz

The handsome Bill Boltz has a secret relationship with Scarpetta in *Postmortem*. Scarpetta indicates that her self-image is a bit low when she says, "Sometimes it was hard for me to believe he was so smitten with me" (p. 134). Although she feels physically attracted to him, their relationship is not complete, "We were not lovers, not completely, and this remained a subtle but uncomfortable tension between us" (p. 139). Furthermore, when he learns that Scarpetta's credibility might be challenged in *Postmortem,* he places his political well-being before their relationship. She later admits to her ambivalence: "My relationship with Bill had been little different from the weather. He marched in with an almost ferocious beauty, and I discovered all I wanted was a gentle rain, something quiet to quench the longing of my heart. I was looking forward to seeing him tonight, and yet I wasn't" (pp. 201–202). "I'd begun scrutinizing him . . . it seemed a symbol of the distance growing between us" (p. 204).

Later in *Postmortem,* Scarpetta learns that Bill slipped a drug into reporter Abby Turnbull's drink and took advantage of her one night. Remembering his forceful sexual advance toward her, she thinks, "I became sickened by the memory of his sudden aggression" (pp. 229–230). When he says their relationship is not working out, at the end of *Postmortem,* she agrees and is surprised at her own sense of relief (p. 341). Bill makes an appearance in *Cruel & Unusual.*

Mark James

Mark is an old boyfriend that Scarpetta met when they were both in law school at Georgetown (p. 31, *Body of Evidence*). He is the "man who had once broken my heart" (p. 31). "He had been my entire emotional focus. At first a part of me had sensed it wasn't mutual. Later, I was sure of it" (p. 36).

Scarpetta is ambivalent about their relationship. "I was alternately thrilled and disgusted with myself. I did not trust him, but I wanted to desperately. . . . And no matter what my mind said, my emotions would not listen" (p. 89, *Body of Evidence*). "I was always waiting to hear him say he was in love with me. He never did" (p. 107). "The emotional distance was never worth the togetherness, and yet I didn't learn. . . . Desire has no reason, and the need for intimacy had never stopped" (p. 108).

She was devastated when he said that he was in love with another woman, "my heart gripped by the worst pain I ever remember feeling" (p. 289, *Body of Evidence*). In reminiscing about their relationship, though, she has strong feelings: ". . . what I could not forget was loving a young man named Mark James more than I had thought it was possible to love anything on this earth" (p. 340).

Although *Body of Evidence* ends with a note from Mark saying, "I love you" (p. 403), Scarpetta and Mark go their separate ways. "'He's stubborn. I'm stubborn . . . I have my career and he has his . . . I had no intention of leaving Richmond and he had no intention of moving to Richmond'" (p. 74, *All That Remains*). He then transferred to Denver. "'He wanted a separation'" (p. 74). They do meet again, however, and still have strong feelings for each other: "Our passion had always been reckless" (p. 216). She later admits to her psychiatrist, Dr. Anna Zenner, "'I still love him'" (p. 273).

In *Cruel & Unusual,* we learn that Mark James has been killed by a terrorist bomb while in London, "while the war was ending in the Persian Gulf" (p. 22). "Mark's death had left a tear in my soul. I had come to realize, incredibly, just how much of my identity had been tied to my love for him" (p. 22). Since his death, "I had withdrawn," and she had turned to her work for solace (p. 167).

"'It's unfinished business, Kay. I have felt this for a long time. You need to bury Mark James,'" Dr. Margaret Foley says to Scarpetta (p. 13, *Unnatural Exposure*). Scarpetta admits to Lucy, "'I haven't gotten over him and probably never will. . . . I guess he was my first love'" (p. 337).

Scarpetta finds resolution when she finds out that he was with a girlfriend, who also was killed, at the time of the explosion (p. 366, *Unnatural Exposure*). He was going to tell Scarpetta, according to Benton Wesley. Scarpetta replies, "'Typical of my relationship with him, in truth. . . . He couldn't commit'" (pp. 366–367).

Benton Wesley

Scarpetta begins a meaningful and important relationship with Benton Wesley, a married man, in the fifth Scarpetta novel, *The Body Farm.* Scarpetta had known him since 1983, when they discussed a case in *Postmortem:* "The first time I met him I had my reservations. He was FBI right down to his Florsheim shoes . . . He was lean and hard . . ." (p. 75). Wesley had also been a friend and teacher of Scarpetta's former lover, Mark James (p. 75, *All That Remains*). In *All That Remains,* she finds him "handsome" but emotionally distant (p. 10). However, in *Cruel & Unusual,* they spend much time working together, sometimes in romantic situations such as sipping cognac at the Homestead, and she admits that she finds him physically attractive. He is the antithesis of Marino. He is neat, physically trim, cares about his appearance, and is polite and sensitive. In *The Body Farm* Scarpetta notices that "Wesley, always meticulous, spooned clam chowder away from him and raised it to his lips without spilling a drop" (p. 27), something she's not exactly used to when eating with Marino. Her eyes linger on him and he touches her lightly when leading her through a door. Later on, they spend the night together (p. 76).

In general, Scarpetta's love life has been unlucky. "I had lost every man I had loved before [Benton Wesley]" (p. 180, *The Body Farm*). She later says, as she reveals her attitude toward love, "I wanted to tell [Lucy] how much I loved her. . . . I tended to hold love hostage in my heart because, if expressed, I feared it might abandon me as many people in my life had" (p. 327).

Scarpetta's illicit affair with Benton, filled with guilt, continues in *From Potter's Field,* where they spend the night together in New York after visiting a crime scene. "[T]his was the first Christmas morning in years when someone other than me had been in my bed" (p. 43). She sums up her ambivalent feelings: "'Guilt, shame, fear, sadness. I get headaches and you lose weight'" (p. 69). Wesley says the magic words in *From Potter's Field:* "'I'm sorry. I love you'" (p. 318).

In *Cause of Death,* Benton is getting a divorce from his wife, Connie, because she is seeing someone else (p. 107). He and Scarpetta continue their romantic relationship while they are in London (p. 274). Yet Scarpetta's relationship with Benton is still hidden and filled with guilt. "I realized how much Lucy and I were alike. We both loved in secret" (p. 275).

In *Unnatural Exposure,* Wesley has divorced his wife (p. 5) and Scarpetta confides, "'He wants to marry me'" (p. 14). During a romantic dinner together, Wesley says, "'I'm in love with you and want to marry you'" (p. 85).

Their romantic relationship extends through five novels, seeming to culminate in *Point of Origin.* Benton Wesley is essentially living with Scarpetta in *Point of Origin,* although they are not married. Scarpetta spends time with Benton and he expresses his love for her. However, she feels their passion ebbing as they even sleep in separate rooms because they are tired: "[M]y heart was dull or felt sweet pain, and I saw myself getting old" (p. 251).

Tragically, Benton Wesley is apparently murdered in a fire in *Point of Origin* (p. 281), and his ashes are scattered by a distraught Scarpetta at Hilton Head (p. 394).

In a letter he wrote to Scarpetta to be delivered in the event of his death, Wesley expresses his love for her, "'Loving you was when my life began,'" his letter states in the preface to *Black Notice*.

Scarpetta spends much time analyzing her past relationship with Benton in *The Last Precinct*. She talks with her friend Dr. Anna Zenner: "'I do know there were deep places in me he never reached. I also never wanted him to, didn't want to get that intense, that close'" (p. 93). Scarpetta secretly feels that Benton had given up on life because he was getting older and disillusioned before he died and she is angry with him for this (p. 96). Their sexual relationship was also getting stale and she felt that it was too cerebral. "[A]fter Benton's murder, I vanished into a dark vortex of frantic, perpetual motion. I stopped seeing friends. I didn't go out or have people in. I rarely exercised. All I did was work" (p. 224).

In *Blow Fly*, Scarpetta is still in love with Benton Wesley. She "can't get over" him (p. 122). She had remodeled her Richmond house in an attempt to "eradicate the past—a past haunted by Benton . . . [an] unbearable loss" (p. 135). One day she just walked out of her house, never to return.

But Benton is still alive; his death had been fabricated to protect Scarpetta. In *Blow Fly*, he has made a turnaround emotionally since his separation from Scarpetta. Through Scarpetta's influence, he now believes "that all kindnesses will be repaid" (p. 138). He is still in love with her. "His sense of her continues to linger like her favorite perfume" (p. 139).

At the end of *Blow Fly*, Scarpetta and Benton are reunited. He is so touched by their reunion that he cries. Scarpetta's feelings are equally deep: "He said her name. And it shakes her to her soul" (p. 463).

Benton admits to some guilt about his relationship with Scarpetta. He is a family man at heart, and had cheated on his wife during his relationship with Scarpetta, "his only sin he won't forgive" (p. 230).

Benton's torment over his fabricated death and subsequent estrangement from Scarpetta and his own family is an important emotional element in *Blow Fly*. He is intent on destroying the Chandonne family, including Jean-Baptiste, who is on death row in Texas; his brother, serial killer Jay Talley, who is in Baton Rouge, Louisiana; and Rocco Caggiano, lawyer for Jean-Baptiste and the Chandonne family. Because he was unsuccessful in doing this before, he ". . . has not yet forgiven himself. . . . But the one time in his career when he needed his acumen and wits the most, he slipped, and the thought of it still enrages him" (p. 191).

Commander Frances Penn

Scarpetta and Frances Penn, a woman, have much in common. Both are overachievers, were the oldest child in their families, and were forced to take on family responsibilities at an early age. Thus relationships are different for both of them (p. 97, *From Potter's Field*). There is a hint that Frances has more than a casual interest in Scarpetta when she invites her over for dinner, saying, "'I would be less than honest if I told you that I didn't want an opportunity for us to get better acquainted'" (p. 97).

Jay Talley

Talley is Scarpetta's link to Interpol in France in *Black Notice*. She finds him attractive from the start, but has her doubts because of his wealth and signs that he is spoiled. She kisses him, they make love, and Cornwell's descriptions are more explicit than in any of her previous novels: "I wanted it raw and without limits. I wanted the violence in me to make love to his violence. . . . I controlled him. I dominated" (p. 367).

When Scarpetta tells him that she is not ready for a relationship, especially since he is so much younger than she is, he drinks too much and is verbally abusive. He calls her old, overbearing, and filled with fear ever since her father's death (pp. 377–378). Scarpetta is angry and leaves him.

However, at the end of the novel, Talley has returned to the United States and is there to comfort Scarpetta when she is attacked.

Scarpetta's attraction to him seems mainly physical. "He is one of the handsomest men I have ever known, his body exquisitely sculpted, sensuality exuding from his pores like musk" (p. 19, *The Last Precinct*). He gazes lustfully at her though she is still upset after her near murder and she thinks, "I realize I don't love him in the least" (p. 20).

In *The Last Precinct,* Scarpetta thinks of Talley when she hears the murderer Jean-Baptiste Chandonne being interviewed. "Talley isn't so different from Chandonne. Both of them secretly hate women, no matter how much they lust for them" (p. 192).

Rudy Musil

Rudy is Lucy's former partner at the FBI. He resigned from the bureau and eventually came to work for her at her private investigative firm, The Last Precinct, in Manhattan, in *Blow Fly*.

Even though Lucy is a lesbian, they have strong feelings for each other. Once, he misinterpreted her intentions and tried to force himself on her sexually, which led to her leaving the FBI, as related in *Blow Fly*. Together, they murder Marino's son, Rocco Caggiano, in *Blow Fly* to prevent Rocco from killing Marino. After killing Rocco, they need each other's emotional support even more. ". . . [T]hey need each other. Each becomes desperate for the other's warm flesh. Lucy lifts his hand to her mouth . . . as she deeply kisses his fingers. . . ." (p. 197). Rudy has always been attracted to her, since he first saw ". . . her fiery beauty as he watched the way she walked with confidence and grace and not a trace of masculinity. . . . Lucy is athletic but definitely feminine and very pleasing to the touch" (p. 336).

Nic Robillard

Nic is a thirty-six-year-old investigator from Zachary, Louisiana; she makes her first appearance in *Blow Fly*. She takes a ten-week course on forensics at the National Forensic Academy and meets Scarpetta, whom she admires. She tries to overcome her small-town upbringing and, like Scarpetta, feels that she is discriminated against as a woman. As the "only woman" on the police force in Louisiana, she feels isolated.

She is attracted to Scarpetta, feeling jealous when Scarpetta's niece, Lucy, is mentioned. She finds Scarpetta, despite her "fiery fearlessness and brilliance," to be "kind and gentle" (p. 10). "The need to impress Scarpetta dominates Nic's life" (p. 150).

As a working single mother, Nic is often depressed. Her father helps her with her son, but she is often filled with "powerlessness, loneliness and despair" (p. 151).

FAMILY AND CHILDHOOD
Dorothy

Scarpetta is estranged from her sister, Dorothy. "Dorothy would say such a thing and, what was worse, she would believe it. I felt a flare of the old anger" (p. 38, *Postmortem*).

Scarpetta feels bad that Lucy's mother, Dorothy, neglects her because of her job, and this brings up painful childhood memories for Scarpetta. Scarpetta's childhood was deprived of much love. When she tries to make things up to Lucy at the end of *Postmortem*, she is flying with her for a vacation in Florida. "We'd do everything I wished I could have done when I was her age" (p. 338). Throughout the book, she often hugs and kisses Lucy and tells her that she loves her.

Speaking of Dorothy in *Cruel & Unusual,* Scarpetta says, "She was simply a failure as a human being" (p. 77).

Dorothy's true feelings about Scarpetta come out in a drunken tirade in *Black Notice.* She resents Scarpetta and her influence on her daughter, Lucy. She thinks Scarpetta is a closet lesbian and has turned Lucy into one as well. Scarpetta reflects, "I wanted to love her. But I didn't. I never had" (p. 282).

Scarpetta's Father

Scarpetta's father, Kay Marcellus Scarpetta III, died when she was a child. She was told that he had leukemia when she was twelve years old (p. 171, *Postmortem*). Her family life was lacking in emotional support as a child, with no real relationship with her mother, father, or sister. "[When] I lost my father I lost [my mother], too. She was . . . consumed by his dying. . . . There was nothing warm-blooded left for Dorothy and me"(p. 173). She also relates having seen her father die of leukemia and cried out in anguish (p. 322); later, she muses, "'I don't cry. . . . I learned not to when my father was dying, because to cry was to feel, and it was too much to feel" (p. 348, *Black Notice*).

Scarpetta remembers her childhood as a time of emotional and material deprivation, and recalls, "I saw my father and the white gold ring he wore on his left hand where a wedding band would have been . . . he had never really lost his wedding ring He had sold it when he did not know what else to do, but to tell Mother was to destroy her" (pp. 179–180, *The Body Farm*).

Scarpetta's Mother

The first somewhat tender mention of Scarpetta's mother occurs in *Body of Evidence:* "I called my mother . . . and for once was relieved to receive the usual lectures and reminders, to hear that strong voice loving me in its no-nonsense way" (p. 75).

In *From Potter's Field,* Scarpetta's mother is on a respirator and has had a tracheotomy, having also suffered from emphysema from smoking (pp. 19, 64).

Scarpetta also has some fond memories of her grandmother: "My heart was tugged by memories of my own grandmother, whose humor was unflagging" (p. 282, *Body of Evidence*).

In *Blow Fly,* it's worth noting that Scarpetta moves south to Florida, near her mother and sister, yet her house is "safely far away" (p. 137).

PART THREE

A DOSE OF REALITY

SHOP TALK:
THE LANGUAGE OF THE
MEDICAL EXAMINER

THE nature of Scarpetta's profession, chief medical examiner, requires Cornwell to include numerous medical terms in both dialogue and the narrative. Some are briefly explained in the novels, but many are not. This section of the book offers interpretations and commentary on medical processes and terminology used by Scarpetta and her colleagues. It is important to note that definitions here are oversimplified to help the reader understand complex medical terms. They are not, under any circumstances, to be used for diagnostic or treatment purposes.

POSTMORTEM

BARR BODIES In a test to determine whether the human swab samples being examined are from a female, Betty, the chief serologist, says to Scarpetta, "'I'll . . . [see] if there are any Barr bodies present'" (p. 188).

In 1949, Murray Barr found that applying a chemical stain to certain cells from a domestic cat resulted in the appearance of a drumstick-shaped form if the cat was a female. Later it was determined that these *Barr bodies*, also appear on cells of human females. Another scientist, Mary Lyon, correctly hypothesized that Barr bodies are actually condensed X chromosomes.

CHLORAL HYDRATE Detective Pete Marino describes how rapists may subdue their victims. "They meet some babe in a bar, buy her a drink and slip in a little chloral hydrate" (p. 242).

Chloral hydrate is a prescription sedative, often used in short-term treatment of insomnia, to relieve anxiety, or to induce sleep before surgery. It is available in capsule form and is usually taken orally with water or juice. It can also be prescribed in suppository form. Before the so-called "date rape" drug Rohypnol gained underground popularity, chloral hydrate was the primary choice for slipping someone a "Mickey."

MAPLE SYRUP URINE DISORDER A fugitive killer has been described as having a strange odor of maple syrup. Scarpetta says, "'[He] may have some sort of anomaly, some type of metabolic disorder. Specifically, "maple syrup urine disease"'" (p. 272).

There really is such a disease, nearly always found in infants and occurring in about 1 in 180,000 births in the United States. It is an enzyme defect related to the accumulation of certain amino acids. In a few populations, such as Pennsylvania Mennonites, it may occur as frequently as in 1 out of 176 newborns. The baby's urine emits an odor resembling maple syrup or burned sugar. If not treated early, the disease can cause death or mental degeneration.

MESENTERY As she conducts an autopsy, Scarpetta says, "I resumed measuring a large tear of the mesentery" (p. 183).

The *mesentery* is a membrane that connects the intestines and their appendages to the dorsal wall (situated on the back) of the abdominal cavity.

NAPHTHYL ACID PHOSPHATE To examine human samples that Scarpetta gives her, Betty, the chief serologist, performs a number of related tests. "Getting out the medicine droppers, she began deftly dripping naphthyl acid phosphate over the filter paper. Then came the fast-blue B salt. We stared, waiting for the first hint of purple" (p. 187).

Naphthyl acid phosphate is a chemical used in testing for the presence of seminal fluid left behind by a perpetrator. Samples of body fluids are taken at the crime scene and preserved. Later, tests are performed in the laboratory to determine whether semen is present. The lab process, developed in 1944, is known as "alkaline phosphatase staining protocol." Sodium-naphthyl acid phosphate is a substance acted on by an enzyme. It is hydrolyzed (split with the use of water) and coupled with another chemical known as fast blue salt, then dropped onto swabs containing collected body fluids. If the sample turns purple, it indicates the presence of seminal fluid.

PETECHIAL HEMORRHAGES A murder victim has been strangled. Scarpetta says, "'She had petechial hemorrhages in the conjunctivae, and facial and neck skin'" (p. 266).

A *petechia* is a pinpoint-sized, purplish-red spot, usually related to capillary hemorrhaging beneath the skin. *Conjunctivae* refers to the mucous membrane lining the eyelids' inner surface. The appearance of petechial hemorrhaging, especially inside the eyelids, is a strong indicator that a deceased person has been smothered, asphyxiated, or strangled. If something soft, such as a pillow, has been used by the perpetrator, the body usually shows no marks of trauma, but petechial hemorrhages give medical investigators strong evidence of homicide.

STRYKER SAW "Wingo's face was bright red as he stabbed the plug of the Stryker saw into the yellow cord reel dangling over the steel [autopsy] table" (p. 180).

This tool, invented in 1945 by American orthopedic surgeon Dr. Homer H. Stryker (1894–1980), is a rapidly vibrating electric saw for cutting bone or plaster casts. Pathologists often use it to cut around the skullcap in order to remove the brain. This saw also shows up in *From Potter's Field* (p. 112) and in *Unnatural Exposure* (p. 130).

SUBDURAL-SUBARACHNOID HEMORRHAGES Scarpetta examines the victim's brain after her assistant has used a Stryker saw to remove the skullcap. She observes, "No subdural or subarachnoid hemorrhages" (p. 181).

A tough, leathery outer covering known as the dura surrounds and protects the brain within the skull. A traumatic blow to the head, though, can tear interior blood vessels. Blood then can accumulate within the space between the brain and dura. This is *subdural hemorrhage*.

A *subarachnoid hemorrhage* is an abnormal, dangerous condition in which blood accumulates beneath the arachnoid mater, a spiderweb-like membrane covering the brain.

TIME OF DEATH Scarpetta examines a corpse and observes, "Time of death is more elusive than most people think. It can't be pinned down exactly unless the death was witnessed or the victim's Timex stopped ticking" (p. 11).

In older movies and in the works of less-exact novelists, the detective or the medical examiner possesses an uncanny skill to unequivocally state a murder victim's *time of death*. Scarpetta is correct about the difficulty in doing this. Determining time of death is an inexact science influenced by a number of factors, and is usually subject to attack by trial defense attorneys.

At the crime scene, a forensic medical examiner gathers information that might help estimate when the victim died. This includes observing environmental factors, taking the victim's body temperature with a rectal thermometer, and then noting *algor mortis, rigor mortis,* and *livor mortis.*

Algor mortis is the term for body cooling after death until it reaches ambient temperatures. Of course, if the victim was killed outside in midwinter, the cooling is accelerated.

Rigor mortis is the chemical process that causes stiffening of muscles after death and is also influenced by temperature and the victim's metabolic rate. The initial signs of rigor, affecting facial muscles, may show up within minutes or may not begin for a few hours. It is usually in full force within ten to twelve hours and begins to fade from twenty-four to thirty-six hours later.

Livor mortis is the settling of blood by gravity into the body's lower regions, causing those sections of the skin to turn purple. It generally starts within two hours and is completed within eight hours. If the skin affected by livor mortis is red, it may indicate poisoning or freezing.

At the autopsy, stomach contents can sometimes help estimate time of death, particularly if information is available about the victim's last meal. But all of these indicators are subject to environmental and circumstantial influence.

BODY OF EVIDENCE

ATHEROSCLEROSIS During the autopsy of a male victim, Scarpetta notes, "'[He's] got calcification of his aorta, moderate atherosclerosis'" (p. 184).

Atherosclerosis causes progressive narrowing and hardening of the arteries over time, partially due to aging, but exacerbated by smoking, diet, diabetes, and genetic history.

COLLAGEN DISEASES Explaining the possible health problems of a deceased woman, Scarpetta says, "'Could be a lot of things, . . . any one of a number of collagen diseases'" (p. 190).

Collagen is a protein contained in connective tissue and bones, once thought related to a large variety of chronic diseases, including rheumatoid arthritis, lupus, progressive sclerosis, and diseases of the skin. Disorders related to collagen are now regarded as inherited genetic conditions resulting in autoimmune diseases. For example, a person who generates antibodies in the lungs will chronically lose respiratory function and may die as a result.

HISTOLOGIC Still searching for answers on the mysterious illness found in the deceased woman, Scarpetta says, "'I won't know anything until I can look at the histologic changes under the scope'" (p. 191).

Histology is the branch of biology dealing with the study of tissues, especially the microscopic structure of organic tissues.

INFARCTS The same victim, says Scarpetta's deputy chief, has "'. . . no evidence of old infarcts, her coronaries clear'" (p. 190).

An *infarct* is a localized area of tissue, generally in the heart, that is dying or dead, having been deprived of blood supply because of an obstruction, embolism, or thrombosis (coagulation of the blood in any one of the many vessels).

LIVER ENLARGED In conference with one of her medical staff, Scarpetta is told that a woman's autopsy revealed that she had an enlarged liver weighing 2500 grams (p. 190). What is normal?

As the largest glandular organ in the human body, the liver can vary in weight, ordinarily from 1400 to 1600 grams in the male and 1200 to 1400 grams in the female. So, a 2500-gram liver in this woman is almost double the volume it should be.

METASTASIS Scarpetta asks about the same woman, "'Any metastases?'" (p. 190).

Metastasis (plural, *metastases*) is an oncological term referring to the spread of cancer cells. They may start in one part of the body, spread to other parts such as the lymph nodes, and finally invade most of the organs.

STENOSIS/LAD In another autopsy, Scarpetta observes, "'He has twenty percent stenosis of his LAD'" (p. 184).

Stenosis means simply a narrowing or stricture of a duct or a blood vessel. *LAD* is an acronym for *left anterior descending* artery.

ALL THAT REMAINS

ANALOGUES OF PCP Listing various drug tests performed on a young couple found murdered, Scarpetta says, "'As for designer drugs, we tested for analogues of PCP, amphetamines'" (p. 183).

Analogues in this context simply means other drugs analogous to, or similar to, PCP. PCP (phencyclidine), or "angel dust," is a synthetic chemical developed in the 1950s, largely for use as an anesthetic in treating animals. It soon became apparent that PCP also had postoperative side effects of confusion and psychosis. Scientists began experimenting with its use on humans in understanding schizophrenia, but this was soon terminated. In the 1960s it became a popular street drug but produced unpredictable behavior. By 1978, it was withdrawn from veterinary use, but still sporadically appears among drug addicts. A close analogue, ketamine, is sold legally as an anesthetic and finds its way to street use. Amphetamines are synthesized drugs structurally related to a natural stimulant found in plants (ephredine) and to adrenaline. Once used medically for weight control or treatment for depression, amphetamines also have evolved chiefly to street usage in the form of powder called "speed" or "crack." It is generally "snorted" (ingested by inhaling through the nose).

BERRY ANEURYSM Reviewing the family history of a murder victim, Scarpetta notes that he was "an only child whose mother had died last year when a berry aneurysm ruptured in her brain" (pp. 19–20).

An aneurysm is a permanent ballooning in the wall of an artery. The pressure of blood passing through can force part of a weakened artery to bulge outward, forming a thin-skinned blister or sac. Some of these bulges can resemble a berry, thus the name *berry aneurysm,* which is usually the result of congenital or inherited weakness in artery walls.

CHINA WHITE Continuing the conversation about street drugs, Benton Wesley asks Scarpetta, "'What about China White?'" (p. 183).

Two types of illegal drugs are referred to as *China White*. One is known as fentanyl, a synthetic opiate analgesic developed in 1962. It became popular as a street drug in 1979 and can be injected, smoked, or snorted. Other names for it are Duragesic, Sublimaze, Actiq, China Girl, TNT, Apache, and Dance Fever. Fifty times more potent than heroin, it can be even more deadly.

White powder heroin from Asia, often smuggled through France, is also sometimes called China White.

METABOLITES OF BENZOYLE-COGONINE The bodies of a badly decomposed young couple are autopsied and tested for drug use. Scarpetta states, "'There was some red tissue left, muscle. That's enough for testing. Cocaine or heroin, for example. We, at least, would have expected to find their metabolites of benzoyle-cogonine or morphine'" (p. 183).

Metabolites are the products of metabolism, the physical and chemical process in an organism by which protoplasm is produced, maintained, and destroyed, and by which energy is made available for the organism to function. *Benzoyle-cogonine* is the chemical residue found in organisms having used cocaine. So, more simply stated, this chemical would be discovered in an autopsy if the deceased person had recently metabolized cocaine.

RIA Still speaking to Wesley, Scarpetta says about China White, "'Less than one milligram can be fatal, meaning the concentration is too low to detect without using special analytical procedures such as RIA.'" She sees a blank expression on his face and explains. "'Radioimmunoassay, a procedure based on specific drug antibody reactions. Unlike conventional screening procedures, RIA can detect small levels of drugs, so it's what we resort to when looking for China White, LSD, THC'" (p. 184).

Wesley may have looked blank because he was thinking of another RIA. The Research Institute on Addictions at the University of Buffalo, New York, has been conducting groundbreaking research on drug addictions for thirty-three years.

LSD, lysergic acid diethylamide, which produces temporary hallucinations and a schizophrenic psychotic state, gained popularity among illegal drug users during the "flower power" heyday of the 1960s.

THC is *tetrahydrocannabinol,* the chemical producing a "high" for someone using the cannabis plant, more commonly known as marijuana.

SPINOUS PROCESS AND PEDICLES Pointing out damage caused when a victim is shot in the back, Scarpetta says, "'The bullet fractured the spinous process and the pedicles'" (p. 96).

Spinous process refers to the long rearward projection from the arch of each vertebra that provides a point of attachment for muscles and ligaments. *Pedicles* are portions of the arch of the vertebra extending from the body.

CRUEL & UNUSUAL

BRADYCARDIA Scarpetta and Marino piece together the forensic pathology clues and come up with a scenario in which someone placed one arm around the victim's neck, then pulled it tight by grabbing that wrist with the other hand. "'This placed pressure eccentrically on her neck, resulting in fracture of the . . . hyoid bone. . . . She would have gotten hypoxic, or air hungry. Sometimes pressure on the neck produces bradycardia, a drop in the heart rate, and the victim has an arrhythmia [irregular heart beat]'" (p. 128).

Bradycardia is a slowing of the heart rate, usually associated with disease or aging. When the heart rate is too slow (usually fewer than sixty beats per minute), not enough oxygen is pumped through the body. This causes dizziness, extreme fatigue, shortness of breath, or fainting. A pacemaker can help correct the symptoms.

COLD WATER IN EARS A young boy, victim of a gunshot, lies critically wounded in an emergency clinic. Scarpetta asks the attending nurse about his condition. She says, "'There's no circulation to the brain, due to the swelling. There's no electroencephalic activity, and when we put cold water in his ears there was no caloric activity. It evoked no brain potentials'" (p. 32).

Among the recommended criteria to diagnose brain death is total unresponsiveness to external visual, auditory, or tactile stimulation. This may be surmised if pupillary responses (in the eye pupil) are absent and eye movements cannot be elicited by irrigating the ears with cold water.

EPINEPHRINE/EPIPEN A briefcase owned by the executed killer comes into Scarpetta's hands. Among the contents she finds "an EpiPen, a .3-milligram epinephrine auto-injector routinely kept by people fatally allergic to bee stings or some foods" (p. 377).

Epinephrine is a hormone produced by the adrenal glands. A commercial form of this substance is used as a stimulant in the case of cardiac arrest from ventricular fibrillation, tachycardia, asystole (absence of a heartbeat), bradycardia, or extreme hypotension. Injection improves coronary and cerebral blood flow.

The *EpiPen Auto-Injector* is a disposable drug delivery system with a spring-activated, concealed needle. It is designed for emergency self-administration to provide rapid, convenient first aid for individuals sensitive to potentially fatal allergic reactions. The active ingredient is epinephrine, which quickly constricts blood vessels, relaxes the bronchi, improves breathing, stimulates the heartbeat, and works to reverse hives and swelling around the face and lips.

FORAMEN MAGNUM Scarpetta's deputy chief speaks to her about a female murder victim: "'Looks to me like [the assailant] pressed the barrel hard against her neck. The bullet enters at the junction of the foramen magnum and C-one and takes out the cervical-medullary junction. Travels right up into the pons.'"

The *foramen magnum* is the large opening in the occipital bone at the base of the skull through which the spinal cord passes.

C-1 refers to the first of seven cervical vertebrae in the spinal column.

The *cervical-medullary junction* is the point at which the spinal cord makes a junction with the medulla oblongata, the lowest-hindmost part of the brain continuous with the spinal cord.

The *pons* is a rounded eminence off the ventral (lower) surface of the brainstem.

The path of the bullet in question could not have been more lethal.

MICROVASCULATURE/EARLY NEPHROSCLEROSIS Continuing her diagnosis of a woman who had been strangled, Scarpetta notes antemortem signs of high blood pressure and says, "'I should find fibrinoid changes in the renal microvasculature or early nephrosclerosis'" (p. 127).

Fibrinoid relates to a homogenous material similar to fibrin (a white, tough elastic protein formed in the coagulation of blood) found normally in the placenta and formed in connective tissue and in the walls of diseased blood vessels. *Renal* refers to kidney functions. *Microvasculature* relates to the portion of the circulatory system composed of the smallest blood vessels. *Nephrosclerosis* is a kidney disease usually associated with hypertension; it consists of sclerosis of the renal arterioles (tiny blood vessels), which reduces blood flow and can lead to kidney failure and heart failure. As Marino puts it, "'You're saying kidney and brain cells get killed off when you got high blood pressure?'" Scarpetta replies, "'In a manner of speaking'" (p. 127). The victim appeared doomed even if someone hadn't strangled her to death.

PARATHYROIDS Dictating the details of an autopsy to an assistant, Scarpetta notes that she found four parathyroids (p. 15).

The *parathyroid glands* are tiny parts of the endocrine system and are located in the neck behind the thyroid. There are four of them normally about the size of a pea. Their sole purpose is to regulate the body's calcium level so that nervous and muscular systems function properly. Even though both parathyroids and the thyroid gland are adjacent and part of the endocrine system, they are otherwise unrelated.

SCOLIOTIC Christmas has nearly arrived and Scarpetta impulsively stops at a Christmas tree lot. "At this late date, there wasn't much of a selection, those trees passed over, misshapen or dying, each destined to sit out the season, I suspected, except for the one I chose. It would have been lovely were it not scoliotic" (p. 160).

Scoliosis is a congenital lateral curvature of the human spine, and the term is applied by Scarpetta to the tree in a touch of dark humor.

STERNOCLEIDOMASTOID MUSCLE Scarpetta gives Marino information in the case of a woman who died mysteriously. "I showed him a photograph of her neck at autopsy—'she's got irregular hemorrhages in the sternocleidomastoid muscles bilaterally. She's also got a fracture of the right cornua of the hyoid'" (p. 126).

The *sternocleidomastoid* is one of two muscles located on the front of the neck that serve to turn the head from side to side. The *hyoid bone,* which happens to be the only jointless bone in the body, is shaped like a horseshoe and is located at the base of the tongue. Forensic investigators nearly always examine it for a fracture, which would indicate that the victim was almost certainly strangled manually. Scarpetta concludes, "'Her death was caused by asphyxia, due to pressure applied to the neck'" (p. 126).

TETANUS, IN TOTAL A prisoner on Virginia State Penitentiary's death row is executed in the electric chair. Scarpetta conducts the autopsy. She states, "Electrocution heats you up. The brain temperatures of smaller men I had autopsied were as high as a hundred and ten. Waddell's right calf was at least that, hot to the touch, the muscle in total tetanus" (p. 14).

This *tetanus* is not the bacterial disease sometimes called lockjaw, but is a state of sustained muscle contraction during which the muscle does not relax to its initial length or tension. Such a condition is induced by a rapid stimulus, such as a lethal jolt of electricity.

VALSALVA MANEUVER The executed convict's nose had bled during the electrocution. Scarpetta notes in a report that it was caused by "the Valsalva maneuver, or an abrupt increase in intrathoracic pressure" (p. 55).

The *Valsalva maneuver* is ordinarily used as a diagnostic measure with patients who have suspected heart abnormalities. The patient forcibly exhales against a closed nose and mouth while bearing down, as if having a bowel movement. Specific changes occur in blood pressure and the rate of blood returning to the heart. It is also occasionally recommended as a first-aid treatment to correct abnormal heart rhythms or relieve chest pains. Nosebleeds often result.

THE BODY FARM

HYPERNATREMIA In a review of the young girl's death, Scarpetta says, "The child would have gone into hypernatremia, finally a coma, and she would have been near death . . ." (p. 323).

Hypernatremia is defined as a serum sodium level over 145 mM. A severe case, above 152 mM, can result in seizures and death.

VITREOUS SODIUM LEVEL An eleven-year-old girl has died under strange circumstances. Scarpetta, discussing the case with Benton Wesley, explains,

"'Her laboratory reports were equally perplexing: vitreous sodium level elevated to 180, potassium 58 milliequivalents per liter'" (p. 18).

Vitreous humor is the transparent gelatinous substance filling the eyeball behind the crystalline lens. The sodium content, an indicator of the body's moisture level, was 180 units, called milliosmoles (mM or mmol), per liter. A normal reading would be 135 to 145 milliosmoles, according to the 1994 edition of *Current Medical Diagnosis & Treatment*. So a reading of 180 is a considerably elevated level.

Medical examiners use measurements taken from the vitreous humor for two reasons: It is an accurate indicator of the blood's contents, including any drug and alcohol content, at the time of death, and it remains in good condition much longer than blood, which quickly deteriorates after death.

Potassium levels should drop no lower than 3.3 mmol per liter, nor exceed 5.2 mmol/L (52 milliequivalents). Thus, a reading of 58 is high.

About the subject of Scarpetta's concern, she says, "'It could mean she was profoundly dehydrated'" (p. 19).

FROM POTTER'S FIELD

COCAETHYLENE A fugitive has left hair at a crime scene. Lab tests indicate traces of drugs. Marino says to Scarpetta, "'. . . the bottom line is they found drugs in his hair. They said he had to be drinking and doing coke for this stuff to have shown up in his hair.'"

She replies, "'They found cocaethylene'" (p. 152).

Cocaethylene is formed by the human body and can be identified in the urine, blood, hair, or liver of individuals who have consumed both cocaine and alcohol in the same time period.

DIPHENYLHYDANTOIN During autopsy of a woman who may have had seizures, one of the doctors says, "'Let's check her for diphenylhydantoin'" (p. 58).

Diphenylhydantoin is a drug used most commonly in the treatment of epilepsy.

CAUSE OF DEATH

ADRENERGIC BLOCKER/FINASTERIDE In a blue mood, Marino confesses to Scarpetta that he is afraid of dying, and admits he has stopped taking his medication. She asks, "'Which medication? Your adrenergic blocker or the finasteride?'" (p. 222).

Her question indicates that Marino has prostate gland problems. An *alpha-adrenergic blocker* is found in any one of various name-brand drugs used for treating benign prostatic hyperplasia (BPH), which is a noncancerous enlargement of the prostate. This small gland increases in size and partially blocks the urethra, obstructing urine flow. It is a common malady in men age sixty and older.

His other medication, *finasteride,* is the chemical name of Propecia, which is sold as a treatment to help delay the onset of male pattern baldness. This may be more important to Marino psychologically than his prostate problems.

HYPOSPADIAS Scarpetta notices something unusual about a victim who died while doing underwater exploration. "[He] had no injuries except several old scars, mostly on his knees. But biology had dealt him an earlier blow called hypospadias, which meant his urethra opened onto the underside of his penis instead of in the center. This moderate defect would have caused him a great deal of anxiety, especially as a boy. As a man he may have suffered sufficient shame that he was reluctant to have sex" (p. 35).

Somewhat rare, *hypospadias* occurs in about 1 of every 350 male births, resulting in abnormal placement of the opening for urine passage, anywhere along the underside of the penis. In *Portrait of a Killer,* Cornwell suggests that Walter Sickert, whom she concludes was Jack the Ripper, may have been born with this disorder (pp. 59–60).

MEDIASTINUM/EXTRAALVEOLAR AIR Proceeding with internal examination of a diver's body, Scarpetta tells Marino that she is checking to see whether the victim had drowned. She describes several steps and adds, "'I'll . . . look at the soft tissue of the mediastinum for extraalveolar air'" (p. 44).

The *mediastinum,* in the middle of the chest cavity, contains the heart and all of the organs except the lungs. *Alveolar* refers to that part of the respiratory system that consists of tiny sacs of air, called *alveoli.* Alveolar air is gas in the pulmonary alveoli, where CO_2 exchange with pulmonary capillary blood takes place. If too much air, or gas, is found inside the mediastinum from ruptured alveoli, drowning may be the cause. Scarpetta points out how it might affect a diver who is breathing inadequately: "'[E]xcessive pressure in the lungs can result in small tears of the alveolar walls, causing hemorrhages and air leaks into one or both pleural cavities'" (p. 44), which could be lethal.

MENDELIAN Marino, visiting Scarpetta in her home, pours a cup of coffee and offers her one.

"'Black, please,'" she says.

"'I think by now you don't have to tell me.'"

"'I never make assumptions . . . [especially] about men who seem to be having a Mendelian trait which precludes them from remembering details important to women'" (p. 127). Perhaps she is hypersensitive to this behavior as it is reminiscent of her former husband, Tony.

Gregor Johann Mendel (1822–1884), an Austrian monk, pioneered studies in genetics through botany studies. Many of his theories are the foundation of long-standing laws of heredity, known as *Mendelian* laws or traits. But they really don't apply to learned behavioral patterns. Scarpetta is just yanking Marino's chain a bit with her implication that some men inherit an inability to remember things important to women.

MRI/TECHNETIUM Marino is worried that he has been exposed to radioactive uranium. Scarpetta, trying to calm him, points out, "'I do know about radioactivity. I know about X-rays, MRIs and isotopes like cobalt, iodine and technetium that are used to treat cancer'" (p. 219).

MRI stands for *magnetic resonance imaging.* Marino, admitting he has a phobia about radioactivity, may have remembered when it was called *nuclear magnetic resonance imaging* in the early 1980s. It has no nuclear or radioactive components. Detailed images of the internal human body are made with MRI using magnetism, radio waves, and a computer.

Technetium is atomic element number 43, discovered in 1937 and isolated in 1962. It is used in medical radioactive isotope tests, radiological bone scans, and other similar functions. Protective containers are used with this metal. Marino would avoid proximity to it.

PALPATE Examining a corpse with help from her assistant, Scarpetta says, "I palpated the scalp some more" (p. 179).

To *palpate* means, very simply, to examine by touch, especially for the purpose of diagnosing disease or illness.

PNEUMOTHORAX/MEDIASTINAL SHIFT/BAROTRAUMA Continuing the diver's autopsy with one of her regional assistants, Scarpetta notes, "[W]hat an X-ray might reveal was pneumothorax or a mediastinal shift caused by air leaking from lungs due to barotrauma" (p. 32).

More commonly known as a collapsed lung, a *pneumothorax* takes place when air escapes from the lungs or leaks through the chest wall into the pleural cavity (the space between the two membranes covering the lungs). As air builds up outside of the lungs, it causes the lung to collapse. Pneumothorax can be precipitated by diseases but usually results from a puncture wound or blunt-force trauma. A *mediastinal shift* can follow. This means that the mediastinum (the cavity between the lungs that contains the heart, large blood vessels, trachea, esophagus, thymus, and connective tissues) may shift toward the collapsed lung and severely compromise pulmonary and cardiac functions.

Barotrauma refers to the pain and damage caused by a sudden change in barometric pressure.

PROCTITIS, EPITHELIUM As Scarpetta continues the diver's autopsy, she comments: "I was almost finished with the external examination, but what was left was the most invasive, for in any unnatural death, it was necessary to investigate a patient's sexual practices. Rarely was I given a sign as obvious as a tattoo depicting one orientation or another, [but] . . . I would still check for evidence of anal intercourse." She explains what she's looking for. " 'Proctitis, anal tunneling, small fissures, thickening of the epithelium from trauma' " (p. 37).

Proctitis, or inflammation of the rectal lining, has several causes, including injury or infection. The *epithelium,* a thin sheet of tissue lining body surfaces including the internal organs, colon, and anus, provides a permeable barrier between the contents of the tract and the body tissues. Anal intrusion can injure the epithelium and cause thickening.

UNNATURAL EXPOSURE

ANTIGENIC/CHORIOALLANTOIC In a meeting of medical experts investigating the potential spread of an epidemic disease, one attendee says, " 'We also got a verification of antigenic identity using agar gel. Now, chick embryo chorioallantoic membrane culture . . . [will] take two, three days. So we don't have those results now, but we do have a PCR. It verified a pox'" (p. 276).

Antigenic describes a class of substances produced by the body, or injected into it, that stimulate production of antibodies (proteins in the blood that react to toxins).

Agar gel is a gelatinous material extracted from red algae and used most frequently as a culture medium, especially for bacteria.

Chorioallantoic refers to chorioallantois, the embryonic membrane fusing the contents of an egg to the shell. Chick embryos are used as a matrix in lab culture experiments.

PCR stands for *polymerase chain reaction,* a process used in amplifying DNA for tests.

BERYLLIOSIS A pulmonary specialist mentions to Scarpetta that an autopsy he performed revealed a rare disorder called mineral dust pneumoconiosis, specifically berylliosis (p. 177).

Berylliosis is a lung inflammation caused by inhaling dust or fumes containing a metallic element called beryllium. It is a metal used in the aerospace industry. The disease may not show up until twenty years after the patient has inhaled the metal.

CORTICAL ATROPHY A female corpse is being autopsied by Scarpetta, who observes, "She had cortical atrophy, widening of the cerebral sulci and loss of the parenchyma, the telltale hints of Alzheimer's" (p. 212).

Cortical atrophy is wasting away or degeneration of the brain's cerebral cortex. This is often a symptom of acquired immune deficiency syndrome (AIDS) and its infection of the central nervous system. *Sulci* are grooves in the cerebral cortex, which become wider with cortical atrophy, and *parenchyma* are delicate cells related to the organ's function. Thus, damage to the cortex and loss of functional cells in the brain can produce symptoms of Alzheimer's disease, including confusion and reduced memory capabilities.

CRYPTOSPORIDIUM A nurse is complaining to Scarpetta about budgetary problems that curtail health care, such as "'Medicaid, air pollution, and tracking the winter flu epidemic or screening water supplies for the Cryptosporidium parasite'" (p. 222).

Cryptosporidium is an intestinal parasite that causes chronic diarrhea. It is particularly dangerous to AIDS patients.

EBOLA/HANTAVIRUS In one scene Scarpetta mentions, "scientists doing open war with Ebola, Hantavirus and unknown diseases for which there was no cure." (p. 210).

Ebola hemorrhagic fever, first identified in 1976 and named after a river in Africa, is a terrifying viral disease affecting humans, monkeys, gorillas, and chimpanzees. Death rates among humans run as high as 90 percent of those infected.

Hantavirus pulmonary syndrome has been recognized as a disease only recently in North America. It is spread to humans by infected rodents via particles from mouse droppings that have been swept into the air and inhaled. So far, it is fairly uncommon and the chances of becoming infected are low. But it is potentially lethal, and immediate intensive care is essential for survival once symptoms appear.

ENTEROHEMORRHAGIC E. COLI At a restaurant with Marino, Scarpetta is disgusted when he orders his "usual grilled hamburger platter," medium rare.

"'Medium,'" she suggests. He reluctantly agrees.

"'Enterohemorrhagic E. coli,'" Scarpetta advises. "'Trust me. Not worth it'" (p. 126).

Enterohemorrhagic *Escherichia coli* is a bacteria that produces a toxin in the digestive system that can cause serious, long-term damage to internal organs. The primary source for the bacteria is contaminated beef. Cooking meat thoroughly will kill the bacteria.

GLUTARALDEHYDE Working in her laboratory, Scarpetta says, "I had fixed liver and spleen sections in glutaraldehyde, which penetrated tissue very rapidly" (p. 179).

Glutaraldehyde is a chemical used as a fixative, especially for electron microscopy.

GUARNIERI BODIES Under a high-power microscope, Scarpetta examines slides of cells taken from a woman who may have died from an epidemic disease. "The smear on the slide came into focus, magnified four hundred and fifty times. . . . I stared at waves of bright red eosinophilic inclusions within infected epithelial cells, or the cytoplasmic Guarnieri bodies indicative of a pox-type virus" (p. 176).

Eosinophilic inclusions refers simply to a red or brown potassium or sodium salt dye used to stain the cells under examination. *Epithelial cells* are the covering of organism surfaces, consisting of cells joined together by small amounts of cementing substances. *Guarnieri bodies,* named for Italian physician Giuseppi Guarnieri (1856–1918), are minuscule bodies found in epithelial cells when smallpox infection might be present. Scarpetta's fears that a smallpox outbreak might be looming seem to be reinforced.

IMMUNOSUPPRESSED Investigating a case involving possible smallpox, Scarpetta tells Marino, "'I've been reexposed, and I'm sick with something, meaning I'm probably immunosuppressed, on top of it all'" (p. 284).

Immunosuppressed means simply having a lowered resistance to disease. AIDS, chemotherapy, chronic illnesses like diabetes and lupus, and sheer exhaustion are among the many various causes that can drastically reduce the effectiveness of a person's immune system.

ISCHEMIC ENCEPHALOPATHY "'[I'm working] on a brain'" (p. 14), Scarpetta tells her angry secretary, whose feelings had been hurt after her boss's unannounced trip to Ireland. The woman forgives Scarpetta, though, and listens when she recites what she's found. "'Swelling, with widening of the gyri, narrowing of the sulci, all good for ischemic encephalopathy brought on by his profound systemic hypotension'" (p. 15).

Gyri, the plural of *gyrus,* are convoluted ridges between grooves in the brain. *Sulci,* the plural of *sulcus,* are the furrows or grooves.

Hypoxic ischemic encephalopathy (HIE) is a term for irreversible brain injury that results from reduced oxygen or blood flow to that organ. *Systemic hypotension* is abnormally low blood pressure throughout the entire body, a condition that can bring on HIE.

LESSER TROCHANTER Examining a badly mangled corpse, Scarpetta says, "'Residual femur on the right measures two inches below the lesser trochanter . . .'" (p. 53).

Lesser trochanter refers to a part of the femur, or thigh bone. It is located on the interior side of the upper leg, to which muscles are attached.

MICROTOME Speaking of various tools used in the microscopic study of tissue, Scarpetta mentions a microtome. This is an instrument for cutting very thin sections of organic tissue to be examined.

MOLLUSCUM CONTAGIOSUM In a discussion of the types of pox viruses, Scarpetta asks, "'Do monkeys get monkeypox or are they just the carrier?'" (p. 253).

Another doctor answers, "'They get it and they give it where there is animal contact, such as in the rain forests of Africa. There are nine known virulent poxviruses on this planet, and transmission to humans happens only in two. The variola virus, or smallpox, which, thank God, we don't see anymore, and molluscum contagiosum'" (p. 253).

The *molluscum contagiosum* virus is a species that causes skin lesions in humans, mostly children, and is transmitted by direct contact with the infected animal or from inorganic carriers such as books or clothing. It can produce large, disfiguring lesions in AIDS patients.

SHIGELLA A colleague of Scarpetta's, also a doctor, discusses various sources of internal infections with her. "'Imagine this,'" he says. "'A resort in Iowa where we've got suspected shigella because a lot of rain overflowed in private wells'" (p. 254).

Shigella is a bacterium that causes dysentery. Contaminated drinking water is the usual source.

VZV One of Scarpetta's assistants helps with an autopsy. When they notice raised, fluid-filled vesicles (small cysts) on the corpse's skin, Scarpetta guesses it is the "herpes zoster virus" (p. 54). The helper (who may have AIDS) is alarmed. Scarpetta asks if he has ever had a VZV vaccination (p. 54).

Herpes zoster is a reactivation of the same virus that is responsible for chicken pox. It causes a painful, blistery red rash generally confined to one side of the body. It affects nerve distribution and can lead to optic nerve damage and blindness.

VZV, varicella zoster virus vaccine, has been shown to have potential benefits in treating herpes simplex and AIDS.

POINT OF ORIGIN

AVULSED Lucy accidentally injures herself, and Scarpetta is giving her medical care. "I . . . washed her hand with bottled water. A thick flap of skin on her thumb was almost avulsed" (p. 282).

Avulsed means having the tissue torn away.

DIABETIC KETOACIDOSIS AND DIABETES MELLITUS Telling a father about his son's death, Scarpetta explains, "'[His] cause of death was acute pneumonia due to acute diabetic ketoacidosis due to acute onset of diabetes mellitus. I'm sorry for your pain'" (p. 233).

Diabetic ketoacidosis sets in with the depletion of insulin, the substance allowing the body to absorb glucose into cells and produce energy. Without insulin, the body compensates by breaking down (metabolizing) fats for fuel. Metabolism of fat produces a by-product called ketone. Too many ketones in the blood result in diabetic ketoacidosis, and can lead to coma and death.

Diabetes mellitus is a disease characterized by changes in insulin production and use by the body. It disrupts the metabolism of carbohydrates.

EXSANGUINATION A woman's dead body is found in a burned house. Scarpetta recognizes it as a homicide. "'She was dead before the fire . . . her cause of death exsanguination'" (p. 110).

Exsanguination is loss of blood.

GALEA/PERIOSTEUM The woman had been not only murdered, but scalped as well. Scarpetta is discussing the unusual aspects with an expert from the Smithsonian Institution. He points out that scalping methods vary. For example, he says, "'There were many ways that Indians scalped the enemy. Usually, the skin was incised in a circle over the skull down to the galea and periosteum so it could be easily removed'" (p. 160).

He refers to the *galea aponeurotica,* a fibrous sheet of tissue attached to muscles over the skull. The *periosteum* is a membrane of connective tissue surrounding the skull.

HYPEROSMOLAR VACUOLIZATION Autopsy results reveal problems with a victim's kidneys. Scarpetta points out, "'[They] show hyperosmolar vacuolization of the proximal convoluted tubular lining cells'" (p. 232).

Hyperosmolarity is an increase in the concentration of fluid that has moved, via osmosis, through a separating membrane. *Vacuolization,* or vacuolation, refers to multiplying spaces or cavities within a cell. These cavities, or vacuoles, may function in digestion, secretion, or excretion processes. Scarpetta finds that the cells in the tubes of the kidney she examined are twisted, malfunctioning, and clear instead of their normal pink color, and are enlarged due to fluids and cavities.

BLACK NOTICE

ADENOSINE TRIPHOSPHATE Asked what causes rigor mortis in a corpse, Scarpetta explains, " 'When you die, your body quits making adenosine triphosphate. That's why you get stiff' " (p. 233).

The human body requires continuing supplies of energy to allow food metabolism, muscle contractions, and other physical functioning. It is carried by an organic compound composed of adenine, the sugar ribose, and three phosphates, making up *adenosine triphosphate,* or *ATP.* When the body stops functioning, this oxidation process ceases, and the muscles stiffen until decomposition takes over.

This process is also mentioned in *Portrait of a Killer.*

CARABELLI, CUSP Discovering peculiar irregularities in the dental work of an autopsied body, Scarpetta notes, " '[T]here was an accessory cusp of the Carabelli. All molars have four cusps, or protrusions. This one had had five.'

" 'What's a Carabelli?' Marino wanted to know.

" 'Some person. I don't know who' " (p. 91).

This dental anomaly is named after Georg von Carabelli, an Austrian dentist (1787–1842).

CARGILLE MELT MOUNT Scarpetta observes one of her assistants at work: "[H]e was making a permanent slide, using a pipette to touch a drop of Cargille melt mount on the edge of a cover slip while other slides warmed up on a hot plate" (p. 391).

A *Cargille Meltmount* (trademarked name) is a mounting medium specifically formulated for use in microscope slide mounting and in other optical applications. The reusable material is fluid at 65°C and requires no solvents. It is also available in a "Quick-Stick" form, which can be applied to a slide on a hot plate for making permanent microscope slide mounts.

CHLORAL HYDRATE/ETHCHLORVYNOL Odors can be important in diagnosing death by poisoning, says Scarpetta. "They have their own story to tell. A sweet smell might point at ethchlorvynol, while chloral hydrate smells like pears. . . . a hint of garlic might point at arsenic" (p. 86).

Ethchlorvynol is a prescription sedative once used primarily for short-term treatment of insomnia. Other drugs have replaced it. Massive use can be deadly.

Chloral hydrate is also a potentially lethal prescription sedative used as a sleeping pill. In capsule form, it can be taken orally or as a rectal suppository. (See also the definition under *Postmortem*.)

CLOSTRIDIA Marino is paranoid about contracting AIDS. Scarpetta advises him, " 'If you're determined to worry about something, try . . . bacteria. . . . Clostridia' " (p. 31).

Clostridia are bacteria that most commonly cause illness via food that has been left at room temperature too long. The symptoms are abdominal pain and diarrhea occurring from eight to twenty-four hours after ingestion. Sometimes this illness is self-diagnosed as the so-called twenty-four-hour flu.

HYPERTRICHOTIC One of the most eerie of all antagonists in the Scarpetta series—the "werewolf," Chandonne—suffers from a strange malady. Scarpetta considers how it must affect him. "I could only imagine his humiliation, his rage. It was typical for parents to shun a hypertrichotic infant at birth" (p. 360).

Hypertrichotic describes a person who has hypertrichosis, excessive growth of hair over the entire body; it's also called *polytrichosis*.

THE LAST PRECINCT

BUSPAR Searching a murder victim's medicine cabinet, Scarpetta finds that the woman hoarded Valium and Ativan. "She had a small amount of BuSpar, too" (p. 333).

BuSpar, or *Buspirone,* is an antianxiety agent not chemically or pharmacologically related to barbiturates or other sedative-type drugs.

VASOVAGAL RESPONSE In her diagnosis after an autopsy, Scarpetta says, "I am . . . inclined to suspect that the compression of blood vessels caused a vasovagal response" (p. 419).

Vasovagal refers to the action of the vagus nerve on blood vessels. This nerve innervates the gastrointestinal tract, heart, and larynx. Excitation of the nerve may cause fainting due to cardioinhibition, or slowing of the heart, which reduces cerebral blood flow.

BLOW FLY

SNEEZE OR COUGH PATTERNS Scarpetta notes unusual blood patterns along the wall of a victim's house (p. 421). Circular dark-rimmed drops of blood with lighter centers indicate bubbles of air in the blood—found when a victim has blood entering the respiratory system. These can be a result of a stabbing, or the victim could merely have blood in the mouth.

TRACE

BURKING Scarpetta refers to this practice of body snatching in connection with Edgar Allan Pogue (p. 402). It was named after William Burke and William Hare, two Scottish immigrants who provided fresh, unmarked corpses to medical students in Edinburgh by murdering their victims through mechanical asphyxia.

CILIATED RESPIRATORY EPITHELIUM Scarpetta checks for these on Gilly Paulsson's bed linens to confirm mechanical asphyxia (p. 119). These are skin cells lining portions of the respiratory tract with cilia on them—cilia are projections from the cell wall that help to move fluids over the cell surface. They would have been expelled from her stressed respiratory system, helping to prove murder by mechanical asphyxia.

DECOMPOSED ROOM Scarpetta uses the Decomposed Room to autopsy Gilly Paulsson's corpse (p. 112). The room is a small mortuary with a special ventilation system for working on particularly noxious or decomposed corpses.

DEXTRO HEAD Benton Wesley is interviewing Henri, and she is furious that an ER doctor called her a Dextro Head (p. 66). A Dextro Head is someone who abuses over-the-counter cold medications containing opiates.

ERECTOR PILI MUSCLES Scarpetta sees a corpse with goose bumps (p. 93). She notes postmortem contractions of these small muscles at the bottom of each hair shaft.

HAVERSIAN CANALS Scarpetta uses these structures to identify bone fragments (p. 308). These are small channels that run through bone to carry nerves and circulatory vessels.

PANNICULUS Scarpetta sees five people struggle to move an enormous corpse onto the stainless-steel autopsy table. She remarks on the size of the panniculus (p. 53). A panniculus is the fold of fat that hangs from the belly of obese people.

PULMONARY EDEMA FLUID Gilly Paulsson, suspected murder victim, has a bruise on her back, just below the scapula. Scarpetta asks to have the linens of the bed on which Gilly was found checked for pulmonary edema fluid and ciliated respiratory epithelium (p. 119). They will provide supporting evidence for death by mechanical asphyxia—where a weight on the chest or back prevents the victim from breathing until he or she dies. Pulmonary edema is a life-threatening condition in which the lungs fill with fluid. Pulmonary edema fluid accumulates in the lungs when circumstances overwhelm the lymphatic system's ability to remove it. It can occur due to medical reasons—like acute cardiac and pulmonary disease. It can also occur due to mechanical asphyxiation. In a mechanical asphyxiation, the victim aspirates the fluid, blowing it out while trying to breathe.

SPIROMETRY Scarpetta comments on Edgar Allan Pogue's disability citing spirometry results (p. 330). Spirometry is the science of interpreting the results from a spirometer, a machine that measures lung function. The patient breathes into the machine, then out. The machine measures the amount of air taken in, as well as the amount of air expelled from the lungs. The air can be measured several ways—either as static (under the patient's own lung power) or forced (the machine blows air into the lungs). The machine gives a number of statistics including lung capacity, peak expiratory flow rate, forced expiratory flow rate, and vital capacity, which is the change in volume from the lungs that are fully inflated to those that are at rest after full exhalation. These measurements can be used to determine the health of the patient's respiratory system.

FORENSICS, FIREARMS, AND FINGERPRINTS

THE pursuit of killers requires not only great investigative skills, but also a broad scope of knowledge about forensic sciences. This includes up-to-date fingerprinting methods, ballistics, and serology, as well as understanding of and familiarity with weapons, including a variety of guns and knives. Scarpetta and Marino demonstrate a wide knowledge in this area, but also recognize that they need expert assistance on occasion.

Following are selected examples of the technical aspects of their jobs, along with supplementary information about the tools of crime and forensic investigation they use.

BLOOD EVIDENCE

At a gory crime scene, Scarpetta examines blood spatter evidence and notes, "The [blood] stains were elliptical, about six millimeters in diameter, and became increasingly elongated the farther they arched left of the doorframe." Marino says, "'Based on the location of this spatter, I'm thinking the drone was right about here. . . . He swings, cuts her again, and as the blade follows through, blood flies off and hits the wall. The pattern, as you can see, starts here'" (p. 16, *Body of Evidence*).

True to their profession, Scarpetta and Marino know that patterns made by spattering blood can reveal all sorts of hidden secrets about the murder. National television audiences were introduced to this subject when Dr. Henry Lee, one of America's foremost experts on the subject, testified for the defense in the notorious O. J. Simpson trial. Dr. Lee, using sentences reduced to the fewest possible words, uttered a jarring phrase: "Something wrong here!" He followed up by demonstrating how the stains from blood can reveal what happened, or what did not happen.

Analysis can tell technicians whether blood fell vertically or flew horizontally, the velocity of its movement, the direction from which it traveled, the angle, and the distance. All of this is influenced by the surface on which it lands, whether that surface is hard or smooth, whether it is wood, fabric, concrete, or something else. Stain sizes and configurations are also an important part of the puzzle.

A Virginia murder case is a good example of this sort of analysis. On February 7, 2000, Officer Mark Jones went to the residence of James Allen Smith, Jr., in Henrico County. He found Tracey L. Chandler lying face up on the bed, with her feet on the floor. Six bullets had slammed into her body: behind her right ear, in the right side of her chest, in her mouth, in her right hand, and above both knees. She had bled to death. Smith was arrested for murder.

At his trial, Smith testified that he had shot Chandler in self-defense when she attacked him with a needle during an argument over her drug use. The defendant said that Chandler was standing when he fired the first three shots and that she sat down and rose once more before he fired again.

A blood spatter expert, Norman Tiller, told jurors that, based on analysis of impact spatter bloodstains on the victim's pants, Chandler was not standing when she was shot.

Scarpetta and Marino would have arrived at the same conclusions.

Smith was convicted and sentenced to prison. He appealed, claiming the court erred in admitting expert opinion testimony on blood spatter analysis. The court's opinion stated, "Because we conclude that blood spatter analysis is a matter for expert testimony and that a sufficient evidentiary foundation for that opinion testimony was established in this case, we will affirm the convictions" (www.courts.state.va.us/opinions/opnscvwp/1021583.doc).

Cases of this type have been replicated countless times across the nation, reinforcing the value of blood spatter evidence as perfectly sound information for juries to consider.

Technology related to other blood forensics is mentioned in *Cruel & Unusual,* in which Scarpetta, Benton Wesley, and a crime-scene technician prepare to use a chemical on surfaces where they suspect bloodstains might exist, but are not visible due to the passage of time. Scarpetta explains, "'Actually, aged and decomposed blood reacts better to luminol than do fresh bloodstains because the more oxidized the blood, the better. As blood ages, it becomes more strongly oxidized'" (p. 320).

Luminol has become a standard weapon in the arsenal of crime-scene investigators. Human blood contains a pigment called hemoglobin, the agent instrumental in distributing oxygen through the blood vessels. Iron in hemoglobin reacts to luminol. The chemical is sprayed onto surfaces where blood may have been. When the room is darkened, the luminol-activated bloodstains give off an eerie blue glow, even if attempts have been made to wash away the telltale stains.

In a California murder case, a young woman had been missing for three years. When her body was found in a freezer stored in the back of a truck in Arizona, the killer was traced. He had used a hammer to beat her to death in a warehouse. Criminalists sprayed luminol on the warehouse floor, which had been scrubbed clean. Even though three years had passed, the luminous glow told investigators exactly where the victim had died. Her assailant wound up on death row (*Cold Storage,* Don Lasseter, Pinnacle Books, 1998).

Early use of blood evidence focused primarily on standard blood typing: A, B, AB, or O. It is still useful in many cases but has certain limitations. In *Postmortem,* Scarpetta is dealing with serial murders. She comments on the use of body fluid evidence found in the investigation, and its connection to blood types. "Seminal fluid was present in all of the cases, yet it was of little serological value. The assailant was one of the twenty percent of the population who enjoyed the distinction of being a nonsecreter" (p. 12).

DNA is now the more reliable method for matching suspects to human tissue or fluids left at a crime scene. Prior to the advent of DNA testing, blood found at a crime scene was, and still is, tested for type to see if it matches the victim or was possibly left by the assailant. If body fluids such as saliva, semen, or mucus are deposited by the killer, they can also be analyzed for blood type. Subsequently, upon arrest of a suspect, his or her blood is tested to see if its type matches crime-scene samples.

The main problem in relying on standard blood typing of fluids (other than blood) found at crime scenes comes from the fact that about 20 percent of humans (this figure varies according to gender and race) are nonsecretors. This means they are unable, by genetic predisposition, to secrete blood-type antigens into saliva, semen, or mucus. Thus, in the case of nonsecretors, lab analysis cannot accurately determine blood type from these fluids. Unless a nonsecretor leaves a collectible amount of blood at a crime scene, he or she cannot be identified as a possible suspect through blood typing. (*Note:* Cornwell uses the spelling *nonsecreters,* while most other references use *nonsecretors.*)

DNA technology has solved that problem in most cases and has become the standard tool in analyzing blood evidence. Understanding DNA is an integral part of Scarpetta's job and it is mentioned in several books. Early in *Postmortem,* she says, "As recently as two years earlier, the killer's nonsecreter status would have been a crushing blow to the forensic investigation. But now there was DNA profiling, newly introduced and potentially significant . . ." (p. 12).

Postmortem was published in 1990, before the nationally televised trial of O. J. Simpson taught viewers far more than they wanted to know about DNA. In regard to being "newly introduced," author Joseph Wambaugh, in *The Blooding,* describes how DNA profiling came about in 1987. Two young women were raped and murdered near the English village of Narborough, three years apart. Earlier, in 1984, geneticist Alec Jeffreys, working at Leicester University, had discovered a process of DNA profiling that would pave the way for its use as forensic evidence. Investigators working the Narborough crimes decided to use Jeffreys's system. They drew blood from more than 4,000 men in the region and systematically began the process of comparison and elimination. Their work finally led to one man, who confessed to the slayings.

In *Postmortem,* Scarpetta talks to the commonwealth's attorney Bill Boltz, who believes the serial killer is leaving no evidence behind. Scarpetta protests by pointing out that he has left ample fluids, which will yield DNA evidence.

Boltz argues, "'DNA printing's only gone to trial a couple of times in Virginia. There are very few precedents'" (p. 138).

Virginia was actually one of the first places in the United States to use

DNA in a murder trial. In 1988, it helped a jury convict Timothy Spencer of killing three women. DNA also cleared a man previously convicted of another murder Spencer may have committed (www.vuac.org/capital/timothyspencer.pdf).

Postmortem contains another mention of DNA. Scarpetta meets with a reporter to request covert help by planting a news story that will cause the killer to become reckless. Explaining the probability of DNA matches within the population, she comments, "'[I]f he's black, then only one out of 135 million men theoretically can fit the same pattern. If he's Caucasian, only one out of 500 million men'" (p. 270).

Significant strides have been made in DNA technology and analysis since 1990. Methods have been developed that narrow the odds down to 1 in 1.7 quintillion. If every planet rotating around the sun had a population the same as Earth's, the DNA pattern would statistically match only one person in the entire solar system!

FIREARMS AND OTHER WEAPONS

A variety of firearms and other weapons are mentioned in the Scarpetta series, and they are used by the bad guys, the police, Pete Marino, Kay Scarpetta, and even her niece, Lucy.

Guns

Scarpetta carries a Colt 38 handgun in her purse and also owns a Ruger .38-caliber revolver, and Marino teaches Lucy to shoot a SIG Sauer P230.

Ruger is one of the products of Sturm, Ruger & Co., Inc., which has been manufacturing handguns since 1949. Located in Southport, Connecticut, the firm is the nation's largest firearms company. The Colt company has been producing firearms since the 1830s.

After discovering and subduing an intruder in her office, Scarpetta jests that the killer may be a reporter. Marino doesn't think her comment is funny. "'Most reporters I know don't pack nine mils loaded with Glasers'" (p. 182, *Body of Evidence*).

The reference to "nine mils" means pistols that fire nine-millimeter ammunition. The diameter of a bullet is measured in decimals of an inch (caliber) or in millimeters. For example, .45-caliber handguns shoot bullets that are .45 inch in diameter.

"Glasers," manufactured by CorBon/Glaser in Sturgis, South Dakota, are bullets composed of a compressed core made up of individual lead pellets and topped with a polymer ball to produce a rounded profile. Upon impact with an inanimate object, the core fractures into a number of pieces. This immediate expansion reduces the penetration and produces immense stopping power. If it strikes animals or humans, it is like a miniature shotgun shell, penetrating into flesh about one-half inch.

Marino notes that the suspect's car had been found and adds, "'Got enough ammo clips and magazines in the trunk to stop a small army, plus a Mac Ten machine pistol . . . He ain't no reporter'" (p. 182, *Body of Evidence*).

A Mac Ten machine pistol is the preferred weapon of terrorists. Machine pistols, some of which are equipped with detachable shoulder stocks, have select fire capabilities, automatic or semiautomatic. Built by the Military Armaments Corporation, the Ingram MAC-10 is named for its inventor, Gordon Ingram. In fully automatic mode, it can fire thirty-two rounds in a nine-millimeter clip. *Fully automatic* means it has the capability to fire a succession of cartridges as long as the trigger is depressed or until the ammunition supply is exhausted. The weapon can also accommodate .38-caliber ammunition. Because of its compact size and its compatibility with silencers and barrel extensions, it is popular among criminals.

In *The Body Farm*, Benton Wesley informs Scarpetta that Lucy has purchased a gun: a "'SIG Sauer P230'" (p. 209).

The SIG Sauer P230 pistol was designed and produced in Germany by the joint venture of J. P. Sauer (Germany) and SIG Arms (Swiss) as a compact police and self-defense pistol. The P230 hit the market in 1977 and was manufactured until 1996, when it was replaced by the P232 pistol.

P230 and P232 SIGs are similar. Both are blowback-operated, hammer-fired pistols, with double-action triggers and manual decocker levers mounted on the left side of the frame, behind the trigger. Both are high-quality, durable, reliable weapons. These guns are well suited for personal defense or for backup weapons carried by law enforcement officers. They offer excellent accuracy and mild recoil.

A notorious firearm appears in *The Last Precinct*. A police officer explains to Marino about a traffic arrest that led to a surprising discovery.

"'Started four months ago with a guy speeding along Route Five just a couple miles from here. A James City cop pulls him. . . . Runs his tag and finds out he's a convicted felon. Plus the officer happens to notice the handle of a long gun protruding from under a blanket in the back seat, turns out to be a MAK-90 with the serial number ground off. . . . As you know, a MAK-90's a popular knock-off of the AK-47'" (p. 295).

The semiautomatic AK-47 was developed in the USSR in 1947 and is regarded as the world's first successful assault rifle. It gained worldwide popularity, especially among paramilitary and underground organizations.

As the officer mentioned, the MAK-90 is a knockoff of the AK-47. It is made in China by a company that calls itself Norinco. It, too, has gained popularity among gun buffs in this country and is especially coveted by illegal users.

In *Cause of Death,* the AK-47 shows up again when Marino reels off a list of weapons owned by a murder victim: "'[H]e's got plenty of guns to choose from, including . . . an AK-47, an MP5 and an M16'" (p. 56).

The MP5 is regarded by many weapons buffs as the best submachine gun ever made. Produced by HK, Heckler & Koch, it is a lightweight, air-cooled, magazine-fed weapon that can be shouldered or hand-fired. Introduced in the 1960s in Europe, it appeared in the United States in the early 1970s.

The United States Rifle, caliber 5.56 mm, M16 series, developed in the early 1960s for the U.S. military services, has undergone a long series of modifications to suit contemporary needs. It is still a general-issue rifle with the U.S. armed forces and widely used by American law enforcement agencies in automatic or semiautomatic form. It is manufactured by several different companies.

Ammunition for all of these firearms is an important element in Cornwell's novels. In *All That Remains,* a bullet has been recovered from the spine of a murder victim during the autopsy, and a spent cartridge case has been located not far from the crime scene. But can they be matched? Scarpetta comments, "'We can't prove that this cartridge case belongs to the bullet I found in Deborah Harvey's lumbar spine, and won't be able to do so unless we recover the pistol. . . . We can't even say with certainty it's from a Hydra-Shok cartridge. All we know is it's nine-millimeter, Federal'" (p. 171).

Federal is an ammunition manufacturer in Anoka, Minnesota. Since 1918 the company has produced a multitude of products, including a line of .45-caliber bullets called Hydra-Shok. This is a copper-jacketed, hollow-point bullet in a nickel-plated cartridge case. It features a small rod in the interior that will cause the bullet to expand when it rips into soft tissue.

Scarpetta is knowledgeable about ammunition. In her narrative, she recalls target practice with Marino. "Loading wadcutters into my revolver, I glanced up as Marino withdrew a 9-millimeter pistol out of the back of his trousers . . . I had fired 9-millimeters before and didn't like them. They weren't as accurate as my .38 special" (p. 278, *Body of Evidence*).

Wadcutters are cylindrical projectiles composed completely of lead used for target shooting. The front of the bullet is flattened, allowing it to cut neat and accurate wads out of the target for clear evidence of scoring.

In *Cause of Death*, Scarpetta performs an autopsy task routine to her, but one that may be chilling to the average person. "I was removing the skull cap in pieces to look at the brain. . . . The bright white shape of the bullet was lodged in the frontal sinus, three inches from the top of the head. . . . The deformed bullet was big with sharp petals folded back like a claw" (p. 179). She and her assistant name possible types the slug might be. "'Maybe Starfire or Golden Sabre?' . . . 'I'm thinking Black Talon because the cartridge case recovered isn't PMC or Remington. It's Winchester. And Winchester made Black Talon until it was taken off the market'" (pp. 179–180).

Starfire ammunition is made by PMC Ammunition. The hollow-point bullet is engineered to expand on impact, which causes it to immediately lose momentum and make shallow penetration. It is designed with five sharp-edged ribs inside the deep hollow-point cavity. The ribs stretch apart on impact, hyperexpanding the bullet to nearly twice its original diameter, with virtually no fragmentation.

Remington's Golden Sabre and Winchester's Silver Tip ammunition also may be acquired with hollow points for similar expansion when the target is struck.

Winchester did indeed produce Black Talon SXT bullets from 1991 until the end of 1993, when the company voluntarily took them off the public market due to adverse publicity. The ammunition was well known for its black color and six serrations in the hollow point, called radial jacket petals, which expanded upon impact. Winchester replaced it on the general market with the Ranger Talon. When this one expands, the copper jacket peels back and forms six sharp jutting points that resemble claws.

Scarpetta described the Black Talon as "'Unbelievably destructive. It goes through you like a buzz saw. Great for law enforcement but a nightmare in the wrong hands'" (p. 180).

Notoriety surrounded another type of ammo mentioned in *Cause of Death*. Marino says, "'I've never seen KTW in Richmond at all . . . Legal or otherwise'" (p. 56). According to Scarpetta's narration, he is referring to a particular brand of Teflon-coated cartridges.

The KTW ammunition firm used the initials of three men—Kopsch, Turcos, and Ward, who founded the company. They invented and manufactured bullets specifically designed for law enforcement officers to use in their handguns. The bullets would penetrate glass, car doors, or other barriers utilized by criminals. The Teflon coating was added to reduce damage to gun barrels. KTW's reported intent was to limit sales to police officers. Somehow, though, the ammunition became notorious as a potential for underground use against body armor worn by cops. A media uproar caused Congress to investigate, after which various states introduced legislation banning KTW ammunition.

Lucy, too, becomes competent with firearms and ammunition after she joins ATF. In *Black Notice* she comments, "'[T]he One-Sixty-Fivers aren't going to survive. . . . And I'm looking forward to that.'"

Scarpetta is puzzled. "'The who?'"

"'The gun-trafficking assholes we're after. Remember, I told you we call them that because their ammo of choice is one-sixty-five-grain Speer Gold Dot. Real high end, hot stuff'" (pp. 69–70).

CCI Ammunition of Lewiston, Idaho, manufactures Gold Dot bullets for all calibers of firearms. One of their products is 165-grain ammunition for .40-caliber Smith & Wesson handguns. It's available in gold boxes containing twenty rounds, which sell for about $15. The company makes a heavier version of the Gold Dot, at 451 grains.

Recognition of ammunition is an important aspect of Scarpetta's autopsy work. In *Point of Origin,* she speaks to an attending detective who has brought in a gun to compare with the bullets used in a victim's shooting death. "'Be sure to note the caliber, make, and model. . . . And is the ammunition ball versus hollow point?'

"'Ball. Remington nine-mill,'" he replies (p. 102).

Ball, the most common type of bullets, refers to a round nose, which allows deeper penetration of solid objects.

If the projectile is hollow point, as mentioned earlier, the forward tip is hollow, creating a mushrooming effect when a target is struck. This produces more damage, particularly to human flesh and tissue. Lucy refers to the Remington Arms Company, which manufactures a variety of ammunition for pistols and revolvers. Among them are *lead round nose,* a versatile, general-purpose bullet for all revolvers; *lead hollow point,* a fast-expanding lead bullet ideal for situations where barrier penetration is not a necessity; *jacketed hollow point,* whose full-length jacket and hollow-point construction provide controlled expansion with good penetration while assuring dependable function in autoloading pistols; and *semijacketed hollow point,* featuring a unique scalloped jacket design engineered to combine optimum expansion with controlled penetration for maximum energy transfer.

Knives

Guns are only one type of weapon Scarpetta and Marino encounter. In *Point of Origin,* while searching a suspect's residence, they discover a secret compartment constructed within the garage. Inside, on a plywood table, they see what Scarpetta characterizes as "the instruments of Joyce's crimes."

She narrates, "Half a dozen knives were lined in a perfect row . . . all . . . in their leather cases."

Marino speaks. "'I'll be damned . . . Let me tell you what these are, Doc. The bone-handled ones are R. W. Loveless skinner knives, made by Beretta. For collectors, numbered, and costing around six hundred bucks a pop. . . . The blue steel babies are Chris Reeves, at least four hundred a pop, and the butts of the handles unscrew if you want to store matches in them'" (p. 375).

Robert W. Loveless has been making custom knives for nearly fifty years in his Riverside, California, shop, using high-precision materials and steel. His knives are famed for beauty and functionality. Loveless collaborated with Beretta, the Italian manufacturer of guns and knives, which has been in business hundreds of years and owns a production facility in Maryland, to produce the Loveless Skinner. It boasts quince wood handles and hollow-ground stainless steel blades. Beretta knives are designed for hunters, collectors, and law enforcement, or for self-protection.

The other brand Marino mentions is named for Chris Reeves, who has operated a small knife-manufacturing company since 1975, renowned for unique design, top-quality steel, sophisticated machining, and high-quality hand craftsmanship. In 1989 he moved from his native South Africa to the United States, where his firm branched out to include product design, research and development, and production oversight. Among the many knives bearing the Chris Reeves stamp is a line made from a single piece of steel with a hollow handle. It is closed with a butt cap of aluminum, which screws into the handle, and sealed by a neoprene O-ring to keep moisture out.

The tools used by killers, guns and knives, require the Scarpettas and Marinos of the world to keep up with the absolute latest on the market.

FINGERPRINTS

Scarpetta's fingerprint expert, Neils Vander, is employed by the OCME, or office of the chief medical examiner. He appears throughout the entire series implementing state-of-the art technology to bring out prints on a variety of surfaces. So do crime-scene technicians who search diligently for prints that might become important clues.

In *Postmortem,* Scarpetta and Marino supervise work in the home of a female murder victim. Scarpetta observes, "An ID officer was busy coating every surface with black dusting powder" (p. 10).

Fingerprints are left at crime scenes for a simple reason. Oil and perspiration residue on the fingers of most people will adhere to smooth surfaces when they are touched. Compression squeezes these substances from between ridges on the skin. The latent (invisible) print remains to be discovered by a technician. The oldest method involves using a soft brush to dust black magnetic powder over crime-scene surfaces. The powder's adherence to oil makes prints visible. Depending on the surface color, lighter shades of dusting powder may be more effective. The prints are then photographed for use as evidence.

During examination with a laser beam of a victim in *Postmortem,* Scarpetta comments, "Theoretically, a fingerprint left on human skin can emit light and may be identified in cases where traditional powder and chemicals will fail. I knew of only one case where prints on skin were found, in south Florida, where a woman was murdered inside a health spa and the assailant had tanning oil on his hands" (p. 23).

The case to which she refers is probably one that happened in 1978 and had remarkably bizarre subsequent twists. Homicide investigator Eddie Stone tackled a triple murder at a North Miami Beach health spa. Using an unprecedented technology, he managed to lift fingerprints from the skin of one victim, an eighteen-year-old woman. These prints became a milestone in forensic science. They matched samples from a karate champion and bodybuilder named Stephen Beattie. Eddie Stone's evidence held up in court. A jury convicted Beattie, and he was sentenced to die in Florida's electric chair. While waiting for his execution date, Beattie committed suicide. In a sad twist, Eddie Stone followed suit five years later. He put the barrel of his handgun in his mouth and pulled the trigger.

Research on lifting prints from human skin continues, with mixed results. Pioneering efforts began in an interesting place. In the early 1970s, FBI specialists arranged with Virginia's chief medical examiner to run an experiment by placing fingerprints on cadavers. They tried a number of methods to lift and preserve the prints with little success, but never ruled out the possibility.

Since then, with advances in science, techniques have improved, including the use of laser beams. Another method, called *cyanoacrylate fuming,* has shown encouraging results. The body is placed in a tentlike chamber that is infused with heated fumes of the chemical used in Super Glue. In many cases, the fumes adhere to latent prints.

Scarpetta's expert, Vander, utilizes the Super Glue method. "I can't even tell you what I could do with cyanoacrylate." He tells Scarpetta that Super Glue reacts to components in human perspiration and is excellent for developing fingerprints difficult to see with the unaided eye.

After a laser wand has revealed something, Scarpetta is hopeful. She observes as he works magic. "Retrieving a jar of powder and a Magna brush, Vander delicately dusted what appeared to be three latent fingerprints left on [the victim's] skin" (p. 23, *Postmortem*). He is able to lift partial prints.

Magna is the brand name of a soft brush used to apply magnetic powder to latent prints for photographing and lifting.

In *The Body Farm,* Scarpetta narrates an interesting aspect of fingerprints most people don't realize. Speaking of a female suspect, Scarpetta says, "'She's not a fingerprint examiner. It's unlikely she would realize that every time a latent print is left, it's reversed. And it matches a ten-print card [an exemplar of all ten prints from any individual] only because those prints are reversed as well" (p. 238). Prints are a mirror image, and this must be recognized by forensic technicians.

Another method for lifting fingerprints involves the use of a chemical called ninhydrin. Scarpetta mentions it in *Postmortem*. "I could always tell when [Vander had] forgotten to put on gloves while using ninhydrin . . . because he'd walk around with purple fingers for a week" (p. 44).

Ninhydrin is used in the collection of latent prints from surfaces such as wallpaper or books, particularly those left months earlier. The chemical is sprayed onto the surface, then allowed to dry. It produces blue-violet tones on the ridges and whorls of fingerprints.

When prints are found and recorded, the next step is to search for a suspect who left them. For many years, this involved arduous and time-consuming manual comparisons. Computers changed all that. Many states have systems in place to search data files and find previously collected exemplars that match those taken from a crime scene. The FBI has one of the largest fingerprint databases.

A reference is made in *Unnatural Exposure* to both Virginia's database and the FBI's system. Neils Vander attempts to find usable prints on a victim's skin and says, "'If I get something, I'll run it through AFIS.'"

Scarpetta replies, "'And I'll start with HALT.'" She explains that HALT is the "Homicide Assessment and Lead Tracking System . . . a Virginia database maintained by the state police in conjunction with the FBI. It was a place to start if we suspected the case was local" (p. 91).

AFIS refers to the FBI's Automated Fingerprint Identification System. It was developed in the 1960s when the bureau began investigating the feasibility of automating fingerprint identification and evolved over the years to include millions of prints. Access is available to state law enforcement agencies.

THAT'S A REAL KILLER

IT is not uncommon for homicide investigators, both in real life and in novels and films, to draw comparisons between their cases and the patterns used by notorious serial killers, assassins, rapists, and other perpetrators of violent crimes. Cornwell realizes this and incorporates into her stories at least twenty-two allusions to criminals who have made headlines in recent decades. She introduces these names into the text by using dialogue between her characters and through Kay Scarpetta's thoughts.

Most of these references to criminals in the Scarpetta series are made by Benton Wesley. He is introduced in *Postmortem* as a "suspect profiler for the FBI" (p. 74). In *Unnatural Exposure* he has been elevated to chief of the FBI's CASKU (Child Abduction Serial Killer Unit), and in *Point of Origin* he is "the retired chief of the FBI's profiling unit" (p. 8). These executive positions and his vast experience certainly make Benton an expert on the behavior patterns of killers.

The great majority of readers will probably recall the following names and crimes, which have been covered extensively by news media, television documentaries, and true-crime books. But for those who may have restricted their reading to fiction, or for those who have forgotten the details, a brief reminder of these criminals and the horrific circumstances of their crimes is offered here.

Ted Bundy

In *Postmortem*, Benton discusses with Scarpetta and Marino the possible future behavior of a certain serial killer under investigation. "'He's becoming increasingly desensitized. . . . Over the subsequent days or weeks, the tension builds until he finds his next target, stalks her and does it again. The intervals between each killing may get shorter. He may escalate, finally, into a spree murderer, as Bundy did'" (p. 80).

Several books, movies, and television documentaries have detailed the bloody trail left by Theodore "Ted" Bundy. He was a law student who was also active in politics. He began his reign of terror against young women near Seattle, Washington, in the 1970s and wound it up in Florida. The victims he targeted bore similar physical characteristics, many wearing long dark hair parted in the middle. As Wesley points out, Bundy gradually increased the frequency of his violent attacks and wound up committing a "spree murder," battering three young women to death in a sorority dormitory near Florida State University.

Scarpetta notes in *From Potter's Field* that "[The killer is becoming] more daring, meaning he's taking greater risks. That's what Bundy did in the end" (p. 220).

Between 1978 and 1980, Bundy faced three murder trials in which he was convicted of slaying seven young women. His final victim was only twelve years old. Sentenced to be executed, Bundy died in Florida's electric chair on January 24, 1989. In the final days of his life, he confessed to killing twenty-eight female victims, but there may have been many more. While waiting on death row, Bundy agreed to be interviewed by Bill Hagmaier, an FBI agent working with the Behavioral Science Unit in Quantico, Virginia. In Cornwell's books, agent Benton Wesley conducts this interview.

Scarpetta narrates, in *Cruel & Unusual*, "When Wesley alluded to the Bundys . . . in the world, he did so theoretically, impersonally, as if his analyses and theories were formulated from secondary sources. . . . He had, in fact, spent long, intimate hours with the likes of Theodore Bundy, David Berkowitz, Sirhan Sirhan, Richard Speck, and Charles Manson, in addition to the lesser-known black holes who had sucked light from the planet Earth" (pp. 220–221).

Sirhan Sirhan

Sirhan Sirhan is not a serial killer, but a political assassin. The story of Sirhan Bishara Sirhan remains riddled with questions. On the evening of June 5, 1968, in an anteroom/pantry of the Ambassador Hotel in Los Angeles, California, this small, innocuous man waited for his prey. Senator Robert F. Kennedy, brother of assassinated U.S. president John F. Kennedy, finished a speech in the ballroom after winning the California primary in the Democratic presidential nominating race. Moments later, a hail of bullets dropped Kennedy to the floor and ended his life the next day. In the ensuing pandemonium, Sirhan was restrained by a half-dozen men.

A native of Jerusalem who emigrated from Jerusalem to California with his parents in 1957, Sirhan kept a journal expressing his outrage at world disorder, especially in the Mideast. He perceived Robert Kennedy as a friend of Israel and noted, "RFK must die . . . must be assassinated." But at his trial, Sirhan denied being Kennedy's killer. A jury disagreed, found him guilty, and recommended life imprisonment rather than execution. Despised, he sits in prison still claiming his innocence and waiting for his next parole hearing. Sirhan is still the subject of persistent conspiracy theories.

Richard Speck

Richard Speck is categorized as a "spree" killer rather than a serial killer. A tattoo on his left forearm proclaimed, "Born to Raise Hell." This motto described his wandering, aimless, alcoholic, troubled life. By 1966, at age twenty-four, he had been arrested thirty-seven times. In July of that year, while waiting in Chicago for a possible berth aboard a merchant ship, he slipped into a two-story townhouse occupied by nine student nurses, six of them American students and three from the Philippines. A few minutes after midnight, he began his bloodbath. Threatening six of the women with a knife, he bound them with strips of bedsheets. Two others arrived home late. Speck kept them separate from the original group. One by one, he began methodically raping and murdering his victims, but somehow lost count. Tiny Corazon Amurao managed to slip under a bunk and elude Speck.

After he departed, she waited until six in the morning, then ran out and screamed for help. A police dragnet finally corralled Speck several days later. Amurao's detailed description of the killer included his distinctive tattoo. Sentenced to death, Speck was the beneficiary of a ruling by the U.S. Supreme Court and his sentence was commuted to life in prison.

A bizarre incident took place in 1988. Someone had smuggled a camcorder into Speck's cell. Illinois authorities were horrified eight years later when the tape was discovered and aired on television. It showed a pale, bloated Speck grotesquely prancing around, wearing nothing but blue panties and showing off his female hormone–enhanced breasts. Grinning lasciviously, he said, "If they only knew how much fun I'm having in here, they would turn me loose." The fun had already ended for Speck in December 1991, when he died of a massive heart attack.

Charles Manson

The third person mentioned by Scarpetta, Charles Manson, is perhaps the most well-known killer of the twentieth century. Yet his conviction was for orchestrating murders, not actually committing them. On August 9, 1969, members of the "Manson Family," three women and one man, invaded the residence of pregnant actress Sharon Tate near Hollywood. They savagely slaughtered Tate along with coffee heiress Abigail Folger, hair stylist Jay Sebring, writer-producer Voytek Frykowski, and teenager Steven Parent. The next night, another attack took the lives of businessman Leno LaBianca and his wife, Rosemary.

In October, Manson and most of his followers were caught and jailed on minor charges. They probably would have been released had Susan Atkins, one of the killers, not been previously arrested. She confided to a cellmate about the murders and the cellmate promptly informed authorities.

A spectacular trial lasted for months. Famed prosecutor Vincent Bugliosi persuaded a jury to find Manson guilty along with his accomplices, even though he had not actually been present inside the homes when the murders were perpetrated. Bugliosi later chronicled the case in his book *Helter Skelter*.

Manson, Susan Atkins, Patricia Krenwinkel, Leslie Van Houten, and Charles "Tex" Watson were all sentenced to die in California's gas chamber, but a 1972 Supreme Court ruling resulted in commutations for all five to life in prison with the possibility of parole. They have all been rejected numerous times following parole hearings.

Dr. Spiro Fortosis, a forensic psychologist, discusses in *Postmortem* the issue of killers craving publicity. "'The public tends to believe the vast majority of people who commit sensational crimes want recognition, want to feel important. . . . These types are the exception, in my opinion. They are one extreme. The other extreme is your Lucases and Tooles. They do what they do and often don't even stick around in the city long enough to read about themselves'" (pp. 257–258).

Earlier Pete Marino also mentions Lucas and sarcastically refers to "'the Green Valley strangler out there in the land of fruits and nuts,'" adding, "'this squirrel we're dealing with ain't a Lucas'" (pp. 82–83, *Postmortem*).

Gary Ridgway

The first of Marino's comments may be a veiled or mistaken allusion to Gary Ridgway, the notorious "Green River" serial killer, who reportedly murdered forty-nine women in Washington state between 1982 and 1984. When Cornwell wrote *Postmortem,* all of those crimes were still unsolved. Not until 2001 was Ridgway arrested and charged with forty-eight of the slayings. He pleaded guilty to all of the charges in 2003 and was sentenced to life in prison without parole.

Henry Lee Lucas

Marino's and Fortosis's reference to "Lucas" probably refers to alleged serial killer Henry Lee Lucas, who was at one time thought to be the most prolific serial killer in history. He confessed to hundreds of murders carried out across the country between 1947 and 1983, some of which involved necrophilia, bestiality, and child molestation. Most of Lucas's allegations turned out to be uncorroborated, but he was finally convicted of killing a young female hitchhiker known as "Orange Socks," a reference to the only garments she wore when her unidentified body was found in a Texas culvert. Facing execution in 1998, Lucas's sentence was commuted to life imprisonment by then–Texas governor George W. Bush because of unanswered questions about the case. Lucas died behind bars of natural causes in March 2001.

During Lucas's cross-country roaming, he was sometimes accompanied by a rough partner named Ottis Toole. Shock rippled across the nation when Toole made an unsubstantiated confession to killing six-year-old Adam Walsh, son of "America's Most Wanted" moderator John Walsh. Not enough evidence could be found to file charges in the Walsh case. Convicted of two other murders, Toole succumbed to liver failure in a prison hospital in September 1996.

Benton also states in *Postmortem,* " 'Take Gacy. We've got no idea how many people he murdered. Thirty-three kids. Possibly it was hundreds'" (p. 85) and " 'Chapman's toting around *Catcher in the Rye* when he wastes John Lennon. Reagan, Brady get shot by some jerk who's obsessed with an actress'" (p. 85).

John Wayne Gacy

The first person Wesley mentions in that passage, John Wayne Gacy, was a Chicago light-construction contractor who lured thirty-three young men into homosexual liaisons by offering them jobs with his firm, murdered them, and buried most of the bodies under his house. His crimes took place from 1972 to 1978. In conjunction with his membership in the Junior Chamber of Commerce, he was active in the community and performed as an entertainer at children's events dressed as Pogo the Clown. He once posed for a photograph with Rosalynn Carter, wife of U.S. president Jimmy Carter. After investigators finally found the decomposing corpses, Gacy was tried in 1980 and sentenced to death. He spent fourteen years appealing his conviction but was finally executed by lethal injection on May 10, 1994.

Following Benton Wesley's initial comments about Gacy, he makes a blunder. He says about Gacy's victims, " 'Strangers, all of them strangers to him. Then he does his mother and stuffs pieces of her down the garbage disposal'" (p. 85). Wesley seems misinformed. Not all of the young men Gacy murdered were strangers to him. Several worked in his contracting business. One was the son of Gacy's business colleague. But the more serious error is about Gacy "doing" his own mother. He certainly did not murder her, nor ever harm her. As an expert criminal profiler for the FBI, it is unlikely Benton would have made such a grievous misstatement. Perhaps he confused Gacy with a California serial killer, Edmund Kemper III, who, after murdering and beheading several coeds, then using their bodies for sexual purposes, did the same thing to his own mother. In a subsequent confession, Kemper said he "humiliated her corpse."

Mark David Chapman

The comment Wesley makes about Chapman toting *Catcher in the Rye* is more accurate. Other references to Mark David Chapman appear in *Point of Origin* and *From Potter's Field*. In the latter, Kay Scarpetta visits New York City and remarks, "I stared up at the Dakota on my left, where John Lennon was killed on a corner years ago" (p. 71).

Chapman shot and killed ex-Beatle John Lennon just outside the musician's New York City apartment building, the Dakota, on December 8, 1980. At the time he pulled the trigger, Chapman carried with him a copy of J. D. Salinger's cult novel. Reporters wrote that Chapman identified with the book's protagonist, Holden Caulfield, a troubled teenager. No death penalty existed at that time in New York, so Chapman was sentenced to life imprisonment. He became eligible for parole in 2000, but to date his applications have been rejected.

John Hinckley, Jr.

The comment Wesley makes about Reagan and Brady getting shot "by some jerk" refers to John Hinckley, Jr., who is also mentioned by name in *Point of Origin*. Hinckley attempted to assassinate President Ronald Reagan on March 30, 1981, outside a Washington, D.C., hotel. Reagan was critically wounded and his press secretary, James Brady, suffered permanently debilitating injuries. Hinckley had previously stalked President Jimmy Carter. According to widespread reports, he also fantasized about having a relationship with actress Jodie Foster after he saw her performance as a young prostitute in *Taxi Driver* and hoped to impress her by killing the president. At the gunman's 1982 trial, he was found not guilty by reason of insanity. The court committed Hinckley to St Elizabeth's Hospital in Washington, D.C., for treatment of his psychotic disorders.

Since 1999, Hinckley has been allowed supervised visits away from the hospital to malls and restaurants. His applications for unsupervised visits were denied until December 2003, when a federal judge granted him the right to a limited number of unsupervised visits with his parents. Hinckley's requests for full release have been consistently denied.

John Joubert

In *Cruel & Unusual,* Benton and Scarpetta discuss the modus operandi of another murderer on the run. Benton says, "'I think this killer is into piquerism'" (p. 212).

Piquerism is a criminal paraphilia that may include sexual mutilation or excessive biting and stabbing of the victim. According to the *Diagnostic and Statistical Manual of Mental Disorders,* fourth edition (DSM-IV), paraphilia involves recurrent, intense sexually arousing fantasies, sexual urges, or behaviors involving 1) nonhuman objects, 2) the suffering or humiliation of oneself or one's partner, or 3) children or other nonconsenting persons, that occur over a period of at least 6 months.

Kay Scarpetta comments about the victim they are discussing being stabbed multiple times, and Wesley agrees.

"'Yes,'" he says. "'I'd say that what was done to her is a textbook example. There was no evidence of rape—not that this means it didn't occur. But no semen. The repeated plunging of the knife in her abdomen, buttocks, and breasts was a substitute for penile penetration. Obvious piquerism. Biting is less obvious, not at all related to any oral components of the sexual act, it is my opinion, but again, a substitute for penile penetration. Teeth sinking into flesh, cannibalism, like John Joubert did to the newspaper delivery boys he murdered in Nebraska'" (pp. 212–213).

John Joubert, a twenty-year-old enlisted man stationed at Offutt Air Force base in Nebraska, confessed to a pair of vile crimes after being apprehended in early 1984. He was caught after loitering around a preschool where an adult challenged him and memorized the license plate of a car in which Joubert fled. It turned out to be a rental vehicle, which authorities soon traced to the young airman. Evidence found in his possession linked him to the death of thirteen-year-old Danny Joe Eberle, who had vanished the previous September while delivering newspapers. When the boy's body turned up, examination revealed extensive stab wounds and bite marks. Another similarly abused victim, Christopher Walden, twelve, had been found nearby in December. He had vanished en route to school.

Eventually, Joubert was convicted of both murders and a third homicide committed in August 1982. Richard Stetson, eleven, had been strangled and stabbed to death near Portland, Maine.

In 1996, Joubert, a former Boy Scout leader, was executed in Nebraska's electric chair.

David Berkowitz

As Wesley and Scarpetta continue their conversation in *Cruel & Unusual*, he has more to say about the subject of piquerism: "'the dynamics, in some instances, become clear. Something penetrating flesh. That was the Son of Sam's thing'" (p. 213).

This is an interesting conclusion by Benton. Piquerism—stabbing, biting, mutilating, and killing for sexual pleasure—involves very intimate, brutal contact with the victim. David Berkowitz, known as the "Son of Sam," did stab two women who were walking in public, neither of them fatally, but used a pistol to shoot most of his victims, all strangers who sat in parked cars.

Berkowitz terrorized New York City for a full year from July 1976 until August 1977. He murdered at least six people and severely injured several more. The peculiar nickname stemmed from Berkowitz's claim that howling demons, sometimes speaking through dogs, ordered him to kill. According to Berkowitz's fevered imagination, a neighbor named Sam, who owned a black Labrador retriever, orchestrated the frenzy of death. "It was Sam who was working through me," he later explained. In a desperate attempt to quiet the demons, Berkowitz shot the dog but only wounded it. Ironically, Berkowitz was finally caught when a woman walking her dog noticed a police officer ticketing a car on the same night of a nearby murder. A record check finally led investigators to the car's owner, David Berkowitz. Declared sane and convicted of a half-dozen murders, he was sentenced to prison for six consecutive terms of twenty-five years to life.

Bernhard Goetz

During a visit to New York City in *From Potter's Field*, Scarpetta takes special safety precautions. As she exits her hotel, she is reminded of one of the most highly publicized and controversial crimes in the city's history. "My Browning [handgun] was in my briefcase, and I hoped Wesley got special permits and did it fast, because I did not wish to be in violation of New York gun laws. I thought of Bernhard Goetz" (pp. 327–328).

To some, Bernhard Goetz was a hero who summoned the courage to lash out against threatening thugs, a feat most surviving victims can usually achieve only in their fantasies. He performed a role of personal vengeance, similar to the one acted by Charles Bronson in his 1974 film *Death Wish*.

To others, Goetz is a reckless vigilante who violated the law. In December 1984, Goetz, thirty-six, sat quietly in a New York subway train. Bespectacled, appearing meek and vulnerable, he didn't respond at first when four young black men surrounded him. But moments after one of them demanded money, Goetz drew a concealed revolver and opened fire. He wounded all four men, permanently paralyzing one of them.

When the train squealed to an emergency halt, Goetz managed to disappear. News media plastered the story everywhere, raising his deed to legendary status and dividing national sympathy. Succumbing to pressure, Goetz finally turned himself in to New Hampshire police on the last day of 1984.

At his trial, evidence revealed that each of the four assailants had criminal records and carried tools that might be used as weapons. According to their stories, they had meant no harm and were simply requesting money to use in video games. Skeptical jurors acquitted Goetz of serious felony charges but found him guilty of violating New York gun laws. He served several months in prison. After release, he kept a low profile and melted into society.

In a civil lawsuit, the paralyzed youth won a judgment of $43 million, but Goetz filed for bankruptcy so will probably pay very little of it. The other three men wounded by Goetz have reportedly been involved in subsequent crimes, one of them a savage rape case.

Scarpetta's desire not to violate gun laws in the state was well grounded.

When her duties once again take her to New York in *Point of Origin,* Scarpetta visits a state psychiatric institution. As she enters, she ruminates about some of the inmates/patients. "They had shot their families, burned up their mothers, disemboweled their neighbors, and dismembered their lovers. They were monsters who had become celebrities, like Robert Chambers of the Yuppie murder fame, or Rakowitz, who had murdered and cooked his girlfriend and allegedly fed parts of her to street people" (p. 344, *Point of Origin*).

Robert Chambers

Robert Chambers inspired lurid headlines for weeks in the late summer of 1986 after he confessed to a shocking homicide near the Metropolitan Museum of Art in Central Park. The body of Jennifer Levin, eighteen, had been found partially disrobed, sexually assaulted, and badly beaten. Chambers, twenty, captivated the news media with his youthful good looks, light blue eyes, and imposing six-four height. News articles reported that Chambers had pretended to be a curious bystander, sitting on a low stone wall next to the museum, watching investigators examine Levin's body. Cornwell makes another reference to this in *Portrait of a Killer.*

Through Levin's friends, investigators learned that she and Chambers had previously dated and that she had left a bar with him the night before her death. While interviewing him, police noticed scratches on his face and chest. Chambers asserted that he and Levin had gone together to Central Park, where she made sexual advances. "She molested me," he claimed, and said they had "rough sex," which led to her accidental death. Reporters dubbed it the "preppie murder" case.

Chambers's videotaped account was introduced during his murder trial. While jurors struggled to reach a verdict after eight days of deliberations, Chambers suddenly agreed to plead guilty to manslaughter. Famed District Attorney Robert Morgenthau made the public announcement. Chambers was sentenced to serve fifteen years in prison. Soon afterward, news watchers were treated to a videotape of Chambers fondling a doll and twisting its head off. Smirking, he said, "Oops, I think I killed it."

He demonstrated the same unrepentant attitude in prison, frequently violating rules. After serving the full fifteen years, Chambers was released on Valentine's Day 2003.

Daniel Rakowitz

The other miscreant on Scarpetta's mind, Daniel Rakowitz, committed a horrific crime that, remarkably, received much less publicity. Few people took Rakowitz very seriously as he drifted around Tompkins Square Park on New York's Lower East Side, among a colorful cross section of subcultures. The scruffy vagabond in his late twenties muttered about religion and social ills while carrying a live chicken on his shoulder. He shared a Ninth Street apartment with a pretty dancer, Monica Beerle. On August 19, 1989, Rakowitz turned brutally violent and killed Beerle. Over the next few days, he decapitated her, carved her body up, and boiled the flesh from the bones. Some reports suggested that he offered the broth to park denizens. To dispose of the remains he stuffed them in a bucket and left it in a public building.

At first, police paid no attention to people who reported Rakowitz's raving confessions. At last, they pursued the grisly rumors and arrested him. Found legally insane, the killer was remanded to the custody of a state hospital.

Wayne Williams

Another famous serial killer is mentioned in *Postmortem* by Pete Marino, who discusses the use of fibers left at crime scenes: "'Ever since Wayne Williams half the world knows fibers can be used to nail your ass'" (p. 100).

When bodies of young African-American murder victims began turning up around Atlanta, Georgia, in 1979, investigators and the general public suspected racially motivated killings perpetrated by one or more Caucasian men. That's why it shocked the community when a black man, Wayne Bertram Williams, twenty-three, an intelligent freelance photographer from an affluent background, was arrested in June 1981. Tiny purple and yellow-green fibers had been found clinging to clothing on most of the victims. Eventually, crime-lab technicians matched this trace evidence to fibers discovered on a floor mat in the station wagon driven by Williams, on carpeting in his home, and on a bedspread he used. At least twenty victims had been found, but Williams was convicted of murdering only two of them. He is serving two life sentences in a Georgia prison. Controversy rages on about his guilt or innocence, but investigators point to a simple fact: the murders stopped after Williams was caught.

Gilles Garnier

The tale of a fictional serial killer begins in *Black Notice,* when a cargo container arrives at Richmond's harbor aboard a ship from Belgium. Scarpetta is summoned to examine a decaying human body inside it. She notices a mysterious scrawl of French words on an interior wall. "'*Bon voyage, le loup-garou*'" (p. 33). Later, at home, she uses a French/English dictionary to learn that *loup* means wolf, but is stumped by *garou*. She telephones the chef at La Petite France and asks, "'What is a *loup-garou*?'"

"'Miss Kay,'" he answers, "'you must be dreaming bad things! . . . I'm so glad it's not a full moon! *Le loup-garou* is a werewolf! . . . In France, hundreds of years ago, if you were believed to be a *loup-garou* you were hanged. There were many reports of them, you see'" (pp. 48–49).

The chef didn't mention that punishment for being a suspected werewolf in those medieval years might also include being burned at the stake, which is what happened to Gilles Garnier.

Garnier is mentioned in *The Last Precinct* by a New York lawyer, Jaime Berger, who becomes a key player in Scarpetta's tangled problems. The two women discuss a murder suspect who appears to have certain werewolf traits. Berger wonders aloud, " 'Was he influenced by the French serial killer Gilles Garnier, who killed little boys and ate them and bayed at the moon? There were a lot of so-called werewolves in France during the Middle Ages' " (p. 312).

The majority of other rogues brought up in the Scarpetta books committed their crimes in the latter part of the twentieth century. Gilles Garnier goes back considerably further, all the way to 1573, in rural France.

Garnier's bizarre stooped walk, pale countenance, drooping gray beard, and Neanderthal eyebrows bristling over deep-set eyes made local farmers think of a werewolf. An incident one evening seemed to confirm their suspicions. The terrified shrieking of a young girl brought several local residents into the woods, where they spotted the child trying to escape from a howling, humanoid creature with animalistic features. It loped away into the night. A few of the witnesses thought the apparition resembled the odd hermit Garnier. Within the next few days, four children vanished: two girls and two boys.

Furious townspeople dragged Garnier from his isolated cabin and accused him of the crimes. They pieced together a horrifying story in which Garnier had strangled the children, torn away their clothing, and eaten their flesh. Found guilty and sentenced to die, Garnier suffered a gruesome execution: the local citizens burned him alive.

One account of the Gilles Garnier crimes calls him Le Loup-Garou.

The casual mention of this fiend by Jaime Berger seems innocuous. Cornwell's fans, though, may wonder if the ghoulish account of Gilles Garnier had planted a seed in the author's fertile mind. Perhaps it inspired the complex case that became the fundamental thread in two books.

Elizabeth Bathory

During the same conversation about werewolves in *The Last Precinct,* Berger brings up another early horror story. " 'There was a Hungarian countess in the early sixteen hundreds, Elizabeth Bathory-Nadasdy, also known as the Blood Countess. . . . She supposedly tortured and murdered some six hundred young women. Would bathe in their blood, believing it would keep her young and preserve her beauty. . . . [T]his countess kept young women in her dungeon, fattened them up, would bleed them and bathe in their blood and then force other imprisoned women to lick all the blood off her body. . . . I'd say there was a sexual component. . . . [I]t's about power and sex'" (p. 311).

According to numerous accounts, Elizabeth Bathory, born into Hungarian aristocracy in 1560 and married at fifteen to Count Nadasdy, ranks among the most cruel women in history. Beautiful and well educated, she took sadistic and sexual delight in torturing young servant girls to death. With the help of a small ring of accomplices, she found inventive methods of beating and inflicting terrible wounds on victims, sometimes dragging them naked and screaming outside in ice-cold weather. On snow-covered ground, she would pour cold water on the helpless girls until they froze. One of Bathory-Nadasdy's favorite companions was a bisexual aunt.

Some doubts have been expressed about her bathing in blood. While records support most of the savage incidents, nothing exists to verify the blood baths. It was reported that she developed an obsession with blood after striking a servant girl and being soaked by the squirting wounds.

In another incident, she didn't feel well enough to leave her bed, so ordered helpers to bring in a girl. Bathory-Nadasdy drew blood by biting the victim's cheeks, shoulders, and breasts. If Benton Wesley had profiled this killer, he would have noted her piquerism.

By 1611, Bathory-Nadasdy had victimized as many as six hundred young women. At first, authorities ignored reports of her sadism, but they finally investigated. The female accomplices were tried, found guilty, and tortured by having their fingers pulled off and then being burned alive. A male aide was decapitated. But Bathory-Nadasdy, as a member of the aristocracy, could not face trial. Instead, she was interred in a small room sealed up by masonry and fed through one of several ventilation holes left in the wall. She died there in 1614.

According to a book by Raymond McNally, *Dracula Was a Woman,* Bathory-Nadasdy was one of the primary inspirations for Bram Stoker's *Dracula.*

Fingerprints occupy Scarpetta's thoughts in a segment of *The Body Farm.* "I recalled from International Association of Identification meetings I had attended over the years that many notorious criminals had made many creative attempts at altering their fingerprints. The ruthless gangster John Dillinger had dropped acid on his . . . while the lesser-known Roscoe Pitts had surgically removed his prints from the first knuckle up" (p. 236).

The training organization to which Scarpetta refers, the International Association for Identification, is the world's oldest and largest forensic organization. Headquartered in Mendota Heights, Minnesota, it has more than 5,600 members from seventy nations. The IAI offers training and educational opportunities in fingerprints, crime-scene investigation, forensic photography and electronic imaging, firearms and tool marks, bloodstain pattern identification, footwear and tire track analysis, documents of unknown origin, polygraph, forensic art, forensic odontology, and innovative and general techniques and laboratory analysis. It was founded in October, 1915. IAI would certainly play an essential part in Kay Scarpetta's training as a chief medical examiner who solves crimes.

John Dillinger

In her IAI training, Scarpetta might have learned of the effort by John Dillinger, legendary in American criminology, to destroy his own fingerprints. To many indigents suffering through the Great Depression during the early 1930s, Dillinger was a Robin Hood who stole from the rich and gave to the poor. In truth, he was a bank-robbing killer who launched his outlaw career while still a teenager and robbed his first bank at age twenty-one. He served nine years in prison for it. Two months after his May 1933 release, he began a string of robberies across Indiana, Ohio, and Pennsylvania. He was captured in September; his October escape resulted in the shooting death of a guard. Caught again in 1934, he used an escape ploy often cited in books and movies. From a piece of wood taken out of a washboard, Dillinger fashioned a fake pistol, dyed it with black shoe polish, and fooled guards into believing it was real. (The fake weapon is on display in the John Dillinger Museum in Hammond, Indiana.) Several more innocent people died in the wake of his crimes, and the FBI joined the hunt for "Public Enemy Number One."

Dillinger hired a Chicago surgeon to obliterate his fingerprints with acid, but as Scarpetta noted, the scars only made them more distinctive. In the long run, it didn't matter. Soon after the operation, on July 22, 1934, a female acquaintance led him into an FBI trap outside Chicago's Biograph Theater. The woman, Anna Sage, became known as "the Lady in Red." Agents shot Dillinger to death in a nearby alley. The Biograph Theater still stands and is the high point of tours that trace the paths of Chicago gangsters.

Robert "Roscoe" Pitts

The other outlaw who altered his fingerprints, Robert "Roscoe" Pitts, remains obscure except for his misguided surgical choice. A petty thief who spent a good part of his life in various jails, he may have heard about Dillinger's efforts and decided to emulate them. Sometime after 1940, he contacted a shady plastic surgeon who excised the skin from Pitt's fingertips, then used grafted skin from the patient's rib cage, under the armpits, to create new fingertips. Each hand, done separately, took about two weeks to heal, so Pitts was virtually helpless for about a month.

Arrested again on Halloween 1941 for another bungled crime, Pitts boasted to the police about his blank fingertips. The officer simply rolled ink on Pitts's skin below the knuckle and compared the images to full handprints left at the scene. They matched.

Pitts had his moment of fame during the Warren Commission hearings investigating John F. Kennedy's assassination. In questioning expert witness Sebastian Latona, commission members inquired about Lee Harvey Oswald's fingerprints on the rifle allegedly used to shoot the president, then asked if fingerprints could be destroyed.

EXCERPT FROM HEARING TRANSCRIPTS:

SEBASTIAN F. LATONA—FBI fingerprint expert

MELVIN A. EISENBERG—Warren Commission Assistant Counsel

ALLEN W. DULLES—CIA Director, 1953–1961; member of Warren Commission

HALE BOGGS—Louisiana congressman; member of Warren Commission

REPRESENTATIVE BOGGS. Is it true that every fingerprint of each individual on earth is different?

MR. LATONA. Yes, sir; that is my sincere belief.[. . .]

MR. DULLES. The same is true of palmprints, isn't it?

MR. LATONA. Absolutely; yes, sir; fingerprints and palmprints and foot-prints.

REPRESENTATIVE BOGGS. Can they be distorted, destroyed?

MR. LATONA. They can be destroyed in the sense that—

REPRESENTATIVE BOGGS. Cut your finger off, that is right?

MR. LATONA. Sure, you can cut your finger off. You can resort to what is known as—they can be transferred. You can slice off a pattern from one finger and place it on another but you will see the scar. They can have what is known as surgical planing.

REPRESENTATIVE BOGGS. That is what I was thinking about.

MR. LATONA. That can be done, too.

REPRESENTATIVE BOGGS. What happens then?

MR. LATONA. What happens is that you lose the ridge area and you will simply have a scar. There will be no more pattern. Now, the pattern is formed by what are known as dermal papilla, which is below the epidermis or outer layer of skin. As long as you only injure the outer surface, the ridge formation will grow back exactly the same as it was before. If you get down to the dermal papilla, which lay like this—

MR. EISENBERG. You are drawing an illustration on the board which shows short, broad, downward strokes.

MR. LATONA. If you destroy or injure these to the extent that there is actual bleeding, you will get a permanent scar. Fingerprints can be destroyed or scarred in such a fashion that we would not be able to successfully classify them.

MR. DULLES. Do criminals do that?

MR. LATONA. Yes; they do. We have had one case, probably the most successful was known as the so-called Roscoe Pitts case. This was a fugitive who in order to avoid identification went to an unscrupu-lous doctor who performed an operation and he did so by virtue of first cutting five slits on one side of his chest. Then he removed the pattern areas, what we call the pattern areas, which would consist of re-moval of the whole core area down to the delta area, sliced that off.

REPRESENTATIVE BOGGS. How much would that be?

MR. LATONA. He would literally have to draw blood. He would have to get down and just slice that off completely. He did that with five fingers. Then he taped the five fingers to the side of his chest and he kept them there for about 2 weeks. The same procedure was gone through with the other hand, and at the end of that time they were taken down and bound up individually. When they finally healed, all he has now is scar tissue for his pattern areas; but all we did in order to identify him was to drop down to the second joint. We made the identification from the second joint. Now, at that particular time—

REPRESENTATIVE BOGGS. After all that business.

MR. LATONA. It didn't do him any good. Literally, the easiest person in our files to identify is Roscoe Pitts. He is the only one that has scar patterns like that. As soon as they see anything like that, everybody that knows anything about our files knows—Roscoe Pitts.

Jeffrey Dahmer

Yet another conversation between Scarpetta and Benton, this one near the conclusion of *Unnatural Exposure,* refers to infamous serial killers. Scarpetta expresses dismay about her failure to realize the killer's identity. "'I should have known.'" Benton replies, "'People who live next door to the Gacys, the Bundys, the Dahmers of the world are always the last to figure it out, Kay'" (p. 361).

Jeffrey Dahmer, another candidate for Benton's piquerism list, murdered his first victim at eighteen, in 1978, shortly after his parents left him to live alone in their Wisconsin home. He picked up a hitchhiking teenager and took him to the lonely house, where he bludgeoned and strangled the lad. A few days later, he dismembered the corpse and buried all but the head, which he kept to act out sexual fantasies. Following a stint in the military, Dahmer occupied a room in his grandmother's home while spending most of his time in a belligerent, alcoholic stupor. An extraordinarily handsome man, he had no trouble attracting other gay men in bars and bathhouses. Several of their dissected bodies wound up buried in his grandmother's basement.

Dahmer continued the pattern after moving into an apartment. He severed the head and genitals of one youth and boiled flesh from the skull. This led to even more repulsive acts in which he resorted to cannibalism. Finally, his eighteenth intended victim escaped and yelled for the police. Investigators discovered a mind-numbing array of gory photos, skulls, and body parts in Dahmer's apartment.

Found guilty of multiple murders in 1992, Dahmer was sentenced to life imprisonment (Wisconsin has no capital punishment). A fellow inmate beat him to death in 1994.

Another reference to killers in *Point of Origin* is made by Benton Wesley. "The hunt for [this suspect] is as big as the one for the Unabomber or Cunanan" (p. 139). References are also made to the Unabomber in *Unnatural Exposure*.

Theodore Kaczynski

The Unabomber mystery kept Americans worried for eight years, from May 1978 until April 1996. This period included a six-year hiatus during which the bomber hid quietly and refrained from any known criminal acts. His terrorism began with an unmarked package's explosion in a Chicago parking lot that injured one person. One year later, a similar blast at Northwestern University wounded another victim. In June 1980, the president of United Airlines opened mail in his home and suffered injuries from an explosion. Two years passed before another incident injured a man at Vanderbilt University in Nashville, Tennessee. Then, the interval shortened to two months when a professor suffered wounds in similar circumstances at the University of California, Berkeley. In May 1985, another person was injured at Berkeley. The following November, two people on the campus of the University of Michigan at Ann Arbor needed treatment for wounds from an exploding package.

Not until December 1985 did the Unabomber cause a fatality when the owner of a computer store in Sacramento, California, died after picking up a bomb-loaded package at the entry to his building.

The first clue to the bomber's identity came when a witness spotted someone leaving a parcel at a Salt Lake City computer store. An artist's conception appeared soon afterwards in the news media, depicting a man in sunglasses wearing a hooded sweatshirt.

Another pair of injuries occurred before two more victims lost their lives in similar events. In December 1994, a New Jersey man was killed. The final bombing took place in April 1995 in Sacramento, California, where a political lobbyist for the timber industry died.

During this sporadic terror, the Unabomber sent a letter to the *New York Times* in which he rationalized his acts on the basis of ecological activism. Later, he forwarded a 35,000-word manifesto titled "Industrial Society and Its Future," demanding its publication in full. In September 1995 the *New York Times* and the *Washington Post* printed the entire text.

The Unabomber's craving to see his work in print led to his downfall. His brother read it, recognized the style and wording, and contacted the FBI. Agents tracked Theodore Kaczynski to a tiny mountain cabin in Montana and arrested him. After more than eighteen months of legal wrangling, he entered a plea of guilty to murder, avoiding a possible death sentence in exchange for life imprisonment.

Andrew Cunanan

The second widespread manhunt Wesley spoke of was for Andrew Cunanan. On July 15, 1997, that hunt intensified dramatically after a shocking murder in Miami, Florida. Many people were stricken when someone shot famed designer Gianni Versace to death near the entry to his home.

Scarpetta refers to this in *Point of Origin* while grieving over the violent death of Benton, the man she loved. Marino, hoping the reports are not true, says, "'He's gonna show up one of these days. . . . You wait. I know that son of a bitch. He don't go down this easy.'"

Scarpetta remains silent, thinking, "But [he] had gone down this easy. It was so often like that, Versace walking home from buying coffee and magazines or Lady Diana not wearing her seat belt" (p. 328).

Within hours after Versace's murder, police suspected that a homosexual gigolo named Andrew Cunanan had pulled the trigger. A widespread search for the fugitive had already been in progress for three months. Cunanan was suspected of killing four other men in three states. But Versace's slaying escalated the manhunt to national headline status.

As it turned out, Cunanan hadn't put much distance between the scene of his last killing and his hiding place. In a Miami marina, he had broken into a luxury houseboat, unused by its owner, where he hid for a week. Police found Cunanan's body there on July 23, bloated from overindulgence in alcohol. He had stuck the barrel of his .40-caliber handgun in his mouth and pulled the trigger.

With Cunanan's death, the chance to find the answers to endless questions evaporated forever.

TIMELINES: CHRONOLOGIES OF THE CORNWELL NOVELS

[Note: This section contains essential plot information that you may not want to know if you have not read all of the books yet.]

FIGURING out when something is going on as compared to the real world can be tricky in Patricia Cornwell's novels, thanks to the author's skill at drawing the reader completely into her world. Here are the books' timelines as they relate to events in real life.

THE SCARPETTA NOVELS

Postmortem

Postmortem begins on Friday, June 6. Although the year is not mentioned, it can be surmised as 1983; this is calculated from Lucy's age of twenty-three in *Cause of Death,* which occurs in 1996. Lucy is ten years old in *Postmortem.* Scarpetta is notified of this serial killer's fourth murder at 2:33 A.M. on Saturday, June 7. She goes to the scene, returns to the OCME to do the exam, and returns home late that night to see her niece, Lucy, whom she had just picked up three days earlier, on Wednesday.

On Monday afternoon, Scarpetta and Marino meet with Benton. Scarpetta later learns that the office database has been hacked. Bill Boltz visits that night for dinner with her and Lucy (p. 128).

On Wednesday afternoon, Scarpetta and Marino drive to the four crime scenes, looking for a pattern (p. 145).

Scarpetta meets with her boyfriend, Bill Boltz, on Wednesday night (p. 179).

Friday night passes without notification of a murder (p. 197).

On Monday, June 16, at 3 P.M., Scarpetta is notified of the fifth murder, which had occurred that past Friday. She performs the autopsy that evening (p. 232).

On Tuesday, June 17, she visits Dr. Fortosis, a forensic psychiatrist at UVa (p. 249).

On Wednesday, June 18, Scarpetta meets with newspaper reporter Abby Turnbull (p. 265). On Thursday, June 19, Scarpetta investigates the bloody blue jumpsuit with Vander (p. 276).

The newspaper headline comes out indicating that the killer has a genetic defect (p. 302).

On Friday, June 20, a sixth murder attempt occurs (p. 323).

On Monday, June 23, Scarpetta and Marino talk about the resolution of the case (p. 328).

On Thursday, June 26, "three days later," Scarpetta is flying with Lucy to Florida for a vacation (p. 337).

MISCELLANEOUS
The homicides in *Postmortem* began two months prior to the fourth murder that opens the novel. The first (Brenda Steppe) was on April 19, the second (Patty Lewis) was on May 10, and the third (Cecile Tyler) was on May 31 (pp. 80, 99).

Body of Evidence

Body of Evidence begins on Halloween 1984, when Scarpetta examines Beryl Madison's body (p. 7). It ends near Christmas. "Rose had crossed everything out through the end of next week. After that it was Christmas" (p. 400). The attorney general mentions at one point that the events in *Postmortem* occurred "a year or so ago" (p. 194).

On day one, Scarpetta goes to the murder scene that afternoon with Marino and meets with Mark James, an old boyfriend, at her home that night (p. 32).

The following afternoon she meets with profiler Benton Wesley (p. 44) and then meets with Mrs. McTigue on her way home (p. 64).

Probably the next day, Scarpetta reviews fiber analysis (p. 77) and then flies to New York that afternoon to meet with lawyer Mark James (p. 88). She stays overnight, meeting with Sparacino the next day, and flies back to Richmond.

On the following day, Saturday, Scarpetta meets with Marino at her home that evening and they watch the videotaped interviews of the supervisor at the car wash where Beryl washed her car (p. 126).

The next day is Sunday (p. 143) and Cary Harper is murdered. The next day, Scarpetta discovers his sister, Sterling, dead in her library (p. 167).

The next morning Scarpetta does the autopsy on Cary Harper (p. 185).

On Friday morning, Scarpetta meets with a fiber expert, Roy Hanowell, in Quantico (p. 209).

On Saturday and Sunday Scarpetta stays home. She meets Marino at Amtrak on Monday to visit Sterling Harper's doctor (p. 241).

The next morning, Scarpetta meets with the attorney general, who warns her against Mark James (p. 266).

A few days later, Scarpetta visits the former psychiatrist of the car wash supervisor (p. 292). The next day, Saturday, she tracks down more details about the car wash supervisor (p. 304).

On Monday evening, Marino's new car is blown up outside Scarpetta's house (p. 333). Early the next morning, Scarpetta flies to Key West to search for Beryl's missing manuscript (p. 338).

Mark James surprises Scarpetta in her hotel room the following evening (p. 364).

Two days later, Scarpetta returns to Richmond, where the killer is revealed (p. 388).

Concerning Beryl Madison's past activities: The prior November, she gave a lecture to the DAR (p. 63).

She started receiving threatening phone calls in January (p. 49).

She suddenly flew out of Richmond to Key West on July 13 (p. 27). She wrote letters to "M" on August 13 and September 30 (p. 1). She returned to Richmond on October 29.

All That Remains

All That Remains occurs over the course of many months. The novel begins on "Saturday, the last day of August" (p. 1), and ends around "the first day of spring" (p. 323), which would be late March. A definite year is not mentioned, and is difficult to pinpoint, although Scarpetta at one point is listening to Bruce Hornsby's *Harbor Lights,* released in 1993. The next novel, *Cruel & Unusual,* occurs in 1990, so this fact is probably incongruous with the general time line. The most likely date for the novel is somewhere between 1984 and 1990, the dates of the books preceding and following this one in the series.

Abby Turnbull, the reporter Scarpetta met in *Postmortem,* shows up at Scarpetta's place three years after she gave notice to the *Richmond Times* (p. 49). Lucy, who was ten years old in *Postmortem,* is "a sophomore in high school" in *All That Remains* (p. 217), suggesting a lapse of at least five years.

The murder of couples began "two and a half years ago on June first" (p. 26). The action moves quickly and soon it is January 20 of the next year when Scarpetta is notified that someone has found the bodies of Deborah and Fred (p. 78).

Scarpetta is at the OCME "the following afternoon" (p. 93), and makes the identification of the body of Deborah Harvey.

The following Sunday (p. 101), Scarpetta was supposed to have dinner with Marino but is unable to do so.

The next day, Monday, Scarpetta drives to Washington, D.C., to bring the bones to the forensic anthropologist at the Smithsonian. On the same day, she visits the reporter Abby Turnbull, who says she is being followed and that her computer, containing information on the previous murders, has been broken into (p. 116).

Scarpetta and Marino fly the next day to see the psychic used by the FBI, in Spartanburg (p. 126).

On January 31, she meets with Dr. Sessions, the commissioner of Health and Human Services, who pressures her to release the autopsy information to the parents.

Scarpetta then meets with Benton Wesley and Mark James at Benton's house and rekindles her relationship with James (p. 214).

On February 10, Scarpetta reads a sensational magazine article that claims she has been forced to release the autopsy results on Deborah Cheney early (p. 216).

No other specific dates are given until "the first day of spring" (p. 323), when Scarpetta and Marino meet with Benton Wesley at Quantico to discuss the profile of the suspected killer.

Cruel & Unusual

Cruel & Unusual begins just two weeks before Christmas 1990 (p. 1). This novel occurs seven years after *Postmortem,* since Scarpetta's niece, Lucy, is now seventeen. (She was ten in the first novel.)

On a Monday in December, Ronnie Waddell is executed and Scarpetta does the autopsy that evening (pp. 3, 217). He had been transported to the Richmond Penitentiary fifteen days before that (p. 219).

Scarpetta does the autopsy on Eddie Heath on December 16 (pp. 39, 217), which is also the night her computer is broken into (p. 217). (These dates don't match up exactly.)

On Saturday night, Scarpetta discovers someone broke into her computer (p. 69).

On Monday, Scarpetta does the autopsy on Jennifer Deighton (p. 117).

On Christmas Eve, Vander video-enhances the blank paper found at Jennifer Deighton's house (p. 152).

Scarpetta has Marino over for dinner on Christmas Day (p. 176). Susan Story is murdered on Christmas Day (p. 184), and her autopsy is done on Sunday (p. 197).

Scarpetta and Wesley scan the old scene of Robyn Naismith's house on New Year's Eve (p. 326).

MISCELLANEOUS
On September 4, ten years before the start of *Cruel & Unusual,* Robyn Naismith had been murdered by Ronnie Waddell (p. 7).

Ten years before the start of *Cruel & Unusual,* Scarpetta was the deputy chief medical examiner in Dade County, Florida (p. 18).

Twenty years before the start of *Cruel and Unusual,* Scarpetta had been in law school at Georgetown (p. 38).

In *Cruel & Unusual,* Lucy is now seventeen (p. 70).

This would be Marino's first Christmas since his divorce from his wife (p. 20).

The Body Farm

The Body Farm occurs two years after the killer Gault went on his killing spree in the previous novel, *Cruel & Unusual* (p. 3). That would make 1992 the most likely date for this novel. A minor discrepancy is that, based on Lucy's age, four years have passed between these two novels. (Lucy is twenty-one in *The Body Farm* [p. 7], whereas she was seventeen in *Cruel & Unusual.*)

The action in *The Body Farm* takes place during the entire month of October. The murder being investigated happens on Sunday, October 1 (p. 2), her body is found on October 7 (p. 13), and the story begins with Scarpetta's involvement on October 16 (p. 1).

The novel ends on Halloween Day, when Scarpetta finds Lucy at a church in Newport, Rhode Island (p. 331).

From Potter's Field

From Potter's Field begins on Christmas Eve of an unspecified year, possibly 1992 (p. 3), with the murder of Anthony Jones in Richmond. The previous novel, *The Body Farm,* took place two months earlier, during October. It can be assumed that it is the same year since Lucy is mentioned as being twenty-one in both novels (p. 100, *From Potter's Field*). She is still a senior at University of Virginia (p. 126).

After Anthony Jones's murder in Richmond, Scarpetta and Marino are flown that same night to New York and spend the early morning of Christmas Day at the murder scene in Central Park (p. 29).

On day two, Christmas Day, Scarpetta witnesses the autopsy of the woman murdered in Central Park (p. 45).

The day after Christmas, Scarpetta and Marino revisit the Museum of Natural History (p. 81). Scarpetta has dinner with Commander Frances Penn that night (p. 89). Jimmy Davila is killed that night and they go to the scene (p. 100).

The next day (two days after Christmas), Scarpetta goes to Davila's autopsy (p. 109), and later returns to Quantico (p. 123). The next day will be Thursday (p. 165). Scarpetta will start her jury duty on Monday (p. 166).

On Thursday, Sheriff Lamont Brown's body is discovered in the morgue, with a pink letter in his pocket (p. 182).

On Friday, the day before New Year's Eve, Scarpetta visits the James Galleries in Shockhoe Slip (p. 252). That same Friday afternoon, Scarpetta is at Quantico discussing the case with Benton Wesley (p. 277).

The climax of the novel occurs on a Saturday. Saturday is the day Mrs. Gault always wires money to her daughter (p. 314). Scarpetta, Lucy, and Benton fly back to Virginia on Monday, which would be January 9 (p. 352).

Cause of Death

Cause of Death begins on New Year's Eve, 1995 (pp. 1, 8, 177), with the murder of reporter Ted Eddings and ends seven days later on January 6, 1996.

Lucy is now twenty-three and has "barely graduated from the FBI academy" (p. 30). This would place this novel two years after *From Potter's Field,* in which Lucy was twenty-one.

At the start of the novel, Scarpetta, Marino, and Lucy spend New Year's Eve together at Dr. Mant's house in the Tidewater district (p. 54).

On New Year's Day, everyone's tires have been pierced (p. 84). That same evening, Scarpetta interviews Eddings's mother (p. 111).

The next day, Scarpetta goes to the OCME (p. 131) and then to St. Bridget's (p. 142).

The next day, Scarpetta performs Danny Webster's autopsy (p. 177).

For the first time, Cornwell mentions a year, although indirectly. In *Cause of Death,* the autopsy number is ME-3096 (p. 177), which means "the thirtieth case of the new year," the year being "96."

The next day, Scarpetta and Marino drive to UVa to test the uranium found in her car (p. 213). Later that day, while they are driving back to Richmond, the terrorist takeover of the nuclear power plant is announced (p. 248).

The next morning, Scarpetta and Wesley fly to London on the Concorde (p. 269). The next morning she meets Dr. Mant, and flies back to Quantico that evening (p. 289). The following morning, Scarpetta then meets the attorney general and Senator Lord (p. 302), they fly to the nuclear power plant, and Scarpetta meets the terrorists for the finale of the novel.

Unnatural Exposure

Unnatural Exposure occurs in 1997, as told by the autopsy number of 1930–97 (p. 68). The story begins a few weeks before Halloween (p. 2) and the action ends sometime in mid-November. In the epilogue, it is New Year's Eve and Scarpetta and Benton Wesley plan a trip to London to visit the site of Mark James's death (p. 359), which they do at the end of the novel on February 18, 1998 (p. 362).

Specifically, the main action of the novel occurs over fifteen days, starting on October 30 when Scarpetta flies from Dublin to Richmond (p. 14).

The next day Scarpetta goes to the scene of Virginia's fifth landfill case (p. 19). The following day she performs the autopsy on that case (p. 43). That evening she prepares a romantic dinner for Wesley (p. 76).

The next day (p. 87), Scarpetta checks the fingerprints found in the e-mail, checks with the expert on fibers (p. 92), and meets with Keith Pleasants (p. 102).

The next day, she flies to Memphis to see Dr. Canter, a forensic anthropologist (p. 121).

"Two days later, on Thursday, November 6," Scarpetta goes to Quantico and explores the e-mailed picture using virtual reality (pp. 141, 162).

The next day, Dr. Hoyt calls Scarpetta at 4 A.M. (p. 170) and she is off to Tangier Island (p. 180).

That evening, Scarpetta is in isolation (p. 204).

She awakens the next day (p. 207), still in isolation.

The next morning (p. 243), she is still in isolation and communicating with *deadoc,* but leaves for Atlanta later that day, then returns to Richmond. She visits Keith Pleasants late the next afternoon (p. 285).

She goes to the bondsman the next morning (p. 307). Next, she flies to Janes Island State Park, where they find the killer's RV (p. 311), and she flies to Dugway the next day at 5 A.M. (p. 335).

After that, "[d]ays crept into the weekend" (p. 346), and Scarpetta then discovers who the killer is.

Point of Origin

Point of Origin begins on Sunday, June 8 (p. 1). The year presumptively would be 1998, since the prior novel, *Unnatural Exposure,* ended in February 1998 (p. 362, *Unnatural Exposure*). It has been five years since Gault's death in *From Potter's Field* (p. 3), although there was no mention of the year in that novel.

On the second day (p. 17), Scarpetta flies by helicopter to Warrenton.

On day three (p. 73), Scarpetta and Marino visit with Kenneth Sparkes.

On day four (p. 90), Scarpetta does the autopsy on Claire Rawley. This is Wednesday, June 11 (p. 138).

On day five, Scarpetta finds a nick in the victim's temporal bone (p. 147).

On day six, Scarpetta and Marino see Dr. Vessey at the Smithsonian (p. 150).

On day seven, a Saturday, Kenneth Sparkes visits Scarpetta at her home (p. 192).

On day eight, Sunday, Scarpetta and Marino visit the farrier (pp. 207, 213).

On day nine (p. 229), Scarpetta is checking on trace evidence at the morgue.

On Wednesday night, Benton Wesley is killed, his body burned in a fire in a grocery store on Walnut Street (p. 284).

"Late Thursday morning" (p. 285), Scarpetta wakes up after a night of grieving over the death of Benton.

"Several hours later" (p. 289), Marino drives Scarpetta and Lucy back to Richmond.

On day thirteen (p. 299), Scarpetta wakes up and has coffee with Lucy. She then goes to the OCME and examines trace evidence of the metal filings.

On day fourteen (p. 329), it is 6 A.M., and Scarpetta later flies to Kirby Forensic Psychiatric Hospital, where Carrie Grethen is imprisoned.

Carrie Grethen had escaped from prison on June 10, which was on day three (p. 346).

MISCELLANEOUS
"Marino was almost fifty-five. . . . We had defended and irritated each other almost daily for more than eleven years" (p. 20).

Black Notice

Black Notice opens on December 6 (p. 1), a Monday (p. 48). Presumably this is 1999, since the next novel, *The Last Precinct,* begins in 1999, less than twenty-four hours after *Black Notice* ends.

Scarpetta goes to the Port of Richmond to investigate a death (p. 13). She later has dinner with Marino (p. 49).

The next morning (p. 64), Scarpetta does the autopsy on the body found in the cargo container (p. 86). Later she visits Rose at her home (p. 131).

The next morning, Wednesday (p. 145), Scarpetta meets Dr. Wagner and confronts Deputy Chief Bray at a restaurant (p. 161).

Presumably the next morning (Thursday, December 9), Scarpetta goes over the victim's body and clothing with a Luma-Lite (p. 184). Christmas is "about two weeks" away. That evening, she goes to the scene of Kim Luong's murder at a convenience store (p. 217).

The next day (Friday, December 10), Scarpetta is snowed in and Marino has to pick her up (p. 241) and she does the autopsy on Luong.

The next day (Saturday, December 11), Scarpetta's burglar alarm goes off (p. 264), and the break-in is on the news that night.

Scarpetta, at home in front of a fire on Sunday evening (p. 274), phones her mother and finds out that Dorothy is in Richmond. She tracks down Dorothy and later Lucy shows up at her house (p. 283).

The next day (Monday, December 13), Scarpetta and Marino fly on a Concorde to Paris, France, on an 8:30 A.M. flight (p. 292).

The next day, after Scarpetta and Marino arrive in Paris (p. 308), it is 5 A.M. They then meet with Secretary-General George Mirot of Interpol (p. 316).

Scarpetta wakes up the next day (Wednesday, December 15) (p. 348), and meets with Dr. Stvan, the chief medical examiner of France.

Scarpetta returns to Richmond the next day (Thursday, December 16) (p. 385).

The next day, she awakens at 2 A.M., tries to write a note to Talley, and then goes to work (p. 389).

Diane Bray is found dead (p. 394), murdered the previous evening. At around midnight, Scarpetta is home when her burglar alarm goes off. Shortly afterward, the Loup-garou knocks on her front door.

MISCELLANEOUS
In *Black Notice,* Wingo died "several years ago" (p. 146). It is stated that November 24 was "two days before the *Sirius* set sail for Richmond" (p. 321), which, when this novel starts, was "two weeks ago" (p. 22).

In *Black Notice,* Benton has been dead for more than a year (p. 370).

The Last Precinct

The Last Precinct begins on Saturday, December 18, 1999. It has been less than twenty-four hours after the end of *Black Notice* (p. 1). The murder of Diane Bray by Chandonne in *Black Notice* occurred just "two days ago, on Thursday" (p. 2). The year is 1999, since the "twentieth century ends in exactly nine days" (p. 88).

On day one, December 18, Scarpetta moves out of her house in Virginia and stays at Dr. Anna Zenner's house. The days pass uncounted. City commonwealth attorney Buford Righter tells Scarpetta that Chandonne might be extradited to New York, and thus avoid the death penalty.

On Wednesday (December 22), Scarpetta and Lucy go Christmas shopping (p. 78).

On Thursday (December 23), Scarpetta is watching Jaime Berger's video-taped interview of Jean-Baptiste Chandonne at MCV (p. 162). Berger asks Scarpetta what she is going to do tomorrow, on Christmas Eve (p. 220). Scarpetta meets with Governor Mitchell (p. 227). She tells the Governor that she plans to resign as Virginia's chief medical examiner (p. 252), and then goes to Anna's house to see Lucy and Teun (p. 237).

On Christmas Eve, Scarpetta does the autopsy on the runner from William & Mary, Mitch Barbosa (p. 257). She later goes to examine Diane Bray's house with Jaime Berger (p. 313).

It is after 9 P.M. on Christmas Eve when Scarpetta and Berger, later joined by Marino, are in Scarpetta's house discussing the crime scene (p. 341).

Scarpetta, Anna, Marino, Lucy, and Teun have Christmas dinner together (p. 390).

The days pass as Scarpetta remains in Anna's house and it is now Monday, January 17 (p. 405). Scarpetta is at the OCME for Benny White's autopsy. She and Lucy then fly to the scene of Benny White's hanging the next day (p. 436).

Scarpetta and Lucy are taken prisoner by Jay Talley and Bev Kiffin. Bev shoots Lucy—who survives, thanks to her body armor. Lucy saves Scarpetta, but Talley and Kiffin escape (pp. 448–455).

On February 1, 2000, which is "two weeks later" (p. 456), Scarpetta testifies before the grand jury and Berger dismisses the case (p. 465).

MISCELLANEOUS

Lucy says that she is twenty-eight in *The Last Precinct* (p. 253). Eighteen years have passed since the first novel, *Postmortem,* when she was ten years old.

In *The Last Precinct,* Scarpetta is in her forties, perhaps around forty-two, since she says, "My father died more than thirty years ago, when I was twelve" (p. 255).

Blow Fly

Blow Fly begins on April 25, 2003, and ends on April 30.

On day one, Scarpetta has an informal party with the students she has taught at the National Academy of Forensics (p. 1).

On day two, the date is April 26, 2003. The Red Notice that Lucy instigated through Interpol for Rocco Caggiano was based on a warrant for his arrest issued April 24, two days before they meet with him in Poland (p. 170).

Lucy takes the Concorde to England to meet Rocco Caggiano, wanted for murder in France and Italy (p. 19).

Scarpetta has breakfast with Nic Robillard (p. 22) and discusses the serial murders in Nic's hometown of Zachary, Louisiana.

The month of April is mentioned as Jay Talley is disposing of body parts near Baton Rouge, Louisiana (p. 40).

On day three, "[t]he next morning" (p. 244), Scarpetta receives the information on Charlotte Dard's autopsy.

On day four, April 28, Rocco Caggiano's body is discovered in the hotel in Poland, "[N]ot even forty-eight hours" later (pp. 273, 280, 299).

On day five, April 29, Scarpetta arrives in Texas and then goes to Baton Rouge (pp. 337, 387).

On day six, April 30, Scarpetta awakes in Dr. Lanier's guesthouse "[t]he next morning" (p. 403), and talks to him about the serial murders. The final shootout scene at Jay Talley's hideout occurs late that night.

MISCELLANEOUS
Scarpetta is forty-six years old (p. 136).

The date of Jean-Baptiste's execution is set for May 7 (pp. 83–84).

It has been six years since Benton Wesley's fake death in a fire (p. 141).

Scarpetta speaks to the National Forensic Academy's class of 2003 at the beginning of the novel. It has been three years since she left office as chief medical examiner of Virginia (p. 121).

At the start of the ten-week course, we learn that Ivy Ford was the first murder victim in Zachary, Louisiana (p. 28).

The Beast's execution is set for "one week before" Chandonne's (p. 219).

Trace

The day before the book begins, Dr. Joel Marcus, the current chief medical examiner of Virginia, calls Scarpetta and asks for her help with a case.

The year is 2005 (p. 5). It is five years after she left Richmond, which occurred in 2000.

Day one (Thursday, December 18) begins two weeks later (p. 2) on a gray December morning (p. 1) at sixteen minutes past eight (p. 8). Scarpetta (with Marino) is back in Richmond, and the first thing they discover is her old building—in the process of being torn down (p. 2). They also discover that Marcus doesn't want her there (p. 26), the staff hates him (p. 31), and the FBI is involved in the case she's supposed to be consulting on

(p. 32). And they are hip-deep in a political morass, with the possible murder of a fourteen-year-old girl named Gilly Paulsson at its center.

Gilly's death occurred on Thursday, December 4, (p. 139). Scarpetta autopsies the girl, and discovers that the cause of death is murder by mechanical asphyxiation (p. 113).

Unbeknownst to Scarpetta, someone has attempted an identical mechanical asphyxiation on Lucy's current love interest (actress-turned-cop-turned-private-investigator Henri Walden) at Lucy's mansion in Los Angeles (p. 63). Lucy has entrusted Henri to Benton Wesley in Aspen (pp. 41–42). Wesley is trying to get to the bottom of what happened to Henri. He knows that a killer is stalking Lucy and Scarpetta, and he fears that the killer is poised to strike at one or both of them by Christmas (p. 46).

Scarpetta and Marino go to interview Gilly Paulsson's mother (p. 133).

Scapetta sets up a meeting for dinner with Dr. Fielding, an old colleague from her days in Virginia, and he doesn't show up (pp. 206–207).

Meanwhile, Marino visits Suzanna Paulsson again. He discovers much about the case, and the two have what Marino thinks is very rough consensual sex play (p. 214).

On day two (Friday), Lucy calls Scarpetta in the morning, awakening her (p. 190).

Scarpetta attends a morning staff meeting at the morgue (pp. 218–221), and discovers that trace evidence from Gilly's corpse (which she was not told about) is identical to trace evidence from the apparently accidental death of a tractor driver working on demolishing the old morgue.

Marino worries that Suzanna Paulsson will accuse him of rape (p. 237).

Day three (Saturday) dawns (p. 291) and Rudy Musil discovers a bomb in Lucy's mailbox.

Scarpetta and Marino drop off soil samples from the tractor accident scene at the trace evidence lab at the morgue (p. 305). The samples contain human bone fragments and paint chips. They then visit the abandoned house opposite Gilly Paulsson's (p. 316) and discover personal items belonging to Edgar Allan Pogue, one of Scarpetta's former employees. Rudy calls and tells them that the latent fingerprints from Gilly

Paulsson match the latents for a case Lucy is working on. Scarpetta tells him to look for Pogue.

Around midnight, Scarpetta and Marino interview Mrs. Paulsson again (p. 340).

Day four, Sunday (p. 374), begins as Lucy visits Dr. Paulsson (p. 347) and proves the rumors that he's taking liberties with his female patients are true. She also interviews him about Gilly. She then flies to Aspen to see Benton Wesley.

On day five, Monday (p. 385, 389), Marino checks out a lead on Pogue (p. 416) and discovers he craves Cuban cigars. Lucy fires Henri (p. 428).

An indeterminate number of days later, Marion catches Pogue at a gun and pawn shop in Florida (p. 431). Later still, Benton and Scarpetta get together again in Aspen (p. 432).

THE BRAZIL NOVELS

Hornet's Nest

Three weeks before the start of the novel, there were three murders, one per week, of men visiting the city. No dates as to month or year are given, although the story is set in the summer.

Day one: Deputy Chief Virginia West meets with Chief of Police Judy Hammer and is told that Andy Brazil, a reporter for the *Charlotte Observer*, will be going on patrol with her that evening (p. 6).

Day two: Brazil publishes a newspaper article calling the serial killer the "Black Widow Killer," to West's chagrin (p. 56). He describes the orange paint sprayed over the victim's genitalia, which the public had not known about previously, and which he had discovered during the previous night's ride-along with West.

The autopsy of the fourth victim takes place (p. 58). West looks up articles on Brazil's deceased father, and Brazil looks up newspaper articles on West (pp. 62–63). He then goes to interview West's former high school tennis coach (p. 64).

Day three: On Sunday, Brazil has written an article on West that appears in the paper (p. 70).

Day ten: The following Sunday, West takes Brazil to a firing range (p. 83).

Day eleven: On Monday (p. 89), Hammer meets with USBank CEO Solomon Cahoon. West and Brazil confront Bubba at a firing range (p. 99).

Day twelve: On Tuesday (p. 110), Officer Johnson runs into a Mercedes, killing an entire family.

Day thirteen: On Wednesday (p. 112), Brazil directs traffic for the Freedom Parade.

Day fourteen: On Thursday (p. 128), Brazil gets a traffic ticket after police officers follow him in his car. He then calls in a burglary in progress that he witnesses (p. 130).

Day fifteen: On Friday (pp. 135, 141), Hammer calls Brazil to apologize for police harassment that was ordered by Jeannie Goode (p. 138).

Later, Hammer and West have lunch at the Presto Grill and then arrest a robber across the street (p. 146). That evening, West and Brazil are on patrol and she makes an arrest at the Fat Man's Lounge (p. 160). Later, they arrest a young boy named Wheatie when he holds up a Hardee's (p. 170). Brazil sits in a park next to Hammer's house at 2 A.M. and watches her on her porch (p. 176).

Day sixteen: Publisher Richard Panesa and Hammer attend a banquet to receive public service awards (p. 187).

Day seventeen: The fifth murder victim, state senator Ken Butler, is found (p. 209). Hammer's husband shoots himself in the buttocks (p. 221).

Day eighteen: Hammer's husband is taken into surgery (p. 231). Brazil talks with Jazzbone, who tells him the killer is probably the pimp Punkin Head (p. 241). An undercover agent, Mungo, thinks Brazil is the killer. Several days pass.

West and Raines go to happy hour on a Thursday (pp. 258, 260).

The next day, Friday (p. 275), Brazil meets with Panesa, who informs him that Brent Webb, the TV reporter, has scooped Brazil's stories and broadcast them the night before they appeared in the paper. Hammer and West attend the trial of Johnny Martino (p. 279).

On Saturday (p. 292), West searches for and finally chases down Brazil, who is upset about his stories being stolen. West and Brazil have a sexual encounter in her car. Bubba discovers them, threatens them with a rifle, and is apprehended (p. 309).

On Sunday (p. 315), Hammer's husband, Seth, dies of an infection from his self-inflicted gunshot wound, with Hammer and their children in attendance (p. 323). West confronts Brenda Bond with the fact that she knows Bond has broken into Brazil's computer, stealing his stories (p. 329). Bond had then given the stories to TV reporter Brent Webb, Deputy Chief Jeannie Goode's boyfriend, at Goode's direction. Bond is also found out to be the one making obscene phone calls to Brazil (p. 332). Judy Hammer fires Jeannie Goode (p. 331).

On Monday (p. 343), Blair Mauney III is the serial killer's sixth victim (p. 348). It is discovered that Mauney has been laundering millions of dollars. That night, Hammer drives to Cahoon's house to tell him the news (p. 354). Also later that night, Brazil looks for Punkin Head's prostitute, Poison. Punkin Head, the serial killer, is ready to kill Brazil when Hammer and West drive up. Brazil shoots and kills Punkin Head and Poison (p. 369).

Southern Cross

The events in *Southern Cross* occur over a one-week period (Monday through Sunday) in March. The year is not mentioned.

Day one: On the last Monday in March (p. 1), Judy Hammer has been hired as police chief to help solve Richmond's severe problems with crime. She had reduced crime in Charlotte but quit that job and applied to the National Institute of Justice to spend a year each in a series of Southern cities with crime problems (p. 4).

Virginia West's cell phone picks up two rednecks, Bubba and Smudge, apparently planning the racially motivated murder of a woman named Loraine (p. 9). However, Bubba also hears the words "Chief Hammer" on his cell phone.

Smoke, a troubled teenager, commits a robbery at an ATM (p. 17).

Andy Brazil is in charge of research. He has created a website and writes an OP-ED piece on crime in Richmond (p. 18).

Hammer, West, and Brazil hold their morning conference with the police department and explain the new computer system to fight crime, COMSTAT (computer statistics), that shows crimes in each precinct (p. 22).

Smoke wants his younger friend, Weed Gardener, to join his gang (p. 30).

West and Brazil go to Godwin High School to give a talk on crime (p. 71).

The abusive Smoke initiates the intimidated Weed into his gang, consisting of Dog, Sick, Beeper, and his girlfriend, Divinity (p. 79). They get him drunk and tattoo his finger with a "slave number" (p. 83).

At 8 P.M. (p. 85), Virginia West discovers that her computer (as well as those of Hammer and Brazil) has been infected with a virus and has a screensaver that shows the crime map of second precinct's beat 219, infected with images of fish (p. 88).

Day two: At 3 A.M. (p. 151), Smoke coerces Weed to paint over the statue of Jefferson Davis in Hollywood Cemetery (p. 154).

Bubba's house is broken into and his guns are stolen (p. 175).

Day three: Lelia Ehrhart calls a meeting of the city leaders about the Jefferson Davis statue (pp. 178, 234). Bubba is stopped by Officer Budget (p. 245).

Ruby Sink is murdered by Smoke (p. 263).

Brazil finds Weed Gardener at the defaced statue and arrests him (p. 295). He realizes that Weed has painted the statue as a tribute to his admired, deceased brother Twister.

Day four: A SWAT team raids the Pikes' clubhouse (p. 337). Weed's arraignment hearing is held (p. 353).

Day six: It is Saturday, the day of the Azalea Parade (p. 363).

Day seven: On Sunday, Weed is cleared of defacing the statue, as rain washes the paint away (p. 382). Hammer decides not to resign as chief of police.

Isle of Dogs

Isle of Dogs takes place in September (p. 25), "several years" after the action in *Southern Cross* (p. 111). The action occurs over six days, ending on a Saturday. The year is not mentioned.

Day one: Unique First attacks Moses Custer (p. 2).

Andy Brazil posts his first daily installment on the website called "Trooper Truth" (p. 9). Unique First murders T.T. on Belle Island (p. 25).

Day two: Brazil goes to Tangier Island and paints a speed trap line (p. 42). Unique First goes back to the scene of the crime (p. 58). Fonny Boy takes the dentist, Dr. Faux, prisoner as a sign of rebellion against mainland Virginia (p. 65).

Detective Slipper identifies the murder victim at Trish Thrash (p. 84).

Day three: On a Wednesday (p. 106), Andy meets the governor at Ruth's Chris Steak House.

Day four: On Thursday (p. 148), Brazil is invited to the governor's house. Major Trader murders Caesar Fender (p. 195). Cruz Morales has a package of stolen guns that Major Trader discovers (p. 238).

Day five: Governor Crimm calls Moses Custer in the hospital (p. 261), and offers to take him to a NASCAR race on Saturday (p. 263).

Day six: On Saturday, Brazil and Hammer meet Smoke at Richmond International Racetrack (p. 392) and then fly to Tangier Island (p. 403). Hammer's dog, Popeye, is recovered, and Smoke is apprehended (p. 410).

LOCATION, LOCATION, LOCATION

B y placing her fictional characters in real and recognizable locations, including various cities, hotels, shops, government offices, parks, and especially restaurants, Cornwell achieves a sense of realism in her books. Of course, she cannot apply the brakes to her fast-moving stories, bring the whole thing to a jarring halt, and digress with description about these sites. Valuable momentum and suspense would be lost. Questions may arise in readers' minds as to whether these sites used by Cornwell really exist or are imaginary. This section of the book lists, in alphabetical order, some of the actual locations she mentions and briefly shows how they fit into the context of the stories being told.

AQUIA HARBOR (*The Body Farm*) Scarpetta telephones a Washington, D.C., scientist at the FBI laboratories and requests a meeting with him. She asks, "'Where do you live?'" He replies, "'Aquia Harbor'" (p. 292).

While preparing to drive there, Scarpetta notes that "a surprising number" of Washington, D.C., agents with families live in Aquia Harbor. She is also interested in the fact that it is a half-hour drive from the home of her friend Benton Wesley.

Aquia Harbor is an authentic location, a gated community in North

Stafford County, Virginia, located on historic Aquia Creek. It is approximately forty-five miles south of Washington, D.C., fifteen miles north from Fredericksburg, Virginia, and seventy miles from Richmond, Virginia. . . . a short commute from Quantico and Fort Belvoir Army Base.

AQUIDNECK LOBSTER COMPANY (*The Body Farm*) In a desperate search for her niece, Scarpetta rushes to Newport, Rhode Island. Soaked by rain as she walks along the wharf, she feels lost and alone. "Water swept down in sheets from a slate-gray sky, and a lady hurrying past gave me a smile. 'Honey, don't drown,' she said. 'Nothing's that bad.' I watched her go inside the Aquidneck Lobster Company at the end of the wharf, and I chose to follow her because she had been friendly" (p. 332).

The Aquidneck Lobster Company buys and sells local seafood, including fish, lobsters, clams, and crabs.

BANNISTER'S WHARF (*The Body Farm*) Kay Scarpetta's search for Lucy Farinelli, her niece, takes her to Bannister's Wharf, a scenic area on the Newport, Rhode Island, harbor. Once a commercial hub of Colonial Newport, it's now an upscale tourist shopping area.

BEE TREE AND LAKE JAMES (*The Body Farm*) Detective Pete Marino is upset about a job reassignment and, in a heated conversation with Scarpetta, threatens to take a position in a North Carolina town where they are investigating a murder. "'And another thing,' he railed on, 'there's a lot of really good places to fish around here. They got Bee Tree and Lake James . . . [and] the real estate's pretty cheap'" (p. 120).

Bee Tree Ridge is a mountain community, elevation 4,000 feet, near Lake Glenville, North Carolina. Lake James is tucked away in the Blue Ridge Mountains in western North Carolina, near Morganton. This scenic body of water, covering 6,510 acres, has 150 miles of shoreline offering vistas of the Blue Ridge and Appalachian Mountains.

BLACK MOUNTAIN, NORTH CAROLINA (*The Body Farm*) A young victim dies in Black Mountain (p. 2) and in the climactic ending, Scarpetta takes a cab from Asheville to meet Marino and Wesley there (p. 296).

Black Mountain is a tourist community in the mountains of western North Carolina.

BUNCOMBE COUNTY COURTHOUSE (*The Body Farm*) Scarpetta arrives in Asheville, North Carolina, to meet a judge. She observes, "The Buncombe County Courthouse was an old dark brick building that I suspected had been the tallest edifice downtown until not too many years before. Its thirteen stories were topped by the jail . . ." (p. 89).

This neoclassical-style building is located in Asheville at 60 Court Plaza. Scarpetta was correct about its relative height, but not the number of floors. Built in 1928, the courthouse towers sixteen stories high, not thirteen, and was the tallest in Asheville until 1964, when the BB&T office building reached eighteen stories.

BURGER KING (*Cruel & Unusual, Point of Origin*) While investigating a murder/arson near Warrenton, Virginia, Scarpetta says, "We bought drive-thru Whoppers and fries at a Burger King on Broadview" (p. 51, *Point of Origin*).

There is a Burger King fast-food restaurant on Broadview Avenue in Warrenton, three-quarters of a mile from the town's center. In *Cruel & Unusual,* Scarpetta alludes to an illuminated sign for the eatery that can be seen from her passing car.

CAFÉ RUNTZ (*Black Notice, The Last Precinct*) In Paris, accompanied by an Interpol agent, Scarpetta enters a restaurant. "Café Runtz was small and quiet, with green checked cloths and green glassware. Red lamps glowed and the chandelier was red" (p. 375, *Black Notice*).

Cornwell pays homage to the eatery again in *Food to Die For:* "the charming Café Runtz at 16 Rue Favart (which I discovered while researching *Black Notice* in Paris, one of many Parisian bistros recommended by my friend Paul Elbling, the chef at La Petite France in Richmond)" (p. 198).

CALHOUN'S (*The Body Farm*) While in Tennessee, Scarpetta checks into her hotel room, then takes a cab to a restaurant. The driver "took me to Calhoun's, which overlooked the Tennessee River and promised the best ribs in the USA" (p. 263). Cornwell repeats this passage in *Food to Die For* (p. 74).

This barbecue restaurant, located at 6515 Kingston Pike, Knoxville, Tennessee, commands a view of the river and does, indeed, claim to have "the best ribs." Owned by Mike Chase, it offers a huge combination platter of barbecued meats. It is the kind of place where patrons should ask for extra wet-naps and wear an old shirt.

CAMP PEARY (*All That Remains*) When several couples are murdered in rural areas during various hunting seasons, Scarpetta investigates. She says, "Within the fifty-mile radius where the couples had vanished and turned up dead were Fort Eustis, Langley Field, and a number of other military installations, including the CIA's West Point, operated under the cover of a military base called Camp Peary. 'The Farm,' as Camp Peary is referred to in spy novels and investigative nonfiction books about intelligence, was where officers were trained in the paramilitary activities of infiltration, exfiltration, demolitions, nighttime parachute jumps, and other clandestine operations" (p. 193).

Camp Peary, nestled between two water inlets near historic Williamsburg, Virginia, is indeed a real place and just as mysterious as Scarpetta suggests. The 10,000-acre site was originally established on the banks of the York River in 1942 to train World War II navy construction battalions known as "SeaBees." An airfield was later installed and is now considered a private landing strip with highly restricted access. Called an "Armed Forces Experimental Training Activity," the camp is owned by the Defense Department but reportedly is where the Central Intelligence Agency provides field training for its agents. Various researchers and military buffs agree that "The Farm" is used by the CIA. Some call it "the Spy Shop." Others say it is no longer in operation for those purposes.

Several armed forces installations, including the Yorktown Naval Weapons Station, Camp Peary, Cheatham Annex, and the U.S. Coast Guard Reserve Training Center, are all in York County near the Williamsburg area. Langley Air Force Base, Fort Eustis, and Fort Monroe are all within an hour's drive from Williamsburg.

CAPITOL BUILDING OF VIRGINIA (*Cruel & Unusual*) Summoned to Virginia's capitol building by the governor, Scarpetta walks through rain to get there. She reflects, "The Capitol resides on Shockhoe Hill and is surrounded by an ornamental iron fence erected in the early nineteenth century to keep out trespassing cattle. The white brick building Jefferson designed is typical of his architecture, a pure symmetry of cornices and unfluted columns with Ionic capitals inspired by a Roman temple" (p. 301).

Inside the building, she takes an elevator to the top of the Rotunda, "where previous governors gaze sternly from oil portraits three floors above Houdon's marble statue of George Washington" (p. 301).

The gleaming white building in Richmond occupies Capitol Square, which is elevated on the hill between Bank and Broad Streets on the north and south borders and Ninth and Governor Streets to the west and east. When Thomas Jefferson sought a model for Virginia's first capitol, he selected the Maison Carré at Nîmes in southern France, an exquisite temple that had been built by Romans early in the Christian era. This building is now the middle structure of the capitol complex, its center rotunda area displaying the life-size Houdon statue of Washington along with busts of seven other presidents born in Virginia. Famed sculptor Jean-Antoine Houdon, 1741–1828, is recognized as one of France's finest artists.

CENTRAL PARK (*From Potter's Field*) A woman has been murdered in Central Park in New York City. It appears to be linked to crimes being investigated by Scarpetta. She journeys to Manhattan and meets with an official who explains, "'As best we can reconstruct what happened to this woman . . . [the assailant] took her to Central Park after leaving the subway. He led her to a section called Cherry Hill, shot her and left her nude body propped against the fountain. . . . We think he may have enticed her into accompanying him into the Ramble.'"

Scarpetta comments that the Ramble "'is frequented by homosexuals'" (p. 27). The official agrees.

Cherry Hill, a circular configuration with a fountain at its center, is located in the lower half of Central Park's 837 acres. If Seventy-second Street crossed the park, it would intersect Cherry Hill. The Ramble is a wooded area just north of Cherry Hill, on the other side of a lake channel, with winding trails that lace through it.

The official says, "'No matter how often you've been [there], you still get lost. It's high-crime. Probably twenty-five percent of all crime committed in the park occurs there. Mostly robberies'" (p. 28).

COMFORT INN, RICHMOND (*Cause of Death*) A former intern of Scarpetta's is in trouble and Marino is asking questions about where he lived while working in Richmond. She says, "'I don't remember where he stayed, but I think it was the Comfort Inn on Broad Street'" (p. 161).

Comfort Inn is part of Choice Hotel International's chain of more than 5,000 hotels, inns, and resorts across the world, with more than 3,500 in the United States. They also include Comfort Suites, Quality, Clarion, Sleep Inn, Rodeway Inn, EconoLodge, and MainStay Suites. There is a Comfort Inn at 7201 West Broad Street in Richmond, Virginia.

CONCH TOUR TRAIN (*Body of Evidence*) In search of a manuscript that might shed light on a mystery, Scarpetta travels to Key West, Florida. "I passed sidewalk art displays and boutiques selling exotic plants, silks, and Perugina chocolates, then waited at a crossing to watch the bright yellow cars of the Conch Tour Train rattle by" (pp. 342–343).

The Conch Tour Train consists of a black locomotive replica pulling a half-dozen open-air, canopy-covered linked trailers in which tourists are seated on benches. It winds through the semitropical Old Town streets of Key West. Narrated by a docent, the tour lasts about ninety minutes and passes the Hemingway House, Mallory Square, Duval Street, and the historic seaport. Perugina chocolates, by the way, are gourmet candies made originally (beginning in 1907) in central Italy's Etruscan town of Perugia. Huge volumes are sold in the United States.

DARIEN, GEORGIA (*From Potter's Field*) Scarpetta has learned that Marino is the father of an adult son. She is curious. "I did not want to push him about his son, but the topic was within reach, and I believed their estrangement from each other was the root of many of Marino's problems."

She asks Marino, "'Where is Rocky?'"

[He replies,] "'An armpit of a town called Darien.'"

"'Connecticut? And it's not an armpit of a town.'"

"'This Darien's in Georgia'" (pp. 82–83).

Darien, Georgia, is a rural community of 9,500 in the coastal wetlands halfway between Savannah and Florida. Employment centers on commercial fishing and forestry. The chamber of commerce boasts excellent hotels, bed and breakfast establishments, and Hird Island, "an unspoiled jewel on Georgia's Gold Coast." Darien is a favorite destination of the yachting crowd, and showed up on *Yachting* magazine's top ten list for cruising destinations.

Marino may have called it "an armpit" due to bitterness over the damaged relationship with his son.

D. C. CAFE (*Point of Origin*) Near Lucy's apartment in Washington, D.C., Scarpetta and Marino stop to pick up some takeout food in the "two thousand block of P Street, where we entered the D. C. Cafe. . . . The cafe was open twenty-four hours a day, and the air was heavy with sautéing onions and beef" (pp. 166–167).

Cornwell tells more about the very real self-serve restaurant and its owner, Ayman Almoualem, in *Food to Die For:* "On the menu are Greek and Mediterranean specialties, including gyros, pita sandwiches, baklava, and Lebanese beer" (p. 186).

ESTERO BAY, FORT MYERS BEACH, FLORIDA (*Cruel & Unusual*) Scarpetta is in Florida to interview Willie Travers, and meets her sister, Dorothy, in Fort Myers at a resort hotel. "The Pink Shell resort was the color of its name. It backed up to Estero Bay and threw its front balconies open wide to the Gulf of Mexico" (p. 371).

Fort Myers is on the west, or Gulf side, of Florida, about one hundred miles from the state's southern tip. Fort Myers Beach occupies a narrow spit of white sand just south of the city. And there actually is a Best Western Pink Shell Beach Resort, one of the better hotels on the island. It's been in business more than fifty years.

FBI ACADEMY (*The Body Farm*) Scarpetta becomes a consultant for the FBI and spends extensive time at the Academy. Benton Wesley works there, as does Scarpetta's niece, Lucy Farinelli.

It is located on the U.S. Marine Corps Base at Quantico, Virginia. The facility, which opened in the summer of 1972, is situated on 385 wooded acres of land, providing security, privacy, and the safe environment necessary to carry out diverse training and operational functions for which the FBI is responsible. The Drug Enforcement Administration also has its training academy at Quantico.

The main complex at Quantico consists of three dormitory buildings, a dining hall, library, a classroom building, a forensic science research and training center, a 1,000-seat auditorium, a chapel, administrative offices, a large gymnasium and outside track, and a fully equipped garage. A mock city on the site known as Hogan's Alley, which is made up of facades replicating a typical small town, is used to train new FBI and DEA agents. Behind the facades are classrooms, audiovisual facilities, storage areas, and administrative and maintenance facilities. A 1.1-mile pursuit/ defensive driving track helps ready agents for the tricky driving challenges they'll face. Firearms training is provided to all FBI/DEA and other law enforcement officers, so the site also features an indoor firing range, eight outdoor firing ranges, four skeet ranges, and a 200-yard rifle range. The FBI academy is a secured facility, not open for public tours.

FBI BUILDING, WASHINGTON, D.C. (*Cruel & Unusual*) Consistent with her FBI association, Scarpetta visits headquarters in the nation's capital. "The FBI Building is a concrete fortification at 9th Street and Pennsylvania Avenue in the heart of D.C. . . ." (p. 251).

Once known as the J. Edgar Hoover building in honor of the long-time FBI chief, the fortresslike FBI structure was recently the subject of a Senate bill "[t]o redesignate the Federal building located at 935 Pennsylvania Avenue Northwest in the District of Columbia as the 'Federal Bureau of Investigation Building.'" The once-popular tours through the complex have been discontinued for security reasons.

FORT LEE, VIRGINIA (*From Potter's Field*) Needing help to identify a bootprint, Scarpetta visits an expert acquaintance at the military post. "As I got closer to Ft. Lee I began to see barracks and warehouses where breastworks once had been built upon dead bodies during this nation's cruelest hour" (pp. 202–203).

South of Richmond, just off Interstate 95, this military installation occupies the site of bloody Civil War battles that raged around Richmond. During World War I, it was named Camp Lee in honor of the famed Confederate general Robert E. Lee. Refurbished for World War II, it became the center for Quartermaster Corps training. New permanent buildings replaced old wooden barracks afterward, and Camp Lee became Fort Lee in 1950. Scarpetta would be particularly interested in the quartermaster facilities, since they include the Mortuary Affairs Center.

GALLAGHER'S (*Body of Evidence*) While in New York City, Scarpetta and her lover, Mark James, stop for dinner. "Minutes later we were walking through the sharp night air. I was grateful I had brought my overcoat. It felt cold enough to snow. In three blocks we were at Gallagher's, the nightmare of every cow and coronary artery and the fantasy of every red meat lover. The front window was a meat locker behind glass, an enormous display of every cut of meat imaginable. Inside was a shrine to celebrities, autographed photographs covering the walls" (p. 91).

Gallagher's Steak House, at 228 West Fifty-second Street, is a real place. Calling itself "America's first steak house," it was the creation of Helen Gallagher, a former Ziegfeld Follies dancer. She was married to Edward Gallagher, who teamed with Al Sheen to make up the famous Gallagher and Sheen vaudeville comedy act. The restaurant opened in 1927 and still maintains some original decorations, a grand circular bar, plank flooring, and portraits of celebrities and sports legends. The management claims it to be "a one-of-a-kind steakhouse for people who demand the real thing." A three-course dinner costs an average of $40 per person.

GLOBE AND LAUREL (*From Potter's Field, All That Remains, The Body Farm*) While visiting the FBI Academy at Quantico, Scarpetta and Marino dine at a nearby restaurant. "We ate at the Globe and Laurel, and as I looked around at Highland plaid, police patches and beer steins hanging over the bar, I thought of my life" (p. 160, *From Potter's Field*).

On another occasion, Scarpetta observes, "There was something reassuring about the Globe and Laurel that made me feel safe" (p. 173, *All That Remains*).

Approximately one mile north of the base, on U.S. Route 1, sits the Globe & Laurel pub/restaurant, which seats about sixty people. The name of the restaurant has been used as a code word in FBI sting operations. When the FBI Academy opened in 1972, several agents who had become pub regulars asked that three shoulder insignia patches be attached to the ceiling over their table. A new tradition was born. Today, patches cover the ceiling. Marine Corps memorabilia donated by patrons, including a Medal of Honor, lend a museum quality. Actress Demi Moore was a regular patron while filming a movie in the region.

In *Food to Die For,* Cornwell praises the restaurant and includes a recipe for French onion soup used by the proprietor, Marine Major Richard T. Spooner.

GRAND HÔTEL (*Black Notice*) As her investigative horizons expand, Kay Scarpetta is summoned to Interpol headquarters in France. She and Marino fly over on the Concorde in late December. Scarpetta observes, "Not much decorating had been done [in Paris] for Christmas, not even in the heart of the city. . . . The season was celebrated a bit more, with poinsettias and a Christmas tree, in the marble lobby of the Grand Hôtel, where our itinerary let us know we were staying" (p. 300). Inside the luxury room, "I pulled back heavy drapes and stared out the window at people in evening dress getting into fine cars. Gilt sculptures on the old opera house across the street flaunted their golden, naked beauty before the gods" (p. 302).

Le Grand Hôtel Paris was built in 1862 at 2 Rue Scribe and soon became a gathering place for the internationally rich and famous. Recently restored as one of the InterContinental chain, it boasts four-star, high-tech accommodation in 477 richly appointed and air-conditioned guest rooms. Views from the room windows overlook the Place de l'Opéra and the world-famous Paris Opera House. Guests may dine in the hotel's Café de la Paix, one of the most famous restaurants in Paris.

Awfully nice travel accommodations for a chief medical examiner and a police detective. Curious readers of *Black Notice* will soon learn why.

GREEN TOP (*The Body Farm, From Potter's Field*) Lucy has been injured in a car wreck, and Scarpetta visits her in the hospital to ask some questions. "'Do you remember anything about dinner . . . or your visit to Green Top? . . . You bought a .380 semiautomatic pistol, Lucy. Do you remember that?'" (p. 220, *The Body Farm*).

"'[T]hat's why I went there,'" Lucy answers. She explains that Marino advised her to make the purchase. "'I called him the other day. He said to get a Sig and said he always uses Green Top in Hanover'" (p. 220).

Green Top Sporting Goods is a huge retail outlet in Glen Allen, Hanover County, Virginia, just a few miles north of Richmond. The firm advertises that it has "one of the best selections of hunting and fishing gear available under one roof" (www.greentophuntfish.com). It has been in business since 1947 and stocks more than 4,000 handguns, rifles, and shotguns. The "Sig" to which Lucy refers is one of many handguns produced in joint development by the Swiss-based SIG Arms company and the Germany-based J. P. Sauer & Sohn company.

HARDEE'S (*The Body Farm*) Cornwell's characters not only eat in top-quality restaurants, but sometimes stop for fast food as well. In a conversation between Scarpetta and Marino, she observes, "Marino . . . opened a steak biscuit from Hardee's" (p. 78).

Hardee's is a fast-food restaurant chain started in Greenville, North

Carolina, by Wilber Hardee in 1960. Today it is a subsidiary of CKE restaurants, owner of the Carl's Jr. chain; there are 2,400 franchised and corporation-owned Hardee's restaurants in thirty-two states and eleven foreign countries. Fifteen Hardee's restaurants are spread around Richmond, Virginia, so Marino would have no trouble finding one when he needs a steak biscuit.

HENRICO (*Cruel & Unusual, Cause of Death*) In a conversation between Scarpetta and Marino, she asks, "Do you know a Detective Trent with Henrico?" (p. 21, *Cruel & Unusual*).

Henrico (pronounced "hen-RYE-co") is a Virginia county covering 244 square miles. It lies between the James and Chickahominy Rivers and encompasses approximately one-third of the Richmond metropolitan area.

HILL CAFE (*Cause of Death*) Scarpetta's missing Mercedes-Benz has been found, but her former intern who was driving it is missing. She and Marino search for him. "[W]e continued east on Broad to the Hill Cafe at 28th Street, and my pulse picked up when I realized the restaurant was but one street from where my Mercedes had been found" (p. 162).

The Hill Cafe, a white brick building with black awnings, is located at the corner of 28th and Broad Streets in the historic Church Hill district. Richmond's Church Hill is the city's highest point. Explorer William Byrd, standing atop the rise in 1737, thought the panoramic view was like his home in Richmond-on-Thames, England, so he named the place Richmond.

THE HOMESTEAD (*Cruel & Unusual*) Under stress, Scarpetta desperately wants to confer with Benton Wesley. She calls him on his mobile car phone. "'I need to talk,'" she says. "'I don't feel it can wait.'"

"'Do you ski?'" he asks. "'Connie [his wife] and I are on our way to the Homestead for a couple of days. We could talk there. Can you get away?'"

"'I'll move heaven and earth to, and I'll bring Lucy'" (p. 203).

Upon their arrival, Scarpetta observes, "The Homestead was situated on fifteen thousand acres of forest and streams in the Allegheny Mountains, the main section of the hotel dark red brick with white-pillared colonnades. . . . tennis courts and golf greens were solid white with snow" (p. 206).

Located in the heavily forested mountains of Virginia's Allegheny

Mountains, The Homestead is a luxury retreat for individual or business and government organizational groups. Beginning as a rustic wooden lodge built around spring pools in 1766, it has grown to a modern complex housed in multistory red-brick buildings. The resort offers a wide variety of activities, including golf, tennis, bowling, swimming, fishing, sport shooting, hiking, equestrian trails, and skiing in the winter. Movies, fine dining, mineral baths, and massages round out the environment in which Scarpetta and Wesley meet.

The Homestead is also mentioned in *Southern Cross.*

HOWARD BEACH (*Postmortem*) Attending a meeting with government officials, Scarpetta listens as the topic inspires a sudden revelation about the case she is examining. "I was sitting so rigidly I was barely breathing. . . . The men continued to talk, to explain. References were made to Howard Beach, to a stabbing in Brooklyn, in which the police were negligent in responding and people died. . . . I was scarcely hearing a word of it. . . . I knew what happened" (pp. 115–116).

Howard Beach is the location of a 1987 New York City crime. Three white teenagers from the Howard Beach section of Queens were later convicted of manslaughter in the death of a black man who was chased onto a highway, where he was struck by a car. A fourth defendant was acquitted. Allegations were made against the police at the time who were accused of responding too slowly.

JANES ISLAND STATE PARK (*Unnatural Exposure*) A telephone call from the killer has been traced by the FBI to a Maryland campground. Scarpetta and Marino board a helicopter to cross Chesapeake Bay to the site. Scarpetta is apprehensive. "[T]here was something else in store for us, and I did not want to imagine what that might be. The trip to Janes Island State Park was less than an hour, but complicated by the fact that the campground was densely wooded with pines. There was nowhere to land. Our pilots set us down at the Coast Guard station in Crisfield . . . where sailboats and yachts battened down for winter bobbed on the dark blue ruffled water of the Little Annemessex River" (pp. 311–312).

Located in southeastern Maryland along the shores of Tangier Sound and the Annemessex River, Janes Island State Park is a 3,147-acre natural resource where canoeing, physical fitness, boating, camping, and crabbing attract visitors. Miles of isolated shoreline and marsh areas are perfect for anglers and paddlesport enthusiasts. There are two distinct areas: a developed mainland and a remote portion accessible only by boat. The original island inhabitants were Native Americans of the Annemessex Nation. Crisfield is a small harbor town on the southern tip of Maryland.

JOHN MARSHALL COURTS BUILDING (*Body of Evidence, Point of Origin*) In the normal course of her duties as chief medical examiner, Scarpetta is often required to appear in court. In *Point of Origin* she narrates, "The John Marshall Courts Building was but a ten-minute walk from our new location, and I thought the exercise would do me good. The morning was bright, the air cool and clean as I followed the sidewalk along Leigh Street and turned south on Ninth, passing police headquarters" (p. 142).

The court building is located at 400 North 9th Street in Richmond. Felony and civil trials are conducted inside by Richmond's Manchester circuit court and general district court. It is named after John Marshall, who was chief justice of the U.S. Supreme Court from 1801 to 1835.

KIRBY FORENSIC PSYCHIATRIC CENTER (*Point of Origin*) A mentally deranged female serial killer once confronted personally by Scarpetta has escaped from the New York KFPC. Scarpetta travels in a helicopter to the facility in search of answers. She observes, "The entrance into the heart of Kirby was typical for a penitentiary, with its airlocked doors that never allowed two of them to be opened at the same time. . . . No matter how adamant politicians, health workers, and the ACLU might be, this was not a hospital. Patients were inmates. They were violent offenders housed in a maximum security facility" (pp. 343–344).

An imposing tan structure standing fifteen stories high, the Kirby Forensic Psychiatric Center is located at 600 East 125th Street, Wards Island, New York. It is a maximum-security hospital of the New York State Office of Mental Health, opened in 1985 to provide secure treatment and evaluation for the forensic patients and courts of New York City and Long Island.

LA PETITE FRANCE (*The Body Farm*) In Richmond, Scarpetta treats her niece to a fine meal. "I took Lucy to La Petite France, where I surrendered to Chef Paul, who sentenced us to languid hours of fruit-marinated lamb kabobs and a bottle of 1986 Château Gruaud Larose" (p. 159).

Patricia Cornwell states in *Food to Die For,* "La Petite France at 2108 Maywill Street is one of my favorite restaurants in Richmond, where you can forget about life as you know it and let yourself be spoiled by Chef Paul Elbling and his wife, Marie-Antoinette" (p. 76).

LUMI (*The Last Precinct*) Scarpetta watches a videotaped interview with a man she hates. He is being questioned by a prosecutor about a woman he is suspected of killing in New York. "He replies that they met in a restaurant called Lumi on 70th Street, between Third and Lexington" (p. 166).

In *Food to Die For,* Cornwell confirms that Lumi is real. "Lumi Restaurant [is] an elegant, romantic regional Italian restaurant housed in a two-story brownstone at 963 Lexington Avenue (70th Street) in New York City. . . . The former private residence is filled with comfortable tables, a fireplace, bay windows, antique mirrors, and candlelight. Chef Hido Holli likes to use fresh seasonal ingredients in his ever-changing Italian menu" (p. 212).

MEDICAL COLLEGE OF VIRGINIA, OR MCV (*From Potter's Field, Unnatural Exposure*) Affiliation with the Medical College of Virginia is an integral part of Scarpetta's life. She spends time there in several of the novels. Her secretary sometimes provides a ride to the premises. "Rose had dropped me off at Eleventh and Marshall streets, at the Medical College of Virginia, or MCV, where I had done my forensic pathology residency when I wasn't much older than the students I now advised and presented gross conferences to throughout the year. Sanger Hall was sixties architecture, with a facade of garish bright blue tiles that could be spotted for miles" (pp. 176–177, *Unnatural Exposure*).

Since 1838, the Medical College of Virginia hospitals have provided health care. In July 2000, the college became part of the Virginia Commonwealth University Health System. Sanger Hall is named after Dr. William T. Sanger, who became MCV's third president in 1925. The sprawling facilities can be seen from Interstate 64 near the Nine Mile Road ramps. Scarpetta arrived at 11th and Marshall, in the complex's southern sector.

MONROE BUILDING (*Postmortem*) Friction flares between Scarpetta and her boss, so she is alarmed when he summons her to his office. "In the past, when he had something to discuss, if he didn't send a memo he sent one of his aides. There was no doubt in my mind his agenda was not to pat me on the back and tell me what a fine job I was doing. . . . He reigned across the street on the twenty-fourth floor of the Monroe Building" (p. 106).

The James Monroe building, within walking distance of the state capitol, is an actual location of many Virginia state government entities. Located at the corner of North 14th and East Franklin Streets, it is one of the taller structures in east Richmond and can easily be seen from Interstate 95. Its construction was completed just nine years before Cornwell wrote *Postmortem*.

NASA AMES RESEARCH CENTER (*Unnatural Exposure*) Lucy Farinelli, Scarpetta's niece, a computer genius even as a child, has advanced to an important assignment with the FBI's Engineering Research Facility (ERF). Demonstrating to Scarpetta certain experiments with virtual reality, she slides a special glove on her aunt's hand. Scarpetta is nervous. "[S]he picked up a helmet-mounted display that was connected to another cable, and fear fluttered through my breast as she headed my way." Lucy explains about the peculiar object. "'Same thing they're using at NASA's Ames Research Center, which is where I discovered it'" (p. 163).

According to its website, "NASA Ames Research Center is located at Moffett Field, California in the heart of Silicon Valley. Ames was founded December 20, 1939 as an aircraft research laboratory by the National Advisory Committee for Aeronautics (NACA) and in 1958 became part of National Aeronautics and Space Administration (NASA). Ames specializes in research geared toward creating new knowledge and new technologies that span the spectrum of NASA interests" (www.arc.nasa.gov/aboutames.cfm).

OLD EBBITT GRILL (*Point of Origin*) Ready to dine out in Washington, D.C., with Marino, Scarpetta chooses a popular old restaurant. "We caught a cab on Constitution and told the driver to head toward the White House and cut over to the six hundred block of Fifteenth Street. I intended to treat Marino to the Old Ebbitt Grill, and at half past five, we did not have to wait in line but got a green velvet booth. I had always found a special pleasure in the restaurant's stained glass, mirrors, and brass gas lamps wavering with flames. Turtles, boars, and antelopes were mounted over the bar, and the bartenders never seemed to slow down no matter the time of day" (p. 163).

Old Ebbitt Grill at 675 15th Street, NW, located near the White House and other historic locations in Washington, D.C., was established in 1856.

Presidents Grant, Cleveland, Harding, and Theodore Roosevelt all dined there. Cornwell writes about the famous Oyster Bar in *Food to Die For* (p. 184).

OUTBACK STEAKHOUSE (*The Body Farm*) Benton Wesley tells Scarpetta, by telephone, that her niece has been injured in an auto accident. "'It happened earlier this evening on Ninety-five just north of Richmond. She'd apparently been at Quantico and went out to eat and then drove back. She ate at the Outback. You know, the Australian steakhouse in northern Virginia?'" (p. 208).

Scores of Outback Steakhouses, an Australian-themed restaurant chain, are spread across the United States, with heavy concentrations on both coasts. Growing rapidly, the company adds sixty-five to seventy new locations each year. From Wesley's description, Lucy probably ate at the Outback in Fredericksburg, Virginia, south of Quantico.

PEABODY HOTEL (*Unnatural Exposure*) On yet another trip to solve a mystery, Scarpetta and Marino find themselves in Memphis, Tennessee. "We arrived in Memphis by noon and checked into the Peabody Hotel. I had gotten us a government rate of seventy-three dollars per night, and Marino looked around, gawking at a grand lobby of stained glass and a fountain of mallard ducks."

Marino speaks up. "'Holy shit . . . I've never seen a joint that has live ducks. They're everywhere'" (p. 125).

Scarpetta describes the scene. "We were walking into the restaurant, which was appropriately named Mallards. . . . There were paintings of ducks on walls, and ducks were on the staff's green vests and ties. They have a duck palace on the roof. . . . And roll out a red carpet for them twice a day when they come and go to John Philip Sousa" (p. 125).

The Peabody Hotel in Memphis is located at 149 Union Avenue. In 1865, Robert Brinkley decided to build a luxury hotel in the city and name it after himself. Just before its grand opening in 1869, Brinkley heard that his best friend, wealthy philanthropist George Peabody, had died, so Brinkley renamed the establishment in honor of his departed associate. When two more hotels were eventually opened in Orlando, Florida, and Little Rock, Arkansas, they bore the same name. The logo and symbol for Peabody hotels is a duck, which has become a tradition. The March of the Peabody Ducks, performed daily at 11 A.M. and 5 P.M., has entertained guests in the Peabody Memphis lobby for more than seventy-six years. In the morning, five mallards, one drake and four hens, leave their private elevator, under the direction of a human Duck Master, and parade down a fifty-foot red carpet across the lobby to a marble fountain, all to John Philip Sousa's "King Cotton March." In the afternoon they reverse direction and return to the rooftop Royal Duck Palace.

PHILIP'S CONTINENTAL LOUNGE (*Cruel & Unusual*) It is finally Marino's turn to choose a restaurant at which he and Scarpetta will eat. "'[W]e can zip over to Phil's,'" he says. "'I'm buying. . . .'"

Scarpetta agrees to join him. "Ten minutes later we were sitting in a corner booth perusing glossy illustrated menus offering everything from spaghetti to fried fish. . . . Philip's Continental Lounge was an old, neighborhood establishment where patrons who had known each other all their lives continued to meet regularly for hearty food and bottled beer" (pp. 238–239).

Opened originally in the 1930s, "Phil's" is located at 5704 Grove Avenue in Richmond, not far from the posh residential area where Scarpetta lives, Windsor Farms. It offers a Delmonico steak dinner for $8.75. Perfect for Marino's budget.

POE'S PUB (*Cause of Death*) Searching for Scarpetta's missing former intern, she and Marino speculate about the direction he might have taken. She says, "'Let's assume he wanted something that was a straight shot from my office, so he stayed on Broad Street.'"

Marino replies, "'Poe's, which isn't on Broad, but is very close to Libby Hill Park . . .'" (p. 162).

Poe's Pub, in a cottage-type building at 2706 East Main Street, is in the historic Shockoe Bottom district. Featuring a variety of food and live music, it is situated about a quarter mile from the James River and adjacent to Libby Hill Park. The park, established in 1851, was named after Luther Libby, who lived nearby and owned a warehouse used during the Civil War as a prison for captured Yankees—the notorious Libby Prison.

P. T. HASTING'S (*Unnatural Exposure*) Driving home through heavy rain, Scarpetta decides to stop for some seafood. "In Carytown, I pulled off at P. T. Hasting's. Festooned with fish nets and floats, it sold the best seafood in the city" (p. 73).

Located in a Richmond suburb called Carytown, P. T. Hasting's Famous Seafood is a favorite stop for local residents. Cornwell notes in *Food to Die For,* "This seafood shop, with two Richmond locations at 3545 West Cary Street and 8121 West Broad Street, offers an abundance of top-quality local fish and seafood." The author adds an interesting postscript. "Both Bev's character and the cocktail sauce were fictional when *Unnatural Exposure* was published, but after P. T. Hasting, Jr., the proprietor, and his staff received so many inquiries about the nonexistent sauce, they started making and selling it" (p. 174).

RICHOUX (*Cause of Death*) In London, Scarpetta and Benton, weary from jet lag and loss of sleep, eat breakfast at Richoux (p. 276). In *Food to Die For,* Cornwell states that it is "a small, pretty restaurant at 41a South Audley Street in Mayfair. For the past ninety-odd years, Richoux has been famous for its all-day breakfast and traditional afternoon tea." She also notes that she discovered the establishment's "beautiful French pastries and chocolates when I had a flat in London several years ago" (p. 164).

RUTH'S CHRIS STEAK HOUSE (*Cruel & Unusual, Isle of Dogs*) Scarpetta agrees to take her niece to an elegant restaurant, but the evening is less than pleasant. "We argued all the way to Ruth's Chris Steak House, and by the time I parked the car I had a headache and was completely disgusted with myself" (p. 138).

Scarpetta and Lucy probably ate in the restaurant in Midlothian, a Richmond suburb located close to the city's western tip. It's an imposing structure, a white mansion with an entry supported by four gleaming columns.

Ruth's Chris Steak House was founded in 1965 by Ruth Fertel in New Orleans. It has expanded to eighty-seven restaurants worldwide. In the United States, a great number of them are clustered on both coasts.

The famed restaurant chain is mentioned in several of Cornwell's novels.

SCALETTA (*From Potter's Field*) With Benton Wesley in New York City during the winter, Scarpetta selects a restaurant. "Around the corner of the Museum of Natural History was the snowcapped pink awning of a restaurant called Scaletta, which I was surprised to find lit up and noisy" (p. 72). This passage is repeated by Cornwell in *Food to Die For,* in which she also describes how she originally found the restaurant. "I thought how remarkable it was that its name was so close to Scarpetta. Since then I've dined there several times and am a real fan of Chef Omer Grgurev."

Scaletta Ristorante, serving Italian cuisine, is at 50 West Seventy-seventh Street in New York, across the street from the Museum of Natural History.

SENTARA NORFOLK GENERAL HOSPITAL (*Cause of Death*) Exploring a mysterious death near Norfolk, Virginia, about eighty miles from her Richmond headquarters, Scarpetta says, "My Tidewater District Office was located in a small, crowded annex on the grounds of Sentara Norfolk General Hospital" (p. 30).

The hospital, on Gresham Drive, is part of a sprawling complex of salmon-colored multistory buildings. They make up a campus of medical buildings including Eastern Virginia Medical School and the Children's Hospital of The King's Daughters.

Her "Tidewater Office" is one of four district office buildings used by the chief medical examiner of the Commonwealth of Virginia in separate cities: the Northern District (Fairfax), the Central District (Richmond), the Western District (Roanoke), and the Tidewater District (Norfolk).

SHOCKHOE [SHOCKOE] SLIP (*Postmortem, The Body Farm, From Potter's Field*) Known also as "Shockhoe Bottom" and the "Slip," this area of Richmond is noted in *Postmortem* as an upscale district of restaurants, shops, hotels, and entertainment venues near the James River, it was once the site of busy tobacco warehouses. About an unknown murderer's profile and habits, Scarpetta speculates, "He is ordinary by most standards, and probably doesn't drive a BMW or grace the bars in the Slip or the finer clothing stores along Main Street" (p. 3).

Though, in *The Body Farm,* Scarpetta notes, "[We drove to Shockoe Bottom and walked along cobblestones beneath lamplight in a part of the city that not so long ago I would not have ventured near" (p. 159).

And in *From Potter's Field,* this is referenced as a quaint, artsy cobble-stoned area in downtown Richmond. Gault buys a cadudeus, the traditional medical wand symbol, here at the James Galleries (p. 252).

SHUFORD MILLS (*The Body Farm*) A piece of orange duct tape becomes an important clue. Scarpetta asks an FBI expert, "'Do you know where the tape was manufactured?'"

He replies, "'Shuford Mills of Hickory, North Carolina. They're one of the biggest duct tape manufacturers in the country'" (p. 171).

Founded in 1880 by Abel Shuford and N. H. Gwyn on Gunpowder Creek near Granite Falls, North Carolina, Shuford Mills gradually expanded to five plants including Hickory, North Carolina, where the company is headquartered today. It manufactures spun yarn products used in upholstery fabrics, woven and knit apparel, industrial fabrics, draperies, carpets, rugs, and other woven materials.

SIX MILE, SOUTH CAROLINA (*All That Remains*) Pursuing answers in yet another mystery murder, Scarpetta and Marino fly to Charlotte, North Carolina; rent a car; and drive down to South Carolina. Scarpetta falls asleep en route and is awakened by Marino's booming voice. "'Welcome to the big town of Six Mile,'" he announces.

Scarpetta is unimpressed. "There was no skyline, not so much as a single convenience store or gas station in sight. Roadsides were dense with trees, the Blue Ridge a haze in the distance, and houses were poor and spread so far apart a cannon could go off without your neighbor hearing it" (p. 134).

Six Mile is an actual place, a small, rural town near Lake Keowee on Route 133 at the northwestern tip of South Carolina.

THE SKULL & BONES (*Cause of Death, Unnatural Exposure*) Retracing the possible steps of a missing intern, Scarpetta drives through a section of Richmond. "I doubted he would have known about The Skull & Bones, where medical staff and students ate" (p. 201).

On the northeast corner of 12th and Marshall Streets stood a restaurant called the Skull & Bones, a favorite eatery for students and staff of the Medical College of Virginia (MCV). After it closed, a new coffee service was opened in the spring of 2003 in the Tompkins-McCaw Library on campus. By popular vote, it was named the Skull & Beans in sentimental reverence to the former gathering site.

Scarpetta was also supposed to have lunch with a medical student advisee here in *Unnatural Exposure* (p. 15).

SLOPPY JOE'S (*Body of Evidence*) In search of information about a murder victim named Beryl, Kay Scarpetta travels to the southern extreme of the eastern United States—Key West, Florida. A letter written by the victim mentions Sloppy Joe's bar. While in the semitropical city, Scarpetta converses with a man who knew Beryl. He recalls, "Next thing, we're walking around Old Town, and end up in Sloppy Joe's. Being a writer and all, she really flipped out, went on and on about Hemingway" (p. 356).

Sloppy Joe's, at 201 Duval Street, Key West, is a well-known bar where Ernest "Papa" Hemingway spent time during his residency in Florida. His drinking pal, Captain Joe Russell, "Sloppy Joe," owned the establishment. Russell was reportedly the inspiration for a few of Hemingway's tales. Memorabilia from the Hemingway era decorate the establishment's interior.

SPRINGFIELD MALL (*The Body Farm*) A suspect is linked to an unusual shop in a prominent mall. Scarpetta is told about it by a confidant. "I looked around for a pencil and wrote as my mind raced. The name of the shop was Eye Spy, and it was in the Springfield Mall, just off I-95" (p. 233).

Scarpetta drives to the mall, which is real. It is on the east side of Interstate 95, off the Franconia exit south of Washington, D.C. But there is no Eye Spy store listed.

STRAWBERRY STREET CAFÉ (*Cruel & Unusual*) With Marino at the wheel speeding madly toward a possible crime scene in which a woman has been killed, Scarpetta is tense. "I was shivering and could not seem to catch my breath. . . . Police had found Susan's car in an alleyway. . . . Marino turned onto Strawberry Street. . . . We passed restaurants and a small grocery store. . . . Near the Strawberry Street Café, the narrow street was lined with cruisers and unmarked units, and an ambulance was blocking the entrance of an alleyway" (pp. 184–185).

There really is a Strawberry Street Café at 421 North Strawberry Street, Richmond. It advertises American food with most entrées around $10.

TANGIER ISLAND (*Unnatural Exposure, Isle of Dogs*) Trying to stem the possible outbreak of an infectious disease, Scarpetta believes it may have started on a tiny rural island where fishing and crabbing are the primary sources of income. She decides to risk investigating at the scene. "The only way to get to Tangier Island was by water or air" (p. 180, *Unnatural Exposure*). She finds the place rustic and primitive, and the people there speak a strange dialect.

Tangier Island is in the middle of Chesapeake Bay, less than twenty miles from mainland Virginia, approximately six miles below the southern Maryland border. It's only one mile wide and roughly three miles long. About 700 residents live in the only town, Tangier.

Patricia Cornwell has thoroughly researched her subject, making Scarpetta's fears of an epidemic quite valid. There really were four deadly outbreaks of diseases on the island between 1866 and the 1880s: cholera, tuberculosis, measles, and smallpox.

Tangier Island is a setting in *Isle of Dogs.* "Tangier was less than three miles long and not even a mile wide. Only six hundred and fifty people lived here" (p. 44).

TATOU (*From Potter's Field*) It is midday in New York and Scarpetta takes time out from her duties. "I took Marino to lunch at Tatou because I thought both of us needed an uplifting atmosphere" (p. 79).

Tatou, at 151 East Fiftieth Street, serves French and Italian food "New York style" and has an extensive wine list. Open for lunch and dinner, it's in the moderate price range, and offers live jazz entertainment.

THE TRELLIS (*All That Remains*) Scarpetta receives a surreptitious telephone call from Abby Turnbull, a female crime reporter friend. They agree to meet. "'I'll be in Williamsburg on Saturday,' she then said. 'Dinner, The Trellis at seven?'" Scarpetta accepts (p. 247).

The Trellis is an actual, award-winning restaurant at 403 Duke of Gloucester Street, Williamsburg, Virginia, serving a variety of meat and fish entrées, plus several vegan and vegetarian platters. But the establishment is especially known for its chocolate delights. Owned by Marcel Desaulniers, who has written several fabulous cookbooks, including the well-known masterpiece *Death by Chocolate,* it's a must for anyone visiting the Williamsburg area.

TRIANGLE, VIRGINIA (*From Potter's Field*) En route to Quantico in Marino's pickup truck, with Lucy as a passenger, Scarpetta observes the area. "The truck got quiet, filled with no voice but its own . . . as Marino drove into the tiny town of Triangle. Roadside diners were lit up, and I suspected many of the cars out were driven by marines" (p. 160).

Scarpetta had good reason to expect Marines. Triangle borders the Quantico base, just across I-95, occupying the narrow stretch of land be-

Patricia with two of her loves—one of her dogs and a helicopter.

Patricia ready for flight.

Patricia at a book signing for *The Last Precinct*.

Patricia is a stickler for authenticity and detail, and here she is shown at work in Paris in preparation for *Black Notice*.

Patricia at a book signing
early in her career.

PHOTOGRAPH OF THE AUTHOR
BY IRENE M. SHULGIN,
© CORNWELL ENTERPRISES, INC.

PHOTOGRAPH OF THE AUTHOR
BY IRENE M. SHULGIN,
© CORNWELL ENTERPRISES, INC.

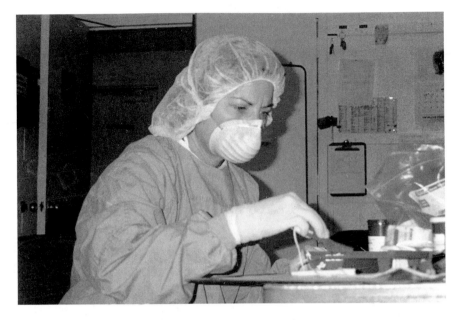

Patricia in the forensics lab (above) and on the firing range (below).

Patricia has always been
interested in animals—
even the most exotic.

Patricia getting to know the
miniature horses while doing
research for *Isle of Dogs*.

Patricia doing research
in the tidal areas near
Baton Rouge, Louisiana.

Patricia examines a gravestone during her investigation of the
Jack the Ripper case, which became *Portrait of a Killer*.

Patricia working a case with The Bureau of Alcohol, Tobacco, Firearms and Explosives (ATF) law enforcement agency.

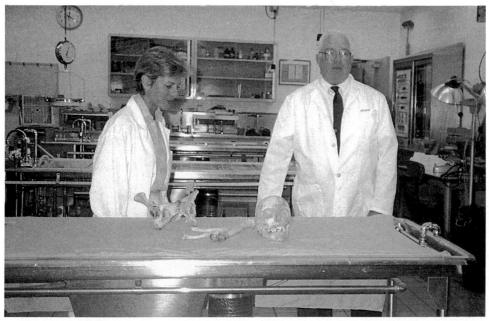

Patricia and legendary forensic anthropologist Dr. Bill Bass in his lab in Knoxville, Tennessee.

The medical examiner's autopsy room (above) and the Bullet Recovery Tank for Firearms and Toolmark Identification (below) in Richmond, Virginia.

GLENN L. FEOLE, M.D.

Dr. Marcella Fierro, the chief medical examiner of Richmond,
Virginia, and role model for Cornwell's Kay Scarpetta, in her office (above)
and an exterior view of the offices of the chief medical examiner (below).

GLENN L. FEOLE, M.D.

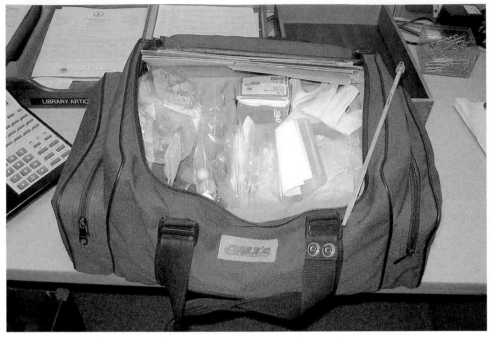

An evidence gathering kit used by a CSI unit at a crime scene.

GLENN L. FEOLE, M.D.

The Arson Lab used for analyzing charred objects with twenty-one
ovens set at 170 degrees Fahrenheit.

GLENN L. FEOLE, M.D.

Patricia participating in a Jamestown, Virginia,
anthropological dig (above and below).

Patricia sifting through evidence in preparation for *Portrait of a Killer*.

Patricia walks the streets of Whitechapel in London
with Scotland Yard's John Grieve.

Patricia left no stone
unturned in her quest to get
to the bottom of the Jack the
Ripper murders. She looked
at thousands of documents.

PHOTOGRAPHS BY IRENE M. SHULGIN,
© CORNWELL ENTERPRISES, INC.

tween the highway and the Potomac River. Fewer than 5,000 residents live there, most of them Marines and their families.

UKROP'S (*Unnatural Exposure, The Body Farm, Black Notice*) Lucy has prepared a home-cooked dinner for Scarpetta, who says, "'The spinach is wonderful. Where did you get it?'"

Lucy replies, "'Ukrops. I'd give anything to have a store like that in my neighborhood'" (p. 114, *Unnatural Exposure*).

Ukrop's is a supermarket chain with outlets located throughout central Virginia, headquartered in Richmond. Founded in 1937 by Joe Ukrop, who decided to start a grocery store based on the Golden Rule. Friendly, attractive, and popular, the chain is known for high-quality produce, fine bakeries, and friendly service. Many of the establishments incorporate cafés, banks, and pharmacies.

Scarpetta mentions shopping at Ukrop's in *Black Notice* (p. 80).

"[Ukrop's] grocery store was mobbed because whenever sleet or snow was predicted, Richmonders lost their minds. They envisioned starving to death or having nothing to drink, and by the time I got to the bread section, there wasn't a single loaf left" (p. 385, *Black Notice*).

U.S. NAVAL AMPHIBIOUS BASE (*Cause of Death*) On the opening page of this book, Scarpetta finds herself staying temporarily in the home of a friend in the Norfolk area. "His weathered cottage was tucked behind a dune . . . between the U.S. Naval Amphibious Base and Back Bay National Wildlife Refuge" (p. 1).

Interstate 64 connects Richmond to Norfolk. In the latter region, the U.S. military maintains a major presence, including the U.S. Navy base in Norfolk, the Naval Amphibious Base and Oceana Naval Air Station in Virginia Beach, Langley Air Force Base in Hampton, Fort Eustis in Newport News, Camp Peary in York County, and the U.S. Naval Weapons Station in James City County. All of these are mentioned in the Scarpetta series. Back Bay National Wildlife Refuge was established in 1938 to provide a habitat for migrating and wintering waterfowl. It contains more than 8,500 acres, situated around Back Bay in the southeastern corner of Virginia Beach.

VIRGINIA BIOMEDICAL RESEARCH PARK (*Cause of Death*) Driving her car at night, Scarpetta passes a construction site. She comments, "It was very dark as I passed construction and empty lots that would soon be Virginia's Biomedical Research Park" (p. 201).

The Virginia BioTechnology Research Park officially opened in December 1995 with the completion of the BioTechnology Center, which houses administrative offices. It is located next to the OCME and the Forensic Laboratories. The complex is still only one-third developed. Originally created as a partnership of Virginia Commonwealth University, the park is home to more than forty-five bioscience companies and research institutes. When completed, it will contain 1.5 million square feet of research, office, and laboratory space in eighteen to twenty buildings.

VIRGINIA STATE PENITENTIARY, SPRING STREET (*Cruel & Unusual, All That Remains*) A man on Virginia's death row is facing execution. Scarpetta watches television news showing protesters outside the prison. She notes, "The camera shifted to the Virginia State Penitentiary, where for two hundred years the Commonwealth's worst criminals had been warehoused along a rocky stretch of the James River at the edge of downtown."

The television reporter says, "'I'd say several hundred people are standing vigil out here. And of course, the penitentiary itself is almost empty. All but several dozen of the inmates have already been transported to the new correctional facility in Greensville'" (pp. 6–7, *Cruel & Unusual*).

In *All That Remains,* Marino is complaining to Scarpetta about the Richmond officials' treatment of police officers. "'[Y]ou're lucky they put gas in your damn car and furnish you with a gun. The squirrels in Spring Street got it better than we do.'"

She observes, "Spring Street was the state penitentiary" (p. 85).

Scarpetta's use of the past tense is now correct. The old state penitentiary on Spring Street in Richmond has been razed. It had been in operation since 1798. Thomas Jefferson commissioned architect Benjamin Latrobe to design it. The cells were arranged in a circular pattern, providing maximum viewing capacity for guards located at the center. A distinctive arch decorated the stone prison's exterior entry. Latrobe used Greek-inspired designs.

A new facility, Greensville Correctional Center, about forty miles south of Richmond, was opened in 1990 to house 3,000 inmates, making it Virginia's largest prison. It also includes the state's death row and execution chamber.

WESTWOOD RACQUET CLUB (*All That Remains*) Pointing out a need for physical exercise to offset the job-related wear and tear to her body, Scarpetta explains that tennis lessons help. "Once a week I took a lesson late at night, when I was less likely to be subjected to the curious stares of the cocktail and happy hour crowd lounging in the observation gallery of Westwood Racquet Club's indoor facility" (p. 90).

Richmond's Westwood Racquet Club was originally Westwood Golf Course in the 1920s, but the 1929 stock market crash forced owners to sell most of the property. It became the Westwood Supper Club until the end of World War II, when it turned into The Officer's Club of Virginia. Finally, in 1967, the tennis facility opened under the Westwood Racquet Club banner. One last change took place in 1994, two years after Cornwell wrote *All That Remains*. It is now simply The Westwood Club. Invitations to petition for membership are extended on a "person to person" basis only, and all petitions are reviewed by the Board of Directors.

WILLARD HOTEL (*The Body Farm*) After a harrowing visit to see a U.S. senator in Washington, D.C., Scarpetta is too weary to drive the 100 miles back to Richmond. "I got a room in the Willard that night" (p. 178).

One writer, reviewing the luxurious Willard, located at the city's center, noted, "This hotel, in fact, may be much more justly called the center of Washington . . . than either the Capitol, The White House, or the State Department. . . . You exchange nods with governors of sovereign states; you elbow illustrious men, and tread on the toes of generals; you hear statesmen and orators speaking in their familiar tones. You are mixed up with office seekers, wire pullers, inventors, artists, poets . . . until identity is lost among them." The author was Nathaniel Hawthorne, who made this assessment while covering the Civil War for the *Atlantic Monthly*.

Cornwell published *The Body Farm* in 1995. In November 2000, the historic Willard InterContinental Washington, at 1401 Pennsylvania Avenue, NW, completed a five-month multimillion-dollar renovation. It now offers 341 modern guest rooms plus 42 suites, and advertises "standard rates from $305."

WILLIAMSBURG, VIRGINIA (*All That Remains*) Several references are made to Colonial Williamsburg in Scarpetta's adventures.

The capital of Virginia from 1699 to 1780, this thriving community anchored political, cultural, and educational functions in the region. When the capital was moved to Richmond, Williamsburg life once again focused primarily on education and the College of William and Mary, chartered in 1693.

Restoration of the city's historic buildings began in the mid-1920s. Eighty-five percent of the community's original area has been restored. Today, visitors may wander along the streets and observe life, customs, and clothing as it was in Revolutionary times. Among more than 100 million people who have toured Colonial Williamsburg in the last sixty-five years are nine U.S. Presidents, scores of foreign government leaders, and various other celebrities.

WINDSOR FARMS (*Body of Evidence, Cause of Death, Unnatural Exposure, Cruel & Unusual, From Potter's Field, The Last Precinct, Southern Cross*) Scarpetta changes her residence more than once in the series. For a period, she lives in one of the most affluent sections of Richmond. When the violent murder of Beryl Madison takes place in the community, on Wyndam Drive, Scarpetta reflects on it: "Windsor Farms was not the sort of neighborhood where one would expect anything so hideous to happen. Homes were large and set back from the street on impeccably landscaped lots. Most had burglar alarm systems, and all featured central air, eliminating the need for open windows. Money can't buy eternity, but it can buy a certain degree of security" (pp. 8–9, *Body of Evidence*).

Scarpetta lives in this exclusive, affluent suburb in the West End of Richmond. "Windsor Farms was quietly rich, with Georgian and Tudor houses neatly arranged along streets with English names, and estates shadowed by trees and surrounded by serpentine brick walls. Private security jealously guarded the privileged, for whom burglar alarms were as common as sprinklers. Unspoken covenants were more intimidating than those in print" (pp. 167–168, *Cruel & Unusual*). It is also mentioned in *The Body Farm* (p. 148).

In *Cause of Death,* Scarpetta has built a new house with high security in this neighborhood (p. 92). To get there, she travels from Malvern to Cary to Old Locke Lane (p. 107). Chief of Police Paul Tucker also lives in Windsor Farms (p. 16, *From Potter's Field*).

Sulgrave Street runs through Windsor Farms: "she lived on the lovely tree-lined street of Sulgrave, which was well known for wealthy estates and the sixteenth-century manors called Virginia House and Agecroft that in the 1920s had been shipped from England in crates" (p. 111, *Cause of Death*).

Lockgreen is mentioned as Scarpetta's neighborhood in Windsor Farms in *The Last Precinct* (p. 338).

Chief Hammer approves a plan to increase patrols in this wealthy area because of the crime in *Southern Cross* (p. 41).

Just west of Interstate 95, on the north bank of the James River, Windsor Farms is a wealthy enclave of homes, many of which can be described as mansions. One of them was reportedly shipped from England, stone by stone, and rebuilt in this neighborhood. Cornwell can write about it from personal experience since she actually lived there at one time.

WORLD TRADE CENTER (*Point of Origin*) Scarpetta lists a series of deadly disasters in which she had worked, including the World Trade Center. Regarding the WTC, new readers might think she is referring to September 11, 2001.

Because *Point of Origin* was published in 1998, she obviously means the first terrorist attack on the buildings. In a grim preview of the 9/11 attack, Islamic terrorists drove a bomb-laden truck into the underground garage below the north tower on February 26, 1993. After they departed, a massive explosion ripped through concrete four floors below, taking six lives and injuring more than a thousand victims. It took several years to round up conspirators and multiple trials to convict them.

DISASTERS AND TRAGEDIES

B Y alluding to several actual disasters, Patricia Cornwell builds yet another matrix of authenticity for fictional events whirling around the center of real-life drama. In *Point of Origin,* Scarpetta states, "In recent years I had worked the World Trade Center and Oklahoma City bombings and the crash of TWA Flight 800. I had helped with the identifications of the Branch Davidians at Waco" (pp. 4–5).

C&O TUNNEL COLLAPSE (*Cause of Death*) Scarpetta and Marino are in the vicinity of the site as a case develops in historic Church Hill. One of Scarpetta's employees, given permission to use her personal car, has vanished. The empty Mercedes turns up near Libby Hill Park. Scarpetta narrates: "Police cruisers with lights throbbing red and blue lined both sides of Franklin Street . . . [M]idway down the steep hill were woods thick and dense where the C&O tunnel had collapsed in the twenties" (p. 150).

In 1871, the Chesapeake & Ohio Railroad began building a tunnel under Richmond's Church Hill. It seemed cursed from the beginning. Two years of labor were marked with frequent setbacks before the project was finally completed. After twenty-nine years of use, the company closed the tunnel and rerouted trains through a viaduct on the James

River. But burgeoning traffic forced them to reconsider, so they began a restoration project in September 1925 to make the tunnel safe for future passage.

On October 2, engineer Thomas J. Mason rolled his steam locomotive and ten flat cars deep into the tunnel where scores of men sweated in the rehabilitation project. At first, a few stones fell from the ceiling, then more, and finally tons of earth and rock tumbled down. Shouting men ran for their lives. Most succeeded, but Mason and at least two workers died immediately. Mason's fireman, Benjamin F. Mosby, managed to escape but succumbed to injuries later that day.

More than 300 laborers frantically shoveled debris trying to reach the lost men, but managed only to retrieve Mason's body.

Railroad executives decided it was economically unfeasible to recover the train, so packed both ends of the tunnel with sand and sealed it up. Today, a train and an unknown number of men rest under Church Hill in the doomed C&O tunnel.

OKLAHOMA CITY (*Cause of Death, Point of Origin*) Six years and six months before the catastrophic horror that collapsed New York's World Trade Center and took thousands of lives, a terrorist bombing in Oklahoma City stunned the nation. It horrified the nation to learn that these terrorists were American citizens.

Lucy refers to that disaster once in *Cause of Death,* and Scarpetta does so twice in *Point of Origin,* in which she recalls working the site. On April 19, 1995, Timothy McVeigh committed the heinous act. An Army veteran of America's first war with Iraq, Operation Desert Storm, McVeigh parked a rental truck in front of the Alfred P. Murrah Federal Building and fled. Four thousand pounds of fertilizer and fuel oil detonated, disintegrating the building's front half and ripping out a vast crescent-shaped section. Nine stories of glass, steel, and concrete plunged down, compressing everything and everyone in its path. Windows shattered and walls crumbled blocks away. Of the 168 victims who perished that day, 19 were small children.

McVeigh was subsequently caught, tried, and executed.

TWA FLIGHT 800 (*Point of Origin*) As the chief medical examiner for the Commonwealth of Virginia, Scarpetta is called upon by the FBI to help at major disasters across the nation, including the tragic crash of Trans

World Airlines Flight 800 on July 17, 1996. Reasons why the Boeing 747 exploded, killing all 230 people aboard, are still being contested today.

Within minutes after taking off from New York's JFK Airport, bound for Paris, the airliner erupted in a ball of flame, thought by a few witnesses to be fireworks. The fuselage shattered and plummeted into the Atlantic Ocean.

Widespread rumors that a missile had struck it infuriated Americans. Eventually, investigators suggested that leaking fuel, ignited by an electric spark, caused the explosion. Disbelievers argue that the missile theory is far more likely, and accuse the government of hiding the true facts.

VINCE FOSTER SUICIDE (*Cause of Death*) The Vince Foster case is mentioned by Benton Wesley in *Cause of Death,* which is an eerily appropriate title particularly in consideration of questionable events surrounding this real case. It's too bad Scarpetta, or someone of her remarkable forensic skills, didn't investigate. Perhaps some of the mysteries would have been cleared up.

Foster, a deputy White House counsel who was also personal legal advisor to President Bill Clinton and his wife, was found dead on July 20, 1993, in Fort Marcy Park, a Virginia suburb of Washington, D.C. He appeared to have shot himself, but questions sprang up almost immediately and still circulate today. Suspicious circumstances abound, including blood evidence, ballistics problems, body position, accusations of a forged suicide note, absence of blood or fingerprints on the gun, inconsistent descriptions of the wound, allegedly sloppy investigation, and a long list of additional questions. Conspiracy theorists suggest a coverup at the highest government levels.

Scarpetta, Marino, and Benton Wesley probably would have found answers.

WACO/BRANCH DAVIDIANS (*Point of Origin*) Another episode of fiery violence costing human lives, perhaps even more controversial, brought Scarpetta to a tragic scene in 1993.

Outside Waco, Texas, a religious group of approximately 100 devotees known as the Branch Davidians occupied a compound of wooden structures. David Koresh (born Vernon Wayne Howell in 1959) had survived a power struggle to become their leader. He reportedly claimed direct connections with God. Federal investigators regarded Koresh as a purveyor of illegal weapons and a child beater who victimized offspring he had fathered by several women in his flock. On February 28, 1993, agents from the Bureau of Alcohol, Tobacco, and Firearms attempted to arrest him.

The encounter turned violent and four ATF agents fell mortally wounded. More than a dozen suffered injuries. No one knows exactly how many followers of Koresh died.

The government sent more armed agents, this time from the FBI. At the compound, negotiators arranged for a few children to come out, but settled nothing else. Reinforcements arrived, including armored vehicles. Weeks of stalemate followed. Preparing for a tear gas assault, the FBI issued warnings but Koresh refused to capitulate. Soon after the attack started on April 19, with armored vehicles crashing into compound walls, fires erupted and a few Davidians made their way out. The flames roared out of control. Seventy-six people inside, including Koresh and more than two dozen children, perished.

In the ensuing controversy, the FBI claimed the Davidians started the fires, while others vilified the government, certain that agents caused the conflagration, deliberately or accidentally.

CELEBRITIES

Dozens of celebrities are mentioned throughout the Scarpetta series, most of them in brief, passing encounters. By inserting these real luminaries into her parade of characters, Cornwell creates a feeling of verisimilitude. If her creations are surrounded by real people, then they, too, seem real. The celebrity references range from political leaders, actors, artists, and authors to controversial figures, some very well known but others more obscure.

MICHAEL BOLTON (*Hornet's Nest*) Michael Bolotin (who later changed the spelling of his name) was born in New Haven, Connecticut, in 1954 and launched his musical career at age twenty-two. His prolific work has sold more than fifty-two million albums and singles. He is the recipient of several Grammys, American Music Awards, and other similar recognitions. The philanthropic singer-songwriter also serves on the boards of several charitable foundations, including Michael Bolton Charities, which he founded in 1993.

MEL BROOKS AND ANNE BANCROFT (*Black Notice*) Scarpetta and Marino are waiting to fly to Paris on the Concorde. En route, Marino glances at other passengers in the lounge and says, "'I'm pretty sure there's somebody famous sitting over there. She's got sunglasses on and everybody's staring. . . . The guy she's with looks famous, too, sort of like Mel Brooks.'"

Unimpressed and not even glancing their way, Scarpetta asks, "'Does the woman in sunglasses look like Anne Bancroft?'

"'Yeah.'

"'Then it's Mel Brooks'" (p. 298).

Mel Brooks—comedian, writer, actor, director, producer, and Academy Award winner—was born Melvin Kaminsky in 1926. His comedic movies have achieved broad success, including *Blazing Saddles, Young Frankenstein,* and his 1968 film *The Producers,* which went on to become a Tony-winning Broadway musical in 2001. He is one of the few people to have earned all four of the major entertainment prizes: an Oscar, a Tony, a Grammy, and an Emmy.

He married Anne Bancroft in 1964. Anne Bancroft, dancer and actress from early childhood, was born Anna Maria Louise Italiano in 1931. She has won the New York Drama Critics award, a Tony Award, Best Actress at Cannes and the British Film Academy, and an Academy Award for her role in *The Miracle Worker.*

No documented evidence is available to prove that the famous couple ever flew on the Concorde, but it's possible that Cornwell may have personally witnessed this.

JIMMY BUFFETT (*Hornet's Nest*) Born on Christmas Day, 1946, in Mississippi, Jimmy Buffett studied journalism in college but launched a music career in 1970. His colorful, tongue-in-cheek lyrics soon caught on with the public. In the mid-seventies, he made an album titled *Changes in Latitudes, Changes in Attitudes,* including a song called "Margaritaville." That song turned into a million-seller as a single. Attracted to the sea and boats, Buffett migrated to Key West, Florida, and turned out more albums through the nineties. His music combines a popular country sound with Caribbean rhythms. His fans, called Parrotheads, still flock to Buffett's concerts.

WARD AND JEFF BURTON (*Isle of Dogs*) A set of racing brothers are the Burtons: Ward, born in 1961, and Jeff, six years younger. They both have won several Winston Cup races.

TRUMAN CAPOTE/TENNESSEE WILLIAMS (*Postmortem*) An early murder suspect in *Postmortem* has written a dissertation about famed playwright Tennessee Williams. The suspect's opening paragraph describes Williams as a person "'whose most successful plays reveal a frustrating world in which sex and violence lie beneath the surface of romantic gentility'" (p. 50).

To Marino, this reinforces suspicions against the suspect, but Scarpetta argues that writing about behavioral aberrations does not imply the author is a criminal. She says, "'Truman Capote wasn't a mass murderer, Sergeant'" (p. 51).

Truman Capote (1924–1984) wrote *In Cold Blood,* the 1966 nonfiction book about a horrific Kansas mass murder in which a pair of young hoodlums slaughtered a farmer, his wife, and their two teenage children. A chilling 1967 motion picture based on the story featured actor Robert Blake as one of the killers who was executed by hanging. (In a strange twist, in 2002 in Los Angeles Blake faced charges of killing his own wife.)

Capote's work pioneered the true-crime genre. Among his six novels was *Breakfast at Tiffany's,* also made into a motion picture with Audrey Hepburn.

Thomas Lanier "Tennessee" Williams (1911–1983), American playwright from Mississippi, was best known for *A Streetcar Named Desire, The Glass Menagerie, Cat on a Hot Tin Roof,* and *Night of the Iguana.* He won two Pulitzer Prizes.

ERIC CLAPTON (*Southern Cross*) A music legend, Clapton is a baby boomer, born in Ripley, England, on March 30, 1945, a few weeks before World War II ended. By 1962, when the Beatles were starting out, he had entered his long career in music as a guitarist. In the early years of his career, he worked with several bands, including the Yardbirds and Cream. After that first success, he broadened his scope to include lead vocals with his new group, Derek and the Dominos. When they broke up, he withdrew from the business for several years, then re-emerged as a star in the mid-seventies. Gold and platinum albums followed. In 1992 he was awarded a remarkable six Grammy awards. His compositions and work with film soundtracks have garnered him even more awards and assured him a permanent niche in the pantheon of music greats. His songs "Tears in Heaven" and "Layla" (written with Jim Gordon) are classics.

DIANA, PRINCESS OF WALES (*Black Notice*) During a mission in Paris, Scarpetta takes a taxi ride. "Our driver this day was sullen and in a hurry. I rubbed my temples as motorcycles sped past in lanes of their imagination, weaving between cars and roaring through many narrow tunnels. I was depressed by reminders of the car crash that killed Princess Diana" (p. 308).

Diana, Princess of Wales, former wife of Prince Charles, died in a Paris limousine accident on Sunday, August 31, 1997. Her companion, Dodi Al Fayed, son of Harrods department store owner Mohammed Al Fayed, was also killed. The accident occurred in a tunnel under the Place de l'Alma in the city center, reportedly while the vehicle was being pursued at high speeds by photographers on motorcycles.

DALE EARNHARDT, JR. (*Isle of Dogs*) Dale Earnhardt, Jr., is the son of racing icon Dale Earnhardt, who was killed in a racing accident on February 18, 2001, and the grandson of Ralph Earnhardt, also a NASCAR driver. The younger Earnhardt, born in 1974, began competing at age seventeen and has taken many Winston Cup victories.

ENYA (*Southern Cross*) Enya is known by the music world under this simple name for a very good reason: At her 1961 birth in northwest Ireland, she was named Eithne Ní Bhraonáin, with a first name pronounced "Enya" in English. She and her eight siblings were heavily influenced by their music-teacher mother. With members of her extended family, she turned professional while she was a teenager, playing instruments. Her first breaks came in writing music for television and movies, but she evolved to performing. Her albums have been bestsellers in Great Britain, Europe, and America. In 2002 she wrote and recorded two songs for the sound track of *The Lord of the Rings: The Fellowship of the Ring*.

GLORIA ESTEFAN (*Hornet's Nest*) In 1959, when Gloria Maria Fajardo was two, her parents fled their native Cuba. Two years later, her father joined the ill-fated Bay of Pigs invasion and spent eighteen months in prison. Even though Gloria, her mother, and her younger sister lived in indigent conditions, she learned to play the guitar. Eventually she worked her way into the University of Miami, where she accompanied a musical group led by Emilio Estefan, whom she married. Their talent soon propelled them into the spotlight. Gloria was severely injured in a 1990 motor vehicle accident, but recovered and continued her sparkling career as the "Queen of Latin Pop."

GERALDINE FERRARO (*All That Remains*) Pat Harvey, a fictional "bright star in Washington," is being discussed by Scarpetta and her reporter friend, Abby Turnbull, who says, "'When it comes to prominent people included on the elite guest lists, Pat Harvey is right up there with the First Lady. It's been rumored that come the next presidential election, Pat Harvey may successfully conclude what Geraldine Ferraro started'" (p. 58).

Geraldine Ferraro's background would appeal to Scarpetta. Born in 1935, she was the youngest child of Italian immigrants to New York. Her father died when Ferraro was only eight. As a teacher, she worked her way through Fordham University Law School, became an assistant D.A. in Queens, and won a congressional seat in 1978. In 1984, she and Walter Mondale ran unsuccessfully against Ronald Reagan and George H.W. Bush for president and vice-president. Afterward, she resumed her law practice.

JEFF AND RICK FULLER (*Isle of Dogs*) Jeff and Rick Fuller are brothers who compete on NASCAR circuits.

KENNY G (*Hornet's Nest*) Kenneth Gorelick, a native of Seattle, Washington, and a specialist with the soprano saxophone, was born in the late 1950s. His high school band went to Europe in 1974. Two years later, he shortened his name and joined an orchestra. After brief stints with other groups, he went solo, eventually performing with stellar names in the musical arts. One of his biggest hits, *Breathless,* released in 1992, sold more than eight million copies.

AMY GRANT (*Hornet's Nest*) A top performer in Christian music who has broken out as a star in the pop world as well, Amy Grant is from Augusta, Georgia, where she was born in 1960. She soon moved to the country music capital, Nashville, Tennessee. While employed at a studio there, she was allowed to make a personal tape of her guitar playing and singing for private use, but a producer heard it and signed her to a contract. Her first album in 1977, titled *Amy Grant,* found a huge audience, and her career took off. Many albums later, she is still immensely popular.

BOBBY HAMILTON (*Isle of Dogs*) Bobby Hamilton, a strong competitor, drove in one of the races depicted in *Days of Thunder,* starring Tom Cruise.

PATTY HEARST (*From Potter's Field*) Scarpetta is in danger from a lurking killer. Marino stands protective guard in her home, but falls asleep. She impulsively sneaks out before dawn and drives to a grocery store. When she returns, Marino yells, "'Je-sus Christ, I can't believe you just did that.'"

Losing her temper, she retorts, "'What do you think this is? . . . Patty Hearst? Am I kidnapped now? Should we just lock me inside a closet?'" (p. 249).

Patricia Campbell Hearst, daughter of Randolph Hearst and granddaughter of William Randolph Hearst, the legendary newspaper magnate of California, was born into wealth in 1954. In February 1974, she was kidnapped by radical members of the so-called Symbionese Liberation Army. Two months later, the nation was stunned when television news aired film of her wielding an assault rifle along with SLA members robbing a San Francisco bank. She appeared to have willingly joined the criminal group.

A south Los Angeles shootout with police in May took the lives of several SLA members, but Hearst had been moved elsewhere. She was finally caught in September 1975. At a controversial trial, jurors found her guilty of bank robbery. Hearst served only twenty-two months in prison while arguments waged across the nation. Those who wanted her freed claimed she had been tortured and brainwashed by the SLA, while others thought she voluntarily participated in criminal behavior. President Jimmy Carter commuted her sentence in 1979.

HOOTIE & THE BLOWFISH (*Hornet's Nest*) This popular quartet consists of Darius Rucker—lead vocalist, guitar, harmonica; Mark Bryan—guitar, mandolin, background vocalist; Jim Sonefeld—drums, guitar, background vocalist; and Dean Felber—bass, background vocalist. The Columbia, South Carolina, group assembled in 1989 and rocketed to national and international fame within five years. Their first three albums sold twenty million copies. In 1996 they won their first Grammy for their hit single "Let Her Cry."

ANTHONY HOPKINS (*Cause of Death*) At a University of Virginia dormitory, Scarpetta visits her niece, Lucy, and comments on the decor. "Heart of pine floors were bare, with no art on whitewashed walls except a single poster of Anthony Hopkins in *Shadowlands*" (p. 229).

Shadowlands, a 1993 British movie starring Anthony Hopkins and Debra Winger, is about an Oxford don in the 1950s whose life is changed by his relationship with a female American poet.

BRUCE HORNSBY (*Hornet's Nest*) Born in the same year as Annie Lennox, 1954, Bruce Hornsby hails from Williamsburg, Virginia, near Scarpetta's turf. He migrated in 1980 to Los Angeles, where he wrote music for a movie studio. Six years later his first album, *The Way It Is,* climbed the charts. After touring in the 1990s with the Grateful Dead, he produced *Harbor Lights* and *Hot House,* followed by *Spirit Trail, Here Come the Noisemakers,* and *Big Swing Face.*

DALE JARRETT (*Isle of Dogs*) "Jarrett" is Dale Jarrett, a North Carolina native born in 1956 who was an all-around high school athlete. He began racing in 1977 and has won thirty-one Winston Cup victories.

Andy Brazil tries to inspire the driver. "'On any given race weekend, . . . any driver can make a big move and win, and I think you're the one to make that big move tonight. You can do it . . . just like Rudd, Labonte, Skinner, Wallace, and Earnhardt, Junior'" (p. 388). To make his point, he recalls a dramatic race. "'Right after an accident in Turn Four . . . Hamilton spun off toward Turn Two and took out Burton and Fuller'" (p. 388).

ELTON JOHN (*Hornet's Nest, Southern Cross*) One of the kings of pop music, Elton John was born in 1947 in England and was named Reginald Dwight. Before he was twelve, he had earned a scholarship at the Royal Academy of Music. Struggling toward fame in the late sixties, he adopted the name Elton John from a pair of musical colleagues. In 1970, he started to receive real recognition for his work and for his offbeat costumes. His popularity has continued to grow ever since. One of his greatest hits was "Candle in the Wind," written initially about Marilyn Monroe and rewritten in 1997 as a tribute to Princess Diana after her death.

WYNONNA JUDD (*Hornet's Nest*) Few people would know the name Diana Ciminella, but most would quickly recognize the name she adopted in the late sixties—Naomi Judd—along with the names of her two daughters, Wynonna and Ashley. Wynonna was born in Ashland, Kentucky, on May 30, 1964. Her parents divorced shortly after the family had moved to California, when Wynonna was seven and her sister Ashley was three. A few years later, using the names Naomi and Wynonna, mother and daughter began singing in Kentucky, and became spectacularly popular as The Judds. In 1991, Naomi retired because of complications brought on by hepatitis C. Wynonna continued her career as a solo artist and has produced fourteen Top Ten hits, including five number-one hits, as a solo act. Wynonna's younger sister, Ashley Judd, is known worldwide to movie audiences for her fine performances in movies such as *High Crimes, The Divine Secrets of the Ya-Ya Sisterhood,* and *Twisted.*

SENATOR TED KENNEDY (*The Body Farm*) In Washington, D.C., Scarpetta visits an old friend, Senator Frank Lord. They eat in the U.S. Senate dining room, surrounded by other legislators. When the table server brings their check, Lord discovers it is the wrong one. He says to her, "'I don't think this is our check. We didn't have four entrées.'" The waitress is apologetic. "'Oh, I sure am sorry, Senator Lord. It's the table there.'"

"'In that case,'" he replies, "'make Senator Kennedy pay both tabs. His and mine . . . He won't object. He believes in tax and spend'" (p. 164).

Senator Ted Kennedy from Massachusetts is the brother of two political leaders, President John F. Kennedy and Senator Robert F. Kennedy. Lord's gentle jibe about Kennedy seems directed at the traditional Democratic image of liberally spending tax money on public programs. But since it is unclear how many people sat with Kennedy at his table, with a bill for four entrées, the humor may be a subtle jest about his tendency to be overweight.

KEYSTONE KOPS (*Postmortem*) The sister of a reporter has been murdered. Scarpetta advises her not to investigate it. The reporter says, "'Somebody's got to! . . . What? I'm supposed to leave it up to the Keystone Kops?'" (p. 267).

She refers to the bungling, pratfalling comic police force depicted in silent movies made by the Keystone film production company in Hollywood in the 1920s. The words *Keystone Kops* have become a way to describe any inept police action.

K. D. LANG (*Hornet's Nest*) Kathryn Dawn Lang was born in Canada on November 2, 1961. She mastered the piano and guitar in her early teens, enabling her to begin performing for audiences. After moderate success, lang switched to the country genre and scored with several hits. In 1992 she "came out" regarding her sexuality and explained the choice of lowercase letters in her name as "generic," apparently meaning that it gives no hint of gender. Her single "Constant Craving" earned a Grammy award.

ANNIE LENNOX (*Hornet's Nest, Scarpetta's Winter Table*) A native of Scotland, born on Christmas Day 1954, Annie Lennox was educated at London's Royal Academy of Music. She achieved huge success with the Eurythmics, then embarked on a solo career in 1992 with an album called *Diva,* which reached platinum status in the United States. This was followed in 1995 with *Medusa,* and in 2003 with *Bare.*

HOWIE LONG (*Cause of Death*) Marino and Scarpetta enter the Hill Cafe in Richmond. Scarpetta observes, "It was a true neighborhood bar, and at this hour, tables were still full, smoke thick in the air, the television loudly playing old Howie Long clips on ESPN" (p. 163).

Howie Long played college football at Villanova before being drafted into professional ranks by the NFL Raiders. For thirteen seasons, until 1993, he excelled as a defensive end. With his good looks, he was a natural to become a television sportscaster and football analyst, a career he enjoys today.

MADONNA (*Hornet's Nest*) She needs no introduction and her name really is Madonna. Madonna Louise Ciccone was born in Michigan on August 16, 1958. She is an accomplished singer, songwriter, and actress, and is frequently referred to as the "Material Girl" because of her 1985 hit with the same title. She's written and recorded monster hits for decades, put together one of the most sensational books ever (*Sex*), and starred in movies from *Desperately Seeking Susan* to *Evita.* She's reinvented her image every few years, with the public watching everything she does with fascination. She is truly a pop icon.

IMELDA MARCOS (*All That Remains*) Benton Wesley discusses the CIA with Scarpetta. He says, "'[W]hen was the last time you read anything positive about the CIA? Imelda Marcos was accused of theft and fraud, and the defense claimed that every transaction the Marcoses made was with the full knowledge and encouragement of the CIA'" (p. 204).

Imelda Marcos, once a beauty queen, and her corrupt husband, Ferdinand Marcos, ruled the Philippines from 1965 to 1986. They fled to Hawaii in 1986 amid accusations of severe financial misconduct. Ferdinand died three years later. She returned to her homeland and tried unsuccessfully to capture the presidency in 1992. Legal actions have been ongoing during the entire period.

MASTER P. (*Southern Cross*) Percy Miller began life in Louisiana on April 29, 1970. He is an entrepreneur who founded a hip-hop record company, expanded to other similar genres such as "gangsta rap," moved to California, and helped develop the market for hardcore rap with underground, antisocial messages. He parlayed success into visual entertainment, then clothing products and sports management.

MEAT LOAF (*Hornet's Nest, Scarpetta's Winter Table*) Marvin Lee Aday was born in Dallas, Texas, on September 27, 1947. His first wide success came with his *Rocky Horror Picture Show* portrayal of Eddie the motorcycle rider. Adopting the name Meat Loaf, a nickname given to him by his high school football coach, Aday teamed with songwriter Jim Steinman to produce *Bat out of Hell*, which skyrocketed up the charts after a slow start and went on to sell more than thirty million copies. His music career was interrupted by financial and vocal difficulties, but he staged a comeback and still tours internationally. He has also turned very successfully to acting. He's appeared in thirty-seven movies to date.

MIKE + THE MECHANICS (*Southern Cross*) English musician Mike Rutherford, a longtime member of Genesis, formed Mike + the Mechanics in 1985 during a hiatus in his Genesis workload. By 1989 the group had a chart-topping hit called "The Living Years." Subsequent albums have fluctuated between near hits and near misses. The group's lead vocalist, Paul Young, died in 2000.

MARTHA MITCHELL (*All That Remains*) Pat Harvey, one of the most powerful women characters in Washington, D.C., in the Scarpetta series, has encountered serious trouble. Benton Wesley, discussing it with Scarpetta, says, "'More worrisome is that she's close friends with an ex–United Nations ambassador who is a member of the President's Foreign Intelligence Advisory Board. Members of the board are entitled to top-secret intelligence briefings on any subject at any time. The board knows what's going on, Kay. It's possible Mrs. Harvey knows everything.'"

Scarpetta asks, "'So she's set up Martha Mitchell-style? . . . To make sure she comes off as irrational, unreliable, so that no one takes her seriously, so that if she does blow the lid, no one will believe her?'" (p. 207).

Martha Mitchell (1918–1975), an Arkansas native, was the wife of President Richard Nixon's attorney general, John Mitchell. The Watergate scandal that ended Nixon's presidency swept Mrs. Mitchell into national prominence. John Mitchell's involvement in illegal activities was sensationalized by reporters. Mitchell's wife began telephoning media representatives to defend her husband, but wound up saying too much, sparking fury from Nixon. Mrs. Mitchell alleged that she was held captive in a hotel room to end her loquacity. She became an object of scorn and political humor, and the couple separated soon afterward. She died in 1975 from cancer.

ROBERT MORGENTHAU (*The Last Precinct*) A prosecutor from New York explains to Scarpetta that her city requires concurrence by the DA's office before police can arrest a homicide suspect. "'Morgenthau's idea,'" she says.

Scarpetta explains, "Robert Morgenthau has been the district attorney in Manhattan for nearly twenty-five years. He is a legend" (p. 161).

Morgenthau is, indeed, a real person as well as a legend. Born in 1919, decorated for U.S. Navy service during World War II, and a Yale law school graduate, he was appointed to a federal judgeship by John F. Kennedy. Elected as district attorney of New York County in 1974, he was still serving in that post as of the end of 2003.

MANUEL NORIEGA (*All That Remains*) International corruption in relation to drug money is the topic of conversation between Scarpetta and a reporter. Pointing out that large contributions from antidrug charities were being diverted, the reporter says, "'I'd been informed by what I considered reliable sources that millions of dollars donated each year were ending up in the pockets of people like Manuel Noriega. Of course, this was before Noriega was arrested'" (p. 121).

Later in the same book, Benton Wesley says, "'Then it came out that Noriega was on the CIA's payroll'" (p. 205).

Panamanian general Manuel Noriega, born in 1934, was considered the *de facto* leader of that country from 1983 to 1989. The United States, under Ronald Reagan and later under George H.W. Bush, regarded Panama as an ally, and sent vast amounts of foreign aid. News reports consistently charged that Noriega, as chief of staff to a succession of presidents, actually controlled the Panamanian government and personally accepted payments from the CIA. Finally, the Drug Enforcement Administration indicted Noriega in 1988 on drug-related charges.

The following year, President Bush sent 27,000 troops to Panama. Noriega fled after several weeks of conflict, but eventually surrendered in 1990. Convicted in the United States of drug trafficking and racketeering, he is serving thirty years in federal prison, but will be eligible for parole in 2006.

ROY ORBISON (*Hornet's Nest*) Perhaps one of the most widely known singers from the golden rock-n-roll era of the 1950s, Roy Orbison still finds new fans long after his December 1988 death from a heart attack. Born in Texas on April 23, 1936, Orbison bounced from rockabilly singer to songwriter. He wrote a tune called "Only the Lonely" in 1960 and offered it to Elvis Presley and the Everly Brothers, both of whom rejected it. So Orbison decided to record it himself. It ascended into the stratosphere and hoisted his fame with it. Known for his trademark black-rimmed sunglasses, Orbison turned out a number of classics, including "Oh Pretty Woman." The tragic tone in his voice is understandable, since he lost his wife in a motorcycle accident in 1966 and his two sons in a house fire in 1968. In 1987, he was inducted into the Rock and Roll Hall of Fame. He staged a major comeback in the late eighties, recording with George Harrison, Tom Petty, Bob Dylan, and Jeff Lynne in The Traveling Wilburys.

JOAN OSBORNE (*Hornet's Nest*) A rock singer and songwriter, Kentuckian Joan Osborne was discovered in a New York bar when someone dared her to stand up and sing. Her impressive talent led to professional work, a contract with a major label, albums, television appearances, and her own record company. Born in 1963, she has earned kudos for a number of songs, including a Top Ten hit titled "One of Us."

DOROTHY PARKER (*Body of Evidence*) In a discussion with Scarpetta about a controversial lawyer, a Virginia official brings up the attorney's early background and says, "'Apparently, the kid visited his father in New York several times a year, was precocious, a prolific reader quite taken with the literary world. On one such visit he managed to persuade his father to take him to lunch at the Algonquin on a day that Dorothy Parker and her Round Table were supposed to be there'" (p. 197).

Dorothy Parker (1893–1967), known for her quick wit, was a prolific magazine writer, drama critic, and political activist. While she worked for *Vanity Fair* in 1919, New York's famed Algonquin Hotel invited her to several functions. The Algonquin Round Table was born as a regular gathering of literary notables such as James Thurber, Robert Benchley, and several others. A socialist, Parker later was questioned in the early fifties by a congressional committee on a witch hunt for communists. She won an Academy Award for her work on the screenplay *A Star Is Born*. She died in New York in 1967.

RICHARD PETTY/DARRELL WALTRIP (*The Body Farm*) Specially designed and produced duct tape becomes a clue in the search for a killer. Scarpetta asks an FBI expert, "Can you give me an example of what sort of person might design his own duct tape?'"

He answers, "'I know some stock car racers do. . . . For example, the duct tape Richard Petty has made for his pit crew is red and blue, while Daryl Waltrip's is yellow'" (p. 172).

Neither Richard Petty nor Darrell Waltrip (note correct spelling) is a suspect in the duct tape case.

Cornwell writes about a number of natives of North Carolina (see the entry on Billy Graham and Thomas Wolfe), the home state of Richard Petty, who was born there in 1937. He grew up to be one of the best-known stock car racers in the country. From his first victory at the Charlotte Speedway in 1960 to his last in 1992, he won a spectacular series of NASCAR and other championships.

Darrell Waltrip, another NASCAR legend, launched his career in 1972. He is enshrined in the Tennessee Sports Hall of Fame, Kentucky Hall of Fame, the Michigan Motorsports Hall, and the National Motorsports Press Association Hall. Waltrip retired from the track in 2000.

THE POINTER SISTERS (*Hornet's Nest*) This quartet, truly sisters, were raised in Oakland, California. Eight years separate them in age: Ruth (born in 1946), Anita (1948), Bonnie (1951), and June (1954). Beginning in church choirs, they progressed to backup status for other artists, then to their own albums featuring old-fashioned harmony. Their song "Fairytale" won a Grammy in 1974. After a temporary parting of the ways, they reconnected and continued turning out hits, eventually appearing in stage musicals.

ELVIS PRESLEY (*Unnatural Exposure*) Marino and Scarpetta travel to a Memphis, Tennessee, medical examiner's office. Marino's devotion to Presley becomes apparent at the morgue when he says, "'I can't believe I'm here. . . . This is where he was posted [autopsied].'"

Scarpetta knows immediately who "he" is. She says, "'No . . . Elvis Presley was posted at Baptist Memorial Hospital. He never came here, even though he should have'" (p. 127). She explains that Presley's death was treated as natural when it should have been handled by the medical examiner as an accident.

When they visit Graceland, Scarpetta notes that Marino regards it with awe, as if it were Buckingham Palace (p. 136).

Elvis Presley, "the king of rock and roll," born in Tupelo, Mississippi, in 1935, died at his Graceland mansion on August 16, 1977, only forty-two years old, of cardiac arrhythmia, reportedly brought on by overuse of prescription drugs.

PUFF DADDY (P. DIDDY) (*Southern Cross*) Sean Combs's personal life and the subjects of his rap music have borne eerie similarities. Born in Harlem, New York, in 1969, he had his first encounter with violent crime when his father was murdered in 1971. As a teenager, he found work as an intern with an entertainment group and soon learned enough to start his own company, which he called Bad Boy Entertainment, in 1993. He worked with some of the biggest names in the rap and pop industry. Trouble came with rivalry from another company and the murders of rappers Tupac Shakur and The Notorious B.I.G. Combs persevered and found success with several solo records. He made headlines because of his relationship with actress and singer Jennifer Lopez. More press followed when he faced charges of assaulting another record industry competitor. He and Lopez broke up after they were linked to a shooting in New York. His career continued with more music and bits in motion pictures, and the introduction of his own clothing line, fragrance line, and New York restaurant.

DAN RATHER (*The Body Farm*) While investigating the case of a young murdered girl, Scarpetta meets an old acquaintance who works in a government office. The woman says she has been following news about the investigation. "'Even Dan Rather was talking about the Steiner girl's case the other night'" (p. 157).

Dan Rather has been anchor and managing editor of the *CBS Evening News* since March 1981. He has also worked on that network's *48 Hours* and *60 Minutes* programs. Born in Wharton, Texas, on October 31, 1931, he began a journalism career in 1950. He still writes a weekly newspaper column and has authored several books.

KEITH RICHARDS (*Hornet's Nest*) An iconic guitarist, singer, and songwriter and a member of the Rolling Stones, Keith Richards was an only child, born in England on December 18, 1943. While still in Wentworth Primary School, he met and befriended a youngster named Mick Jagger. After performing with another group, Richards joined his old schoolmate with the Stones in 1962, and the rest is history.

LENI RIEFENSTAHL (*The Last Precinct*) Temporarily staying with her female psychiatrist friend, Scarpetta contemplates the woman, who had immigrated to the U.S. after World War II. "Anna takes the chair across from me, elbows on the table, leaning into our conversation. She is an amazingly intense, fit woman, tall and firm, a Leni Riefenstahl enlightened beyond her time and undaunted by the years" (p. 32).

Leni Riefenstahl gained international notoriety for her production of two propaganda films for Nazi Germany glorifying Aryan youth and Nazi ideology: a rousing record of Hitler's Nuremberg rallies in *Triumph of the Will* (1934) and a tribute to the 1936 Berlin Olympics in *Olympia* (1938). As an actress, she starred in several German films before developing her own motion picture company. It was widely believed, despite her denials, that she was also Hitler's mistress. After release from imprisonment by the American army, she began a successful career as a still photographer. Riefenstahl died in September 2003 at age 101.

RICKY RUDD (*Isle of Dogs*) Ricky Rudd, born in 1956, has collected twenty-three Winston Cup victories.

GEORGE BEVERLY SHEA (*Hornet's Nest*) Renowned as one of America's top gospel singers for sixty years, George Beverly Shea is Canadian by birth. The son of a Methodist minister, he was born in Winchester, Ontario, on February 1, 1909. He joined evangelist Billy Graham in 1943 and earned international fame for his beautiful delivery of religious hymns, scores of them recorded on albums and compact discs. He has been the recipient of multiple Grammy nominations and won the award in 1965.

O. J. SIMPSON (*Point of Origin, Black Notice, The Last Precinct*) Orenthal James Simpson—college football Heisman Trophy winner, spectacular professional running back in the NFL, film star, and television commercial pitchman—was acquitted of killing his wife and her friend in the "trial of the century." He is mentioned in three of Cornwell's books. In *Point of Origin,* some events are similar to the killing of Simpson's wife. Marino brings up the comparison. "'Sounds like O.J. again, you ask me. Rich, powerful black guy. His white former girlfriend gets her throat slashed. Don't the parallels bother you just a little bit?'" (p. 212).

In *Black Notice,* Scarpetta takes extra precautions with a case. "I never left an investigator alone with an unexamined body, certainly not since the badly botched O. J. Simpson trial, when it became the vogue for everyone except the defendant to be impeached in court" (pp. 86–87).

A prosecutor from New York also mentions the case in *The Last Precinct*. "'We have a mountain of evidence, but then so did the prosecution in the O.J. case'" (p. 312).

MIKE SKINNER (*Isle of Dogs*) Mike Skinner had a late start in NASCAR and was the 1997 Winston Cup Rookie of the Year.

MARTHA STEWART (*Unnatural Exposure*) Depressed, Scarpetta tries to forget her problems by concentrating on a television program. "I watched the *Today* show, which I ordinarily never got to do. Martha Stewart was whipping up something with meringue while I picked at a soft-boiled egg. . . . I could not eat" (p. 207).

Martha Stewart, the expert on gracious living and homemaking, earned her fortune when a catering business expanded to books, magazines, and television shows. Admired, imitated, and parodied, she was already a household name when Scarpetta watched her on the *Today* show. Stewart faced serious problems starting in 2002, five years after *Unnatural Exposure* was published. An insider stock trading scandal resulted in a trial and a criminal conviction in 2004. She relinquished her position as CEO of her company, but continued in a consulting capacity.

RANDY TRAVIS (*Hornet's Nest*) Randy Bruce Traywick, a North Carolina native born in 1959, had early encouragement in his musical education from his father, a devoted fan of country music. Randy and one brother soon learned to play the guitar, while a third sibling strummed the bass. They appeared at local clubs. Randy's distinctive voice gained attention in Nashville. A record producer noticed him in 1985 and changed his name to Travis. Randy's music started selling well and garnered awards. By the early nineties, several of his records had reached number one on country charts. In 2003 he registered another top hit with "Three Wooden Crosses."

RUSTY WALLACE (*Isle of Dogs*) Rusty Wallace, one of three brothers driving race cars, born in 1956, has taken 54 Winston Cup victories. Over a period of sixteen years he never suffered a shutout from the win column until 2002.

ROBIN WILLIAMS (*Cause of Death*) Arriving at her home, Scarpetta is surprised to find her niece, Lucy, there. "She was . . . stretched out on the couch in the gathering room. The fire was on, and she had a blanket over her legs, and on TV, Robin Williams was hilarious at the Met" (p. 170).

One of the funniest men alive, as well as a fine dramatic actor, Robin Williams was born in Chicago, Illinois, on July 21, 1952. Known for wild improvisation, he has made several dozen movies, won an Academy Award, entertained extensively on television, and made numerous live appearances, including a side-splitting performance at New York's Metropolitan Opera house. For the audio recording of this comedy performance, "A Night at the Met," which Lucy was watching, he won a Grammy Award.

THOMAS WOLFE/BILLY GRAHAM (*The Body Farm*) A murder investigation takes Scarpetta to western North Carolina. She observes, "Notorious criminals and their crimes had never been a concern in this picturesque part of the world known for Thomas Wolfe and Billy Graham" (p. 3).

American novelist Thomas Clayton Wolfe (1900–1938), from Asheville, North Carolina (where his home is open to tourists), is one of the most respected American authors. His best-known works, *Look Homeward, Angel* and *You Can't Go Home Again,* are literary classics. He died of tuberculosis not long before his thirty-eighth birthday.

The world-renowned evangelist Billy Graham was born on November 7, 1918, and spent much of his youth on a dairy farm outside Charlotte, North Carolina. He married Ruth McCue Bell in 1943. (See *Ruth, A Portrait: The Story of Ruth Bell Graham.*)

BOB WOODWARD (*All That Remains*) A reporter and friend of Scarpetta has been reassigned to more menial work at the *Washington Post.* Scarpetta wonders why. The woman answers, "'I'm not Bob Woodward'" (p. 124).

Bob Woodward, paired with Carl Bernstein at the *Post,* broke the news of the Watergate scandal with government-shaking investigative journalism. They wrote the bestselling book *All the President's Men* about their work that culminated in toppling Richard Nixon's presidency. The book was made into a 1976 motion picture starring Robert Redford as Woodward and Dustin Hoffman as Bernstein. (Woodward continues to write bestselling nonfiction, including *Bush at War* and *Plan of Attack.*)

WU-TANG CLAN (*Southern Cross*) The Wu-Tang Clan is one of the great rap groups. Their 1993 debut album, *Enter the Wu-Tang (36 Chambers),* went platinum, and the group's founding members, among them Ol' Dirty Bastard and Method Man, have been influential in the development of the art form. Heavily influenced by Asian martial arts and Islam, they used their interests to bring a whole new rhythm to the art of rhyming.

FINE THINGS

SCARPETTA not only occupies elegant homes in the finest sections of Richmond and drives a black Mercedes-Benz, but she also demonstrates superior taste in art, furnishings, fine wine and liquor. Perhaps this reflects the tastes of her creator, Patricia Cornwell.

Here are a few of the premium objects Scarpetta uses and observes:

BIEDERMEIER (*The Last Precinct*) While a guest in the home of a friend, Scarpetta admires the furniture. "The guest room where I am to stay . . . is dominated by a large yew wood bed that, like much of the furniture in her house, is pale gold Biedermeier" (p. 41).

Biedermeier furniture was manufactured in Austria between 1815 and 1848 and exhibits a clean, elegant design that can still look modern even today.

BREITLING AEROSPACE (*Point of Origin*) Benton Wesley is dressing as Scarpetta looks on. "The stainless steel Breitling Aerospace watch I had given to him for Christmas was on the table. He picked it up and snapped it on" (p. 2).

Breitling is an expensive wristwatch made by a Swiss company in

France. The firm started production in 1884. Popular among pilots, this watch has reportedly been seen on the wrists of astronaut Scott Carpenter as well as celebrities Jerry Seinfeld, Mel Gibson, and Bruce Willis.

CHIPPENDALE (*Body of Evidence*) A wealthy murder victim's home and furniture impress Scarpetta while she visits his family. "I was fairly certain the sofa was a Chippendale, and I had never touched, much less sat on, a genuine Chippendale anything before" (p. 150).

Named for English cabinetmaker Thomas Chippendale (1718–1779), Chippendale furniture is among the most prized of all antique pieces, and its decorative elements are still widely used and copied today in expensive reproductions as well as more mass-produced furniture. The gracefully carved wooden chairs with ball-and-claw feet typical of Chippendale's masterpieces are true classics. Scarpetta didn't offer much detail about the sofa, but if it still had its original upholstery, it was probably covered in a rich patterned silk or brocade, in cream or brown colors, perhaps a delicate blue-green. Or, in very rare cases, it might have been upholstered in tapestry cloth.

GREGG CARBO PRINTS (*All That Remains*) Scarpetta stands at the open door of a reporter's home and notices the decorations. "Through her open doorway I could see arctic white furniture, pastel throw pillows, and abstract monotype Gregg Carbo prints" (p. 113).

Gregg Carbo is a Richmond artist trained at Virginia Commonwealth University; he is now associated with the faculty there. His works have been exhibited around the city and have been recognized by the Virginia Commission for the Arts.

MONT BLANC PENS (*Body of Evidence, The Body Farm*) Men who impress Scarpetta use Mont Blanc pens on at least three occasions in the series.

Mont Blanc fountain pens got their start in Europe in 1906. Known the world over for their distinctive black-and-gold styling, the expensive pens can be recognized by the unique white star that straddles the top of the pen. It allegedly represents the snowcapped peak of the French mountain for which the pens are named.

ORIENTAL RUGS (*nine books in the Scarpetta series*) Scarpetta seems obsessed with Oriental or Middle Eastern–made rugs, which are mentioned at least twenty times in nine books. She's extraordinarily observant in noticing every detail of the carpets. The first rug pops up in *Postmortem*: "The polished hardwood floor was almost completely covered with a dhurrie rug of pale blue and green geometrical designs against a field of white" (p. 214). A dhurrie rug is a fringed, usually rectangular, cotton rug manufactured in India.

Other references include the following: "an Indian rug dominated by designs in rose and deep plum" (p. 31, *All That Remains*). "Covering the hardwood floor was an Iranian Dergezine rug with a brightly colored floral design that turned the entire room into a garden" (p. 304, *All That Remains*). "[A] large vibrant Persian rug that I suspected cost more than the house I had just visited on the other side of the river" (p. 168, *Cruel & Unusual*). "A small Bakhara rug was in the middle of the parquet floor" (p. 222, *Cruel & Unusual*). "I had hidden the tile floor with a Sarouk prayer rug that was machine-made but bright" (p. 135, *Cause of Death*). She finally deviates in *The Last Precinct*: "Just off the entry hall . . . are two rather stiff parlors of Brussels carpet" (p. 223).

Dergezine refers to an Iranian-made carpet, Bakhara to a Pakistani product, and Sarouk to a tightly woven Iranian rug with soft colors and usually a central design element.

VALOY EATON (*The Body Farm*) Admiring artwork on the walls of Benton Wesley's office, Scarpetta says, "My favorite was an expansive landscape by Valoy Eaton, who I believed was as good as Remington and one day would cost as much. I had several Eaton oil paintings in my home, and what was odd was that Wesley and I had discovered the Utahan artist independent of each other" (p. 142).

Valoy Eaton, a native of Vernal, Utah, born in 1938, paints in oil and watercolor, turning out realistic landscapes with wide vistas and picturing people involved in everyday activities. Frederic Remington (1861–1909), a painter and sculptor, created vividly realistic action scenes of the American West.

Wine and Liquor

BARBANCOURT RHUM This rum is made in Haiti from fermented sugar-cane juice rather than cane molasses. Scarpetta spots a bottle while visiting Key West in *Body of Evidence*.

BLACK BUSH This seems to be her favorite Irish whiskey. Black Bush is a rich, dark blend from the world's oldest licensed distillery, Old Bushmills in County Antrim, Ireland. It is composed entirely of single malt whiskey, making it a regular selection for aficionados. When Benton Wesley is going to grocery shop for their vacation in *Point of Origin,* Scarpetta instructs, "'Make sure there's plenty of Black Bush and Scotch'" (p. 12). In *Unnatural Exposure,* he shows up with a bottle of it in his hand.

BOOKER'S BOURBON This bourbon is from Kentucky, and advertised to be the only bourbon bottled straight from the barrel, uncut and unfiltered. In *Black Notice,* Scarpetta pours a glass of Booker's for her niece.

CHIVAS REGAL This is a popular upscale Scotch whiskey. James Chivas and his brothers began blending it in Scotland about 1857. Scarpetta is flying to New York in *Body of Evidence:* "For the next hour I sipped Chivas on the rocks" (p. 89).

DEWAR'S This high-grade Scotch whiskey has been blended in Aberfeldy, Scotland, since 1886. At a restaurant in *Cruel & Unusual,* a waiter appears to take drink orders. "'Dewar's and soda,'" Scarpetta says (p. 139).

GLENFIDDICH This is a highly regarded Scotch single malt whiskey. In *Body of Evidence,* Scarpetta offers a drink to her male guest: "Retrieving the Glenfiddich from the bar, I automatically fixed his drink exactly as I had so long ago. . . ." (p. 32).

GLENMORANGIE This single malt whiskey comes from Scotland, distilled by the shores of the Dornoch Firth. The company also produces a rich sherry. As a guest in a friend's home, in *The Last Precinct,* Scarpetta notes, "She has thoughtfully left on a light . . . near a crystal tumbler and the bottle of Glenmorangie, just in case I needed a sedative" (p. 365).

GREY GOOSE This vodka is made in Cognac, France, by an American company. Lucy chides Marino in *The Last Precinct* for using moonshine in the Bloody Mary he prepares in Scarpetta's presence. "'Gag,'" she says. "'At least use Grey Goose'" (p. 384).

HOOPER'S HOOCH This malt-based beverage contains real fruit juice, lemonade in this case. In *Unnatural Exposure,* Scarpetta recalls, "We walked hand in hand and bought bottles of Hooper's Hooch because one could drink alcoholic lemonade on the streets of England" (p. 367).

WILD TURKEY This potent bourbon is distilled in Kentucky. It is mentioned in a conversation between Scarpetta and Marino in *Black Notice.*

In the first chapter of Cornwell's novelette, *Scarpetta's Winter Table,* Kay cooks Christmas dinner for Lucy and Marino. Lucy remembers the first time Marino made eggnog for them, made with Wild Turkey and eggnog laced with 100-proof Virginia Lightning corn liquor.

A variety of wines please Scarpetta's palate as well:

CAKEBREAD CHARDONNAY This white wine comes from Cakebread Cellars, Napa Valley, California. It is made from the vinifera grape, which is one of the few grapes in the world that does not require blending. Wesley brings Scarpetta a bottle in *Unnatural Exposure.*

CHABLIS Chablis is a white wine. The first mention of Scarpetta's drinking comes in Chapter 1 of *Postmortem* when she arrives home and states, "I went to the refrigerator and poured myself a glass of Chalis. . . . I shut my eyes for a moment and sipped" (p. 32).

CHAMBERTIN GRAND CRU This red wine comes from Côte de Nuits in France. In *The Last Precinct,* being served dinner in a friend's home, Scarpetta observes, "McGovern uncorks a Chambertin Grand Cru red burgundy while Anna sets the table" (p. 383).

CÔTE RÔTIE This red wine is made in France's Rhone Valley. While cooking in *Cause of Death,* Scarpetta says, "I turned the oven on low and opened a bottle of Côte Rôtie, which was for the cook to sip as she began her serious work. I would serve a Chianti with the meal" (p. 54).

MAD DOG WINE Scarpetta didn't drink any of this potent (18 percent alcohol) inexpensive red grape wine bottled in New York. The Mad Dog 20/20 label has been dropped in favor of MD 20/20. It is mentioned in *Postmortem.*

FINE THINGS 211

MASSOLINO BAROLO This "big, bold" red wine is from the Vigna Rionda vineyard in northern Italy. In *The Last Precinct*, Scarpetta watches videotape of a killer being questioned about meeting his victim in an expensive restaurant while consuming a meal. He mentions ordering a bottle of Massolino Barolo. Scarpetta notes that it is her favorite Italian wine.

OPUS ONE This wine comes from a Napa, California, vintner. In *The Body Farm*, Scarpetta is in a restaurant with Benton Wesley, who suggests they have a bottle of Opus One with dinner.

More references to wine include these: In *The Last Precinct* Scarpetta tells of visiting France with Benton: "[W]e toured the Grands Vins de Bourgogne and Dugat, and tasted from casks of Chambertin, Montrachet, Musigny and Vosne-Romanée" (p. 62). In *Unnatural Exposure,* she tells of her tastes: "I like pinot noir because it's light. Not heavy like a merlot" (p. 115).

Scarpetta's taste also extends to fine champagne. In *Cause of Death* she notes, "I was interested in a single bottle of Louis Roederer Cristal Champagne" (p. 97). She also likes Veuve Cliquot, a French product sometimes called "La Grande Dame de la Champagne."

Scarpetta is not above quaffing a beer now and then. In *Point of Origin*, she selects Samuel Adams, a fine beer from the Boston Beer Company. In *Cruel & Unusual,* she picks a brand brewed in Mexico. Dos Equis, paradoxically, was started by a German immigrant in 1897, who called it "Siglo XX," meaning the twentieth century, signifying the approaching millennium. It was later changed to Dos Equis, meaning two Xs. Lucy also enjoys a cool one. In *Cause of Death,* she sits at a counter sipping Peroni, a top-selling lager popular in Italy for more than 150 years.

COP CODES:
TEN-CODES COMMONLY USED
BY PUBLIC SAFETY OFFICERS

PATRICIA Cornwell's books are filled with authentic vernacular. As a consequence, some of the police "ten-codes," the official shorthand for radio communication describing common situations in which law enforcement officers find themselves, appear at various points in the books. The following list is not exhaustive, nor is it universal. Local variations in coding are common, but this covers the codes that appear in the books of Patricia Cornwell.

10-1	Unable to copy, change location
10-2	Receiving well or signal good
10-3	Stop transmitting
10-4	Okay, message received
10-5	Relay message
10-6	Busy—stand by, unless urgent
10-7	Out of service, leaving air
10-8	In service, subject to call
10-9	Repeat message

10-10	Fight in progress, or, in some locations, negative
10-11	Animal problem
10-12	Stand by
10-13	Weather or road report
10-14	Prowler report
10-15	Civil disturbance
10-16	Domestic disturbance
10-17	Meet complainant
10-18	As soon as possible
10-19	Return to
10-20	What is your location?
10-21	Call by telephone
10-22	Disregard
10-23	Arrived at scene
10-24	Assignment completed
10-25	Report or meet the person
10-26	Detaining subject
10-27	Driver's license information/Vehicle registration information
10-28	Identify your station
10-29	Check—is subject a wanted person?
10-30	Unnecessary use of radio
10-31	Crime in progress
10-32	Person with gun
10-33	Emergency
10-34	Riot
10-35	Major crime alert/Backup needed
10-36	Correct time
10-37	Investigate suspicious vehicle
10-38	Stop suspicious vehicle
10-39	Urgent—use lights and siren

10-40	Silent run—no lights or siren
10-41	Beginning tour of duty
10-42	Ending tour of duty
10-43	Information
10-44	Permission to leave for (insert reason here)
10-45	Animal carcass/dead animal
10-46	Assist motorist
10-47	Emergency road repairs
10-48	Traffic signal repair
10-49	Traffic signal out of service
10-50	Accident (fatal, personal injury, property damage)
10-51	Tow truck required
10-52	Ambulance needed
10-53	Road blocked at (insert location here)
10-54	Animal(s) on highway
10-55	Suspected DUI
10-56	Intoxicated pedestrian
10-57	Hit and run (fatal, personal injury, property damage)
10-58	Direct traffic
10-59	Convoy or escort
10-60	Squad in vicinity
10-61	Isolate self for message
10-62	Reply to message
10-63	Prepare to make written copy
10-64	Message for local delivery
10-65	Net message assignment
10-66	Message cancellation
10-67	All units comply
10-68	Dispatch information
10-69	Message received

10-70   Fire

10-71   Advise nature of fire

10-72   Report progress of fire

10-73   Smoke report

10-74   Negative

10-75   In contact with (insert name here)

10-76   En route

10-77   Estimated time of arrival (ETA)

10-78   Need assistance

10-79   Notify coroner

10-80   Chase in progress

10-81   Breathalyzer

10-82   Reserve lodging

10-83   Work school crossing at (insert location here)

10-84   If meeting _____, advise

10-85   Delayed due to (insert explanation here)

10-86   Officer/operator on duty

10-87   Pick up/distribute

10-88   Present telephone number of (insert name here)

10-89   Bomb threat

10-90   Bank alarm

10-91   Pick up prisoner/subject

10-92   Improperly parked vehicle

10-93   Blockage

10-94   Drag racing

10-95   Prisoner/subject in custody

10-96   Mental subject

10-97   Check or test signal

10-98   Meet at (insert location here)

10-99   Wanted/stolen or Officer needs help

PATRICIA CORNWELL
AND JACK THE RIPPER

SPECULATION about Jack the Ripper's identity has occupied authors, crime buffs, and armchair sleuths for more than 115 years. The elusive serial killer began murdering London prostitutes in August 1888. His violent use of a razor-sharp weapon to slash and eviscerate his victims spread a pall of fear in the slums of Whitechapel, a section of England's capital city, and led to sensational press coverage at the time.

No one knows for certain how many women he killed. Most literature on the subject names five dissolute, aging, indigent hookers: Mary Ann Nichols, Annie Chapman, Elizabeth Stride, Catherine Eddows, and Mary Jane Kelly. Just as the actual number of victims murdered by Ted Bundy may never be known, Jack the Ripper's full tally may also remain uncertain. If this notorious killer had been caught, the story might have faded into obscurity, but the failure of investigators to locate or arrest any suspects has immortalized the crimes. Over the decades, writers have suggested the Ripper might have been someone with medical training, a barrister who committed suicide, an insane Polish Jew, or even a member of Queen Victoria's family.

Patricia Cornwell has entered the arena by gathering a great deal of circumstantial and forensic evidence, and concluded that Jack the Ripper was famed artist Walter Richard Sickert. Born in Germany in 1860, when America's Civil War started, he lived until 1942 when his adopted country, England, was in the midst of World War II. Cornwell has researched the case diligently, examined historic documents, conducted interviews, traveled widely, purchased items for evidentiary use, and even paid for expensive scientific tests and experiments.

In *Portrait of a Killer: Jack the Ripper—Case Closed,* Cornwell doesn't keep the reader waiting long for her solution. She solves the mystery on page two! This is an interesting reversal of the usual sequence in which authors first hook the reader with clues, plant a few red herrings, and rely on tension to maintain growing interest before finally revealing the killer's identity. Cornwell names the man she believes is Jack the Ripper, then offers supporting evidence in a matrix of history, sociology, and forensic procedures.

Her arguments are often persuasive, especially in view of the mountainous obstacles she faced. It is not easy to accurately reconstruct events distorted and faded by the passage of more than a century. Yet her research is impressive. Much of Cornwell's examination focuses on the 211 letters purportedly written by Jack the Ripper to newspapers and police organizations. She commissioned scientific tests on several, and offers the results as evidence that some were indeed written by Sickert.

As might be expected, skeptics of Cornwell's conclusions express concern with "shaky evidence," "too many assumptions," and "inconclusive, circumstantial evidence." To Cornwell's credit, she acknowledges that modern defense attorneys in a court of law could probably undermine the evidence she offers. This happens even when prosecutors present a powerful case against defendants who are guilty.

Readers can be even more incredulous than lawyers. Some of them may base their skepticism on the author's frequent use of speculative language such as "it is possible," "could be," "I suspect," "I don't know," "may have," "might have," "perhaps," and other similarly equivocal expressions.

All nonfiction writers wrestle with this problem. None of them can possibly know every precise detail of a crime nor every fact about the criminals they portray. It is a necessary part of the process to offer educated guesses about certain elements. As long as the majority of facts presented are supported by documented resources such as court records, police reports, and interviews, connective interpretation is understandable. Cornwell has obviously conducted comprehensive probing for material she has discovered, and is candidly honest about inevitable gaps.

One aspect of the book that will delight her fans is her revelation of a few personal matters about her own life and thoughts as she first learns details about the Ripper and as she conducts her intensive research.

Cornwell makes numerous references to famous artists, actors, writers, or other personalities who were Walter Sickert's contemporaries and, in some cases, his friends. Readers will recognize many of the names, but not all of them. Thirteen are listed in one sentence, tied to Cornwell's comment that "Sickert . . . was a star stalker. He somehow managed to hobnob with the major celebrities of the day" (p. 3).

To amplify a bit on Sickert's contemporaries and the names from history, here are brief reminders:

AUBREY BEARDSLEY An illustrator and art editor for several magazines and books, Beardsley is known for something that might have appealed strongly to Sickert: a tendency to the grotesque and erotic. They couldn't have known each other very long, since Beardsley died in 1898 at age twenty-five.

SIR HENRY MAXIMILIAN BEERBOHM Critic and caricaturist whose work appeared in numerous periodicals and books. Cornwell gives no detail regarding the timing or nature of contact between the two men. Born in 1872, Beerbohm was twelve years younger than Sickert, so their paths would have crossed well after the spate of Whitechapel murders. Beerbohm died in 1956.

CLIVE BELL Cornwell notes that "Victorian writer and critic Clive Bell's relationship with Sickert was one of mutual love-hate" even though Bell characterized Sickert as "the greatest British painter since Constable" (pp. 314–315). Born in 1881, Bell authored several books about artists. He died in 1964.

John Constable (1776–1837) is regarded as one of the finest English painters of landscapes and rural life.

JACQUES-ÉMILE BLANCHE French artist specializing in portraits. Among his many works were portraits of Beardsley and Proust. Cornwell, commenting on Sickert's skill at disguises, notes that his friend Blanche wrote of Sickert's "'genius for camouflage in dress, in the fashion of wearing his hair, and in his manner of speaking'" (p. 4). Blanche was one year younger than Sickert, and died the same year, 1942.

JEAN-BAPTISTE-CAMILLE COROT (1796–1875) Mentioned only in the suggestion by Cornwell that Sickert would probably have paid a shilling "for a peek at the masterpieces of Corot, Diaz, and Rousseau in the high priced galleries" (p. 15). French painter Corot preceded and inspired later Impressionists.

EDGAR DEGAS (1834–1917) French Impressionist best known for his paintings of ballet dancers and the sculpture of a young ballerina. Cornwell notes that Sickert was a "disciple" of Degas.

NARCISSE-VIRGILE DIAZ DE LA PEÑA (1808–1876) was a French landscape painter who specialized in scenes of Fontainebleau forests.

ÉDOUARD-ÉMILE-LOUIS DUJARDIN (1861–1949) A contemporary of Sickert, Dujardin was a French journalist and author.

ANDRÉ DUNOYER DE SEGONZAC (1884–1974) Establishing that Sickert lived in close proximity to the London murders, Cornwell cites certain correspondence: "In a letter from Paris, November 16, 1968, André Dunoyer de Segonzac, a well-known artist . . . wrote . . . that he had known Walter Sickert around 1930 and had very clear memories of Sickert claiming to have 'lived' in Whitechapel in the same house where Jack the Ripper had lived, and that Sickert had told him 'spiritedly about the discreet and edifying life of this monstrous assassin'" (p. 56).

Dunoyer de Segonzac, a French painter and engraver, was known for realistic landscapes, figure paintings, and portraits.

HENRY FIELDING (1707–1754) Offering historic background of criminality in England and efforts to control it, Cornwell writes, "It wasn't until 1750 that times began to change. Henry Fielding, better known as an author than a magistrate, gathered a faithful group of constables under his command" (p. 92).

Novelist and playwright Fielding became a justice of the peace for Westminster and Middlesex in 1748

ANDRÉ-PAUL-GUILLAUME GIDE (1869–1951) French author of books, satires, and fables.

EDWARD WILLIAM GODWIN (1833–1886) Sickert had apprenticed with artist James Whistler before they had a falling out. In describing reasons for Sickert's angst, Cornwell writes, "Sickert's feelings could only have been inflamed by Whistler's marrying the widow of architect and archaeologist Edward Godwin, the man who had lived with actress Ellen Terry and fathered her children" (p. 6). Godwin is noted for his design of several notable buildings throughout the United Kingdom and Ireland. He also designed a residence for Whistler. Other artistic endeavors included furniture and theatrical sets, which would have caught the attention of Sickert, who started as an actor and later spent a great deal of time attending theater performances. As a companion to actress Ellen Terry, Godwin fathered her son, Edward Gordon Craig, who became a noted actor.

WILLIAM HOGARTH (1697–1764) Sickert, said Cornwell, "[o]ccasionally . . . posed himself on the bed with a wooden lay figure—mannikin— that supposedly had belonged to one of [his] artistic idols, William Hogarth" (p. 76). A lay-figure mannikin is a jointed wooden figure of the human body used by artists in the absence of a live model. Hogarth, an English painter and engraver, is remembered not only for his remarkable oil masterpieces but also his book illustration plates, portraits, and prints.

SIR HENRY IRVING (1838–1905) Cornwell wrote, "The sensuously beautiful Ellen Terry was one of the most famous actresses of the Victorian era, and Sickert was fixated on her. As a teenager he had stalked her and her acting partner, Henry Irving" (p. 6). This noted English actor was the first theater figure ever to be knighted. He was seen in a number of Shakespearean productions with Ellen Terry and gained even more fame when he toured America. Irving is among the immortals buried in Westminster Abbey.

CLAUDE MONET (1840–1926) Among the most renowned of French Impressionist painters, Monet was a master at rendering light and color.

Nearly blind at the end of his career, he still turned out magnificent works. He is particularly noted for giant paintings of water lilies and the Japanese bridge over a pond at his country home near Giverny.

CAMILLE PISSARRO (1830–1903) One of the early pioneers of French Impressionism, he experimented also with pointillism (made famous by Georges Seurat). A prolific artist, he painted more than 1,600 landscapes and scenes of urban life in addition to portraits.

MARCEL PROUST (1871–1922) French novelist. Cornwell's psychological analysis of Sickert follows in the pioneering steps of Proust, who introduced study of the human mind into fiction writing. Proust was eleven years younger than Sickert, so any interaction between the two men would probably have been near the turn of the century.

PIERRE-AUGUSTE RENOIR (1841–1919) A favorite among fans of French Impressionist art, Renoir is revered for his use of rosy colors, particularly in portraits. His still-life paintings of flowers and scenes of people relaxing resonate with vibrant hues.

AUGUSTE RODIN (1840–1917) Prolific French sculptor whose bronze figures have been collected by museums across the world. The most famous is a sitting figure with a hand under the chin, known as *The Thinker*.

HENRI ROUSSEAU (1844–1910), also French, painted Impressionistic, primitive scenes of tropical jungles and animals.

PHILIP WILSON STEER (1860–1942) Again substantiating allegations that Sickert liked to disguise himself, Cornwell states, "In a portrait Wilson Steer painted of Sickert in 1890, Sickert sports a phony-looking mustache that resembles a squirrel's tail pasted above his mouth" (p. 4). Steer, an English painter who generally produced Impressionistic-style portraits, landscapes, and nudes, was born and died in exactly the same years as Sickert.

DAME ALICE ELLEN TERRY (1847–1928) Well-known actress in the Victorian era. Married to George F. Watts from 1864 to 1877, she was later companion to Edward Godwin and had a son by him. A few years after his death in 1886, she was involved, mostly by correspondence, with famed playwright George Bernard Shaw. At the beginning of the twentieth century, she traveled worldwide on Shakespearean lecture tours. Cornwell, placing Sickert in locations from which "Ripper" letters may have originated, such as Regent Street, wrote, "Regent Street . . . would have been familiar to Walter Sickert. In 1881, he tagged along with Ellen Terry as she hit the shops of Regent Street in search of gowns for her role as Ophelia at the Lyceum" (p. 63).

JAMES ABBOTT MCNEILL WHISTLER (1834–1903) Known to many for the painting titled *Arrangement in Black and Gray: The Artist's Mother* (not *Whistler's Mother* as is commonly believed), this American-born artist studied painting in Paris before moving to London. He is mentioned several times as an influence on Walter Sickert. "[Sickert] was a painter, an etcher, a student of James McNeill Whistler" (p. 2). The famous artist had "persuaded Sickert to stop wasting his time with art school and come to work in a real studio with him" (p. 312). Cornwell attributes part of Sickert's personality problems to treatment by Whistler. "Whistler had fallen deeply in love with the 'remarkably pretty' Beatrice Godwin" (p. 4). When Whistler married the widow of William Edward Godwin, his former apprentice, Sickert, wasn't invited to the wedding. "By the time of Whistler's engagement their friendship had cooled" (pp. 4–5). Later, when Sickert began writing "Ripper" letters, he often used the words "Ha ha." Cornwell notes, "The . . . much used 'ha ha's' were favorites of . . . James McNeill Whistler . . . [his cackle] was often described as a much dreaded laugh that grated against the ear of the English" (p. 53).

OSCAR WILDE (1854–1900) Author of *The Picture of Dorian Gray*, which was made into a 1945 motion picture, Wilde was married and the father of two sons when he was convicted of sodomy and spent two years in prison (1895–1897), after which he lived in Paris under a different name.

In this detailed study of Jack the Ripper, Patricia Cornwell has found most of the pieces of a gigantic picture puzzle and meticulously put them together. In the blank spaces, she has sketched credible entries to complete a compelling portrait of one of the world's most enduring serial killers.

PART FOUR

FINAL INVENTORY

PEOPLE

Patricia Cornwell has created nearly six hundred characters in her novels to date. The most frequently used names are Wilson (five), Jones (four), Jackson (three), Davis (three), and ten names beginning with "Mc." There are two Popeyes and two Bubbas. The four different Jones characters appear in four different novels.

AARON The ever-present, graceful butler at the governor's mansion, in *The Last Precinct*.

ABLE, OCTAVIUS A deputy who searches Judy Hammer and Virginia West before they enter the courtroom, in *Hornet's Nest*.

ABRAMS, RON An officer at the Texas prison that houses Jean-Baptiste Chandonne, in *Blow Fly*. He is killed by Jean-Baptiste during his escape.

ADAMS, JEAN The office administrator, in *Black Notice*.

AIMS, FRANK ETHAN (AKA "FRANKIE") Friend and fellow psychiatric inmate of Al Hunt, and an airport worker, in *Body of Evidence*.

ALBRIGHT, DICK NationsBank president and a city leader invited to the Commonwealth Club, in *Southern Cross.*

AMBURGEY, DR. ALVIN Commissioner, in *Postmortem.*

ANDERSON, DETECTIVE RENE A new detective and a friend of the new deputy chief of police, Diane Bray, in *Black Notice.* She is at the scene where a body is found in a cargo container.

ANDERSON, DR. A new female forensic pathologist that Scarpetta has hired, in *From Potter's Field.*

ANDREWS, MR. An alias for Benton Wesley while he is in Louisiana, in *Blow Fly.*

ANN A former policewoman who owns a bar called Rubyfruit on Hudson that Lucy likes to go to in New York, in *Black Notice.*

APOLLONIA A black woman that Carrie picks up and parties with, an activity associated with their use of cocaine, in *From Potter's Field.*

ARANOFF, BARRY His license plates are stolen and placed on the car that follows Scarpetta and Abby Turnbull, in *All That Remains.*

ARMANDO First husband of Scarpetta's sister, Dorothy. She married Armando when she was eighteen, in *Postmortem.*

AXEL, TOMMY The music critic for the *Charlotte Observer,* as well as the not-so-secret admirer of Andy Brazil, in *Hornet's Nest.*

BAIRD, OFFICER T. C. A local officer who gives a ride to Scarpetta and Marino, in *The Body Farm.*

BARBOSA, MITCH A murder victim and undercover FBI agent, who had gone jogging near William & Mary College, in *The Last Precinct.*

BARNES, JIM Former therapist of Al Hunt and Frank Aims, in *Body of Evidence.*

BASS, DR. BILL A forensic anthropologist and mentor of Dr. Canter, in *Unnatural Exposure.*

BATES, ALICE A crime-scene technician, in *Southern Cross.*

BEAN, LINTON A burglary detective with the Richmond Police Department, in *Southern Cross.*

BEAST An inmate on death row in the Texas penitentiary, in *Blow Fly.* He is an acquaintance of Jean-Baptiste and wants him to help him escape before Beast is put to death.

BEATRICE A cleaning lady at the OCME, in *Black Notice.*

BECKER A police officer who helps Marino interview Petersen, in *Postmortem.*

BEEPER An elementary school student who is involved in crime, in *Southern Cross.*

BEGLEY, JUDGE He orders the exhumation of Emily Steiner, in *The Body Farm.*

BENEDETTI, TONY Kay Scarpetta's ex-husband, in *All That Remains* and *Point of Origin.*

BENELLI, FRANK An alias used by the killer Gault, in *From Potter's Field.*

BENNETT A pathologist at the OCME, in *Black Notice.*

BENNETT, JAY A dentist in Seattle who tells Scarpetta about gold foil restoration, in *From Potter's Field.*

BENNY A homeless crack addict who has some of the clothing associated with the murder in Central Park, in *From Potter's Field.*

BERGER, JAIME Head of the sex crimes division of the Manhattan district attorney's office, in *The Last Precinct.* She eventually quits that job and practices law. Berger is also a close personal friend, as well as legal consultant, of Lucy in *Blow Fly*. Lucy does not like Jaime's husband, since she often sees the couple fighting. There is some sexual attraction between the two women as well.

BERTHA Scarpetta's housekeeper and babysitter for Scarpetta's niece, Lucy, in *Postmortem*. She is also Scarpetta's maid in *All That Remains*.

BETTY She runs the serology lab in the Forensic Science Building, in *Postmortem*.

BEV She works at the seafood store P. T. Hasting's in Carytown, giving recipes to Scarpetta, in *Unnatural Exposure*.

BIBB, TREATA An ambulance driver who picks up Caesar Fender, in *Isle of Dogs*.

BILLY-BILLY Scarpetta's bulldog, in *Blow Fly*.

BIRD, GIL A special agent at Quantico, in *Hornet's Nest*.

BLACKSTONE, ED The Blue Ribbon Crime Commissioner, in *Southern Cross*.

BLAND, T. M. Hotel manager of Harbor Court, where Sterling Harper used to stay, in *Body of Evidence*.

BLANK, JACOB A children's book illustrator and the older husband of Scarpetta's sister, Dorothy, in *Postmortem*.

BLAUSTEIN, SUSAN The legal aid lawyer for Carrie Grethen, who also supplied her with money and support, in *Point of Origin*.

BLEDSOE, HUGH A city councilman who, for the sake of publicity, is also a ride-along with the Charlotte police, in *Hornet's Nest*.

BOATWRIGHT, DR. One of the odontologists, a forensic dentist, for the OCME, in *Black Notice*.

BOLTZ, BILL The commonwealth's attorney for Richmond, and boyfriend of Scarpetta, in *Postmortem*. He also appears in *Cruel & Unusual*.

BOND, BRENDA A systems analyst and computer geek at the *Charlotte Observer,* who likes Andy Brazil, in *Hornet's Nest.* She changes his password when he tells her that someone is breaking into his computer, but, ironically, she turns out to be responsible for the break-ins.

BONITA The security guard for the New York City morgue, in *From Potter's Field.*

BOOTH, DR. CHRIS Director of student counseling at the University of North Carolina at Wilmington; she invites Scarpetta down to talk about her counseling sessions with Claire Rawley, in *Point of Origin.*

BOOTH, MRS. The aged librarian for the *Charlotte Observer,* in *Hornet's Nest.*

BOVINE, JUDGE TYLER A female judge who oversees the trial of Johnny Martino, whom Hammer and West had apprehended, in *Hornet's Nest.*

BOWLS, JUDGE A friend of Scarpetta's who nevertheless lets her get harshly cross-examined in a court case, in *Point of Origin.*

BRANDY Jo Sanders's alias while working for the DEA, in *Black Notice.*

BRAY, DEPUTY CHIEF DIANE A new deputy chief of police, in *Black Notice.*

BRAY, ERIC Brother of deputy chief of police Diane Bray, in *The Last Precinct.*

BRAZIL, ANDY The reporter for the *Charlotte Observer* who attends the police academy and goes out on patrol as a volunteer, in *Hornet's Nest.* He becomes a police officer, with Chief Judy Hammer as his mentor. In *Southern Cross,* he is an officer in the Richmond Police Department who also writes a police update on the Web. In *Isle of Dogs* he is a state trooper who uses a daily column on the Web to capture a vicious hijacking group.

BRAZIL, DREW Andy's father, a police detective who was shot and killed while only in his thirties, in *Hornet's Nest.*

BRAZIL, MURIEL Andy's obese, alcoholic mother, in *Hornet's Nest.*

BREES, WINDY Judy Hammer's secretary, in *Isle of Dogs*.

BRENT A waiter at Louie's, in *Body of Evidence*.

BRETT, DONNY A NASCAR driver who helps apprehend Smoke, in *Isle of Dogs*.

BREWSTER, RONALD An undercover agent and detective in the Charlotte Police Department, in *Hornet's Nest*.

BRIDDLEWOOD, CLYDE A security officer at Davidson College and friend of Andy Brazil; he had known Andy Brazil as a young boy, in *Hornet's Nest*.

BRIDGES, SETH Judy Hammer's husband, in *Hornet's Nest*.

BROWN, MAYO He is the victim of a previous case involving a poisoning, in *The Last Precinct*.

BROWN, SHERIFF LAMONT (AKA "SHERIFF SANTA") He is corrupt, but seeks publicity by giving presents to the poor, in *From Potter's Field*. He is involved in drugs, has shot Anthony Jones, and is later murdered by Gault.

BUBBA (AKA BUTNER FLUCK IV) A redneck devoted to his confederate flag, in *Southern Cross*. His partner is Smudge.

BUBBA (AKA JOSHUA RICKMAN) A redneck who first confronts Virginia West and Andy Brazil at The Firing Line, in *Hornet's Nest*.

BUDDY Investigator Nic Robillard's five-year-old son, in *Blow Fly*.

BUDGET, OFFICER JACK He pulls over Bubba, issues him a warning, and later arrests him, in *Southern Cross*.

BURGESS The assistant director of the FBI at Quantico, in *From Potter's Field*.

BURGESS, ANTONY B. The bus driver whose bus is being robbed when Judy Hammer and Virginia West apprehend the robber, in *Hornet's Nest*.

BUTLER, J. F. A female police officer who shows up at Scarpetta's house when her burglar alarm goes off, in *Black Notice*. She reminds Scarpetta of her niece, Lucy.

BUTLER, KEN A state senator from Raleigh, North Carolina, and the fifth murder victim, in *Hornet's Nest*.

BUTTERFIELD, OFFICER He is at the scene of the murder of Diane Bray, in *Black Notice*.

CAGGIANO, ROCCO Marino's son, who has changed his name out of spite for his father. He is a disreputable criminal defense attorney who takes on the defense of serial killer Jean-Baptiste Chandonne, in *The Last Precinct*. In *Blow Fly,* he is a killer and fugitive wanted in Italy and France, whom Lucy Farinelli tracks down. Rocco is also the lawyer for the Chandonne family.

CAGNEY Scarpetta's predecessor as chief medical examiner, in *Postmortem*.

CAHOON, SOLOMON A CEO who tries to dictate policy to Judy Hammer, in *Hornet's Nest*. They eventually share a friendship when Hammer tells him that a senior vice president at his company, Blair Mauney, was killed by the serial killer, and that Mauney had been laundering millions of dollars.

CALLEY, JEFF The second serial murder victim in Charlotte, North Carolina, at the start of *Hornet's Nest*.

CALLOWAY, OFFICER M. I. She questions Scarpetta at Scarpetta's house after the attack by Chandonne, in *The Last Precinct*.

CANTER, DR. DAVID A forensic anthropologist who helps Scarpetta analyze saw marks in bone, in *Unnatural Exposure*. His wife is Jill.

CARLESS, NURSE She takes care of the beating victim, Moses Custer, in *Isle of Dogs*.

CARLISLE A student of trace evidence at the Forensic Institute, in *Black Notice*.

CARMICHAEL, DR. An elderly medical examiner who incorrectly fills out death certificates, in *Black Notice*.

CARSON, DEPUTY CHIEF AL Head of investigations, in *Black Notice*.

CARTER, BRUCE A district court judge who lives near Scarpetta, in *Cruel & Unusual*. His wife is Nancy.

CARTWRIGHT, JACK The director of crime labs in Washington, D.C., in *The Body Farm*.

CAT A member of Smoke's gang, in *Isle of Dogs*.

CATLETT The probable killer of Dwain Shapiro, in *Cause of Death*. He had Shapiro's New Zionist bible, known as *The Book of Hand*.

CHABAUD, OLIVIER AND CHRISTINE The alleged foster parents of Jean-Baptiste Chandonne, in *The Last Precinct*.

CHAN, MARY She works in the forensics labs with trace evidence, in *Point of Origin*.

CHANDONNE, JEAN-BAPTISTE (AKA LOUP-GAROU, THE "WEREWOLF") He is a serial killer and attacks Scarpetta at the end of *Black Notice*. His name is revealed at the start of *The Last Precinct* (p. 1). In *Blow Fly,* he is in prison on death row in Texas. He fantasizes about killing Scarpetta. He is also the twin brother of the serial killer Jay Talley, aka Jean-Paul Chandonne.

CHANDONNE, JEAN-PAUL (AKA JAY TALLEY) He first appears in *Black Notice*. He turns out to be a serial killer, in *Blow Fly*. His twin brother is Jean-Baptiste Chandonne.

CHANDONNE, THIERRY The father of Jean-Baptiste, in *The Last Precinct*.

CHANDONNE, THOMAS The victim found in the cargo container, in

Black Notice. He is connected with the crime cartel that Thierry heads. He turns out to be Jean-Baptiste's cousin.

CHEDDAR, SUE The public defender for Weed Gardener, in *Southern Cross.*

CHENEY, FRED A murdered teenager, in *All That Remains.*

CHONG, DAN A medical student rotating through the OCME, in *Black Notice.* He is later referred to as Dr. Chong in the next novel, *The Last Precinct,* and performs an autopsy.

CISSY The waitress who serves Danny Webster at the Hill Cafe, in *Cause of Death.*

CITRON, DARREN An eighteen-year-old who, while fishing, discovers a human arm hanging as alligator bait in the swamps near Baton Rouge, in *Blow Fly.*

CLARK, CAPTAIN He is a member of the U.S. Army Medical Research Institute of Infectious Diseases, in *Unnatural Exposure.*

CLARK, DETECTIVE A detective in Zachary, Louisiana, in *Blow Fly.*

CLARY, MYRA Jennifer Deighton's neighbor who calls the police, in *Cruel & Unusual.*

CLETA A clerical worker at the front desk of the OCME, in *Black Notice.*

CLICK, MR. The elderly boyfriend of Windy Brees, in *Isle of Dogs.*

CLOT, IMA AND UVA Neighbors of Barbie Fogg, in *Isle of Dogs.*

CLOUD, CAPTAIN A member of the Richmond Police Department, in *Southern Cross.*

COFFEY, SHERIFF An officer mentioned in *Isle of Dogs.*

COLDWELL, TOD A trial lawyer who defends a client in a drug-related murder, in *The Body Farm.* He does not particularly like Scarpetta.

CONNORS, REPRESENTATIVE He supports legislation that would place the OCME under the control of Public Safety, which also controls the police force, as opposed to the Department of Health and Human Services, in *Black Notice*.

COOPER, TIM The toxicologist who works in the trace department at the OCME, in *Point of Origin* and *Black Notice*.

CORIAN The housekeeper of Elizabeth Glenn, who also cleans Ted Eddings's house occasionally, in *Cause of Death*.

CORPS, MAURICE The dentist for Jean-Baptiste Chandonne, in *The Last Precinct*.

CORRELL, GINNY She poses as Scarpetta's driver, but in reality is a police officer, in *Point of Origin*.

COUNCIL, BETTY Bubba's supervisor at Philip Morris, in *Southern Cross*. She encourages competition between Bubba and Smudge.

CRIMM, GOVERNOR BEDFORD, IV Governor of Virginia, in *Isle of Dogs*. He is almost blind, has a poor constitution, and his mental capacity is diminished. His wife is Maude Crimm, who obsessively collects trivets. He has four daughters: Constance, Grace, Faith, and Regina.

CRIMM, LUTILLA The mother of Governor Crimm, in *Isle of Dogs*.

CROCKETT, DAVY The chief of police on Tangier Island, in *Unnatural Exposure*.

CROCKETT, GINNY A native of Tangier Island who charges tourists to look at her male blue crab, in *Isle of Dogs*.

CROW, REVEREND The pastor at the Presbyterian church that Mrs. Steiner attends, in *The Body Farm*.

CROWDER, DR. PHYLLIS A microbiologist and friend of Scarpetta, in *Unnatural Exposure*. Also, unfortunately, a killer.

CUDA A member of Smoke's gang, in *Isle of Dogs*.

CURRY, MR. The band director at Godwin High School, in *Southern Cross*.

CUSTER, MOSES A truck driver who is attacked by Unique First, in *Isle of Dogs*.

CUTCHINS, OFFICER HORACE He drives Officer Patty Passman to jail in the detention wagon, in *Southern Cross*.

CUTLER, BETTY The night editor at the *Charlotte Observer*, in *Hornet's Nest*.

DAIGO A female bartender at the Hill Cafe, in *Cause of Death*.

DAMMIT A dog shot with a bullet similar to the one that killed Deborah Harvey, in *All That Remains*.

DAN, GIG Bubba's boss at Philip Morris, in *Southern Cross*. They are in competition to see whose module can produce the most cigarettes on a given shift. Gig Dan always wins, using foul play.

DARD, CHARLOTTE A murder victim, investigated by coroner Dr. Lanier eight years prior to the start of *Blow Fly*. She died from a supposed drug overdose. Dr. Lanier enlists Scarpetta's help with the case. Her absent husband is the wealthy Jason Dard. There is also a young son named Albert. Her mother, whose maiden name is Sylvie Gaillot De Nardi, was born in Paris, where the Chandonne family resides.

DAVILA, JIMMY (AKA "JIMBO") A murdered transit policeman, in *From Potter's Field*.

DAVIS, JEFFERSON He frequents the Presto Grill, in *Hornet's Nest*. A statue of a different Jefferson Davis, President of the Confederacy, is defaced, in *Southern Cross*.

DAVIS, JUDGE MAGGIE The judge who tries Weed Gardener, and ultimately acquits him, in *Southern Cross*.

DAVIS, TERRY JENNIFER Lucy's alias while working in Miami with the ATF, in *Black Notice*.

DEEDRICK, JEFF The seventeen-year-old who discovers the fourth murder victim, in *Hornet's Nest*.

DEIGHTON, JENNIFER An astrologer and initially an apparent suicide, in *Cruel & Unusual*.

DENVER, PATTY An attractive television reporter, in *Unnatural Exposure*.

DERSHIN, HARLOW Secretary of public safety and uncle of Investigator Ring, in *Unnatural Exposure*.

DE SOUZA, DETECTIVE GLORIA A lesbian police officer who searches Patty Passman, in *Southern Cross*.

DEVON A burglar caught by Andy Brazil, in *Hornet's Nest*.

DIESNER The chief medical examiner in Chicago and a colleague of Scarpetta's, in *Body of Evidence*.

DINWIDDIE, REPRESENTATIVE MATTHEW Detective Stanfield's brother-in-law, in *The Last Precinct*.

DIVINITY The girlfriend of Smoke, in *Southern Cross*.

DIZE, MATTIE A native of Tangier Island, in *Isle of Dogs*.

DONAHUE, FRANK The warden at the Virginia State Penitentiary, in *Cruel & Unusual*.

DOREEN A classmate of Susan Story's, supposedly a witch, who put a curse on Susan's twin sister, Judy, in *Cruel & Unusual*.

DOROTHY Scarpetta's sister, who writes children's books. She is also Lucy's mother.

DORR, HUGHEY The farrier (a person who shoes horses), in *Point of Origin*.

DOWNEY, MINOR A specialist in hairs and fibers at the FBI labs, in *Cruel & Unusual*. He specializes in feathers.

DOZIER, WREN Deputy chief of administration under Judy Hammer, in *Hornet's Nest*.

DUCK, OFFICER One of the officers in charge of Jean-Baptiste Chandonne while he is on death row in a Texas prison, in *Blow Fly*.

ECKLES, BETSY A forensic scientist who runs a scanning electron microscope, in *Cause of Death*.

EDDINGS, JEFF Brother of Ted, in *Cause of Death*.

EDDINGS, THEODORE ANDREW (TED) A news reporter who is found dead while diving in the Inactive Naval Shipyard, in *Cause of Death*.

EDWARDS, MRS. She is in charge of social services at St. Bridget's, in *Cause of Death*.

EGGLESTON, AL A crime-scene technician, in *Black Notice*.

EHRHART, LELIA An upper-class, snobbish member of the board of Hollywood Cemetery, in *Southern Cross*. She insists that the person who defaced Jefferson Davis's statue be found. Her husband is millionaire dentist Dr. Carter "Bull" Ehrhart, a philanderer.

ELSEVIER, DR. A retiring forensic pathologist who is a consultant to the FBI's Behavioral Unit. She is replaced by Scarpetta, in *Cruel & Unusual*.

ENDO, JUDGE NICHOLAS A circuit court judge, in *Southern Cross*.

ENSOR, DR. LYDIA The director of Kirby Forensic Psychiatric Hospital where Carrie Grethen is imprisoned, in *Point of Origin*.

ESCUDERO, OFFICER He videotapes the killer Jean-Baptiste Chandonne for prosecutor Jaime Berger, in *The Last Precinct*.

ESKRIDGE, DAISY She works as a cashier at the only market on Tangier Island, in *Isle of Dogs*.

ETHRIDGE THOMAS, IV The attorney general of Virginia, in *Body of Evidence*.

EUGENIO The maitre'd of Scaletta, in *From Potter's Field*.

EVANS A lax guard at the morgue who lets someone deliver an unauthorized body (Sheriff Brown) in the middle of the night, in *From Potter's Field*.

FARBER, MARLENE The woman who died in the fire at Venice Beach, in *Point of Origin*.

FARINELLI, LUCY Scarpetta's niece, who is introduced at age ten in *Postmortem*. Scarpetta takes care of Lucy and the two remain close—despite their differences—throughout the series. Her last name is mentioned in *Unnatural Exposure*.

FAUX, DR. SHERMAN The corrupt dentist from the mainland of Virginia, who travels to Tangier Island to do substandard dental work on the residents, in *Isle of Dogs*. He is held hostage in retaliation for the speed traps the governor has ordered painted on the island.

FENDER, CAESAR He is fishing and is killed by Major Trader, in *Isle of Dogs*.

FERGUSON, MAX An investigator from the State Bureau of Investigations, in *The Body Farm*. He is found dead from autoerotic asphyxia.

FEUER, GOVERNOR MIKE The governor of Virginia, in *Southern Cross*. His well-educated wife is named Ginny.

FIELDING, DR. JACK Scarpetta's muscular deputy chief medical examiner, in *Body of Evidence* and *Trace*. His wife, Ginny, is pregnant, in *Cause of Death*. He is divorced in *Black Notice*.

FIGGIE, CHEF The chef for Governor Crimm, in *Isle of Dogs*.

FIRST, DR. ULYSSES Unique First's father, in *Isle of Dogs.*

FIRST, UNIQUE She acts as a decoy for Smoke's gang, in *Isle of Dogs.* She considers herself to have a Purpose and believes her spirit is possessed by a Nazi. She attacks people and cuts their bodies.

FLING, OFFICER WALLY Administrative assistant to Judy Hammer, in *Southern Cross.* He is in charge of giving the COMSTAT computer program a Web address so that the public can easily access it. The address is incredibly long, taking detours at such sites as those of Senator Orrin Hatch, the FBI, and the DEA.

FLUCK, DR. BUTNER, III The father of Bubba, in *Southern Cross.*

FOGG, BARBIE A friend of the tollbooth operator, Hooter Shook, in *Isle of Dogs.* Her husband is Lennie. Their twin girls are Mandie and Missie. Barbie works at the Baptist Campus Ministry at the University of Richmond.

FOLEY, DR. MARGARET The forensic pathologist in Ireland who has worked on all five murder victims in Dublin, in *Unnatural Exposure.*

FONNY BOY SHORES (AKA DARREN SHORES) A native of Tangier Island who ties up the dentist who has been performing bad dental work on the people of the island, in *Isle of Dogs.*

FORBES, AMY A medical student rotating through the OCME, in *Black Notice.* In the next novel, *The Last Precinct,* she is referred to as Dr. Forbes.

FORD, IVY The second murder victim in Nic Robillard's town of Zachary, Louisiana, in *Blow Fly.* She is a bank teller and disappears from her home.

FORT, LONNIE The male sports trainer that the elderly Lelia Ehrhart tries to seduce, in *Southern Cross.*

FORTOSIS, DR. SPIRO A forensic psychiatrist, in *Postmortem.*

FOSTER, BETTY Kenneth Sparkes's horse trainer, in *Point of Origin.*

FRANKEL A member of VICAP (Violent Criminal Apprehension Program) who meets with Scarpetta at Quantico, in *Unnatural Exposure*.

FRANKEL, OFFICER JENNY She discovers that Deputy Chief Jeannie Goode and reporter Brent Webb are having an affair, in *Hornet's Nest*.

FREAKLEY, BETTY A police dispatcher, in *Isle of Dogs*.

FRED The security guard at the morgue, in *Postmortem*.

FREDDIE A homeless person, in *From Potter's Field*.

FRISKY The Crimm family dog, in *Isle of Dogs*.

FROST, HENRY He is new at the firearms lab, in *Cause of Death*.

FUJITSUBO, COLONEL JOHN Head of the U.S. Army Medical Research Institute of Infectious Diseases, where Scarpetta is isolated, in *Unnatural Exposure*.

GAIL A search dog handler, in *All That Remains*.

GALLWEY, NICK Head of the FBI's Disaster Squad, in *Unnatural Exposure*.

GANT, PYLE A man murdered in a convenience store, in *Black Notice*.

GARA, GEORGE A painfully shy histologist at the OCME, who also has tattoos, in *Black Notice*.

GARDENER, WEED A high school student at Godwin whom Smoke coerces into his gang, the Pikes, in *Southern Cross*. He enjoys art and is forced by Smoke to paint the statue of Jefferson Davis in Hollywood Cemetery. He paints the statue as his adulated, deceased brother, Twister, who was a black basketball player at the University of Richmond before he was killed.

GARMON, JERRI A worker in the trace lab who discovers that the silicone found in bathing caps will burn down to a pink residue as found on the bodies of the murder victims, in *Point of Origin*.

GAULT, LUTHER Temple's uncle, a general in the army, in *From Potter's Field*.

GAULT, PEYTON AND RACHAEL Temple's father and mother, in *From Potter's Field*.

GAULT, RACHAEL JAYNE (AKA JANE) The murder victim, and sister of Temple Gault, in *From Potter's Field*.

GAULT, TEMPLE BROOKS (AKA HILTON SULLIVAN) A murderer, in *Cruel & Unusual*. He is also seen in *The Body Farm* and in *From Potter's Field,* where Lucy and Scarpetta confront him.

GEORGE, WASHINGTON A cordial AP reporter, in *The Last Precinct*.

GERDE, DR. ABRAHAM A forensic pathologist on the case of Kellie Shephard who was trained by Scarpetta three years previously, in *Point of Origin*.

GIN RUMMY A taxi driver who eats often at the Presto Grill, in *Hornet's Nest*.

GITTLEMAN, MISS JAYNE She is the assistant public information officer at the Texas prison housing Jean-Baptiste Chandonne, in *Blow Fly*.

GLENN, ELIZABETH The mother of Ted Eddings, in *Cause of Death*. Her husband was Arthur.

GLOVER, STEVEN LEONARD An alias for Benton Wesley when he is in New York City, in *Blow Fly*.

GOODE, JEANNIE A female deputy chief police officer and head of patrol, in *Hornet's Nest*.

GORELICK, NANCY The D.A. of Charlotte, in *Hornet's Nest*.

GRADECKI, MARCIA The U.S. attorney general who investigates the take-over of the nuclear power plant, in *Cause of Death*.

GRANNIS, MRS. She teaches Weed Gardener's art class, in *Southern Cross*.

GRANT, DR. A new fellow in forensic pathology, in *Unnatural Exposure*.

GREEN, CAPTAIN He is part of the Navy Investigative Service (NIS) and gives Scarpetta a hard time at the murder scene, in *Cause of Death*.

GREENWOOD, MR. Scarpetta's banker, in *The Last Precinct*.

GRETHEN, CARRIE A co-worker of Lucy's at Quantico, in *The Body Farm*. She has some relationship to the killer Temple Brooks Gault from *Cruel & Unusual,* and uses Lucy's thumbprint to break into secret files at Quantico. She is also an accomplice to Gault in *From Potter's Field*. She is imprisoned but escapes in *Point of Origin*.

GRIGG, DETECTIVE A member of the Sussex County Sheriff's Department, in *Unnatural Exposure*.

GRIMES, HELEN (AKA "HELEN THE HUN") A female prison guard, in *Cruel & Unusual*. She is also involved with "Hilton Sullivan," one of Temple Gault's aliases, in *Cruel & Unusual*.

GRUEMAN, NICHOLAS A lawyer defending the prisoner Ronnie Waddell, in *Cruel & Unusual*. He had been a teacher of Scarpetta's while she was in law school at Georgetown.

GUIDON, MRS. EVELINE Sister of the deceased, and probably murdered, Charlotte Dard, in *Blow Fly*. She is also matron of the house and looks after Charlotte's son, Albert.

HALE, CHARLIE A bomb victim (along with Mark James) to whom Scarpetta sends money in heartfelt appreciation of his aid to Mark before he died, in *Cruel & Unusual*.

HALF SHELL Bubba's dog, in *Southern Cross*.

HAM, GARY A crime-scene technician, in *Black Notice*.

HAMILTON, HENRY A star high school baseball pitcher and schoolmate of Weed Gardener, in *Southern Cross*.

HAMM, JONI She runs the trace and drug analysis lab, in *Body of Evidence*.

HAMMER, JUDY The chief of police of the Charlotte Police Department, in *Hornet's Nest*. Her subordinate is Deputy Chief Virginia West. In *Southern Cross,* she is hired as chief of police in Richmond to solve the crime problem. She thinks of quitting being a police officer at one point because of all the crimes being commited under her jurisdiction, but changes her mind at the end of this novel. In *Isle of Dogs,* Hammer is a state police superintendent of the Richmond Police Department.

HAND, JOEL Leader of the Zionist cult that takes over a nuclear power plant, in *Cause of Death*.

HANGER, MAJOR A member of the Richmond Police Department who is in charge of the first precinct, in *Southern Cross*.

HANOWELL, ROY An FBI special agent, a fibers expert, in the Microscopic Analysis Unit in Quantico, in *Body of Evidence*.

HARPER, CARY A murder victim, a famous writer, and the mentor of the murdered Beryl Madison, in *Body of Evidence*.

HARPER, STERLING Sister of Cary; she died at home, in *Body of Evidence*.

HARRINGTON, JILL A young lawyer who is one of two women murdered prior to the "couple killings," in *All That Remains*. She had a lesbian relationship with Elizabeth Mott.

HARRIS, CHIEF RODNEY Richmond police chief; he visits the crime scene of Diane Bray's murder, in *Black Notice*. He also appears in *The Last Precinct*.

HARSTON, DR. VANCE The chief medical examiner of Philadelphia, who did the autopsy on Benton Wesley, in *Black Notice*.

HART, AUSTIN A fourth-year medical student who died in a fire that started in a bathroom, with no accelerants; his death is deemed a homicide, in *Point of Origin*.

HARVEY, DEBORAH A murdered teenager, in *All That Remains*.

HARVEY, PAT Mother of the murder victim, Deborah, in *All That Remains*. She is the National Drug Policy Director; her husband is Bob.

HARVEY, SANDRA Neighbor of murder and arson victim Kellie Shephard, in *Point of Origin*.

HAVILAND, TOM One of several aliases for former FBI agent Benton Wesley, in *Blow Fly*. His death has been fabricated to protect Scarpetta and he is in the witness protection program.

HAYES, JOSHUA A farmer whose Commonwealth Power and Light account was broken into by computer hackers, in *Cause of Death*.

HEATH, EDDIE A thirteen-year-old murder victim, in *Cruel & Unusual*.

HERBERT, IRA The police reporter for the *Richmond Times-Dispatch*, in *Black Notice*.

HIGGINS An excellent lawyer and friend of Scarpetta's, recommended to Keith Pleasants, in *Unnatural Exposure*.

HILGEMAN, MR. He owns the gallery where the picture painted by Sterling Harper was framed by Clara, in *Body of Evidence*.

HODGES, RICK A police officer who works security at the Ninth Street Executive Office Building, in *Black Notice*.

HONEY Bubba's wife, in *Southern Cross*.

HORGESS, FRED A captain of the Charlotte Police Department, reporting to Judy Hammer, in *Hornet's Nest*.

HOROWITZ, DR. New York City's chief medical examiner and long-time friend of Scarpetta, in *From Potter's Field*.

HOYT, DR. FRED A local medical examiner from Norfolk, in *Unnatural Exposure.*

HUNNEL, WOODROW The taxi driver who brings Beryl Madison home, in *Body of Evidence.*

HUNT, AL Supervisor at a car wash who remembers seeing Beryl Madison there, in *Body of Evidence.*

HURRICANE Fonny Boy's father, in *Isle of Dogs.*

INMAN, MAJOR He replaces Al Carson as deputy chief of investigations, in *Black Notice.*

ISMAIL, DR. The oncologist at Johns Hopkins who treats Sterling Harper's leukemia, in *Body of Evidence.*

IVAN The Interpol connection who meets Scarpetta and Marino in Paris, in *Black Notice.*

JACKSON, HENRY The OCME is accused of stealing property off his body, in *Body of Evidence.*

JACKSON, REVEREND SOLOMON A city leader invited to the Commonwealth Club, in *Southern Cross.*

JACKSONS, THE Racist brothers who dislike Kenneth Sparkes, in *Point of Origin.*

JAKE He works at the security desk at the OCME, in *Black Notice.*

JAKES, DETECTIVE An officer murdered and placed in the crematorium, in *From Potter's Field.*

JAMES, ELMER Owner of the James Gallery in Shockoe Slip; he sells the killer Gault a caduceus, in *From Potter's Field.*

JAMES, MARK A former boyfriend of Scarpetta's when they were in law school together at Georgetown, in *Body of Evidence.* In *All That Remains,* he worked for the FBI with Benton Wesley, his close friend, at Quantico. He is a supposed member of the law firm Orndorff & Berger, and is later killed by a terrorist bomb, in *Cruel & Unusual*.

JAMESON An excellent lawyer and friend of Scarpetta's, recommended to Keith Pleasants, in *Unnatural Exposure*.

JANET A friend of Lucy's at Quantico, in *From Potter's Field*. She is Lucy's lover in *Cause of Death* and *Unnatural Exposure*.

JAZZBONE The owner of a jazz club in Charlotte who points Andy Brazil in the direction of the serial killer, in *Hornet's Nest*.

JED The driver for the governor, in *Southern Cross*.

JEFF A search-dog handler, in *All That Remains*.

JENNIFER A clerk who works at the front office of the OCME and had seen Gault at a local club, in *From Potter's Field*.

JENRETTE, DR. JAMES A local pathologist from Asheville who does the autopsy on Emily Steiner, in *The Body Farm*.

JEROD A Navy diver who helps Scarpetta, in *Cause of Death*.

JILL A resident pathologist at the OCME, in *Black Notice*.

JOE A security guard at the gate of Scarpetta's neighborhood, in *The Last Precinct*.

JOHNSON, OFFICER MICHELLE A police officer for the Charlotte Police Department who runs into a Mercedes while on a chase, killing the occupants, in *Hornet's Nest*.

JONAS, DR. A forensic pathologist at the scene of Davila's murder, in *From Potter's Field*.

JONES, ANTHONY A drug dealer who kills a woman whose surname is King, in *From Potter's Field*. He is then shot by Sheriff Lamont Brown.

JONES, JONAH A murder victim who happened to be high on cocaine and alcohol, in *The Body Farm*.

JONES, PETER (AKA PJ) Gay partner of Walt. He is a friend of Beryl Madison in Key West, in *Body of Evidence*.

JONES, SONNY Marino's partner and a policeman on the case of the Robyn Naismith murder, in *Cruel & Unusual*. He commits suicide.

JONESTON, ELLA An elderly, poor African-American woman. She is arrested for drunk and disorderly conduct by Virginia West, with Andy Brazil in tow, in *Hornet's Nest*. Her grandson, Efrim, son of Lorna, had died that day of gunshot wounds.

JORDAN, ELLEN The clerk at the 7-Eleven that Deborah and Fred stopped at before they were murdered, in *All That Remains*.

JOSH The stablehand for Sparkes who had quit several months previously, in *Point of Origin*.

JOYCE, DR. NEWTON A psychotherapist who was treating Claire Rawley, a student at the University of North Carolina at Wilmington, in *Point of Origin*.

JOYCE, MR. Owner of the dog named Dammit that was shot and killed, in *All That Remains*.

JUAN The doorman at the building where Susan Pless lived, and where Jean-Baptiste Chandonne took her for a drink, in *The Last Precinct*.

JULIE An assistant manager at Pleasants Hardware who explains to Scarpetta the particular use of a masonry hammer that she finds there, in *Black Notice*. The hammer turns out to be the murder weapon.

JUSTICE, REVEREND PENTIUS A minister on the University of Richmond campus, in *Isle of Dogs*.

KATZ, DR. THOMAS His lab is known as The Body Farm. His interests are time of death and fingerprints obtained from skin and other difficult surfaces. He fumes the scene for fingerprints, in *The Body Farm*.

KELSEY, ROB, JR. He recalls his father giving a friend of Charles Steiner some of the blaze orange duct tape for hunting purposes, which is connected to the murder, in *The Body Farm*.

KIFFIN, MRS. BEV The caretaker at The Fort James Motel, in *The Last Precinct*. Her husband is Marcus. In *Blow Fly,* she is the lover of the sadistic murderer Jay Talley. She is his accomplice and is also on the FBI's Most Wanted List.

KILBY, GEORGE He works at the crime labs in Washington, D.C., in *The Body Farm*.

KING Last name of a woman who was slain by a drug dealer, in *From Potter's Field*.

KITCHEN, CLAY A maintenance worker at Hollywood Cemetery who discovers the defacement of the Jefferson Davis statue, in *Southern Cross*.

KITCHEN, MR. He owns the landfill where the body of the fifth murder victim is found, in *Unnatural Exposure*.

KOSS, AARON An expert in microscopic fibers, residues, paints, and explosives, in *Unnatural Exposure*.

KOSTYLO, JOHNNY An Assistant Special Agent in Charge, or ASAC, in Philly taking care of public relations regarding the fire, in *Point of Origin*.

KUHN, JAMIE He is a forensic technician who works in the DNA lab, in *Black Notice*.

LAMB, MAYOR STUART The mayor of Richmond, in *Southern Cross*.

LAMONIA An almost-blind woman who still drives a car, in *Isle of Dogs*. She drives over the body of Caesar Fender and knocks the stretcher into the river.

LAMPKIN, WILL An attorney who dislikes Scarpetta and exposes her relationship to Benton Wesley during a court case, in *Point of Origin*.

LANDON, SALLIE A native of Tangier Island who once had her safe stolen, in *Isle of Dogs*.

LANIER, DR. SAM Coroner for East Baton Rouge Parish, in *Blow Fly*. He is a friend of investigator Nic Robillard and had investigated the death of Charlotte Dard, eight years prior. He enlists Scarpetta's help in this case.

LAPOINTE, PHIL A recent graduate of the Forensic Institute, specializing in image enhancement, in *Black Notice*.

LÉGER, PASCAL Alias used by the killer, Loup-Garou, in *Black Notice*.

LEVINE A new forensic pathologist, in *Point of Origin*.

LEWIS, PATTY The second victim of the strangler, in *Postmortem*.

LILLY, MRS The principal of Weed Gardener's high school, Godwin, in *Southern Cross*.

LINDA A firearms examiner, in *All That Remains*.

LINDSEY, CREED A janitor at Emily Steiner's school. He likes her and gives her flowers, in *The Body Farm*.

LLOYD, JUDSON The chaplain who conducts Benton Wesley's funeral at Hilton Head, in *Point of Origin*.

LORAINE The grandniece of Ruby Sink and daughter of Frances, in *Southern Cross*. Ruby Sink is murdered while babysitting Loraine.

LORD, SENATOR FRANK A good friend of Scarpetta's, in *The Body Farm* and other books. He is responsible for helping Lucy get a job at the FBI. In *Blow Fly,* he gives Benton Wesley, who is in the witness protection program, covert assistance.

LOVING, BUBBA A trucker who gets mad at Hooter Shook, the toll-booth attendant, in *Isle of Dogs.*

LOVING, GLORIA A friend of Scarpetta's and the state registrar for Virginia, in *The Body Farm.*

LUBY, CARY The third serial murder victim in Charlotte, North Carolina, in *Hornet's Nest.*

LUCERO, TOM The officer on the case of Susan Story's murder, in *Cruel & Unusual.*

LUCY BOO Nickname Scarpetta gave Lucy as a toddler, in *Point of Origin.*

LUONG, KIM A woman killed at a convenience store, in *Black Notice.*

MACOVICH, TROOPER THORLO He is the helicopter pilot for Governor Crimm, in *Isle of Dogs.* He is African-American.

MADISON, BERYL STRATTON (AKA "STRAW") An author, murdered in *Body of Evidence.* Her pseudonyms are Adair Wilds, Emily Stratton, and Edith Montague.

MAGIL, SERGEANT A fellow student at the National Academy of Forensics, along with Nic Robillard, in *Blow Fly.* He is from Houston and is known as "Magilla the Gorilla."

MAGPIE A street person, in *Postmortem.*

MAIER, DETECTIVE He is in charge of the footprint casts, in *From Potter's Field.*

MANHAM, ZACH Lucy's chief of staff for her investigative firm, The Last

Precinct, in *Blow Fly*. He used to be a detective for the New York District Attorney's Office. He is six feet tall and close to fifty years old. He is in good physical shape and is "irresistibly attractive" to women. He and Lucy have a close, professional relationship.

MANT, DR. PHILIP Deputy chief medical examiner in the Tidewater District, an area that Scarpetta is covering for as medical examiner, in *Cause of Death*.

MARGARET Scarpetta's programming analyst, in *Postmortem*.

MARIE Scarpetta's housekeeper, in *Black Notice*.

MARINO, DETECTIVE SERGEANT PETE The loud, chauvinistic, bigoted, but endearing detective investigating Lori Petersen's murder, in *Postmortem*. He is a central character in every Scarpetta book. He turns out to be one of Scarpetta's best friends and supporters. In *Blow Fly*, he is working for Lucy and also is in the process of moving from Richmond and joining a police department in Florida.

MARINO, ROCCO (AKA "ROCKY") See **Caggiano, Rocco.**

MARLER, GLENDA The first murder victim in Zachary, Louisiana, in *Blow Fly*. She was a high school teacher there, her car having been found abandoned in the school parking lot.

MARTHA A grade school classmate of Scarpetta's who accused Scarpetta of cheating, in *The Last Precinct*.

MARTIN, DR. BRET An infectious-disease expert at the CDC, in *Unnatural Exposure*.

MARTINEZ, RON The station chief for the Coast Guard who takes Scarpetta to Tangier Island, in *Unnatural Exposure*.

MARTINO, JOHNNY The robber whom Hammer and West arrest on a bus, in *Hornet's Nest*.

MASTERSON, DR. WARNER Al Hunt's psychiatrist, in *Body of Evidence.*

MATOS, ROSSO (AKA "THE CAT") The hit man killed at the Fort James Motel and Camp Ground, in *The Last Precinct.*

MATTHEWS, DR. ALFRED A professor of nuclear physics who analyzes Scarpetta's uranium, in *Cause of Death.*

MAUNEY, BLAIR, III (AKA JACK MORGAN) A senior vice president of US-Bank in the Carolinas, in *Hornet's Nest.* He eventually is the serial killer's sixth victim. It is discovered that he is laundering money through the Cayman Islands.

MAX A worker in the Café Esplanade in Boston, where he has contact with Benton Wesley, in *Blow Fly.*

MAXWELL, WREN A boyfriend of Emily Steiner, who had seen her the day she died, in *The Body Farm.* His father is named Lee.

MAYEUX, ANNIE Nic Robillard's mother, who was murdered in Baton Rouge eight years before the current serial killings started, in *Blow Fly.* Her autopsy report suggests that she may have been murdered by Jean-Baptiste Chandonne. She owned an antiques store and was a friend of another victim, Charlotte Dard.

MAYFAIR, LINDA A reporter who was fed misinformation suggesting that Scarpetta was intoxicated and had been in a car accident, in *The Body Farm.*

MAZZONELLI, SERGEANT Reporter Artis Roop calls this New York City police officer to confirm that COMSTAT is also frozen in New York, in *Southern Cross.*

MCCOMB, LOREN Eddings's girlfriend, who breaks into CP&L's computer files, in *Cause of Death.*

MCCORKLE, ROY A communications officer for Richmond, in *Postmortem.*

MCELWAYNE, R. I. A police officer who shows up at Scarpetta's home when her burglar alarm goes off, in *Black Notice*.

MCFEE, JULIE Mark James's girlfriend, a fact unknown to Scarpetta. Julie and Mark both die in a bomb explosion, in *Unnatural Exposure*.

MCGOVERN, T. N. (TEUN) An arson expert and the team leader in the investigation of Kenneth Sparkes's fire. She is also Lucy's mentor, in *Point of Origin*.

MCINTYRE, JILISON She is with the ATF, and is undercover as Mitch Barbosa's girlfriend, in *The Last Precinct*.

MCKEE, INVESTIGATOR An experienced investigator who helps Scarpetta evaluate Lucy's car accident, in *The Body Farm*.

MCKUEN, COUNCILMAN His daughter is the victim of a hit-and-run, in *Unnatural Exposure*.

MCLAUGHLIN, ROBERT A world-renowned diatomist who trained Larry Posner, in *Black Notice*.

MCTIGUE, MRS. J. R. She had asked Beryl Madison to give a lecture to the DAR, in *Body of Evidence*. Her husband is a friend of Beryl's literary mentor, Cary Harper.

MEANEY, TINKY The lesbian cellmate of incarcerated Officer Patty Passman, in *Southern Cross*.

MENENDEZ, DR. The chief medical examiner in Seattle, Washington, who is familiar with a dental society that specializes in gold foil restorations, in *From Potter's Field*.

MERLE A cleaning lady at the OCME, in *Black Notice*.

MICHAEL, JAY The commonwealth's attorney involved in Weed Gardener's case, in *Southern Cross*.

MICHELLE She works for the Department of Criminal Justice Services and helps Scarpetta and Lucy evaluate Waddell's computerized fingerprints via AFIS, in *Cruel & Unusual*. She is Benton Wesley's daughter and also appears in *Point of Origin*.

MILES, COMMISSIONER The health commissioner and Scarpetta's boss, in *Unnatural Exposure*.

MILLER, JUNE The lieutenant governor of Virginia, in *Southern Cross*.

MILTON, REBECCA A murder victim of Bev Kiffin, in *Blow Fly*. She is a neighbor of Nic Robillard and her house is mistaken for Nic's.

MIROT, SECRETARY-GENERAL GEORGE The head of Interpol who lives in Lyon, in *Black Notice*.

MITCHELL, MIKE AND EDITH The governor of Virginia and his wife, friends of Scarpetta's, in *The Last Precinct*.

MOLLY Marino's girlfriend, in *From Potter's Field*.

MONTANA, CAPTAIN R. P. A police officer who took photographs at the scene of the murder of Jill Harrington and Elizabeth Mott, which happened prior to the other "Couple Killings," in *All That Remains*.

MONTGOMERY, JOHNNY Investigator on the case of the fire in Baltimore that killed Austin Hart, in *Point of Origin*.

MONTY, PAUL The statewide director of the forensic labs, in *The Last Precinct*.

MORALES, CRUZ A twelve-year-old Mexican boy who is transporting guns when Officer Macovich chases him, in *Isle of Dogs*.

MORGANTHAU, ROBERT Legendary district attorney in New York under whom Jaime Berger works, in *The Last Precinct*.

MORGUE ADMINISTRATOR FOR THE OCME Though never mentioned by name, "[M]y administrator was a retired sheriff who loved cologne and snappy suits" (p. 65, *Unnatural Exposure*).

MORRELL, JAY A neophyte investigator at the crime scene, in *All That Remains.*

MOSSBERG, OFFICER He was at the scene of the murder in Central Park, in *From Potter's Field*.

MOTE, LIEUTENANT HERSHEL A local police officer of Black Mountain who is assigned to the Steiner case, in *The Body Farm*.

MOTH One of the inmates at the Texas prison where Jean–Baptiste Chandonne is on death row, in *Blow Fly*.

MOTT, ELIZABETH A young salesperson; one of two women murdered prior to the "Couple Killings," in *All That Remains*. She had a lesbian relationship with the other murdered victim, Jill Harrington.

MOWERY, JIM Special agent who helps Lucy fly the helicopter, in *Point of Origin*.

MULLINS, FREDERICK An alias for Rudy Musil when he flies home from Europe with Lucy after killing Rocco Caggiano, in *Blow Fly*.

MULLIS-MUNDI, MRS. The executive secretary to CEO Solomon Cahoon, in *Hornet's Nest*.

MUNGO An undercover agent investigating drug dealing at the Presto Grill, in *Hornet's Nest*.

MURPHY, ERIC The chief death investigator who works with coroner Dr. Lanier, in Zachary, Louisiana, in *Blow Fly*.

MUSIL, RUDY Lucy's former partner at the FBI. He resigned from the Bureau and eventually came to work for her at her private investigative firm, The Last Precinct, in Manhattan, in *Blow Fly*. Even though she is a lesbian, they have strong feelings for each other. Once, he misinterpreted her intentions and tried to force himself on her sexually. Together they murder Pete Marino's son, Rocco Caggiano, in *Blow Fly*.

MUSKRAT (AKA "SCRAT") Bubba's friend at Muskrat's Auto Rescue, in *Southern Cross*.

MYRE, LIZ A profiler on the case, in *The Body Farm*.

NAISMITH, ROBYN An anchorwoman murdered by Waddell, in *Cruel & Unusual*.

NILES Virginia West's Abyssinian cat, in *Hornet's Nest* and *Southern Cross*.

NOBLE, LIEUTENANT Commander of the second precinct in the Richmond Police Department, in *Southern Cross*.

NORRING, GOVERNOR JOE Governor of Virginia, who attempts to replace Scarpetta as chief medical examiner, in *Cruel & Unusual*.

ODOM, DR. WAYNE The Charlotte medical examiner, in *Hornet's Nest*.

O'CONNOR, FATHER A priest at St. Bridget's, in *Cause of Death*. He presides over Diane Bray's funeral, in *The Last Precinct*.

O'CONNOR, FRAN Sister of murder victim Cecile Tyler, in *Postmortem*.

O'DONNELL, OFFICER T. L. A police officer at the scene of the murder in Central Park, in *From Potter's Field*.

OGREN, FATHER The priest who takes Lucy in, in *The Body Farm*.

OLSON, CHUCK The FBI's senior legal attaché for Great Britain, in *Cause of Death*.

OZIMEK, HILDA A psychic used by the parents of Deborah Harvey and by Scarpetta and Marino, in *All That Remains*.

PACKER, ED The editor at the *Charlotte Observer* who doesn't command much of Andy Brazil's respect, in *Hornet's Nest*.

PANESA, RICHARD The publisher of the *Charlotte Observer* who first hires Andy Brazil, in *Hornet's Nest*.

PARKS, THELMA A native of Tangier Island, in *Isle of Dogs*.

PARKS, WHEEZY A native of Tangier Island who likes to pay for things with pennies, in *Isle of Dogs*.

PARSONS, CARL The fourth murder victim, from Spartanburg, South Carolina, in *Hornet's Nest*.

PARTIN, SCOTT The son of Senator Partin; he witnesses Scarpetta and Mark James at Gallagher's, in *Body of Evidence*.

PARTIN, SENATOR JOHN Mentioned in *Body of Evidence*.

PASSMAN, OFFICER PATTY She is the overweight and unliked communications officer in charge of the dispatches in *Southern Cross*. She receives a commendation from Chief Hammer of the Richmond Police Department. She eventually attacks an officer who keeps giving her parking tickets and is incarcerated with a lesbian cellmate.

PATTERSON, ROY Attorney general for Virginia who prosecutes Scarpetta, in *Cruel & Unusual*.

PEELER, VINCE The bail bondsman on Broad Street that Scarpetta uses, in *Unnatural Exposure*.

PENN, COMMANDER FRANCES A New York Transit Police officer in charge of the murder in Central Park, in *From Potter's Field*.

PEPPER The arson dog trained to sniff out petroleum products at fire scenes, in *Point of Origin*.

PERLEY, KEN A. The killer was using his identity, in *Unnatural Exposure*.

PETERSEN, DR. LORI The third murder victim of the serial killer, in *Postmortem*. She is a graduate of Brown and Harvard Medical School.

PETERSEN, MATT Husband of the murder victim, Lori, in *Postmortem*.

PHARAOH, MOSES Patty Passman's former boyfriend, in *Southern Cross*.

PIGEON An older homeless man who befriends Weed Gardener, in *Southern Cross*.

PIKES, THE Smoke's gang, which Weed is forced to join, in *Southern Cross*.

PINN, A. P. A prison guard who is ambushed by Smoke, who then escapes, in *Isle of Dogs*.

PIT, JOHN An expert at applying tattoos, in *Black Notice*.

PLEASANTS, KEITH A worker at the landfill associated with the murders, in *Unnatural Exposure*. He is incorrectly accused of the murder.

PLESS, SUSAN A murder victim in New York, killed two years before the action in *The Last Precinct*. The details of her murder are similar to the "werewolf" murders in Virginia that occurred in *The Last Precinct*.

POE, JUDGE A friendly, experienced Southern judge, in *The Body Farm*.

POISON (AKA ADDIE JONES) Punkin Head's prostitute, who is killed by Andy Brazil, in *Hornet's Nest*.

POLLY A clerical worker at the front desk of the OCME, in *Black Notice*.

PONY The butler for Governor Crimm of Virginia, in *Isle of Dogs*.

PONZI, LIEUTENANT AUDREY She is on the Richmond Police Department, in *Southern Cross*.

POPEYE A fellow student of Nic Robillard at the National Forensic Academy, in *Blow Fly*.

POPEYE Chief Judy Hammer's dog, a Boston terrier, in *Southern Cross*. Hammer is very devoted to her dog.

POSNER, LARRY A trace evidence expert, in *Black Notice*.

POSSUM (AKA JEREMIAH LITTLE) A member of Smoke's gang, the Pikes, in *Isle of Dogs*.

POTEAT, DETECTIVE The detective at the scene of Cary Harper's murder, in *Body of Evidence*.

POTTER, PROFESSOR SAM An unkempt professor of German at the University of Richmond; he has rented the house where Robyn Naismith was murdered ten years prior, in *Cruel & Unusual*.

PRICE, JEB He is armed and found going through files and taking pictures in Scarpetta's office, in *Body of Evidence*.

PRUETT, BUNK An FBI agent, in *The Last Precinct*.

PRUITT, DIPPER She works at an ice-cream shop on Tangier Island, in *Isle of Dogs*.

PRUITT, LILA She dies from exposure to the poxvirus on Tangier Island, in *Unnatural Exposure*.

PUNKIN HEAD A pimp who takes charge of Addie Jones ("Poison"), a prostitute, in *Hornet's Nest*.

QUINN, SONNY An eleven-year-old son of Christian Scientists, he died from diabetic ketoacidosis, in *Point of Origin*.

RADAR The dispatcher assigned to Virginia West, in *Hornet's Nest*.

RADER, DR. LEWIS A friend of Scarpetta's and a forensic pathologist in New York who does the autopsy on the woman slain in Central Park, in *From Potter's Field*.

RAINES, DENNY A paramedic and handsome romantic interest of Virginia West, in *Hornet's Nest*.

RAVAL, BO Head coach of the University of Richmond's basketball team, in *Southern Cross*.

RAWLEY, CLAIRE A former girlfriend of Kenneth Sparkes; she is found killed in his burned home, in *Point of Origin*.

RAY, LUCIAS The funeral director for Emily Steiner, in *The Body Farm*.

RAYNAUD, MONSIEUR A physician who took care of Jean-Baptiste Chandonne as a child, in *Blow Fly*. He was the only physician allowed to see him when Chandonne was growing up.

REBA The roommate of Nic Robillard in *Blow Fly*. She is a crime-scene technician from San Francisco and is also taking the ten-week course in forensics at the National Forensic Academy along with Nic.

REED, JIM The Richmond police officer who responded to Beryl Madison's complaint about threatening phone calls, in *Body of Evidence*.

REEVE, WAYNE The public information officer at the Polunsky Unit of the prison in Texas where Jean-Baptiste is being held on death row, in *Blow Fly*.

RENQUIST, OFFICER A security officer for the governor's mansion, in *The Last Precinct*.

RHOAD, OFFICER OTIS The recipient of a commendation by Chief Hammer of the Richmond Police Department, in *Southern Cross*. He is obsessive about handing out traffic tickets and is physically attacked by Officer Patty Passman when he gives her a ticket.

RICHARDS, DR. The medical examiner for Albemarle County, in *Black Notice*.

RICHARDS, SETH He works at the crime labs in Washington, D.C., in *The Body Farm*.

RICK He drives Lucy's Suburban, in *Cause of Death*.

RICKMAN, MRS. The overweight wife of Bubba, aka Joshua Rickman, in *Hornet's Nest*.

RIGHTER, BUFORD The city commonwealth's attorney, in *The Last Precinct*.

RILEY, DR. Assistant chief medical examiner, in *Black Notice*.

RILEY, DR. ALAN Wingo's doctor at MCV, in *Unnatural Exposure*.

RING, CLIFFORD A reporter from the *Washington Post* who is investigating the murder of Deborah Harvey, in *All That Remains*. He writes a devastating exposé of the case.

RING, INVESTIGATOR PERCY Scarpetta does not like his aggressive manner or his advances to her niece, Lucy, in *Unnatural Exposure*.

RITA One of the security guards at the gate to Scarpetta's Windsor Farms neighborhood, in *Black Notice* and *The Last Precinct*.

RO A burglar caught by Andy Brazil, in *Hornet's Nest*.

ROBERTS A guard at the state penitentiary who shows Scarpetta and Marino the electric chair, in *Cruel & Unusual*.

ROBILLARD, NIC A police officer and investigator from East Baton Rouge Parish, Louisiana, in *Blow Fly*. She is called "Nic the Hick" during her training at the National Forensic Academy, Class of 2003. She investigates the serial murders of women there. She is separated from her husband, Ricky, and has a five-year-old son, Buddy.

She is enamored with Scarpetta during her training at the academy and develops a friendship with her.

Nic's mother had been murdered within several days of Charlotte Dard's death from an overdose, eight years before the start of *Blow Fly*.

ROCHE, DETECTIVE C. T. An officer at the scene of the diver's death in *Cause of Death*. He sexually harasses Scarpetta.

ROOP, ARTIS A reporter for the *Richmond Times-Dispatch* who is first to hear about the anticrime computer program COMSTAT being frozen by the fish screensaver, in *Southern Cross*.

ROSE Scarpetta's longtime secretary. She continues to be her secretary after Scarpetta is fired as chief medical examiner in Virginia and accompanies her to Florida in *Blow Fly*.

ROY, SHERIFF ROB Sheriff of Sussex County, and greatly respected by Scarpetta, in *Unnatural Exposure*.

RUDI Dr. Anna Zenner's violin-playing lover, in *The Last Precinct*.

RUFFIN, CHUCK The morgue supervisor, in *Point of Origin* and *Black Notice*.

RULE, JAY The first serial murder victim in Charlotte, North Carolina, in *Hornet's Nest*.

RUMBLE, FLOYD He chisels words and designs on gravestones, in *Southern Cross*.

SABAT, DON Director of the FBI and friend of Senator Frank Lord, in *Blow Fly*.

SAMMY Scarpetta's albino squirrel that steals her birdseed, in *Body of Evidence*.

SANDERS, JO Lucy's girlfriend, in *Black Notice*.

SANDERS, OFFICER He was at the scene where Scarpetta's tires had been pierced, in *Cause of Death*.

SANTA, SERGEANT He is in charge of crowd control for the Azalea Parade, in *Southern Cross*.

SAUNDERS, TROY An officer in the Charlotte Police Department who trails Hammer and West to the Presto Grill, in *Hornet's Nest*.

SAWAMATSU, DR. The new Japanese assistant chief medical examiner of Virginia, in *Isle of Dogs.*

SCARPETTA, DR. KAY She is the chief medical examiner for the Commonwealth of Virginia introduced in *Postmortem,* and the protagonist of Cornwell's series of thirteen books. She attended Cornell on a full scholarship, went to Johns Hopkins for medical school and Georgetown for law school. Her residency was at Johns Hopkins in pathology. Her knowledge of pathology, both of the living, and of the dead, is unparalleled.

SCARPETTA, KAY MARCELLUS, III Scarpetta's father, mentioned in *The Last Precinct.*

SCARPETTA, MRS. Scarpetta's mother, first mentioned in *Postmortem.*

SCATES, MARLEY Scarpetta's lab partner in medical school, and the source of her computer username, *Marley,* in *Cruel & Unusual.*

SCHURMER, ROB The attorney prosecuting the case against Carrie Grethen, in *Unnatural Exposure.*

SCROGGINS, DETECTIVE From the Wilmington Police Department; he accompanies Scarpetta, Lucy, and Marino as they search Dr. Newton Joyce's house, in *Point of Origin.*

SEARCH, MAYOR CHARLES The mayor of Charlotte; originally from Charleston, South Carolina, in *Hornet's Nest.*

SESSIONS, DR. PAUL As the commissioner of health and human services, he is Scarpetta's boss, in *All That Remains.*

SESSIONS, MAJOR GENERAL LYNWOOD He is in charge of handling the takeover of the nuclear power plant, in *Cause of Death.*

SHADE, DR. LYALL An anthropologist who does forensic experiments at The Body Farm for Dr. Katz, in *The Body Farm.*

SHAPIRO, DWAIN Murdered in a carjacking, he was the owner of the New Zionist bible found under Eddings's bed, in *Cause of Death.*

SHAW, JIMMY The morgue supervisor in Dublin, in *Unnatural Exposure.*

SHAW, JOE The port director, in *Black Notice.*

SHEDD, MR. Registrar at the University of North Carolina at Wilmington, in *Point of Origin.*

SHEPHARD, KELLIE A murder victim whose house was also set on fire, in *Point of Origin.*

SHIRLEY Dr. Canter's receptionist in Memphis, in *Unnatural Exposure.*

SHOOK, HOOTER A tollbooth operator who has a drink with Trooper Macovich, in *Isle of Dogs.*

SIMMONS, OFFICER The driver for Deputy Chief Bray, in *Black Notice.*

SINCLAIR, OFFICER ANDREW D. A rookie police officer who makes several mistakes in evaluating Lucy's car accident, in *The Body Farm.*

SINCLAIR, RICH He is in charge of the firearms and toolmarks lab, in *Point of Origin.*

SINK, RUBY The elderly landlady of Andy Brazil in *Southern Cross.* She is overly attentive to him, much to Virginia West's chagrin, and he tends to ignore her. She is later murdered by Smoke. Virginia West's empathy with Brazil's remorse at not having spent more time with her leads to the rekindling of their relationship.

SKRZYPEK, GEORGE A maintenance worker in the Polish hotel where Rocco Caggiano is murdered, in *Blow Fly.* He discovers the body earlier than expected.

SLEETH, JIMBO (AKA "STICKS") One of Weed's musical friends, in *Southern Cross.*

SLIPPER, DETECTIVE He is in charge of investigating the murder of T.T. on Belle Island, in *Isle of Dogs.*

SMATHERS, TIMOTHY A murder victim whose family accuses the medical examiner's office of stealing his personal valuables, in *Body of Evidence*.

SMOKE (AKA ALEX BAILEY) A troubled, violent teenager who moves to Richmond from North Carolina, in *Southern Cross*. He is head of a gang called the Pikes, recruits Weed Gardener to deface the Jefferson Davis statue, and eventually murders Ruby Sink. His girlfriend is Divinity.

SMUDGE (AKA JOE BRUFFY) Bubba's close friend, in *Southern Cross*. They both work at Philip Morris and go coon hunting together.

SOCKS The stray kitten buried with Emily Steiner, in *The Body Farm*.

SONG, HOWIE Driver of a Dodge Dart who causes a commotion at the intersection where Andy Brazil is directing traffic, in *Hornet's Nest*.

SOO, KI A Navy diver who accompanies Scarpetta in recovering the body, in *Cause of Death*.

SOPHIE Andy Brazil's wealthy girlfriend at Davidson, in *Hornet's Nest*.

SPARACINO, ROBERT A lawyer with the firm Orndorff & Berger, in *Body of Evidence*. He is consulted by Beryl Madison in her dispute with Cary Harper.

SPARKES, KENNETH Owner of a horse farm that is burned down, in *Point of Origin*. He is African-American and a well-known newspaper tycoon.

SPIKE The cook at the Presto Grill, where Judy Hammer and Virginia West go every Friday, in *Hornet's Nest*.

SPURRIER, STEVEN The owner of a bookstore called The Dealer's Room in Williamsburg, and a serial murderer, in *All That Remains*.

STANFIELD, DETECTIVE The less-than-competent detective working on the case of the burn victim found in the Fort James Motel and Camp Ground, in *The Last Precinct*.

STEELS, CHIEF Chesapeake's chief of police, in *Cause of Death*.

STEINER, DENESA Mother of Emily, in *The Body Farm*. Her deceased husband is Charles; their one-year-old, Mary Jo, died of SIDS one year before the birth of Emily.

STEINER, EMILY An eleven-year-old murder victim, in *The Body Farm*.

STEPPE, BRENDA The first victim of the strangler, in *Postmortem*.

STEVENS, BEN Scarpetta's administrator at the OCME who also turns out to be a conspirator, in *Cruel & Unusual*.

STORY, SUSAN A morgue supervisor who is murdered, in *Cruel & Unusual*. Her husband is Jason.

STUCKEY, INVESTIGATOR He investigated the fire that killed Marlene Faber, in *Point of Origin*.

STVAN, MADAME RUTH The chief medical examiner of France, who did the autopsies on eight of Loup-Garou's victims, in *Black Notice*. Her maiden name is Dürenmatt, and her husband's name is Paul.

SULLIVAN, HILTON Alias for Temple Brooks Gault, a murderer, in *Cruel & Unusual*.

SWAN, JEROME He held an ambulance hostage and was taken into custody by Virginia West, in *Hornet's Nest*.

SWEET, LETITIA A woman with whom Trooper Macovich has one date, in *Isle of Dogs*.

TALLEY, JAY He is the ATF liaison at Interpol in France who calls Scarpetta in *Black Notice*. They start a romantic relationship in *Black Notice*. It turns out that he is also the twin brother of the incarcerated murderer Jean-Baptiste Chandonne. His actual name is Jean-Paul Chandonne. In *Blow Fly*, he is a serial killer and takes victims out in his boat in the bayou near Baton Rouge, Louisiana.

His accomplice is his lover, Bev Kiffin, who is on the FBI's Most Wanted List. He fantasizes about making love to, and killing, Scarpetta.

TANDA Marino attempts to date this woman after his divorce from his wife, in *Cruel & Unusual*.

TANNER, NORMAN The director of public safety, in *Postmortem*.

TAXI A pit bull that belongs to John Pit, in *Black Notice*.

TED The tennis pro who gives Scarpetta lessons, in *All That Remains*.

TERESA, SISTER One of Scarpetta's judgmental grade school teachers, in *The Last Precinct*.

TERRY, DR. SAM A forensic odontologist, in *The Last Precinct*.

THRASH, TRISH (AKA T. T.) A murder victim in *Isle of Dogs*.

TILLER An employee at Philip Morris, in *Southern Cross*.

TILLY, CHAD The owner of a funeral home who has trouble driving through an intersection at which Andy Brazil is directing traffic, in *Hornet's Nest*.

TIN MAN A robot created by Lucy and controlled by virtual reality and fiber optics, in *Unnatural Exposure*.

TITTLE, VINCE The magistrate, in *Southern Cross*.

TOTO The robotic dog invented and operated by Lucy, in *Cause of Death*.

TRADER, MAJOR The corrupt press secretary for Virginia's Governor Crimm, in *Isle of Dogs*. He is cooperating with Smoke and his gang, the Pikes, and arranges to have Hammer's dog, Popeye, kidnapped by them.

TRAVERS, WILLIE Ex-husband of the murder victim Jennifer Deighton, in *Cruel & Unusual*. Jennifer had given him a key piece of evidence to keep.

TRENT, DETECTIVE JOE A detective for Henrico County who investigates the Eddie Heath case, in *Cruel & Unusual*.

TREVI The orphaned son of a woman named King who is slain by a drug dealer, in *From Potter's Field*.

TRIXIE In *Blow Fly,* Marino is living with this thirty-year-old woman with brittle, platinum hair. He feels that she doesn't really know him and walks out on her, vowing never to return to Richmond.

TUCKER, CHIEF PAUL The newly appointed chief of police of the Richmond Police Department, in *From Potter's Field*.

TURKEL, LAURA A morgue attendant, in *The Last Precinct*.

TURNBULL, ABBY A prizewinning police reporter and sister of Henna Yarborough, in *Postmortem*. She also shows up in *All That Remains*.

TYLER, CECILE The third strangling victim, in *Postmortem*.

VANDER, NEILS The fingerprints examiner in *Postmortem, All That Remains,* and *Cruel & Unusual*. His wife is Edith.

VESSEY, DR. ALEX A world-renowned forensic anthropologist at the Smithsonian, in *All That Remains* and *Point of Origin*.

WADDELL, RONNIE JOE An inmate convicted of murdering Robyn Naismith; he is executed and autopsied, in *Cruel & Unusual*.

WAGNER, SINCLAIR Secretary of health and human services, who has the capacity to hire or fire the chief medical examiner, in *Black Notice*. He is a psychiatrist who used to be on the faculty of MCV and also has a law degree.

WALT Gay partner of Peter Jones and a friend of Beryl Madison in Key West, in *Body of Evidence*.

WASHBURN, DEBORAH A young girl who is related to Creed Lindsey, in *The Body Farm*.

WATTS, DR. A medical examiner in Williamsburg, notorious for not showing up at the scene of a crime and for avoiding the paperwork involved, in *Body of Evidence.*

WEBB, BRENT A reporter for television station Channel 3 in Charlotte, North Carolina, in *Hornet's Nest.* He is called "The Scoop" since he brazenly steals crime reports at the Police Department.

WEBBER, CAPTAIN He is on the Richmond Police Department, in *Southern Cross.*

WEBSTER, DANNY The morgue assistant for the Tidewater District, in *Cause of Death.* He is murdered driving Scarpetta's car from Tidewater District to Richmond.

WEED, OFFICER She questions Andy Brazil after he witnesses a burglary in progress, in *Hornet's Nest.*

WEINSTEIN A police reporter who writes a derogatory, falsified article impugning the reputation of chief of police Judy Hammer, in *Hornet's Nest.*

WESLEY, BENTON A friend of Mark James, he is a suspect profiler from the FBI. He appears in *All That Remains* and *Cruel & Unusual.* He has a romantic relationship with Scarpetta and later fabricates his own death in order to protect her. In *Blow Fly* he is in Boston in the witness protection program. His wife is Connie; they are in the process of getting a divorce in *Cause of Death.*

WEST, BRETT A vice-president at Virginia's utility company, CL&P, whose account is broken into by computer, and who is assumed to be involved in the takeover of the power plant, in *Cause of Death.*

WEST, VIRGINIA The deputy chief of police in Charlotte, North Carolina, and the protagonist in *Hornet's Nest.* Her boss is chief of police Judy Hammer. In *Southern Cross,* she has moved to Richmond, Virginia, to help Judy Hammer solve the problem with high crime there. She has a relationship with Andy Brazil in *Hornet's Nest* that ends when they move to Richmond. By the conclusion of *Southern Cross,* they have resumed their romantic relationship.

WHEAT, DR. A forensic pathologist from Topeka, in *The Body Farm.*

WHEAT, DR. DOUGLAS A female doctor who runs the DNA lab in the Seaboard Building (a forensics lab) in Richmond, in *Unnatural Exposure*.

WHEELON, REMUS A cook at the Cadillac Grill, where the prostitute Addie Jones hangs out, in *Hornet's Nest*.

WHIT Pilot of the helicopter that flies Scarpetta to a crime scene, in *The Body Farm*.

WHITE, BENNY A young murder victim who is brought to the morgue, in *The Last Precinct*. Scarpetta links his death to Mitch Barbosa's, which then leads to Jay Talley's exposure as a killer.

WHITE, DR. A surgeon who operates on Judy Hammer's husband, Seth, in *Hornet's Nest*. She is an admirer of Judy Hammer.

WILL He is in charge of documents examination, in *Body of Evidence*.

WILLIS, REX An editorial columnist, in *Point of Origin*.

WILLS, BONITA A crime-scene technician investigating the death of Ruby Sink, in *Southern Cross*.

WILSON, AGENT The FBI liaison with Interpol, in *Black Notice*.

WILSON, JEANIE SAMPLE The therapist who takes care of Al Hunt when he is hospitalized at Valhalla Hospital, in *Body of Evidence*.

WILSON, PHILLIP An officer at the Texas prison that houses Jean-Baptiste Chandonne, in *Blow Fly*. He is killed by Jean-Baptiste during the convict's escape.

WILSON, RUTH Scarpetta's computer analyst, in *Black Notice*.

WILSON, TONY An alias for Benton Wesley while he is in Baton Rouge, in *Blow Fly*.

WIND Kenneth Sparkes's horse that ran in the Derby and later dies in the fire at Sparkes's estate, in *Point of Origin*.

WINGO An autopsy technician and the morgue supervisor in *Postmortem*. He is also gay, and eventually dies from exposure to the poxvirus during an autopsy, in *Unnatural Exposure*.

WINN, WELDON A U.S. attorney in *Blow Fly*. He is arrogant and power hungry and takes an interest in the murder investigation in East Baton Rouge Parish for his own self-advancement. He is connected with the corrupt Chandonne family and their cartel.

WITTIKER, LUELLEN She calls West and Brazil when her adopted teenage son is missing, in *Hornet's Nest*. Her son is Wheatie, her daughter is Tangine, and her drug-dealing ex-boyfriend is Jerald.

WORTH, DR. GRAHAM An orthopedist and friend of Scarpetta's, in *Black Notice*. He takes care of Lucy's girlfriend, Jo Sanders, at MCV.

WRIGHT, DR. Scarpetta's deputy chief medical examiner in Norfolk, in *Cruel & Unusual*. He does the autopsy on Susan Story.

YANCEY, MAJOR JIM A major at the U.S. Marine Corps base, where Scarpetta visits Benton Wesley, in *All That Remains*.

YARBOROUGH, HENNA The fifth murder victim in *Postmortem;* she worked at VCU. Sister of Abby Turnbull.

YATES, INTAKE OFFICER CHARLIE He admits Weed Gardener to the jail for juvenile offenders, in *Southern Cross*.

YOUNG, OFFICER S. T. A prank caller to Scarpetta, in *Cause of Death*.

ZENNER, DR. ANNA Scarpetta's psychiatrist and friend, in *All That Remains*. She is also a violinist in the Richmond Symphony.

PLACES

THE various locations in the novels of Patricia Cornwell are organized first by city. Then, within each city's listing, the locations are listed alphabetically by name. For more information on sites that actually exist in the real world, see the location section, beginning on p. 153.

RICHMOND, VIRGINIA

"It remained fiercely loyal to its defeated cause, still flaunting its battle flag, the Southern Cross" (p. 2, *Southern Cross*).

Southern Cross presents a Richmond with many problems, especially dealing with crime and racism. "Its homicide rate had climbed as high as second in the nation. . . . Residents and department stores had abandoned downtown. . . . The tax base was shrinking" (p. 2). Racism was still rampant in Richmond. Judy Hammer, in *Southern Cross,* "knew it wasn't so long ago that blacks couldn't join various clubs or live in certain neighborhoods. They couldn't use golf courses or tennis courts or public pools. . . . When the future first black governor of Virginia tried to move into an exclusive neighborhood, he was turned down. When a statue of

Arthur Ashe was erected on Monument Avenue, it almost caused another war" (p. 187).

Scarpetta mentions the "four quadrants" of the city: the Northside, the Southside, the West End, and the eastern part of Richmond (p. 72, *Postmortem*).

AGECROFT HALL Located in Windsor Farms; Scarpetta and Berger drive past it on Christmas Eve (p. 338, *The Last Precinct*).

AMTRAK STATION Railroad station on Staples Mill Road (p. 241, *Body of Evidence*).

BELLE ISLAND An island in downtown Richmond where concerts and gatherings are held. It is the site of T.T.'s murder by Unique First (p. 25, *Isle of Dogs*).

BENNY'S A Richmond restaurant (p. 10, *Point of Origin*).

THE BERKELEY "I soon found that Dorothy had checked into the Berkeley in the historic area of the city known as Shockhoe Slip" (p. 276, *Black Notice*). This hotel is elegant, with much atmosphere, nestled against the shop-lined, cobblestoned Cary Street as it enters Shockhoe Slip. "The small, elegant hotel had an intimate, dark bar with high-backed leather chairs and a quiet clientele. The bartender wore a white jacket and was very attentive when I went up to him" (p. 276).

BERKLEY AVENUE, NO. 5602 Site of the murder of Lori Petersen (p. 2, *Postmortem*). It is located in Berkley Downs, Southside.

BLILEY'S FUNERAL HOME In *Point of Origin* (p. 140). [Author's Note: This is a very cordial funeral home that I often visited for viewings as an M.E. in Richmond.—GF]

BROOKFIELD HEIGHTS "It's one of the older parts of town the young professionals have begun to take over during the last ten years. The streets are lined with row houses, some of them dilapidated and boarded up, most of them beautifully restored, with intricate wrought-iron balconies and stained-glass windows" (p. 157, *Postmortem*).

BUCKHEAD'S "[T]he city's finest chophouse"; a restaurant at the Beverly Hills Shopping Center (p. 157, *Black Notice*).

CAPITOL SQUARE "[O]n 9th Street, the capitol glows like an egg through the bare branches of ancient trees, the pale yellow mansion next to it elegant with candles in every window" (p. 133, *The Last Precinct*). Scarpetta goes to the governor's mansion in *The Last Precinct,* and pulls "into Capitol Square, cruising past the up-lit statue of George Washington astride his horse, and winding around the south portico of the building Thomas Jefferson designed . . . The early-nineteenth-century executive mansion is pale yellow stucco with white trim and columns. According to legend, it was saved by a bucket brigade when Richmonders burned their own city at the end of the Civil War. In the understated tradition of Virginia Christmases, candles glow and fresh wreaths hang in every window, and evergreen swags decorate black iron gates" (p. 221, *The Last Precinct*).

CARYTOWN Scarpetta often mentions driving through this interesting area of stores at the outskirts of downtown (p. 73, *Unnatural Exposure*).

CHAMBERLAYNE GARDENS A retirement home near downtown Richmond, and residence of Mrs. J. R. McTigue (p. 65, *Body of Evidence*).

CHETTI'S A restaurant in Richmond frequented by Marino (p. 107, *Black Notice*).

CHURCH HILL, THE SUGAR BOTTOM AREA In *Southern Cross,* Cornwell states that this is the "city's original site . . . with iron fences and porches, and slate and false mansard roofs, and turrets, stone lintels, chased wood, stained glass, scroll-sawn porches, gables, raised so-called English and picturesque basements, and thick chimneys" (p. 3). It was in Church Hill that Patrick Henry gave his "Give me liberty or give me death" speech at St. John's Episcopal Church, as well as where Edgar Allan Poe had begun his second courtship with Elmira Royster Shelton (p. 166).

Judy Hammer's house is in Church Hill: "They followed East Grace Street to where it ended at an overlook that was the most popular observation point in the city. On one side of the precipice was the radio station WRVA, and on the other was Hammer's nineteenth-century Greek

Revival house, built by a man in the tobacco business about the time the Civil War ended. Hammer loved the old brick, the bracketed cornices and flat roof, and the granite porch. She craved places with a past . . ." (p. 3, *Southern Cross*).

COMMERCE ROAD An industrial street on the Southside of Richmond that parallels I-95. It is traveled by Bubba, who works at Philip Morris, located in the same vicinity (pp. 98–99, *Southern Cross*).

THE COMMONWEALTH CLUB An "ivy-draped eighteenth-century club," as Scarpetta describes it. "Women could not join the prestigious Commonwealth Club, where half of the major business deals and politics affecting Virginia were made by male power brokers with old family names. . . . They bartered and pontificated in the locker room, a forum where women weren't allowed" (p. 170, *Black Notice*).

The Commonwealth Club's chauvinistic elements are also mentioned in *Southern Cross:* "[W]omen could not be members, but as guests of husbands or male friends were welcome to enjoy all amenities except the Victorian bar, Men's Grill, swimming pool, gym, steam and sauna rooms, squash and racquetball courts and reading rooms" (p. 235).

THE COUNTRY CLUB OF VIRGINIA "[Hampton Hills] was across Cary Street from the Country Club of Virginia, which would not have wanted Mr. Brown for a member" (p. 196, *From Potter's Field*).

Rose tells Scarpetta and Marino, "'I drove to where Grove ends at Three Chopt and took a left, him still behind me. The next right was the Country Club of Virginia, and I turned in there and drove straight to the entrance where the valets were. Needless to say, whoever it was vanished'" (p. 259, *Black Notice*).

In *Isle of Dogs*, Cruz Morales abandons his car here. Located off of Three Chopt Road, CCV has "a long driveway that led to the stately country club with its elegant clubhouse, tennis and paddleball courts, and sprawling golf course. CCV . . . was in a very wealthy neighborhood where many of the homes were as big as the governor's mansion" (p. 303, *Isle of Dogs*).

DU JOUR A café in the West End, off Grove Avenue, where Scarpetta occasionally has Sunday brunch (p. 131, *Black Notice*).

EXECUTIVE OFFICE BUILDING On 9th Street, where the offices of the secretary of health and human services and the attorney general are located (p. 145, *Black Notice*).

THE EYE INSTITUTE An establishment on Cary Street just south of the Huguenot Bridge, where Scarpetta gets her glasses adjusted and where she gets picked up by helicopter (p. 17, *Point of Origin*).

THE FAN "We drove east along Monument Avenue into the district known as the Fan, where gracious mansions lined historic avenues and college students crowded old homes. At the statue of Robert E. Lee, [Marino] cut over to Grace Street" (p. 95, *Cause of Death*).

In *Southern Cross,* both Andy Brazil and Virginia West have houses in this desirable, downtown neighborhood near VCU. Virginia West is on Park Avenue, and Brazil on Plum Street. "The neighborhood *fanned out* several miles west of downtown, spreading fingers of quaint streets with names like Strawberry, Plum and Grove. Homes and town houses of distinctive designs were brick and stone with slate and shingle roofs, stained glass transoms, elaborate porches and parapets, finials and even medallions and domes. Styles ranged from Queen Anne to Neo-Georgian and Italian Villa" (p. 85).

Some restaurants in the Fan that are casually mentioned are Helen's, Joe's Inn, Soble's, Konsta's, Commercial Tap House, and Southern Culture, some of which have changed ownership and names since this novel was published (p. 103, *Southern Cross*).

THE FAN FREE CLINIC Wingo worries that he will wind up dying at this free clinic if he gets AIDS (p. 70, *Unnatural Exposure*).

FARMER'S MARKET An area in downtown Richmond on 17th Street that is known for selling produce during the summer, as well as hosting arts and crafts booths. It is mentioned in *Southern Cross* as being the site of stalls run by Russians that might be selling stolen air bags (p. 38).

GINTER PARK "[T]he oldest residential neighborhood in Richmond. There are monstrous three-story Victorian houses with wraparound porches wide enough to roller-skate on, and turrets, and dentil work along the eaves.

Yards are thick with magnolias, oaks and rhododendrons. Grape vines climb over porch posts and arbors in back" (p. 159, *Postmortem*).

Bubba Fluck had been raised there (p. 9, *Southern Cross*).

GLENBURNIE A neighborhood in Richmond, home of the Dawsons (p. 189, *Cruel & Unusual*).

GODWIN HIGH SCHOOL Smoke goes to school here (p. 31, *Southern Cross*)

HAMPTON HILLS An attractive neighborhood near the Country Club of Virginia (p. 196, *From Potter's Field*). "Hampton Hills was a mixture of mansions and modest homes tucked in woods" (p. 196).

HAVANA '59 A restaurant at the farmer's market (p. 38, *Southern Cross*).

THE HILL CAFE AT 28TH STREET "Known for its Bloody Marys and chili, the cafe was on the corner, and over the years had been a favorite hangout for cops" (p. 163, *Cause of Death*). Marino calls it "'The joint that makes the best steak sandwich in town'" (p. 163).

HOLLYWOOD CEMETERY "Richmond's most formidable city for the dead, some forty acres of rolling hills, streams, and stands of hardwood trees north of the James River. Curving streets were paved and named, with speed limits posted, the sloping grass crowded with granite obelisks, headstones, and angels of grief, many of them more than a century old. Buried here were Presidents James Monroe and John Tyler, and Jefferson Davis, and tobacco magnate Lewis Ginter. There was a soldiers' section for the Gettysburg dead" (p. 375, *All That Remains*).

In *Southern Cross*, Hollywood Cemetery is the site of the defacement of Jefferson Davis's statue. This famous and beautiful cemetery is located in downtown Richmond, at South Cherry and Spring Street in Oregon Hill. Twenty-five generals from the Confederacy are buried here, along with five governors and two presidents of the United States (p. 236). There is also a ninety-foot-tall Confederate Monument pyramid, built in 1868 from granite, that is dedicated to the 18,000 slain Confederate soldiers buried there (p. 159).

HUGUENOT BRIDGE "[T]he James River [is] a plain of darkness below the Huguenot Bridge as I pass into the south side of the city" (p. 237, *The Last Precinct*).

I-95, GOING SOUTH FROM RICHMOND "There were many trucks and much construction along a stretch of I-95 South that I always found bleak. Even the Philip Morris plant with its building-high pack of Merits was stressful, for the fragrance of fresh tobacco bothered me" (p. 202, *From Potter's Field*).

"It seemed as if this stretch of I-95 near Petersburg had been under construction since the Civil War" (p. 202, *Black Notice*).

JAMES CENTER "In front of the James Center, people have pulled over to explore a blaze of reindeer sculpted of light" (p. 133, *The Last Precinct*).

JEFFERSON HOTEL Novelist Beryl Madison gives a lecture to the Daughters of the American Revolution here, in this gorgeous building in downtown Richmond, one of its premier hotels (p. 62, *Body of Evidence*).

Scarpetta calls the Jefferson Hotel in *Black Notice* to see if her sister, Dorothy, was staying there, since it was one of "the obvious hotels" that one would want to stay at in Richmond (p. 276, *Black Notice*).

Lucy says, "'Actually, I'm downtown at the Jefferson'" in *The Last Precinct* (p. 8). Scarpetta thinks, "The Jefferson is the grandest hotel in the city, and I don't know why she would go to a hotel at all, much less an elegant, expensive one" (p. 8). Marino's take on the hotel: "'The Jefferson? . . . You gotta be kidding! She win the lottery or something?'" (p. 9).

JOHN MARSHALL COURTS BUILDING Scarpetta gives court testimony here (p. 43, *Body of Evidence*). This is also the site of the scene where Scarpetta is prosecuted (p. 381, *Cruel & Unusual*).

LA PETITE FRANCE A restaurant that Scarpetta takes Lucy to in *The Body Farm* (p. 159). It is also mentioned in *Point of Origin* (p. 10). The restaurant's chef and his wife are friends of Scarpetta's, whom she calls in *Black Notice* (p. 48). The restaurant is also frequented by Governor Feuer in *Southern Cross* (p. 92).

LIBBY HILL PARK This "was on one of Richmond's seven hills in an area where real estate was now considered prime. Century-old row houses and Greek Revival homes had been brilliantly restored by people bold enough to reclaim a historic section of the city from the clutches of decay and crime" (p. 150, *Cause of Death*).

LINDEN ROW INN Scarpetta and Marino meet here to discuss the case in *Cause of Death* (p. 205). It has an "'enchanted garden' . . . where Edgar Allan Poe used to play when he was a boy in Richmond" (p. 207).

LOCKGREEN Scarpetta's neighborhood in Windsor Farms, in *The Last Precinct* (p. 338).

THE LUCKY STRIKE TOWER A large water tower on the Philip Morris property, seen from I-95, which is painted like a Lucky Strike cigarette (p. 99, *Southern Cross*).

LUCKY'S CONVENIENCE STORE A chain of stores in Richmond (p. 59, *Cruel & Unusual*).

MAMMA'ZU "[R]eputed to be the best Italian restaurant this side of Washington, D.C." (p. 305, *Southern Cross*). It is located in a section of downtown Richmond called Oregon Hill.

MARINO'S HOUSE "Marino's small aluminum-sided white house was on Ruthers Road, around the corner from Bon Air Cleaners and Ukrop's. He had a large American flag in his front yard and a chainlink fence around the back, and a carport for his camper" (p. 209, *Point of Origin*). Marino's showy Christmas display "had made it into Richmond's official *Tacky Tour*" (p. 209).

MCGEORGE MERCEDES Scarpetta had bought her new 500E Mercedes at this dealership in Richmond (p. 226, *The Body Farm*). A friendly salesman named Walter replaces Scarpetta's car in *Cause of Death* (p. 199).

MCV The Medical College of Virginia, located downtown. In *Postmortem,* the term *VMC* was used instead of *MCV.* In the later novels, the correct term familiar to Richmonders is introduced; Scarpetta is on staff at MCV. The real-life chief medical examiner and model for the character of Kay Scarpetta, Dr. Marcella Fierro, is on staff at MCV. The Department of Forensic Pathology is a part of the Department of Pathology at MCV.

The "werewolf" killer, Jean-Baptiste Chandonne, is treated here and interviewed by Jaime Berger in *The Last Precinct*.

MIDLOTHIAN TURNPIKE The main thoroughfare through the Southside, filled with many deteriorating businesses as it approaches the city, and more upscale malls and shops as it approaches the suburb of Midlothian; it is the scene of a car accident in *Point of Origin* (p. 141).

Pete Marino lives in a "blue-collar neighborhood, right off Midlothian Turnpike on the wrong side of the James River in Richmond" (p. 268, *Blow Fly*).

MONUMENT AVENUE "I drove along Monument Avenue, where statues of Confederate generals on horses loomed over traffic circles. . . . Her office was in her house, a lovely old white frame where the street was blacktopped cobblestone and gas carriage lamps glowed after dark" (p. 269, *All That Remains*).

THE MORGUE Located in downtown Richmond (currently at the Office of the Chief Medical Examiner). "The white clock face floated like a full moon in the dark sky, rising high above the old domed train station, the railroad tracks and the I-95 overpass" (p. 18, *Postmortem*).

There is a parking space at the OCME labeled "Chief Medical Examiner" that Scarpetta uses (p. 14, *From Potter's Field*).

"The conference room . . . seemed very cozy with its deep blue carpet, long new table and dark paneling. But anatomical models on tables and the human skeleton beneath his plastic shroud were reminders of the hard realities discussed in here. Of course, there were no windows, and art consisted of portraits of previous chiefs, all of them men who stared sternly down at us from the walls" (p. 174, *Cause of Death*).

[Author's Note: I presented my cases from the weekends here, in the "hot seat" to the right of the chief medical examiner, Dr. Fierro. It was as described: cozy with its dark paneling and long table, but nevertheless intimidating. The table sat perhaps twelve people and all seats were usually taken for the morning conference. As mentioned in *Cause of Death,* present were the chief medical examiner, the deputy and assistant chiefs, two fellows doing their one-year fellowship in forensic pathology, the chief and assistant administrators, the chief toxicologist of the division of forensic science, and the occasional medical student and visiting patholo- gist . . . and me, the lowly medical examiner.—GF]

The old morgue/OCME (Office of the Chief Medical Examiner) was located "on Fourteenth and Franklin" (p. 114, *Point of Origin*). The new morgue/OCME is "on Jackson Street, between the restored row houses of Jackson Ward, and the Medical College of Virginia campus of Virginia Commonwealth University" (p. 92, *Point of Origin*).

MOSBY COURT "[O]ne of seven low-rent housing projects in the city" (p. 133, *The Last Precinct*).

OCME (OFFICE OF THE CHIEF MEDICAL EXAMINER) See **the morgue.**

THE OMNI A plush hotel in downtown Richmond, mentioned in *Black Notice* (p. 276).

OREGON HILL An artsy section of Richmond, filled with row houses, that borders the famous Hollywood Cemetery, in *Southern Cross.*

THE PEKING An elegant Chinese restaurant in the Slip, in downtown Richmond (p. 141, *Postmortem*).

PHILIP MORRIS "Even the Philip Morris plant with its building-high pack of Merits was stressful, for the fragrance of fresh tobacco bothered me" (p. 202, *From Potter's Field*). Scarpetta goes through high security when she goes to the Port of Richmond, which is near the Philip Morris plant, the reason being "the threats of terrorism, crime and lawsuits" (p. 17, *Black Notice*).

In *Southern Cross,* Bubba and Smudge work devotedly at Philip Mor- ris. "The grounds of the 1.6-square-mile administrative offices and man- ufacturing plant were immaculate. . . . Shrubs were perfectly sculpted" (p. 99–100).

PLEASANTS HARDWARE A hometown, friendly hardware store, a favorite of many Richmonders, known for having almost anything you want, including older items. "I . . . cut over to West Broad Street, where I occasionally went to Pleasants Hardware on the twenty two hundred block It was an old neighborhood store that had expanded over the years and tended to carry more than just the standard tools and garden supplies" (p. 430, *Black Notice*).

POE'S PUB A bar with live acoustic music that Scarpetta and Marino visit in *Cause of Death* (p. 162).

POLICE HEADQUARTERS This building is "built of stucco that is almost indistinguishable from the concrete in the sidewalks. Pale and pasty . . ." (p. 311, *Postmortem*).

PORT OF RICHMOND A body is found inside a cargo container here, in *Black Notice.*

THE PROJECTS "[T]here was a drug-related shooting from one of the housing projects on the fringes of what had become a more civilized and healthy downtown. In the last several years, the city had been ranked as one of the most violent in the United States, with as many as one hundred and sixty homicides in one year for a population of less than a quarter of a million people" (pp. 229–230, *Point of Origin*).

In *Southern Cross,* the projects are near Judy Hammer's house in Church Hill. There are "five federal housing projects, with two more on Southside. If one told the politically incorrect truth, all were breeding grounds for social chaos and violence and were clear evidence that the Civil War continued to be lost by the South" (p. 4).

QUIK CARY A convenience store and site of a murder, off Cary near Libbie (p. 217, *Black Notice*).

REGENCY MALL A popular mall in Richmond. Scarpetta and Lucy go Christmas shopping here (p. 78, *The Last Precinct*).

RICHMOND INTERNATIONAL RACEWAY NASCAR races are held here. Cat, a member of Smoke's gang, goes here often and likes to dress up in NASCAR clothing (p. 178, *Isle of Dogs*).

RIVER CITY DINER Chuck Ruffin, the morgue supervisor, meets the new deputy chief of police, Diane Bray, and Detective Anderson here (p. 200, *Black Notice*).

ROBINS CENTER This houses the basketball court for the University of Richmond. Bobby Feeley, the U. of R. basketball player with the same number as that painted on Jefferson Davis's defaced statue, practices here (p. 191, *Southern Cross*).

ROSE'S HOUSE Scarpetta's secretary lives on the third floor of an apartment building off Grove Avenue in the West End, near a café called Du Jour (p. 131, *Black Notice*).

RUTH'S CHRIS STEAK HOUSE This is one of the premier restaurants and desirable locales in general in all of Richmond. Scarpetta takes Lucy here for dinner in *Cruel & Unusual* (p. 138). It is located, incidentally, right next to Patricia Cornwell's former office in Midlothian and next to a grassy lot that served as her helipad when she had a helicopter.

In *Isle of Dogs,* Governor Crimm eats here on Wednesday nights (p. 85). He is flown here by helicopter.

SAINT BRIDGET'S A Catholic church on Three Chopt Road and Grove Avenue, visited by Scarpetta in *Cause of Death* (p. 142). Scarpetta is actually a member of this church (p. 82, *The Last Precinct*).

Scarpetta attends Deputy Chief Diane Bray's funeral, which is held here (p. 129, *The Last Precinct*).

SANGER HALL A part of the Medical College of Virginia, and where Scarpetta has tissue analyzed with an electron microscope (p. 176, *Unnatural Exposure*). Its exterior is not attractive. "Sanger Hall was sixties architecture, with a facade of garish bright blue tiles that could be spotted for miles" (pp. 176–177, *Unnatural Exposure*).

[Author's Note: I have often used this landmark while driving to do a viewing from the OCME. It's hard to miss Sanger Hall. The morgue for MCV is in the bowels of the building, and I parked below ground. As I walked through the building, reminiscent of my medical school days, I would still get that thrill of medical research as I passed through the old halls with signs for the physiology lab, the anatomy department, and biochemistry with huge murals replicating recent, esoteric papers submitted as research.—GF]

SCARPETTA'S HOUSE IN WINDSOR FARMS Located near the intersection of Canterbury Road and West Cary Street (p. 24, *The Last Precinct*). See **Lockgreen.**

SCHWARZCHILD'S JEWELERS Scarpetta has a necklace made for Lucy here (p. 84, *The Last Precinct*).

THE SIXTH STREET MARKETPLACE "The Sixth Street Marketplace is a Bayside without the water, one of these open, sunny malls built of steel and glass, on the north edge of the banking district in the heart of downtown" (p. 70, *Postmortem*).

SOUTHSIDE, OR SOUTH OF THE JAMES "I had forgotten she lived in Southside, where I rarely went and was inclined to get lost. Traffic was worse than I feared, the Midlothian Turnpike choked . . . Parking lots swarmed with cars, stores and malls so garishly lit up . . ." (p. 162, *Cruel & Unusual*).

"[Marino] lived south of the James in a neighborhood with wooded lots just off the strip-mall-strewn corridor called Midlothian Turnpike, where one could buy handguns or motorcycles or Bullet burgers, or indulge in a brushless carwash with or without wax" (p. 209, *Point of Origin*).

STATUE OF ROBERT E. LEE Located on Monument Avenue, it is mentioned in *Cause of Death* (p. 95).

STONYPOINT SHOPPING CENTER Mentioned by Scarpetta in *The Last Precinct* (p. 27).

SUGAR BOTTOM See **Church Hill.**

TOBACCO COMPANY A well-known restaurant and bar in Richmond. "I walked back outside and crossed the cobblestone street to the Tobacco Company, an old tobacco warehouse that had been turned into a restaurant with an exposed glass and brass elevator constantly gliding up and down through an atrium of lush plants and exotic flowers. Just inside the front door was a piano bar with a dance floor" (p. 276, *Black Notice*).

Located in Shockhoe Slip, this is "an upscale restaurant and bar in a renovated old tobacco warehouse not far from the river" (p. 23, *Isle of Dogs*). Unique First meets T.T. here (p. 24).

UNIVERSITY OF RICHMOND Murder victim Robyn Naismith's house was near the campus in *Cruel & Unusual*. The university is described as "a splendid collection of Georgian buildings surrounding a lake between Three Chopt and River roads" (p. 314).

Deputy Chief Virginia West jogs at the track at U. of R. with Andy Brazil, in *Southern Cross*. She admires the college's "slate roofs of handsome collegiate Gothic buildings" (p. 5).

VCU Virginia Commonwealth University is located downtown (p. 209, *Postmortem*). "'I flunked the first two tests in chemistry one-oh-one at VCU,'" Larry Posner, a trace evidence expert, says (p. 196, *Black Notice*).

VENICE RESTAURANT On Cary Street, mentioned in *Black Notice* (p. 167).

VIRGINIA COMMONWEALTH UNIVERSITY See **VCU.**

VIRGINIA HOUSE Located in Windsor Farms; Scarpetta and Berger drive past it (p. 338, *The Last Precinct*).

VMC The medical school in downtown Richmond, referred to as *VMC* in *Postmortem,* but changed in later novels to the actual name that everyone in Richmond uses: *MCV* or *Medical College of Virginia*.

THE WEST END Affluent suburbs of Richmond where Scarpetta lives (p. 33, *Postmortem*).

WHITCOMB COURT This area is located in the projects in Richmond (p. 5, *From Potter's Field*). It is also mentioned in *Cause of Death* as where an officer lost a gun later used in the shooting of Danny Webster (p. 191).

WINCHESTER PLACE, NO. 498 The home of Abby Turnbull (p. 235, *Postmortem*).

WINDHAM DRIVE The scene of Beryl Madison's murder (p. 11, *Body of Evidence*).

WINDSOR FARMS "[T]he city's wealthiest neighborhood" (p. 257, *Unnatural Exposure*). Windsor Farms was also the scene of Beryl Madison's murder on Wyndam Drive in *Body of Evidence*. "Windsor Farms was not the sort of neighborhood where one would expect anything so hideous to happen. Homes were large and set back from the street on impeccably landscaped lots. Most had burglar alarm systems, and all featured central air" (p. 8).

WINDSOR ON THE JAMES "[The Harveys] lived near Windsor on the James in a palatial Jeffersonian house" (p. 22, *All That Remains*).

ANNA ZENNER'S HOME An "imposing Greek revival . . . on the southern bank of the James River" (p. 28, *The Last Precinct*).

WILLIAMSBURG, VIRGINIA

CULPEPER'S TAVERN A bar frequented by Cary Harper (p. 149, *Body of Evidence*).

CUTLER GROVE A famous eighteenth-century plantation on the James River in Williamsburg, and home of Cary Harper (p. 38, *Body of Evidence*).

MARSHALL-WYTHE LAW SCHOOL OF WILLIAM & MARY COLLEGE Mitch Barbosa was jogging here before he was killed (p. 297, *The Last Precinct*).

CHARLOTTESVILLE, VIRGINIA

BOAR'S HEAD Scarpetta and Lucy have many dinners here while she is a student at the University of Virginia (p. 224, *Cause of Death*).

THE IVY Scarpetta and Lucy often eat here while Lucy is a student at the University of Virginia (p. 224, *Cause of Death*).

THE ROTUNDA Located on the campus of the University of Virginia, it is "brilliant white in sunlight and my favorite building Thomas Jefferson had designed. I followed old brick colonnaded walkways beneath ancient trees, where Federal pavilions formed two rows of privileged housing known as the Lawn.

"Living here was an award for academic achievement" (p. 228, *Cause of Death*).

SCOTT STADIUM Scarpetta and Marino pass by this stadium p. 223, *Cause of Death*).

NEW YORK, NEW YORK

BARBIZON HOTEL Jean-Baptiste Chandonne stays here in New York (p. 168, *The Last Precinct*).

CENTRAL PARK The beautiful and expansive public green space in the middle of Manhattan where a body is found in a fountain, in a section called Cherry Hill (p. 27, *From Potter's Field*).

THE DAKOTA The prestigious apartment building facing Central Park and site of John Lennon's murder; Gault stayed here (pp. 71 and 319, *From Potter's Field*).

HELIPORT In *Blow Fly,* Lucy flies her Bell 407 helicopter from the Thirty-fourth Street heliport, which is on the Hudson, "midway between the Statue of Liberty and the Intrepid" (p. 275).

THE LAST PRECINCT, NEW YORK, NEW YORK (AKA INFOSEARCH SOLUTIONS) This is Lucy Farinelli's private investigative agency, located in Manhattan at Lexington Avenue and Seventy-fifth Street, Suite 2103 on the twenty-first floor (p. 189, *Blow Fly*).

LUCY'S APARTMENT IN NEW YORK Located on the Upper East Side, on Sixty-seventh and Lexington (p. 86, *The Last Precinct*).

MUSEUM OF NATURAL HISTORY Gault and the murder victim walk around here before she is murdered in Central Park (p. 26, *From Potter's Field*).

NEIL'S A café across from Lumi where Chandonne claims he ate breakfast (p. 194, *The Last Precinct*).

NEW YORK ATHLETIC CLUB This club is on Central Park South; Scarpetta, Benton Wesley, and Marino sleep here after visiting the crime scene (p. 36, *From Potter's Field*).

NEW YORK CITY MORGUE, OPPOSITE BELLEVUE Mentioned in *From Potter's Field* (p. 45).

POTTER'S FIELD A cemetery for the homeless and unidentified; Jayne Gault is initially buried here, but is moved after she is identified (p. 352, *From Potter's Field*).

PRIMOLA The favorite restaurant of New York D.A. Jaime Berger (p. 78, *The Last Precinct*).

RUBYFRUIT ON HUDSON A bar that Lucy likes to frequent in Greenwich Village, New York City (p. 387, *Black Notice*). It is owned by Ann, a former cop.

WASHINGTON, D.C.

BLACKIE'S STEAKHOUSE Near Lucy's apartment in D.C. (p. 166, *Point of Origin*).

THE FIREPLACE Near Lucy's apartment in D.C. (p. 166, *Point of Origin*).

LAW CENTER OF GEORGETOWN UNIVERSITY Scarpetta meets here with her former law professor Nicholas Grueman (p. 261, *Cruel & Unusual*).

MR. P'S Near Lucy's apartment in D.C. (p. 166, *Point of Origin*).

NATIONAL MUSEUM OF NATURAL HISTORY Visited by Scarpetta and Marino in *Point of Origin* (p. 156). It also is mentioned in *All That Remains.*

THE WESTPARK This building houses Lucy's apartment in D.C., in the two thousand block of P Street (p. 169, *Point of Origin*).

HILTON HEAD, SOUTH CAROLINA

Scarpetta's friend Dr. Anna Zenner lets her use her house here in *From Potter's Field.* Hilton Head is also the site of Scarpetta's and Benton's vacation in *Point of Origin.*

CHARLIE'S A favorite restaurant of Scarpetta and Benton (p. 11, *Point of Origin*).

LA POLLAS A favorite restaurant of Scarpetta and Benton (p. 11, *Point of Origin*).

CHARLOTTE, NORTH CAROLINA

Charlotte is the setting of *Hornet's Nest,* featuring deputy chief of police Virginia West. Cornwell describes it: "Like a boy in puberty, it was rapidly unfolding and clumsy at times, and a little too full of what its original settlers had called pride" (p. 1). It is a city "[v]oted the most attractive city to live in nationwide, third largest banking center in the country, with an appreciation of the arts" (p. 43).

DAVIDSON COLLEGE A small private college about twenty miles away; Andy Brazil went to school here and continues to exercise on its track (p. 6, *Hornet's Nest*).

DAVIDSON, NORTH CAROLINA Cornwell describes Davidson as a "charming college town. Homes were genteel, white frame and brick, with ivy and sprawling porches and swings" (p. 25, *Hornet's Nest*).

FOURTH WARD A beautiful restored neighborhood in Charlotte filled with old Victorian homes (p. 173, *Hornet's Nest*). Chief of police Judy Hammer has a home here.

LAW ENFORCEMENT CENTER Located on Trade Street, this is where chief of police Judy Hammer and deputy chief of police Virginia West work (p. 2, *Hornet's Nest*).

MECKLENBURG COUNTY MEDICAL EXAMINER'S OFFICE Located on North College Street (p. 58, *Hornet's Nest*). Dr. Odom does the autopsy on the fourth murder victim here.

PHILADELPHIA, PENNSYLVANIA

PENN'S LANDING This is visible to Scarpetta from the Sheraton (p. 247, *Point of Origin*).

SOCIETY HILL Scarpetta and Wesley stay at the Sheraton there (p. 246, *Point of Origin*).

BATON ROUGE, LOUISIANA

BATON ROUGE, LOUISIANA The site of the serial murders by Jay Talley in *Blow Fly*. Scarpetta, Lucy, Marino, and Benton Wesley all converge here during the investigation.

"'By far, Baton Rouge has the highest rate of unsolved homicides in the entire country'" (p. 405, *Blow Fly*). "'Organized crime?' 'Fifth largest port in the country, the second largest petrochemical industry, and Louisiana produces some sixteen percent of the nation's oil'" (p. 405).

BOUTIN'S A restaurant mentioned in *Blow Fly* (p. 414).

EAST BATON ROUGE PARISH CORONER'S OFFICE Overlooking the Mississippi River and the state capitol (p. 31, *Blow Fly*). Dr. Sam Lanier, the coroner, works here; his office is on the fifth floor of the Governmental Building (p. 31).

OLD GARDEN DISTRICT Nic Robillard's father lives here (p. 155, *Blow Fly*). The Wal-Mart that is the site of an abduction is near here.

RADISSON HOTEL Benton Wesley stays here in *Blow Fly*. "The hotel is the finest one in Baton Rouge, its staff accustomed to accommodating a lot of people from all over who do not use the valets, preferring to come and go discreetly" (p. 401).

SPANISH TOWN The historic district of Baton Rouge where Rocco Caggiano has a house (p. 411, *Blow Fly*).

SWAMP MAMA'S This restaurant on 3rd Street in Baton Rouge "is a popular hangout for students" (p. 410, *Blow Fly*). "[It] smells like beer, with old vinyl booths and a stained, unvarnished wooden floor" (p. 413). Scarpetta, Eric Murphy, and Dr. Lanier eat there.

SWAMPS AND LAKES IN BATON ROUGE Lake Maurepas, Blind River, and Dutch Bayou (p. 412, *Blow Fly*).

WAL-MART, NEAR LSU Site of an abduction in *Blow Fly* (p. 330).

TEXAS

TEXAS DEPARTMENT OF CRIMINAL JUSTICE, POLUNSKY UNIT Site where Jean-Baptiste is on death row in *Blow Fly* (p. 57). Scarpetta flies down and meets with him here.

FLORIDA

DELRAY BEACH Scarpetta has moved here in *Blow Fly*. It is "barely an hour's drive north of Miami, where she was born" (p. 99).

KEY WEST "Beneath a blue sky that went on forever, huge palms and mahogany trees cradled houses and shops in spreading arms of vivid green as bougainvillea and hibiscus wooed sidewalks and porches with bright gifts of purple and red" (p. 341, *Body of Evidence*). Beryl Madison fled here to escape her stalker, and Scarpetta comes to Key West to find Beryl's missing manuscript.

LONDON, ENGLAND

ATHENAEUM HOTEL ON PICCADILLY Scarpetta and Benton Wesley stay here in *Unnatural Exposure* (p. 367).

BRIGHTON The scene of Mark James's bombing death, which was visited by Scarpetta and Benton Wesley in *Unnatural Exposure* (p. 363).

DORCHESTER HOTEL Scarpetta and Wesley stay in a flat near here in *Cause of Death* (p. 273).

GROSVENOR HOTEL Mark James is killed in an explosion near this hotel (p. 363, *Unnatural Exposure*).

VICTORIA TAVERN Mark James and his girlfriend were killed near here (p. 363, *Unnatural Exposure*).

PARIS, AND LYON, FRANCE

Scarpetta flies to Paris to talk with the Interpol in *Black Notice*.

BALANJO, THE A bar in Paris near where Jean-Baptiste Chandonne claims he met his cousin Thomas (p. 200, *The Last Precinct*).

BAR AMÉRICAIN, THE A bar in Paris near where Jean-Baptiste Chandonne claims to have met his cousin Thomas (p. 200, *The Last Precinct*).

BOULEVARD DES CAPUCINES Along this street, "shops turned into designer boutiques for the very rich" (p. 300, *Black Notice*).

CAFÉ DE LA PAIX Mentioned in *Black Notice* (pp. 344–345).

CHARLES DE GAULLE AIRPORT Scarpetta and Marino fly on the Concorde to this airport in *Black Notice* (p. 299).

COUR DES TROIS FRÈRES A bar in Paris near where Jean-Baptiste Chandonne claims to have met his cousin Thomas (p. 199, *The Last Precinct*).

LE DOME A famous Paris restaurant mentioned in *The Last Precinct* (p. 187) and *Black Notice* (p. 353).

L'EMBARCADÉRE Mentioned in *Black Notice* (p. 309).

FAUBOURG SAINT ANTOINE A place in Paris where "the young artists and nightclubs are" (p. 199, *The Last Precinct*) and where Jean-Baptiste Chandonne claims to have met his cousin Thomas.

GARE DE LYON A Paris railway station mentioned in *Black Notice* (p. 309).

ILE SAINT-LOUIS " 'The people there call themselves Louisiens, and are very proud, very elitist. Many don't consider the island part of Paris, even though it's in the middle of the Seine in the heart of the city. Balzac, Voltaire, Baudelaire, Cézanne . . . Just a few of its better-known residents' " (p. 320, *Black Notice*). The Chandonne family lives here.

INSTITUT MÉDICO-LÉGAL The morgue where Scarpetta meets Dr. Stvan, near the Gare de Lyon, off the Quai de la Rapée (p. 348, *Black Notice*).

LYON PART-DIEU A Lyon train station mentioned in *Black Notice* (p. 310).

OPÉRA-COMIQUE Mentioned in *Black Notice* (p. 368).

PARC DE LA TÊTE D'OR Mentioned in *Black Notice* (p. 313).

PÈRE-LACHAISE "[T]he most famous cemetery in Paris" where Jean-Baptiste Chandonne claims he stole a wallet for traveling money, in *The Last Precinct,* p. 200.

PLACE DE LA CONCORDE Mentioned in *Black Notice* (p. 309).

QUAI DE L'HORLOGE The block where Jean-Baptiste Chandonne's foster parents supposedly live in Paris (p. 170, *The Last Precinct*).

RELAIS HACHETTE Mentioned in *Black Notice* (p. 309).

SANS SANZ A bar in Paris mentioned in *The Last Precinct* (p. 200).

LA TOUR ROSE A hotel in Lyon, off the Rue du Boeuf, which Tally recommends to Scarpetta in *Black Notice* (p. 340).

DUBLIN, IRELAND

THE CORONER'S OFFICE The morgue located at No. 3 Store Street (p. 6, *Unnatural Exposure*).

SHELBOURNE HOTEL A hotel in Ireland where Scarpetta stays at the start of *Unnatural Exposure* (p. 1).

TRINITY MEDICAL SCHOOL This is where Scarpetta gives a series of lectures and also investigates a group of unsolved murders (p. 3, *Unnatural Exposure*).

SZCZECIN, POLAND

RADISSON HOTEL Lucy and Rudy Musil find and murder Rocco Caggiano here (p. 160, *Blow Fly*).

MISCELLANEOUS LOCATIONS

ASHLAND, VIRGINIA "I wondered about the people living in the prim white frame homes facing the tracks. Windows were dark, bare flagpoles greeting us with stark salutes from porches. We passed sleepy storefronts—a barbershop, a stationery store, a bank—then . . . we curved around the campus of Randolph-Macon College with its Georgian buildings" (p. 244, *Body of Evidence*).

BEACON HILL, BOSTON In *Blow Fly,* Benton Wesley is living here, near Storrow Drive, in the witness protection program (p. 69).

CDC The Centers for Disease Control in Atlanta, Georgia, is the definitive source of medical information about infectious diseases, as every doctor knows; Scarpetta visited it in *Unnatural Exposure* (p. 248).

HOMESTEAD INN, GREENWICH, CONNECTICUT Scarpetta was in hiding here after leaving her home in Richmond, having been fired as chief medical examiner (p. 135, *Blow Fly*).

NATIONAL FORENSIC ACADEMY, KNOXVILLE, TENNESSEE Scarpetta gives a lecture here during the last week of a ten-week course in forensics in *Blow Fly.* She meets and develops a friendship with Nic Robillard, an investigator from East Baton Rouge Parish, Louisiana.

NEWPORT, RHODE ISLAND Scarpetta is searching for Lucy in Newport at the end of *The Body Farm* and mentions many different places, such as Inntowne Inn, Christie's, the Black Pearl, Bannister's Wharf, Anthony's, the Brick Alley Pub, the Inn at Castle Hill, Bowden Wharf, and Aquidneck Lobster Company (pp. 331–332).

QUANTICO, VIRGINIA Site of the FBI Academy's profiling unit, where Benton Wesley and Mark James used to work; mentioned in *Blow Fly, Cause of Death,* and *Unnatural Exposure.*

U.S. ARMY QUARTERMASTER MUSEUM Located in Fort Lee, Virginia. Scarpetta observes "displays of field dress, mess kits, and a World War II trench scene with sandbags and grenades. I stopped at Civil War uniforms that I knew were real" (p. 203, *From Potter's Field*).

UNIVERSITY OF NORTH CAROLINA AT WILMINGTON "The campus was an immaculate collection of modified Georgian buildings tucked amid palms, magnolias, crepe myrtles, and [loblolly] and long-leaf pines. Gardenias were in bloom and when we got out of the car, their perfume clung to the humid, hot air and went to my head. I loved the scents of the South" (p. 366, *Point of Origin*).

WARRENTON, VIRGINIA The site of the fire and suspected death of Kenneth Sparkes in *Point of Origin*.

WRIGHTSVILLE BEACH Where Claire Rawley used to live, with such places as Sweetwater Surf Shop on South Lumina, Vito's, Reddog's, and Buddy's Crab (p. 195, *Point of Origin*).

GENERAL CONCORDANCE

SOME specific references found in the pages of Cornwell's books are explained in previous sections of this book. This concordance offers supplementary information about a selection of those terms that don't fit into the categories already covered.

ACE OF SPADES (*All That Remains*) A playing card is found inside a murder victim's car. A reporter mentions it to Scarpetta and asks, "'Are you familiar with the ace of spades, with how it was used in Vietnam?'" Scarpetta doesn't know. The reporter explains, "'When a particular outfit of American soldiers wanted to make a point after making a kill, they would leave an ace of spades on the body. In fact, a company that manufactures playing cards supplied this unit with boxes of the cards just for this purpose'" (p. 118).

This story is true, confirmed by the United States Playing Card Company (USPC), which manufactures several brands including Bee, Aviator, and Bicycle.

ACLU (*Postmortem*) About the possibility of developing a DNA database, Betty, the chief serologist, says, "[It will] never happen as long as the ACLU has a thing to say about it" (p. 98).

The American Civil Liberties Union, founded in 1920, works through the legal system to defend individual rights.

ACR (*Unnatural Exposure*) In preparation for a cargo plane to land on a makeshift runway, "the team set out sixteen ACR remote control landing lights" (p. 328).

ACR Electronics of Fort Lauderdale, Florida, has produced electronic life support and signaling equipment since 1956.

AP (*Cause of Death*) Referring to a snooping reporter, Scarpetta says, "As in the one who works for AP" (p. 7).

The Associated Press (AP), the world's largest news-gathering organization, was founded in 1848 and is headquartered in New York City. It serves 1,700 newspapers and 5,000 radio and TV stations in the United States and many more worldwide.

A PRIORI (*Body of Evidence*) About a former psychiatric patient, his psychiatrist says, "He sensed what others thought or felt and sometimes seemed to possess an inexplicable *a priori* knowledge of what they would do or what they had already done" (p. 297).

This Latin term, literally translated as "from the former," means existing in the mind prior to and independent of experience.

CA (*Postmortem*) Questioned by a commonwealth's attorney, the county's top prosecutor, about who has access to certain records, Scarpetta replies evenly, "Copies are sent to the CA and the police" (p. 120).

A commonwealth's attorney, elected in each Virginia county, is responsible for representing the people and presenting evidence in court against people charged with committing crimes.

C. A. DILLON TRAINING SCHOOL (*Southern Cross*) The novel's major antagonist, a youthful gang leader, has a history of antisocial behavior. At one time, he was "locked up in C. A. Dillon Training School in Butner" (p. 16).

The C. A. Dillon facility (now the Dillon Youth Development Center) in Butler, North Carolina, opened in 1968. It provides custody and treatment for males ranging in age from ten to eighteen. On eighty-eight acres, thirty of which are fenced in, the campus consists of four residential units, a cafeteria, an academic school, and an administrative building.

Treatment programs include programs for violent offenders, sex offenders, and substance abusers. Academic instruction is part of the program, along with music, art, and vocational training.

The North Carolina Department of Juvenile Justice and Delinquency Prevention announced on October 30, 2000, that "the department's Detention Division, which encompasses the State's five training schools and detention centers, will be referred to as the Youth Development Division . . . [and] the State's Training Schools will now be called Youth Development Centers" (www.ncdjjdp.org/djjdp_news/2000/october30_2000.htm)

CCRE (*Cruel & Unusual*) With the help of her niece, Lucy, Scarpetta analyzes computer records to solve a mystery involving a convicted killer. Lucy discovers discrepancies in the fingerprint data. She says, "'We're talking about three records. One was completely dropped or deleted. The SID number of another was altered. . . . I logged into CCRE and ran the SID numbers of [the records]'" (p. 310).

SID refers to the state identification number assigned to each offender. CCRE is Virginia's Central Criminal Records Exchange, a data bank housing criminal history records. It is available to authorized personnel who are legally cleared to access the data. The information can be correlated with AFIS, the Automated Fingerprint Identification System.

CERENKOV RADIATION (*Cause of Death*) At a university physics lab, Scarpetta sees interesting phenomena. "At one end of the lighted pool, Cerenkov radiation caused the water to glow a fantastic blue" (p. 225).

Cerenkov radiation, in a simplified definition, is caused by light slowing down while associated cosmic ray particles do not. Normally light travels in a vacuum at 300 million meters per second. When light passes through any material such as glass, air, or water, it tends to slow somewhat while the cosmic ray particles do not lose velocity. These high-energy particles emit faint flashes of blue light. The effect is named after Russian physicist Pavel Cerenkov (1904–1990).

CHINCH BUG (*Postmortem*) Scarpetta's mother, unhappy because her daughter is childless, is quoted as saying, "'You'll dry out like a chinch bug, Kay'" (p. 39).

The tiny winged insect, less than one quarter inch long, with a black body and red legs, is usually found on grassy lawns. It eats grass rapidly and can inflict severe damage on large sections of turf within a few hours, leaving it with an appearance of being burned.

CHRYSOBERYL (*Postmortem*) A test in Scarpetta's laboratory produces a colorful result: "Instantly spitting from the wand was a rapidly flashing synchronized light as brilliant as liquid chrysoberyl" (pp 21–22).

Chrysoberyl is a mineral gemstone. One variety is known as "cat's-eye" due to its yellowish-green coloring.

CLOISONNÉ (*Postmortem*) Scarpetta notices her boss fidgeting during a meeting. "Idly picking up a cloisonné letter opener, he ran his thumb along the blunt edge" (p. 122).

Cloisonné refers to a decorative application of inlaid enamel in which colored areas are separated by thin metal bands. It is Chinese (and sometimes Japanese) in origin.

COMPSTAT (*Black Notice*) A Richmond police official who would like to recruit Lucy tells Scarpetta, "You know, we're implementing COMPSTAT and need a computer expert." Scarpetta's narration explains the acronym as "computer-driven statistics, . . . a new model of enlightened, technologically advanced policing devised by the New York Police Department" (p. 163).

According to the NYPD, "the CompStat Unit was created to provide the Department with snapshots of preliminary crime statistics which allow tactical planning and deployment of resources to fight crime" (www.nyc.gov/html/nypd/html/chfdept/compstat.html). It provides information to the police commissioner and chief by compiling and analyzing preliminary statistics related to homicide and other crimes. It also generates electronic "pin maps" of citywide crime locations and geographic analysis related to homicides, shootings, and other crimes. In addition, the unit gauges crime-fighting effectiveness.

COMSTAT (*Southern Cross*) New York's earlier computerized statistics system, a predecessor for COMPSTAT.

CORONERS (*Postmortem, Point of Origin, Black Notice, Portrait of a Killer*) When someone confuses Scarpetta's title of *chief medical examiner*, with the title of *coroner*, she points out the difference. "I was not a coroner. Coroners are elected officials. They usually aren't forensic pathologists. You can be a gas station attendant and get elected coroner in some states" (p. 207, *Postmortem*). In *Point of Origin*, she adds, "some coroners were consummate politicians who did not know an entrance from an exit wound, or care" (p. 254).

While this may be true in many places, a notable exception is Dr. Thomas Noguchi, who was Los Angeles County coroner from 1967 to 1982. He personally conducted or oversaw autopsies on Marilyn Monroe, Robert F. Kennedy, John Belushi, and other celebrities, and became known as "coroner to the stars." Noguchi wrote two books about his activities in the field of forensic pathology. Cornwell acknowledges the Los Angeles coroner's duties in *Portrait of a Killer*.

COURTS OF JUSTICE COMMITTEE (*All That Remains*) In the state capitol complex, Scarpetta converses with a power broker from Washington, D. C. They discuss a bill before the legislature and Scarpetta comments about pressure that would be placed on "the Courts of Justice Committee" (p. 78).

In the Senate branch of Virginia's legislature, the general assembly, a "standing" or permanent committee is convened periodically to study and make recommendations regarding the state's criminal justice system. Fifteen senators, including the chairperson, make up the Courts of Justice Committee.

CRT (*Postmortem*) A lab technician "rested his fingers on the keyboard and stared into the CRT display" (p. 46).

CRT stands for *cathode ray tube*, a technology used in early computer monitors.

DRMS (*Cause of Death*) An FBI expert explains U.S. military organizations. Scarpetta asks, " 'What is D-R-M-S . . . ?'" (p. 257).

Defense Reutilization and Marketing Service is the place to obtain original U.S. government surplus property. Originally established in 1972 to consolidate the different military services' disposal operations, the Defense Property Disposal Service (DPDS) was renamed the DRMS in

1985. It is part of the Defense Logistics Agency (DLA), based in Fort Belvoir, Virginia.

ECTOPIC PREGNANCY (*Postmortem*) Discussing the medical history of a homicide victim, Scarpetta says, "she'd been treated five years earlier for an ectopic pregnancy" (p. 286).

This refers to the development of a fertilized ovum outside the uterus.

EOT/TEN-CODES (*Postmortem*) EOT means *end of tour,* announced on radio to dispatcher by Detective Marino. The dispatcher answers, "'Ten-four, seven-ten'" (p. 167). Ten-four means "Okay, message received." The "seven-ten" response doesn't seem to fit in this context. He may have meant "ten-seven," which is "Out of service—leaving the air," or perhaps seven-ten is his identification number. Ten-codes are generally used by public safety communicators. The FCC regulates citizens band radio, but not the meanings of ten-codes. Marino also refers to code "ten-twenty-eight," which means "Identify your station." (For a full listing of ten-codes, see the section titled "Cop Codes: Ten-Codes Commonly Used by Public Safety Officers.")

EPHIS/IIDS (*Isle of Dogs*) Andy Brazil comments about a particular helicopter's capabilities: "'That thing was made to fly through clouds. Why do you think it's got auto-pilot, IIDS, and EPHIS?'" (p. 108).

Brazil presumably means EFIS, which stands for *Electronic Flight Instrument System,* instrumentation that provides displays for most of the aircraft's navigational systems, including color displays of pitch and roll, navigational maps, weather, radio altitude and decision height, autopilot, and flight path information.

IIDS stands for *Integrated Instrument Display System,* which provides a convenient and accurate means of viewing engine-related data that can easily be communicated to the air crew. It displays fuel quantity, status of hydraulic and electrical systems, caution and warning messages, and other essential information.

EPU (*Southern Cross, Isle of Dogs*) Trooper Thorlo Macovich, as a member of the Executive Protection Unit (EPU), is assigned to fly the Virginia governor's helicopter.

EPU is a real Virginia agency, a branch of the Virginia State Police.

ERF (*The Body Farm, From Potter's Field*) Described by Scarpetta as the FBI's "recently built Engineering Research Facility, an austere complex on the same grounds as the Academy" (p. 7, *The Body Farm*), ERF is the division to which Lucy is assigned to help develop CAIN, the Crime Artificial Intelligence Network.

CAIN is fiction. ERF is real, a part of the FBI's Information Resources Division, the bureau's research arm. Opened in 1992, it works with the latest electronic and information technology. Engineers and other specialists also explore the latest computer developments and devise ways to defeat cyberattacks on the United States.

ESA (*Point of Origin*) Scarpetta is "well acquainted" with a computer network related to the Bureau of Alcohol, Tobacco, Firearms and Explosives. "ESA . . . was an acronym for Enterprise System Architecture, the result of ATF being mandated by Congress to create a national arson and explosive repository. Two hundred and twenty sites were hooked up to ESA, and any agent . . . could access the central database" (p. 176).

ESA provides ATF with the ability to collect, clarify, and communicate the information needed to accomplish its mission to reduce violent crime, collect revenue, and protect the public. It supports approximately 4,100 employees and 1,200 contractor workstations nationwide. Field personnel—agents, inspectors, and auditors—use notebook PCs with docking stations; and employees and contractor personnel assigned to offices are equipped with desktop PCs. All employee workstations are connected via local area networks (LANs). The LANs are connected via a high-speed, wide-area network that serves as the electronic backbone of ATF's data communications.

EVIDENCE BUTTONS (*Postmortem*) Scarpetta uses these containers for collecting and transporting fiber evidence (p. 12).

Forensic technicians at crime scenes usually package such evidence in paper bags of assorted sizes, metal cans (for arson debris), glass vials, glassine envelopes, or folding pillboxes. These boxes may sometimes be called *evidence buttons*. It is usually recommended that fibers be packaged in paper to prevent condensation damage.

FMP (*Postmortem*) Scarpetta describes the fingerprint matching processor: "The sleek, upright unit most closely resembling a set of washers and dryers was the [FMP], its function to match unknown prints against the multimillion fingerprint data base stored on magnetic disks" (p. 44).

Since *Postmortem*'s 1990 publication date, the computerized methods of matching fingerprints have improved drastically and no longer resemble "washers and dryers."

FOP (*All That Remains, Cruel & Unusual, Point of Origin*) Marino makes several references to the FOP. In *All That Remains*, he says, "Good thing I don't give a dime to nobody except the FOP" (p. 43). Elsewhere, he mentions bringing dates to the FOP dances.

The *Fraternal Order of Police*, founded in 1915, is the world's largest organization of sworn law enforcement officers, with more than 314,000 members in more than 2,100 lodges. They are committed to improving the working conditions of law enforcement officers and the safety of the people they serve.

FORMALIN (*Black Notice, The Last Precinct, Cruel & Unusual*) A killer enters Scarpetta's home and is threatening her. She snatches a glass container previously brought from her laboratory. As he raises a weapon, she "dashed a quart of formalin in his face. He shrieked and grabbed his eyes and throat as the chemical burned and made it difficult for him to breathe" (p. 438, *Black Notice*).

Formalin is a solution of formaldehyde in water, used as a disinfectant or to preserve biological specimens. Most people think of formaldehyde as a liquid, but it is actually a mixture of water and formaldehyde gas, sometimes stabilized by adding methyl alcohol. The mixture tossed in someone's face certainly would disable the person temporarily.

FROOT LOOPS (*Postmortem*) Marino speaks of a female assault victim for whom he has little respect. "'The girl had the morals of a guppy and was either a Froot Loop or else she made a stupid mistake, laid herself wide open, so to speak, for getting a number done on her'" (p. 147).

Froot Loops is a multigrain breakfast cereal of various colors in the shape of tiny donuts with artificial fruit flavors.

GLASSINE (*Point of Origin*) Scarpetta's assistant takes evidence photographs for her. "[He] slid them into glyassine envelopes" (p. 316).

She probably meant *glassine* evidence envelopes, which are breathable, transparent containers designed to eliminate static electricity and other evidence packaging problems. These are perfect for protecting microparticle evidence such as hair, fibers, glass shards, paint chips, and vegetation.

GODWIN HIGH SCHOOL (*Southern Cross*) A criminal gang leader "turned into the parking lot of Mills E. Godwin High School, named after a former governor of Virginia and home of the Eagles" (pp. 31–32).

This is a real school in the affluent Tuckahoe District; it is located on Pump Road in Richmond. Opened in 1980, it was named for Mills E. Godwin, Jr. (1914–1999), who served as governor from 1966 to 1970 and again from 1974 to 1978. He is noted for reinstating the death penalty and reorganizing the penal system. The school's student body has grown from 450 to more than 2,000. The school mascot is an eagle and the athletic teams' colors are red and white.

GRC (*Cause of Death*) Discussing ballistics sciences, an expert says, "I'm going to enter that into the GRC" (p. 182).

The initials stand for *general rifling characteristics,* which are contained in an FBI data bank available to most law enforcement agencies to help identify specific firearms.

GRE (*Point of Origin*) Needing expert advice, Scarpetta visits the University of North Carolina at Wilmington, along with Marino and Lucy, to confer with the school's director of student counseling. Describing their arrival, she says, "A receptionist was expecting us and showed us down a corridor, past . . . spaces for GRE testing" (p. 366).

Graduate Record Examinations (GREs) are taken by applicants to graduate schools. Since the program was founded more than fifty years ago, the number of graduate students in the United States has grown from 50,000 in 1948 to more than 1.2 million today. Large numbers of them come to the United States from virtually every country in the world. Under the direction of the GRE board, composed primarily of graduate deans from across the country along with several experts in the field of testing and psychometrics, the tests are based on extensive research and on careful monitoring of conditions and results.

HANOVER TOMATOES (*Postmortem*) While driving, Scarpetta listens to the radio. "I heard . . . that the Hanover tomato crop was going to be damaged if we didn't get some more rain" (p. 201)

Hanover tomatoes, reportedly very high quality, are named for the Virginia county in which they are grown. A summer celebration, the Hanover Tomato Festival and Heritage Fair, is held annually in Mechanicsville, Virginia. Cornwell mentions these tomatoes again in *Food to Die For* (p. 150).

HAUSER, KASPAR (*Black Notice*) While a colleague speaks of the bizarre history and freakish appearance of a killer, Scarpetta is reminded of a historical figure. "I wasn't listening. I was thinking of Kaspar Hauser. He spent the first sixteen years of his life in a dungeon because Prince Charles of Baden wanted to make sure Kaspar didn't have any claims to the crown. . . . At age sixteen he was found by a gate, a note pinned to him. He was pale like a cave fish, nonverbal like an animal. A freak. He couldn't even write his name without someone's guiding his hand" (p. 356).

Kaspar Hauser lived from 1812 to 1833. At age sixteen he turned up in Nuremberg, Germany, alone, ragged, incoherent, and illiterate. Two strange letters in his possession gave sparse information. One from his mother said the boy had been born in 1812 and that his military father was dead. The other purportedly came from a laborer who raised the boy in close confinement. Controversy surrounded Hauser during his subsequent residency with a schoolmaster. After a mysterious attack in which he suffered head wounds, he was sent to be educated by a doctor. In 1833, he was again attacked and suffered lethal stabbing injuries. The story has been retold and enhanced through the ages. In one version, Hauser was the son of grand duke Charles of Baden and had been kidnapped by Charles's first wife so her son would succeed the duke. Other accounts dispute this and suggest that Hauser's bizarre past and odd behavior drove him to self-inflict the fatal stab wounds. He has been the subject of great speculation and countless writings.

HEPA (*Unnatural Exposure*) Describing the interior of a special laboratory in which biological hazards are studied, Scarpetta speaks of the necessity for clean air. "It was checked by HEPA filters before it entered our bodies or the atmosphere" (p. 210).

HEPA stands for *high efficiency particulate air.* This filter technology was developed by the Atomic Energy Commission to free environments of hazardous air particulates. The filters, manufactured by several companies, are used in laboratories, surgery rooms, and other places needing clean air.

HHSD (*Postmortem*) About placing the OCME's data into Virginia's computer system, Scarpetta observes, "To have everything dumped in a central computer shared by dozens of other HHSD agencies was an invitation to a colossal security problem" (p. 90).

She refers to Virginia's Health and Human Services Department.

HIDTA (*Black Notice, The Last Precinct*) Lucy and her lover Jo work for the ATF and DEA, respectively, helping implement a special program. Scarpetta defines it "High Intensity Drug Trafficking Area. A squad made up of different law enforcement agencies working violent crimes. ATF, DEA, FBI . . ." (p. 33, *The Last Precinct*).

HIDTA is a component of the White House Office of National Drug Control Policy (ONDCP) established by the Anti–Drug Abuse Act of 1988. It enhances and coordinates drug control efforts among local, state, and federal law enforcement agencies. The program provides these groups with coordination, equipment, technology, and additional resources to combat drug trafficking in critical regions of the United States.

HMMWV (*Unnatural Exposure*) The U.S. Air Force loads material and vehicles needed for a special operation: "the HMMWV towed the camper inside the C-17" (p. 331).

A C-17 Globemaster is a military cargo jet aircraft. The HMMWV, or High Mobility Multipurpose Wheeled Vehicle, which entered Army service in 1985, is a light, highly mobile, diesel-powered, four-wheel-drive vehicle equipped with an automatic transmission. With various conversion kits, it can be configured to carry troops, armament, shelters, wounded personnel, or missiles. It is air-transportable and droppable by parachute. Commonly known as a Humvee or a Hummer, the vehicle has gained popularity for civilian use.

HOBBS METER (*Isle of Dogs*) Helicopter pilot Macovich explains, "There's a little Hobb's Meter in the cockpit . . ." (p. 146).

A *Hobbs meter* is an electronically driven device that records the aircraft's flight time in hours and fractions of hours.

HORNETS (*Hornet's Nest*) The Hornets are mentioned at least four times. They were Charlotte, North Carolina's National Basketball Association (NBA) team until 2002, when they moved to New Orleans. *Hornet's Nest* is not named for them. Instead, as explained by the author, it relates to a statement made in 1780 by British general Lord Cornwallis. Disturbed by hostility among the city's population, he called Charlotte "the hornet's nest of America" (p. 1).

HRT (*The Body Farm, Cause of Death, Unnatural Exposure*) Lucy escorts Scarpetta through a section of the FBI Academy in Quantico, Virginia, and mentions HRT.

The FBI's Hostage Rescue Team (HRT), a branch of its Critical Incident Response Group (CIRG), is a full-time, national-level tactical team headquartered in Quantico. The HRT mission is to be prepared for deployment to any location within four hours of notification by the FBI and conduct a successful rescue of hostages held by terrorists or criminals. Since its inception in 1983, the team has deployed more than two hundred times.

ICD-9 (*Cruel & Unusual*) While searching computer records listing causes of death, Scarpetta says, "I jotted down case numbers and ICD-9 codes" (p. 68).

The International Statistical Classification of Diseases and Related Health Problems is a three-volume set of reference books listing causes of death. Volume I, more than 1,000 pages, itemizes the classifications. Volume II is an instruction manual, and Volume III provides an alphabetical index. It was started in 1893 as the Bertillon Classification or International List of Causes of Death; the contents are periodically updated. When Scarpetta used her books, they were in the ninth revision, ICD-9, made in 1994. ICD-10 has since been issued.

IN SITU (*Postmortem*) At a murder crime scene, Scarpetta meticulously examines evidence. "Next I got out my camera and took several photographs of the body *in situ*" (p. 11).

This Latin term means "in its original place."

ION CHROMATOGRAPHY (*Postmortem*) A murder suspect has left traces indicating that he has washed his hands with borax soap. Scarpetta explains, "'The labs determined it through ion chromatography'" (p. 306).

This is a laboratory process using specialized equipment for the purpose of analyzing nitrates, sodium, ammonium, potassium, chloride, and other substances to determine their chemical and mineral makeup.

JAILING (*Hornet's Nest*) "He was jailing, jeans at low tide in that cool lockup look of six inches of pastel undershorts showing. The fashion statement got started in jail when inmates had their belts confiscated so they wouldn't hang themselves or someone else. The trend had crossed over every racial and socioeconomic line until half of the city's pants were falling off" (p. 3).

This was an interesting and welcome explanation of how and why young men began wearing loose, droopy pants. The information made sense too, since a large segment of American youth seems to take delight in imitating the appearance of convicts with tattoos, shaved heads, goatees, knitted stocking caps, and other apparel. But the source of Cornwell's information is unclear. A search of contemporary online slang dictionaries yielded only one similar definition. A website called A Prisoner's Dictionary, at dictionary.prisonwall.org, lists "Jailin'" and defines it as "(1) Someone who's in the hole (aka in jail). (2) Wives or girlfriends who visit regularly—'That's our lifestyle—jailin!'"

KEL-LITE (*Postmortem*) "Cops milled around . . . aimlessly probing the grass with their powerful Kel lights" (p. 17).

Kel-Lite is the brand name of a heavy-duty portable flashlight favored by many field police agencies.

KUDZU (*All That Remains, Unnatural Exposure*) In a rural area where a double murder has taken place, Scarpetta and Marino search the heavily vegetated area for clues. "The police had dug and sifted maybe ten feet in this direction before running into an infestation of kudzu . . . over the better part of an acre. . . . Every living bush, pine, and plant was slowly being strangled to death" (p. 160, *All That Remains*).

First introduced into the United States from Japan in 1876, kudzu vines were used decoratively, then for animal grazing. Later, it gained popularity in its use as erosion control. Unfortunately, kudzu adapted too well to the climate and soil of the southern United States. By the midtwentieth century, the kudzu invasion had grown beyond control, covering millions of acres, strangling forests, enveloping utility poles, and blanketing pastures. The U.S. Department of Agriculture declared it a weed in 1972. Efforts to curb it have mostly met with failure, although some claim that goats might be used to contain it.

KUKRI (*Portrait of a Killer*) While researching clues about weapons Jack the Ripper could have used, Cornwell says, "I discovered the following Victorian weapons at a London antiques fair and at the homes of two antique dealers . . . daggers, kukris . . ." (p. 37).

A *kukri* is a large knife used for hunting and combat purposes by Nepalese Gurkhas. The weapon has a heavy, curved blade sharp on the concave side.

LANUGO HAIR (*The Last Precinct*) One of the strangest of Scarpetta's antagonists is cursed with a peculiar hirsute affliction: "'This dog-faced congenital anomaly, almost every inch of his face, his body covered with long lanugo hair, pale baby-fine hair . . .'" (p. 38).

According to Webster's, *lanugo* means "a coat of delicate, downy hairs . . . with which the human fetus or infant is covered."

MOLINEUX APPLICATION (*The Last Precinct*) Preparing a legal case against a murderer, Scarpetta and a New York prosecutor discuss procedures. Says Scarpetta, "'[Y]ou're going to try to drag in his other bad acts, aren't you? . . . A Molineux application'" (p. 214).

In New York criminal law, evidence of uncharged crimes is generally inadmissible at a defendant's trial. The prosecutor must focus on the specific charges the defendant faces, rather than past crimes, charged or uncharged. An exception to this rule relates to the 1901 decision of *People v. Molineux,* in which a court of appeals decided that certain uncharged crimes may be introduced if the court decides that the probative value outweighs the prejudicial effect to the defendant.

MP-4 POLAROID CAMERA (*Postmortem*) After Scarpetta's fingerprint expert brings out latent prints, "he began taking photographs with an MP-4 Polaroid camera" (p. 23).

This is a special modular instant camera mounted on a stand, often used in conjunction with recording collected fingerprints. It is especially useful with the cyanoacrylate (superglue) method, accomplished by inserting the object of evidence inside a container. A few drops of superglue are placed on a heating device near the evidence. The heated fumes will adhere to prints, which may then be photographed with the MP-4 Polaroid camera.

MSUD POWDER (*Postmortem*) Trying to locate a suspect who might have a strange disease, Scarpetta advises investigators to check pharmacies for anyone buying MSUD powder, which is a formula of amino-acid-free powder for the dietary management of infants or children suffering from maple syrup urine disease (p. 279). (See the section titled "Shop Talk: The Language of the Medical Examiner.")

NAVSEA (*Cause of Death*) Marino and Scarpetta investigate a mystery at a U.S. Navy facility. An officer mentions NAVSEA to them. Marino asks, "'NAVSEA? What the hell is that?'" (p. 257).

NAVSEA is an acronym for Naval Sea Systems Command, the largest of the navy's five systems of commands. NAVSEA engineers, builds, and supports America's fleet of ships and combat systems. It accounts for nearly twenty percent of the navy's budget.

NCIC (*All That Remains*) A serial killer is victimizing young couples. Scarpetta says, "The cases . . . were inexplicable, and no one seemed to have a clue or credible theory, not even the FBI and . . . VICAP . . . [B]y the time VICAP could be notified, by the time the National Crime Information Center, or NCIC, could even wire descriptions to police departments across America, the missing teenagers were already dead and decomposing in woods somewhere" (p. 3).

NCIC is a computerized index of criminal justice information (criminal record history information, fugitives, stolen property, missing persons). It is available to federal, state, and local law enforcement and other criminal justice agencies and is operational 24 hours a day, 365 days a year.

The concept came about in 1965, in response to an increasing crime rate, when the FBI recognized that law enforcement officers all over the country had a critical need for instant access to the steadily increasing pool of criminal data. The bureau took the initial steps toward the development of a nationwide electronic center that would provide that data quickly. NCIC came online in January 1967. By 1971, all fifty states and the District of Columbia were hooked up. Today, the system has grown to more than 80,000 law enforcement and criminal justice agencies. An NCIC Advisory Policy Board made up of state and local law enforcement representatives is responsible for making sure the needs of state and local police are being met.

NIC112 (*Postmortem*) Busily checking computer file printouts, Scarpetta finds an important one. "The winning candidate was impersonally listed as NIC112" (p. 45).

NIC is an acronym for the brand name New Internet Computer. 112 is a file number.

NIS (*Cause of Death*) Scarpetta is confronted by an officious U.S. naval officer who announces he is with the Navy Investigative Service. She asks, "'You're with NIS?'" (p. 10).

She may have made an error. The U.S. Naval Criminal Investigative Service is the NCIS. Australia's Naval Investigative Service is the NIS. The U.S. Navy also has a security branch, Naval Security Group (NSG).

NOW (*The Body Farm*) Fictitious senator Frank Lord mentions to Scarpetta that he is facing more fund-raisers, "'the usual brush fires. NOW's picketing, and my opponent remains very busy painting me as a woman hater with horns and a pointed tail'" (p. 235).

If he were a woman hater, he would be in serious trouble with NOW. The *National Organization for Women* is the largest association of feminist activists in the United States, with a half-million contributing members and 550 chapters.

O, A, OR V (*Postmortem*) Opening an envelope containing slides recording fluid samples taken from a murder victim, she notes, "Inside were four slides, three of which were definitely smeared with something, but they were not hand-marked with the standard 'O,' 'A,' or 'V'" (p. 185).

These are designations for "oral," "anal," or "vaginal."

OCME *(Postmortem, Cause of Death, Unnatural Exposure)* Lucy, Scarpetta's smart ten-year-old niece, has been experimenting with Scarpetta's home computer terminal. "Lucy understood the seriousness of her ever attempting to access the OCME data" (p. 97).

The letters stand for Office of the Chief Medical Examiner, where Scarpetta's confidential case files are stored.

PANTHERS *(Hornet's Nest)* Several references are made in this novel to the Panthers. The Carolina Panthers are the National Football League's twenty-ninth franchise, awarded to Charlotte in 1993.

PDR *(Point of Origin)* Scarpetta, upon entering her assistant's office, admires his physique and then observes his movements. "He slid out an outdated PDR and set it on the floor" (p. 141).

There is very little context to help determine what this PDR is, but it's probably a *Physician's Desk Reference,* a thick book that provides a source for drug prescription information, drug identification, and prescription drug side effects. It's now available in a compact electronic format.

PERK *(Postmortem)* Marino comments about a rape suspect. " 'He's in hot water because her PERK's positive' " (p. 147).

A physical evidence recover kit, or *PERK,* is also known as a rape kit. It is designed to assist crime-scene investigators and the examining clinician in the collection of evidence specimens for analysis. Generally the kit contains swabs, similar to large Q-tip swabs, used for collecting semen or sperm from body orifices, and containers in which to seal the used swabs. Such evidence should be collected within twenty-four hours of the crime. The fluid samples are later lab-tested for verification of blood, semen, sperm, and other evidence.

PFIAB *(All That Remains)* Deeply concerned about a female reporter's activities and her safety, Scarpetta muses "No wonder she suspected her phones were being bugged, that she was being followed. The CIA, the FBI, and even the President's Foreign Intelligence Advisory Board . . . had a very good reason to be nervous about what [she] was writing" (p. 208).

The *President's Foreign Intelligence Advisory Board (PFIAB)* "provides advice to the President concerning the quality and adequacy of intelligence collection, of analysis and estimates, of counterintelligence, and of other intelligence activities. The PFIAB, through its own Oversight Board, also advises the President on the legality of foreign intelligence activities.

"The PFIAB currently has 16 members selected from among distinguished citizens outside the government who are qualified on the basis of achievement, experience, independence, and integrity" (www.whitehouse.gov/pfiab/).

In 2003, many Americans questioned the quality of intelligence advice the president received prior to invading Iraq.

PICAROON (*Isle of Dogs*) A Tangier Islander complains that the dentist "was a picaroon, which was the Tangier word for pirate" (p. 63).

It not only is the Tangier word, but is also in Webster's. The dictionary defines it as "a rogue, thief, or brigand . . . a pirate or corsair." Its root is the Spanish word *picarón*.

PRO FORMA (*Postmortem*) In a discussion with Scarpetta about his choice not to inform her of an important meeting, the commonwealth's attorney says, "'I didn't see any point in telling you. All it would have done is worry you, and it was my impression the meeting was *pro forma*'" (p. 133).

This Latin term means "as a matter of form."

PROJECT EXILE (*The Last Precinct*) The NYC special prosecutor asks Marino about Richmond's former reputation for the drugs-and-guns trade. "'Oh yeah,'" he replies. "'Before Project Exile got going and slapped those drones with time in federal prison if they were caught with guns, drugs. Yeah, Richmond used to be a real popular place to do your business'" (p. 158).

Project Exile was launched in 1997 with the help of Richmond's U.S. Attorney's Office. Criminals using drugs and guns had been beneficiaries of a generous parole system in Virginia. Federal laws provided longer sentences with far less chance of parole. So a decision was made to "exile" these offenders from state courts to the federal level. With the media's help, it became public knowledge that "an illegal gun will get you five years in federal prison." The Virginia legislature jumped on the bandwagon to amend gun and drug laws. Project Exile has reportedly had a significant effect in reducing these types of crimes.

RACAL HOOD (*Unnatural Exposure*) In a sterile, secured room, Scarpetta waits for a doctor to vaccinate her against a possible epidemic disease. She describes the doctor: "He wore a Racal hood and heavy blue vinyl suit, which he plugged into one of the coiled air lines" (p. 204).

A *Racal hood* provides respiratory protection against biohazards. It is manufactured by Racal Health & Safety, Inc., of Frederick, Maryland.

REEFER (*Isle of Dogs*) A large truck full of pumpkins is hijacked and the driver wounded. The leader of the perpetrating gang, nicknamed Smoke, makes a joke when a local TV personality mentions the crime: " 'He take the reefer or just the cab?' " Smoke replies, " 'I didn't take no reefer. . . . Wish it *had* been full of reefer, though' " (p. 114). A third person adds that the vehicle was a " 'Great Dane reefer' " (p. 114). The author explains that the phrase was "trade talk for the top-of-the-line freight van that had been filled with pumpkins and hitched to the Peterbilt eighteen-wheeler truck" (p. 114).

Reefer is a slang word for "refrigerator," and generally applies to refrigerated railroad cars. Its early use applied to old-fashioned insulated railroad cars packed with ice in compartments at either end and used to transport fresh fruits and vegetables packed in wooden boxes. Modern reefers have mechanized air cooling. Contemporary use of the word may also apply to enclosed, refrigerated trailers pulled by trucks, called "tractors." "Great Dane" alludes to the giant vehicle size. It's not likely the "van" would have been "hitched to a Peterbilt eighteen-wheeler truck," since an eighteen-wheeler is already made up of tractor and trailer. In a few states, though, trucks are allowed to pull multiple trailers.

ROUGH RIDER CONDOMS (*The Body Farm*) An FBI agent is dead, possibly of autoerotic asphyxiation, and Scarpetta examines his bedroom. "His pistol, wallet, credentials, and a box of Rough Rider condoms were on the table" (p. 51).

Rough Rider condoms, according to advertisements, "are studded for those of you who like a bumpier ride."

SAR (*Isle of Dogs*) Two people who have been stranded in a small boat are rescued by a Coast Guard helicopter crew. One of the officers says, " 'We spotted two subjects in a boat and brought them on board. . . .

They fired flares at our aircraft, and a post SAR boarding showed they were not in compliance. No fire extinguishers or life jackets'" (p. 324).

SAR, in this context, stands for Sea–Air Rescue.

SAT (*Hornet's Nest*) Virginia West reflects on her college days. "She couldn't have afforded to go to a college like Davidson and doubted her SATs would have impressed anybody" (p. 25).

SAT was once an acronym for Scholastic Aptitude Test; in 1993, the name of the test was changed to just SAT. Many colleges and universities use the SAT as one indicator among several, including class rank, high school grade point average, extracurricular activities, personal essay, and teacher recommendations. All of these are weighed to determine a student's readiness for college-level work.

SEM (*Postmortem*) Alluding to analysis of substances related to a murder, Scarpetta says the material "all came up as flat-out sodium in SEM" (p. 206).

Scanning electron microscope (SEM) technology was developed in the 1960s and uses electrons instead of light to produce better images of the sample being examined.

SHINGON (*Hornet's Nest*) Judy Hammer is in the lobby of a corporate building. "[S]he passed rich wood paneling and famous fresco paintings depicting the Shingon philosophy of chaos, creativity, making, and building" (p. 92).

Shingon is a form of Buddhism founded in 806 in Japan. The religion holds that secrets of the body, speech, and mind must be explored in order to become at one with Buddha. It is a mystic philosophy that does not allow written instruction or group teaching, meaning it must be passed on directly from teacher to pupil in an osmosis-like fashion. Believers are widespread in Japan.

SIDS (*The Body Farm*) In the Health Department's Division of Vital Records, Scarpetta asks an old friend for help. "'I need to track down a SIDS that allegedly occurred in California around twelve years ago'" (p. 158).

SIDS is an acronym for Sudden Infant Death Syndrome. Approximately 2,500 infants die each year from this syndrome.

SIGMET (*From Potter's Field*) Aboard an FBI helicopter en route to New York, the pilot uses the intercom to inform Scarpetta and Marino, "'The FAA's issued a SIGMET.'

"'What the hell is that?' Marino asked.

"'A warning about turbulence. It's windy in New York City'" (p. 24).

SIGMET is a radioed announcement of Significant Meteorological Information. Weather service to aviation is a joint effort of the National Weather Service (NWS), the Federal Aviation Administration (FAA), the military weather services, and other aviation-oriented groups and individuals. A centralized aviation forecast program originating from the Aviation Weather Center (AWC) in Kansas City was implemented in October 1955. In the contiguous United States, all in-flight SIGMETs and other information are now issued by AWC.

SINE QUA NON (*Body of Evidence*) Remembering her teen years, Scarpetta recalls, "I excelled in science and was intrigued by human biology. I was poring over *Gray's Anatomy* by the time I was fifteen, and it became the *sine qua non* of my self-education" (p. 168).

Sine qua non is a Latin phrase meaning "something essential; an indispensable condition."

SPCA (*Postmortem*) Richmond citizens are nervous about a serial killer on the loose. Scarpetta observes, "The sale of handguns and deadbolt locks went up fifty percent the week after the third murder, and the SPCA ran out of dogs" (p. 4).

Richmond's *SPCA,* Society for the Prevention of Cruelty to Animals, the only full-service humane society in Central Virginia, implements a "long-range plan to end the killing of adoptable animals." They care for about 200 animals each day, providing vaccinations, food, shelter, and medical care. More than 3,500 of their wards are adopted each year. This would include larger dogs used by new owners to protect their homes.

SQL (*Postmortem*) Lucy, Scarpetta's young niece, knows everything about computers. She tells her aunt, "'You get into SQL . . . and then you can create anything you want'" (p. 293).

SQL stands for Structured Query Language, which is used to communicate with a database. According to ANSI (American National Standards Institute), it is the standard language for relational database management systems. SQL statements are used to perform tasks such as updating or retrieving data in a database.

STAR CHAMBER (*Cruel & Unusual*) At a meeting prior to a court hearing, Scarpetta's attorney advises her. "'I believe we can count on Jason Story testifying. . . . And, of course, Marino. I don't know who else Patterson will include in this Star Chamber proceeding of his'" (p. 383).

In fifteenth-century London, the king's councilors held special judiciary meetings in Westminster Palace. The sessions were known as the Court of the Star Chamber, referring to painted stars decorating the ceiling. The council's power and scope expanded from its role as a court of last resort to one that superceded common-law trials. Contrary to popular belief, the council did not deliver death sentences.

A 1983 movie titled *The Star Chamber* featured Michael Douglas as a judge frustrated with legal technicalities allowing killers to go free. He joins a covert group of self-appointed jurists who decide on guilt and capital punishment for defendants who benefitted from legal loopholes. The term *Star Chamber* has become synonymous with legally unfair trials.

STAT (*Body of Evidence, From Potter's Field, The Last Precinct*) In three books, Scarpetta uses this term, all in reference to blood toxin levels found in autopsies: In *Body of Evidence* (p. 183), Fielding says of a corpse, "'Her STAT alcohol's only point oh-three, nothing in her gastric that tells me much.'" "'She's got a STAT alcohol of .23'" (p. 257, *From Potter's Field*); "a STAT carbon monoxide showed he was no longer breathing when he was set on fire" (p. 195, *From Potter's Field*); and "I draw blood from the iliac veins and vitreous fluid from the eyes, and test tubes [go] to the third-floor toxicology lab for STAT alcohol and carbon monoxide tests" (pp. 113–114, *The Last Precinct*).

STAT is a medical term used by doctors who want an immediate lab report or procedure. The word is derived from the Latin term *statim,* which means "without delay." In addition, I-STAT and STAT-American manufacture and distribute medical diagnostic and drug screening equipment, used in determining the level of alcohol in body fluids.

STR (*Isle of Dogs*) Scarpetta makes an appearance and comments about a bit of evidence retrieved from an envelope. "[U]sing STR we recovered DNA from the envelope . . ." (p. 289).

STR stands for *short tandem repeats,* which are repeated short sequences of DNA and are important in the process used for analyzing tissue or fluid evidence.

SYLLABI (*Postmortem*) In the home of a murder victim who has been educated in medicine, Scarpetta scans the furnishings and notices the contents of a particular book case. "Tomes straight from a medical school's syllabi lined two shelves" (p. 6).

Syllabi is the plural form of *syllabus,* a book containing summaries of leading cases in a professional field. It also refers to an outline for a course, listing the topics to be covered and materials needed for study.

TANAPOX (*Unnatural Exposure*) A medical expert is worried about a possible epidemic originating on Tangier Island in Chesapeake Bay. He tells Scarpetta, "'This outbreak must be contained. . . . We've got to worry about houseflies hovering around patients, and crabs headed for the mainland. How do we know we don't have to worry about the possibility of mosquito transmission, as in Tanapox, for God's sake?'" (p. 282).

The reader may at first glance think the doctor is making up a new virus by using the first three letters of *Tangier* and adding *pox.* But there really is a virus called Tanapox generally seen in Kenya and Zaire, Africa. Epidemics spread in 1957 and 1962, but how the infections spread is still mostly unknown.

TARHEELS (*Hornet's Nest*) Virginia West considers North Carolina's procedures for conducting autopsies. "It was probably all about sports again. Hornets fans stayed in Charlotte, Tarheels got [theirs] in the big university town" (p. 58).

The "big university town" is Chapel Hill, site of the University of North Carolina. Not only does the university use the nickname "Tarheels," but the entire state as well. One version of the name's origin stems from soldiers retreating during the Civil War. Someone allegedly claimed that Jefferson Davis planned to apply tar to their heels so they would "stick better" in the next fight.

TMJ (*Southern Cross*) Bubba is advised to chew gum in lieu of smoking cigarettes. He retorts, "'You forget I got TMJ. My jaws are killing me'"

(p. 62). He clicks his jaws from side to side. Later in the story, another character also worries about getting TMJ.

Temperomandibular joint syndrome, or *TMJ,* is an affliction causing problems in the joint of the jaw or mandible. Symptoms include clicking and popping of the joint, grinding sounds, headaches, dizziness, ringing in the ears, pain in the neck, and earaches. It can sometimes be treated with a special device placed in the jaw, without surgery.

TRAUMA REGISTRY (*Cruel & Unusual*) Investigating the death of a child who was subjected to torture, Scarpetta directs her secretary to ask the computer analyst to conduct a search for similar crimes. "'Codes to look for would be *cutting, mutilation, cannibalism, bite marks.* . . . And ask her to see what the Trauma Registry's got'" (p. 35).

It is unclear which Trauma Registry Scarpetta means. There are Trauma Registry data centers in several states, including Virginia. In addition, the National Pediatric Trauma Registry (NPTR) was formed to study the etiology of pediatric trauma and its consequences. It provides information to authorized individuals about children who have experienced various trauma and those survivors who have been discharged from acute-care facilities. Perhaps she meant both, with special focus on the NPTR.

TROJANS (*Postmortem*) Marino and Scarpetta search the residence of a murder suspect. "Out of the same dresser drawer came a box of Trojans" (p. 15).

Trojans are a brand name of condoms sold in most drugstores.

UNIX (*Cruel & Unusual, Unnatural Exposure, From Potter's Field*) When Scarpetta receives bizarre computer messages from someone who has mysteriously learned her password, Lucy's knowledge is helpful. Speaking of the sender, Lucy says, "'He could use a UNIX password-encryption program'" (p. 120, *Unnatural Exposure*). UNIX plays a central role in *Cruel & Unusual.*

UNIX is a pioneering computer operating system developed in 1970.

USAMRIID (*Unnatural Exposure*) Desperate for support to prevent a possible pox epidemic, Scarpetta telephones for military assistance. ". . . A woman answered the phone at the U.S. Army Medical Research Institute of Infectious Diseases, or USAMRIID, at Fort Detrick, in Frederick, Maryland" (p. 193).

As the Department of Defense's lead laboratory for biological warfare defense, *USAMRIID* conducts research to develop vaccines, drugs, and diagnostics for laboratory and field use. It also investigates any diseases or illnesses that occur naturally if they pose a serious public health threat or require special containment procedures. While the institute's primary focus is on protecting military service members, its research programs benefit society as well.

UT (*Unnatural Exposure*) Needing help from a forensic anthropologist, Scarpetta travels to UT, the University of Tennessee.

VAC (*Black Notice*) At a crime scene, Scarpetta needs electricity for some of her equipment. She tells Marino, "'Maybe Mr. Shaw can help you find somewhere to plug it in. Has to be a grounded receptacle, one-fifteen VAC.'

"'I love it when you talk dirty,'" Marino replies (p. 26).

Hardly dirty, *VAC* stands for Volts Alternating Current.

VAN ECK RADIATION (*From Potter's Field*) With Lucy's help, Scarpetta tries to solve the mystery of how someone broke into her computer system. Says Lucy, "'theoretically [they] could use a receiver to pick up keyboard input via Van Eck radiation. Some Soviet agents were doing that not so long ago'" (p. 148).

The Van Eck radiation theory is that electromagnetic emissions from personal computers can surreptitiously be picked up by a radio receiver and reconstructed. Some intelligence communities deny that it really works. Reportedly, though, the technology was used by the CIA in its surveillance of a turncoat agent, Aldrich Ames, in 1993. This may be the reference Lucy makes to "Soviet agents."

VCIN (*Black Notice*) A vehicle license tag number provides a clue for Scarpetta and Marino. Scarpetta says, "He relayed the tag number to the Virginia Criminal Information Network, or VCIN, and asked for a 10-29" (p. 142).

The *Virginia Criminal Information Network (VCIN)* "functions as a service facility under the management control of the Virginia Department of State Police, providing operational support to the entire criminal justice community. The primary mission of VCIN is to provide a means of rapid communications for criminal justice agencies throughout the Commonwealth of Virginia.

"Information made available via the network is as near an officer in the field as his radio. In addition to the VCIN data files, the system also provides user access to data bases maintained by the Virginia Department of Motor Vehicles (DMV) and the National Crime Information Center (NCIC). In addition, VCIN accesses the National Law Enforcement Telecommunications System (NLETS)" (www.vsp.state.us/cjis_vcin.htm).

It is unclear why Marino asked for a 10-29. In the radio ten-codes used by law enforcement agencies, 10-29 is a warrant check for a person (in most states). Since he and Scarpetta had no suspect name yet, it seems more likely he would have asked for a 10-27, vehicle registration information. Then, if a name came up, he could proceed to the 10-29 request.

VFR (*The Last Precinct, Isle of Dogs*) With Lucy at the helicopter controls, Scarpetta is navigating and operating the radio. "Richmond air traffic control comes over the air, telling us radar service is terminated and we can squawk VFR" (p. 437, *The Last Precinct*).

VFR, visual flight rules, applies when an aircraft is not being flown under instrument flight rules. Under VFR, the pilot generally controls the attitude of the aircraft by relying on what can be seen out the window, although this may be supplemented by referring to the instrument panel. The aircraft must keep a certain distance from clouds and stay where there is adequate visibility. The pilot takes responsibility for avoiding other aircraft or objects such as skyscrapers, peaks, antennas, and high towers.

VICAP (*Postmortem, All That Remains, Unnatural Exposure*) Introducing FBI profiler Benton Wesley, who plays a major role in several Scarpetta books, she says, "When he wasn't on the road, he was usually . . . teaching death-investigation classes and doing what he could to coax VICAP through its rocky adolescence" (p. 74, *Postmortem*).

The Violent Criminal Apprehension Program, according to the FBI website, "is a nationwide data information center designed to collect, collate, and analyze crimes of violence—specifically murder. Cases examined by VICAP include:

- solved or unsolved homicides or attempts, especially those that involve an abduction; are apparently random, motiveless, or sexually oriented; or are known or suspected to be part of a series

- missing persons, where the circumstances indicate a strong possibility of foul play and the victim is still missing; and

- unidentified dead bodies where the manner of death is known or suspected to be homicide.

"For VICAP to work effectively, it needs an invitation and coordination with local law enforcement. Therefore, the FBI provides, free of charge, the software to set up the VICAP database. The program has been embraced by many agencies, with busier operation in cities including Los Angeles, Chicago, Detroit, Dallas, and Kansas City. Other cities, including New York City, are in the process of becoming fully operational" (www.fbi.gov/hq/isd/cirg/ncavc.html).

VPL EYEPHONE HRX (*Unnatural Exposure*) In her laboratory at Quantico's FBI Academy, Engineering Research Facility, Lucy demonstrates technology she has been researching. Scarpetta narrates, "She carefully pulled a DataGlove over my left hand. . . . [then] she picked up a helmet-mounted display that was connected to another cable, and fear fluttered through my breast as she headed my way."

Lucy speaks. "One VPL Eyephone HRX, same thing they're using at NASA's Ames Research Center" (p. 163).

VPL Research of Palo Alto, California, pioneered developments in virtual reality and 3D graphics, both software and hardware, beginning in 1984. The owner, Jaron Lanier, is credited with coining the term *virtual reality.* Among the products his company produced were the DataGlove, a glove-based input device, and the Eyephone HRX, an apparatus resembling a diving mask that attaches to the head with elastic bands. It creates a high-resolution, wide-angle, three-dimensional visual field for its color display system, giving the user a feeling of existence in a completely separate environment.

VPL (which reportedly stands for *Visual Programming Language*) and all of its assets were sold in 1998 to Sun Microsystems, which still offers many of the products.

WORLD HEALTH ORGANIZATION (*Unnatural Exposure*) After identifying the source of a possible pox epidemic, Scarpetta notifies an international agency. "[T]he World Health Organization put out another international alert . . . WHO reassured people that this virus would be eliminated" (p. 306).

The *World Health Organization,* the United Nations' specialized agency for health, was established in April 1948. WHO is headquartered in Geneva, Switzerland; its objective is "the attainment by all peoples of the highest possible level of health," defined as "a state of complete physical, mental and social well-being and not merely the absence of disease or infirmity" (www.who.int/about/en).

DEATH BY THE NUMBERS:
A STATISTICAL ANALYSIS
OF DEATH IN THE
CORNWELL BOOKS

THE following table of victims in Cornwell's first fifteen novels (the Scarpetta and Brazil series) reveals that there are one hundred and one deaths, or 6.7333 deaths per book.

The most common cause of death is by gun (forty-two), closely followed by twenty-one knifings. Some victims had both methods performed on them, skewing the statistics slightly. Only two people were killed by poison. The three most interesting methods were five deaths by poxvirus, one by dehydration, and one by a kick. In the following chart, some victims had more than one means of death applied to their bodies.

METHODS OF DEATH

METHOD OF DEATH	NUMBER OF VICTIMS
Shooting	42
Knifing	21
Torture	14
Beating	8

METHOD OF DEATH	NUMBER OF VICTIMS
Fire	6
Strangulation	6
Poxvirus	5
Drugs	2
Electrocution	2
Hanging	2
Poison	2
Asphyxia	1
Dehydration	1
Drowning	1
Kick	1

As far as reasons for these deaths, thirty-one involved a serial killer, the most common rationale. Only six were overtly for revenge, and six occurred during burglaries. Only eleven of the one hundred and one killings were of a sexual nature, barely nudging out self-defense (10 percent) or the impetus to quiet someone who knew too much (8 percent).

The most interesting motives were Munchausen's syndrome (1 percent) as well as two mistaken identities, including a victim who was supposed to be Scarpetta herself. Ten percent of the deaths were the result of self-defense, some by police officers in the line of duty.

Gone are the days of killing out of revenge (6 percent), jealousy (0 percent), or during a burglary (6 percent). These anachronistic motives are no longer politically correct, it seems. The motives of the modern age are more likely to be of psychotic, sexual, or serial-killing nature (45 percent).

REASONS FOR DEATH

REASON	NUMBER OF VICTIMS
Serial killing	31
Sexual	11
Self-defense	10
To keep quiet	8

REASON	NUMBER OF VICTIMS
Revenge	6
Burglary	6
Protect turf	6
Psychosis	4
Anger	3
Protection	3
Accidental	2
Escape	2
Grief	2
Mistaken identity	2
To prevent murder	2
Accidental	1
Autoerotic	1
Guilt	1
Munchausen's syndrome	1
Sadism	1
State execution	1

How many victims succumbed to Scarpetta herself? Surprisingly, only three (3 percent). She shot all three victims and also used a knife on the third. Scarpetta's niece, Lucy, has followed in her aunt's footsteps, with three killings to her name, including deaths preceeding the books, but integral to the action of the plot.

In terms of numbers of deaths per book, Cornwell started out slowly in *Postmortem* with six deaths, and culminated thirteen years later with an amazing twenty-four deaths in the 2003 novel *Blow Fly,* the highest body count in all of her novels. The lowest number was in *Southern Cross* (one).

DEATHS PER NOVEL

NOVEL	NUMBER OF DEATHS
Postmortem	6
Body of Evidence	5
All That Remains	14
Cruel & Unusual	7
The Body Farm	3
From Potter's Field	7
Cause of Death	2
Unnatural Exposure	7
Point of Origin	6
Black Notice	4
The Last Precinct	4
Blow Fly	24
Hornet's Nest	8
Southern Cross	1
Isle of Dogs	3
Total	101

A LIST OF VICTIMS
The Scarpetta Series

VICTIM	PERPETRATOR	WEAPON	REASON	BOOK
Brenda Steppe	Roy McCorkle	strangulation	sexual	*Postmortem*
Patty Lewis	Roy McCorkle	strangulation	sexual	*Postmortem*
Cecile Tyler	Roy McCorkle	strangulation	sexual	*Postmortem*
Lori Petersen	Roy McCorkle	strangulation	sexual	*Postmortem*
Henna Yarborough	Roy McCorkle	strangulation	sexual	*Postmortem*
Roy McCorkle	Marino	gun	defense	*Postmortem*

VICTIM	PERPETRATOR	WEAPON	REASON	BOOK
Beryl Madison	Frankie Aims	knife	psychotic	*Body of Evidence*
Cary Harper	Frankie Aims	pipe	psychotic	*Body of Evidence*
Sterling Harper	self	overdose	sadness	*Body of Evidence*
Al Hunt	self	hanging	knowledge of killings	*Body of Evidence*
Frankie Aims	Scarpetta	gun	self-defense	*Body of Evidence*
Jill Harrington and Elizabeth Mott	Steven Spurrier	knife and gun	serial killer, social isolation	*All That Remains*
Bruce Phillips and Judy Roberts	Steven Spurrier	knife	serial killer, social isolation	*All That Remains*
Jim Freeman and Bonnie Smyth	Steven Spurrier	knife	serial killer, social isolation	*All That Remains*
Ben Andersen and Carolyn Bennett	Steven Spurrier	knife	serial killer, social isolation	*All That Remains*
Mike Martin and Susan Wilcox	Steven Spurrier	knife	serial killer, social isolation	*All That Remains*
Fred Cheney and Deborah Harvey	Steven Spurrier	knife and gun	serial killer, social isolation	*All That Remains*
Abby Turnbull	Steven Spurrier	gun	accident	*All That Remains*
Steven Spurrier	Pat Harvey	gun	revenge for daughter's murder	*All That Remains*
Robyn Naismith	Ronnie Joe Waddell	knife	burglary, on drugs	*Cruel & Unusual*
Ronnie Waddell	Commonwealth of Virginia	electrocution	justice	*Cruel & Unusual*
Eddie Heath	Hilton Sullivan★	gun	serial killer	*Cruel & Unusual*
Jennifer Deighton	Hilton Sullivan★	strangling	accident	*Cruel & Unusual*
Susan Story	Hilton Sullivan★	gun	to keep quiet	*Cruel & Unusual*
Frank Donohue	Hilton Sullivan★	gun	to keep quiet	*Cruel & Unusual*
Helen Grimes	Hilton Sullivan★	knife	sadism	*Cruel & Unusual*

★*AKA Temple Brooks Gault.*

VICTIM	PERPETRATOR	WEAPON	REASON	BOOK
Emily Steiner	Denesa Steiner	dehydration and gun	Munchausen's syndrome	The Body Farm
Max Ferguson	self	autoerotic asphyxia	autoerotic	The Body Farm
Denesa Steiner	Scarpetta	shotgun	self-defense	The Body Farm
Anthony Jones	Sheriff Lamont Brown	gun	drugs	From Potter's Field
Jayne Gault	Temple Gault	gun	psychotic	From Potter's Field
Jimmy Davila	Temple Gault	gun	serial killer	From Potter's Field
Sheriff Lamont Brown	Temple Gault	gun	drugs	From Potter's Field
Detective Jakes	Temple Gault	blow to the chest	serial killer	From Potter's Field
Detective Maier	Temple Gault	electrocuted	serial killer	From Potter's Field
Temple Gault	Scarpetta	knife, gun	self-defense	From Potter's Field
Ted Eddings	unknown, New Zionists	cyanide poisoning	to keep quiet	Cause of Death
Danny Webster	unknown, New Zionists	gun	mistaken for Scarpetta	Cause of Death
Mother of Phyllis Crowder	Phyllis Crowder	gun (suspected)	revenge	Unnatural Exposure
Lila Pruitt	Phyllis Crowder	poxvirus	revenge	Unnatural Exposure
A mother and daughter on Tangier Island	Phyllis Crowder	poxvirus	revenge	Unnatural Exposure
Wingo	Phyllis Crowder	poxvirus	revenge	Unnatural Exposure
Phyllis Crowder	self	poxvirus	revenge	Unnatural Exposure
unidentified man who broke into Crowder's RV	Phyllis Crowder	shotgun	burglary	Unnatural Exposure

VICTIM	PERPETRATOR	WEAPON	REASON	BOOK
Claire Rawley	Carrie Grethen and Newton Joyce	fire, knife	serial killer	*Point of Origin*
Kellie Shephard	Carrie Grethen and Newton Joyce	fire, knife	serial killer	*Point of Origin*
Benton Wesley (survived)	Carrie Grethen and Newton Joyce	fire, knife (faked)	serial killer	*Point of Origin*
Marlene Farber	Newton Joyce	fire	serial killer	*Point of Origin*
Austin Hart	Newton Joyce	fire, knife	serial killer	*Point of Origin*
Carrie Grethen	Lucy Farinelli	assault rifle	self-defense	*Point of Origin*
Newton Joyce	Lucy Farinelli	assault rifle	self-defense	*Point of Origin*
Thomas Chandonne	Le Loup-Garou	drowning	serial killer	*Black Notice*
Pyle Gant	unknown	gun	serial killer	*Black Notice*
Kim Luong	Le Loup-Garou	gun, beating	serial killer, sexual	*Black Notice*
Diane Bray	Le Loup-Garou	beating	serial killer, sexual	*Black Notice*
Rosso Matos	Jay Talley	torture, fire	to keep quiet	*The Last Precinct*
Mitch Barbosa	Jay Talley	carbon monoxide poisoning, torture, secondary arrhythmia	to keep quiet	*The Last Precinct*
Susan Pless	Le Loup-Garou	beating	serial killer, sexual	*The Last Precinct*
Benny White	Jay Talley	hanging	to keep quiet	*The Last Precinct*
Glenda Marler	Jay Talley	torture	serial killer	*Blow Fly*
Ivy Ford	Jay Talley	torture	serial killer	*Blow Fly*
Eight other women	Jay Talley	torture	serial killer	*Blow Fly*
Katherine Bruce	Jay Talley	torture	serial killer	*Blow Fly*

VICTIM	PERPETRATOR	WEAPON	REASON	BOOK
Carlos Guarino	Rocco Caggiano	gun	to protect the Chandonne family	*Blow Fly*
Emmanuelle La Fleur	Rocco Caggiano	gun	to protect the Chandonne family	*Blow Fly*
Annie Mayeux	Jay Talley	knife, beating	sexual	*Blow Fly*
Charlotte Dard	Jay Talley	drug overdose	witness to Mayeux murder	*Blow Fly*
Rocco Caggiano	Lucy Farinelli and Rudy Musil	gun, fake suicide	to protect Pete Marino and to hurt the Chandonne family	*Blow Fly*
Officer Phillip Wilson	Jean-Baptiste Chandonne	beating	escape	*Blow Fly*
Officer Ron Abrams	Jean-Baptiste Chandonne	beating	escape	*Blow Fly*
Rebecca Milton	Bev Kiffin	stabbing, beating	mistaken for Nic Robillard	*Blow Fly*
Attorney General Weldon Winn	Benton Wesley	gun	self-defense	*Blow Fly*
Eveline Guidon	Benton Wesley	gun	self-defense	*Blow Fly*
Bev Kiffin	Rudy Musil	gun	self-defense	*Blow Fly*
Jay Talley, aka Jean-Paul Chandonne	(Rudy Musil)	(gun)	probable self-defense	*Blow Fly*
Agent Riley Minor	Jay Talley	torture	serial killer	*Blow Fly*

The Brazil Series

VICTIM	PERPETRATOR	WEAPON	MOTIVE	BOOK
Jay Rule	Punkin Head	.45 pistol Silvertip ammo	to protect turf	*Hornet's Nest*
Jeff Calley	Punkin Head	.45 pistol Silvertip ammo	to protect turf	*Hornet's Nest*
Cary Luby	Punkin Head	.45 pistol Silvertip ammo	to protect turf	*Hornet's Nest*
Carl Parsons	Punkin Head	.45 pistol Silvertip ammo	to protect turf	*Hornet's Nest*
Ken Butler	Punkin Head	.45 pistol Silvertip ammo	to protect turf	*Hornet's Nest*
Blair Mauney III	Punkin Head	.45 pistol Silvertip ammo	to protect turf	*Hornet's Nest*
Punkin Head	Andy Brazil	gun	to prevent a murder	*Hornet's Nest*
Poison	Andy Brazil	gun	to prevent a murder	*Hornet's Nest*
Ruby Sink	Smoke	gun	robbery	*Southern Cross*
Trish Thrash ("T. T.")	Unique First	box cutter	sexual	*Isle of Dogs*
Caesar Fender	Major Trader	flare gun	altercation	*Isle of Dogs*
Clerk at 7-Eleven	Unique First	gun	robbery	*Isle of Dogs*

ACKNOWLEDGMENTS

To my wife, Tina, for the many days and innumerable hours we drove all over Richmond taking pictures for this book. And for her editorial comments on the pictures that sent me scurrying back again and again, for "just one more" shot.

To Dr. Marcella Fierro, chief medical examiner, close friend of Patsy Cornwell. For attempting to educate a naive "pediapod" as an M.E., for her warm encouragement for the first book I wrote as an M.E., which I shyly showed her, upon which she promptly marched down to the waiting morning conference, held it up and, in her inimitable style, loudly and proudly announced that "we now have another writer in our midst. Most people say they're going to write a book. Almost none do. And Glenn did it." I won't forget your smile. And many thanks for generously opening up the OCME for me to take pictures "of anything you want." And thank you for our long subsequent conversation about this book, your encouragement of Patsy Cornwell's evolution as a writer, and your gentle but persistent encouragement of my writing. Remember, a clean desk is the sign of a sick mind.

To Marty Greenburg, my "book presenter extraordinaire," who sold my very first book, which was on the mystery writer Lawrence Block, and then actually persevered with this current project on Patricia Cornwell, literally doing the footwork in getting it sold to Putnam's via Cornwell's agent, Esther Newberg.

To all the people at the Forensic Lab who generously spent many hours with me as they demonstrated and explained the myriad pieces of equipment and computers.

To Paul Ferrara, Director of the Forensic Laboratories at the OCME, for his encouragement in guiding me to those who could explain the many pieces of lab equipment and computers.

To Eileen Davis, Forensic Section Chief, Trace Evidence Section, at the Forensic Laboratories, who gave me a general overview of the lab. Thank you for sharing the story of how you and Patricia Cornwell burned innumerable pink bathing caps to see if a pink residue would remain, and if those remains could be analyzed by mass spectrometry, as used in *All That Remains.*

To John H. Willmer, Forensic Scientist, Firearms and Tool Mark Identification, for explaining ballistic fingerprinting and the NIBIN system to me.

To H. Michael Moore, Forensic Scientist Section Chief, Questioned Document Section, who interrupted his lunch to kindly spend much time demonstrating the analysis of indented writing with the ESDA, and for his many anecdotes about interesting cases of hand-writing analysis and attempted forgery. It was a Bond-like "Q" moment for me.

To Josh Kruger, the director of the Trace Labs, who spent many patient hours with me at the Forensic Lab, showing me innumerable machines and explaining the science behind their operation.

To members of the OCME in Richmond for your help:

To Vicki Shelar, histologist at the OCME, for all your patience and kindness while I was a medical examiner, asking for tissue samples and for your demonstrations of staining techniques and for showing me the use of the microtome.

To Evelyn Henson, Central District Administrator, who kindly took me into her office, offered me tea as I downloaded my photos, and helped with photographing the autopsy lab, giving me many stories in the process. Your kindness will always be remembered. I'm sorry I talked you into having your picture taken, but your kindness couldn't go unnoticed.

To Larry Cortez, a neighbor and computer whiz, who helped me switch to a new computer when my voluminous manuscript was making my antiquated computer smoke.

And to all my children's wonderful friends, who always greeted me with an encouraging, "And how's 'the book' going?" I will always remember you.

To two wonderful M.E.'s, Jose Abrenio and Takeshi Imajo, "Taki," from Japan, with whom I worked at the OCME in Richmond. Thank you for taking me under your wings and showing me your great gentleness, sensitivity, and humor, as you walked me through many crime scenes and exams.

To Sally Owen at Otto Penzler's The Mysterious Bookstore in New York City, who started my life in publishing. She is the epitome of the kindly bookstore owner, who patiently found some out-of-print Lawrence Block books for me, and then surprisingly took the time and interest to ask what I was writing. If she hadn't repeatedly insisted that I send her the manuscript so she could forward it to Lawrence Block, my writing career would not have happened.

To George "Corky" Plews, my Princeton roommate, best man and best friend, who gave me invaluable advice on publication contracts. Yes, it's thirty-four years and counting, and we are still waiting for The Great American Novel from each other.

To Tom Connor, literary agent, writer, and friend, who unselfishly gave me much advice and help on all aspects of publication.

To Judith Marks-White, another Westport friend and writer, for reading and professing enjoyment at my reams of pediatric anecdotes.

To my Connecticut patients, friends, and staff, who listened for years to my anecdotes and read my poetry, encouraging me along the way.

And lastly and most importantly, to my mother and father, Ben and Pauline Feole, who encouraged and tolerated my voracious reading from a ridiculously early age. For kindly answering my repeated questions about your favorite authors with, "*You* are my favorite author." For providing hundreds of books in their Rhode Island living room during my grade school days, most of which I covertly read while lying wheezing in my bed, home from school, starting with *One Day in the Life of Ivan Denisovich* and ending with *The Agony and the Ecstasy*. Now you finally know how I endured my asthma.

INDEX

(Page numbers in bold indicate tables)

ABOUT THE AUTHORS

Glenn Feole attended Princeton University, '74, and majored in philosophy and pre-medical studies. He studied existentialism under Professor Walter Kaufmann, writing a thesis on Sartre's *Being and Nothingness*. Nothing prepared him for medical school, and he was accepted at Columbia University College of Physicians and Surgeons but deferred his medical studies to play bass in a jazz band. He later graduated from the University of Cincinnati College of Medicine and completed a pediatric residency at Children's Hospital Medical Center in Cincinnati. As an aspiring writer, he was drawn to William Carlos Williams's and Allen Ginsberg's hometown of Paterson, New Jersey, where he served two years in the public health service. While there he published his first pieces of poetry, one of which, "Aequanimitas," was published in *JAMA* as well as in a textbook of the Osler Society of America. He spent the next eleven years in private practice. Nine of those years were spent as an anachronistic, house-call making solo pediatrician with an office in his home in Westport, Connecticut. For the next six years, he lived in Richmond, Virginia, where he worked part-time as a medical examiner, did volunteer pediatric work in the inner city, substitute taught at inner-city high schools, and wrote five books. He has since returned to full-time pediatric work, devoting himself to clinics that care for the underserved, uninsured, and Medicaid patients, and has a special interest in serving migrant Hispanic workers. He is currently working for Eau Claire Cooperative Health Clinics in Columbia, South Carolina, at a satellite clinic called Pediatrics of Batesburg-Leesville, while sneaking off to English lectures at USC in the evenings. He and his wife, Tina, have been happily married for twenty-six years and have four children. His last two books include a book of poetry and a book of pediatric anecdotes, *First Words,* as a solo pediatrician.

Don Lasseter, California native and resident, has authored more than fifty magazine articles and a dozen nonfiction books about notorious crimes and criminals. A World War II historian, he has photographed sites of most major battles and penned a book detailing the adventures of downed airmen in France.